Teller and Tale
in Joyce's Fiction

John Paul Riquelme is associate professor of English
at Southern Methodist University.

TELLER AND TALE IN JOYCE'S FICTION

Oscillating Perspectives

John Paul Riquelme

THE JOHNS HOPKINS UNIVERSITY PRESS
Baltimore and London

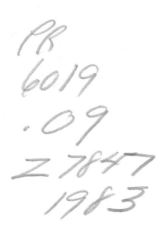

This book has been brought to publication with the
generous assistance of Dedman College of
Southern Methodist University.

The Johns Hopkins University Press, Baltimore, Maryland 21218
The Johns Hopkins Press Ltd., London

Library of Congress Cataloging in Publication Data

Riquelme, John Paul.
Teller and tale in Joyce's fiction.

Includes index.
1. Joyce, James, 1882–1941—Technique
2. Narration (Rhetoric) 3. Point of view
(Literature) I. Title
PR6019.O9Z7847 823'.912 82–7805
ISBN 0–8018–2854–6 AACR2

I dedicate my book with gratitude
to my parents
and
to three teachers
Wolfgang Iser, J. Hillis Miller, and Hayden V. White
Stand me now and ever in good stead.

Labour is blossoming or dancing . . .
. . . .
How can we know the dancer from the dance?
    —W. B. Yeats, "Among School Children"

The very being of writing (the meaning of the
labor that constitutes it) is to keep the
question *Who is speaking?* from ever being
answered.
    —Roland Barthes, *S/Z*

You are trying to reconcile the book and the
author. A book is the writer's secret life,
the dark twin of a man: you can't reconcile
them.
    —William Faulkner, *Mosquitoes*

Contents

Acknowledgments

In reaching back to describe the origins and the development of this study, I find myself in the fortunate position of having many people to thank for substantial assistance. I owe my deepest debts to those mentioned in the dedication, my parents and Professors Wolfgang Iser, J. Hillis Miller, and Hayden V. White. Others have generously taken time out of their busy lives to read and comment on all or part of the typescript at various stages of completion: Bernard Benstock, Steven V. Daniels, Louis O. Mink, Michael O'Dea, Michael Seidel, Fritz Senn, and Philip Solomon. Fritz Senn's criticism, especially his objections to the term *narrator*, and Louis Mink's reactions to the first version of chapter one and to part of chapter two saved me from numerous blunders. Their comments led to some significant reformulations of my positions. Steve Daniels's careful scrutiny often enabled me to recast and strengthen my arguments. If I were to try tracing Michael Seidel's lengthy career of reading, hearing about, and encouraging my work on Joyce, I would have to go back nearly to the book's beginning and stop only at the writing of this page.

Several of my teachers besides those already named influenced my approach in ways that I surely cannot now specify precisely, including Richard Ellmann, Charles Feidelson, Martin Price, Monroe K. Spears, and David Thorburn. I want to thank Professor Ellmann especially for a suggestion at an early stage that became important later. Monroe Spears did me the great service of teaching me that the nature of writing is revision and that literary expression can be allusive in some extravagant ways. I wish also to acknowledge gratefully the influence of John T. Irwin through conversations long ago and more recently through his writings.

Numerous professional groups and the scholars directing them gave encouragement by allowing me to deliver parts of this study at a variety of forums: Richard Lehan and the executive committee of the Twentieth-Century English literature division of the Modern Language Association (MLA Convention, 1977); Hans Rudnick and the executive committee of the Prose Fiction division (MLA, 1977); David Leon Higdon, organizer of a special session at the 1978 MLA Convention; Moris Beja and the executive committee of the American Committee for Irish Studies (MLA, 1979); Michael Seidel and the organizers of the 1978 Joyce Colloquium in Erie, Pa.; Fritz Senn and the program directors, Phillip Herring and Bernard Benstock, of the Seventh International James Joyce Symposium (1979); Sidney Feshbach and Stanley Sultan, chairmen of panels at the Provincetown Joyce Colloquium (1980); and Richard Stamelman, director of the Center for Humanities, Wesleyan University (1980).

Financial support for the research and writing that contributed to this study came from various institutions, whose aid I wish to recognize with gratitude. The School of Criticism and Theory, University of California at Irvine (Murray Krieger, director), provided a fellowship and an arena for study and debate in the summer of 1978. The American Council of Learned Societies provided a travel grant and a grant-in-aid during 1979. The National Endowment for the Humanities provided funds administered by both The School and the ACLS. Southern Methodist University funded a fruitful research leave as well as abundant clerical help. The Andrew W. Mellon Foundation provided a humanities fellowship for teaching and research administered by the Center for Humanities, Wesleyan University. Richard Stamelman, his staff at the center, and my colleagues during my year at Wesleyan (1979–80) created an ideal environment for thinking, writing, and talking freely about ideas. This study would not have been possible in its present form without all these generous benefactors, whom I warmly thank.

Help from Southern Methodist University and Wesleyan University made possible the producing of typescripts. I want to thank Bennett Miller at SMU in particular for the efficiency of his word-processing center. Pat Camden and Shirley Lawrence at Wesleyan and Emy Souther at Southern Methodist University typed versions of this study, putting up good-naturedly with my proliferating revisions. Sheryl St. Germain and Kathleen Triplett did the word-processing for the final version. June Schelling did the typesetting and Jamie Woods did the page make-up, both with great patience, at the graphics lab of Dedman College, Southern Methodist University. Two of my former students, Tom Eagle and David Plott, read the proofs. Jon Crawford helped with the drawings. I wish to thank Dean R. Hal Williams of Dedman College for authorizing use of the graphics lab, but also for his encouragement during the years I worked on this book. Bennett Miller and Randy Phillips of the dean's office made the arrangements for the typesetting to proceed. Dedman College also provided a generous subsidy for a portion of the publishing costs.

I used the resources of several libraries extensively in pursuing the research for this study: the British Library, Bridwell Library (Perkins School of Theology), Fondren Library (Rice University), Fondren Library (SMU), and Olin Memorial Library (Wesleyan University). Decherd Turner, then the director at Bridwell, gave me full access to the library's splendid collection of Joyce materials. John Kelleher of the manuscripts department at the British Library allowed me to examine thoroughly the note sheets for *Ulysses*.

The help of several people at The Johns Hopkins University Press enabled improvement of the manuscript and made the process of publication a rewarding experience for me. I want to thank especially Alan Carter,

James Johnston, William Sisler, and Jane Warth for their conscientious attention to the details of publication and for their thoughtful advice.

The editors of the *James Joyce Quarterly* have kindly granted permission for me to reprint material in chapter two that appeared originally in their journal (vol. 18, Spring 1981) in another version. An earlier version of part of chapter one appeared in *James Joyce: An International Perspective*, ed. Bernard Benstock and Suheil Badi Bushrui (Totowa, N. J.: Barnes and Noble, 1982). An earlier version of the opening of chapter four appeared in *The Seventh of Joyce*, ed. Bernard Benstock (Bloomington: Indiana University Press, 1982).

Finally, I want to acknowledge the help of my most faithful listener, my wife, Louise Ellen. I never would have seen this project into print without her unflagging belief that the work was worth doing and redoing.

Conventions of Reference

I have adopted these abbreviations and editions for references contained in this study. With some slight modification, I follow the practice of the *James Joyce Quarterly*.

CW   Joyce, James. *The Critical Writings of James Joyce*, ed. Ellsworth Mason and Richard Ellmann. New York: Viking Press, 1967.

D   Joyce, James. *Dubliners*, ed. Robert Scholes, in consultation with Richard Ellmann. New York: Viking Press, 1967.
Joyce, James. *"Dubliners": Text, Criticism, and Notes*, ed. Robert Scholes and A. Walton Litz. New York: Viking Press, 1969.

FW   Joyce, James. *Finnegans Wake*. New York: Viking Press, 1939; London: Faber & Faber, 1939. These editions have identical pagination. I identify passages in the *Wake* by page and line numbers. I identify chapters by book and chapter numbers, e.g., I.1 (book I, chapter 1). For II.2, the Schoolroom chapter, I refer to right and left marginal notes and to footnotes by preceding the number of the note with the letter "R", "L," or "F."

JJ   Ellmann, Richard. *James Joyce*. New York: Oxford University Press, 1959.

Letters   Joyce, James. *Letters of James Joyce*. Vol. I, ed. Stuart Gilbert. New
I, II, III   York: Viking Press, 1957; reissued with corrections, 1965. Vols. II and III, ed. Richard Ellmann. New York: Viking Press, 1966.

P   Joyce, James. *A Portrait of the Artist as a Young Man*. The definitive text corrected from the Dublin Holograph by Chester G. Anderson and edited by Richard Ellmann. New York: Viking Press, 1964. I refer to sections by part and section numbers, which I list in Appendix 1.
Joyce, James. *"A Portrait of the Artist as a Young Man"; Text Criticism, and Notes*, ed. Chester G. Anderson. New York: Viking Press, 1968.

SH   Joyce, James. *Stephen Hero*, ed. John J. Slocum and Herbert Cahoon. New York: New Directions, 1944, 1963.

U   Joyce, James. *Ulysses*. New York: Random House, 1934 ed. reset and corrected 1961.

WD   *The Workshop of Daedalus: James Joyce and the Raw Materials for "A Portrait of the Artist as a Young Man,"* ed. Richard M. Kain and Robert Scholes. Evanston: Northwestern University Press, 1965.

Brief Argument

This study deals with the styles, techniques, structures, and conceptual implications of narration in Joyce's fiction. I begin with a chapter on *Finnegans Wake* to define some ends toward which Joyce's writing tends, but which are discernible much earlier in his career. The three chapters that follow deal in turn with *A Portrait of the Artist as a Young Man*, with *Stephen Hero* and *Dubliners*, and with *Ulysses*. The order of the chapters violates conventional notions about developmental sequences that Joyce's texts encourage us to question. His narration is often retrospective, prospective, or even preposterous in the etymological sense of the word. By providing a retrospective orientation, my intention has been to give a strong reading of all Joyce's fiction, to read it with a fresh eye, not a naive eye, but one fresh from reading *Finnegans Wake*.

By juxtaposing *A Portrait* with *Finnegans Wake*, I emphasize the connections between Joyce's early fiction and his late writing. The relationship is closest in the following areas: the representation of the artist as character and as narrator, the linking of ends to beginnings, and the attempt to present the source of writing. In both *A Portrait* and the *Wake*, the teller is literally in the tale in extravagant ways. In addition, I choose *A Portrait* as the subject for the second chapter in order to introduce Joyce's use of *le style indirect libre* (also known as *erlebte Rede* and as narrated monologue) as early as possible after the discussion of the *Wake*. Focusing on that stylistic technique, I continue the exploration of reading and writing initiated in chapter one. Joyce's employment of the device is a recurring subject in the remainder of the study. In chapter three I move back to the beginnings of Joyce's stylistic development in his short stories and in his draft of a novel, *Stephen Hero*. I describe in detail how his style develops toward *A Portrait*. In the chapter's conclusion, I argue that the complex narration of "The Dead" points beyond the developments of *A Portrait*, toward the mythic implications of style in the later works. By beginning the final, and longest, chapter with a detailed discussion of "Circe," I link it to "The Dead" as another descent into the underworld. I treat the visit to the dead as one of several metaphors for the narrative and the narration of *Ulysses* provided within the book itself. The remainder of the chapter concerns other such metaphors and Joyce's styles in *Ulysses*: consciousness as metaphor for textuality, the title as epic structural simile for the narration, Joyce's continuing development of (and away from) *le style indirect libre,* and the Homeric arrangement of the styles. By describing the configuration as Homeric, I bring the study back to the issues introduced in my commentary on *Finnegans Wake*.

xiv

The term I have used in the subtitle refers to a cluster of related structures and implications of Joyce's narration that appears regularly in my descriptions of how we may understand our relation and the teller's to the tale. The analogies and evidence I cite in presenting the oscillating perspectives in Joyce's work include the following: puns as figurative equivalent, the Möbius strip as geometrical model, certain kinds of optical illusion as perceptual equivalents, and *le style indirect libre* as characteristic narrating technique. In addition, interactions of singular with iterative, contemporary with mythic, mental with cultural, initial with ultimate mark Joyce's fluctuating viewpoints. For reader and writer, the oscillations involve the reader's assumption of the writer's role and the writer's adoption of his precursors' personae. In Joyce's recasting of the myth of Daedalus, the artist's adopting of those personae is also the child's attempt to emulate his father and to father himself. In Joyce's version of the myth of Odysseus, the writer enacts the wandering hero's attempt to reach his lost home and copulate with his estranged spouse, who is also his Muse. When we take language as the context for oscillation, we see writing trying to stand in for the unwritten and the nonverbal. In that case, oscillation results because writing and language always stand in the way of our experiencing their ostensible opposites at the same time as they provide the vehicle for our standing where those opposites have been. Through reading and writing as roles in revolution, we enact a version of the narrative Freud defines in his famous dictum about id and ego, which we can read in one way as a comment on the relation of the unconscious to the conscious mind: *Wo Es war, soll Ich werden*. By means of our acts of reading, where the writer has been and where writing comes from there shall we be.

In exploring that narrative, I try to do justice to the complicated double movement in Joyce's career: the development of a style for representing consciousness in fiction and for representing a cultural consciousness as well, the conscience of his race that Stephen Dedalus knows, in the journal of *A Portrait*, he has yet to create. As I suggest in my commentary on "The Dead," Joyce discovers in the writings of W. B. Yeats the possibility of representing a cultural consciousness. But in order to achieve such a representation in fiction, only adumbrated at the end of "The Dead," Joyce must develop his style further by moving beyond the techniques for representing mind that he has mastered in writing that story. He moves beyond even the technical and conceptual achievements of *A Portrait* to produce post-Romantic epics written in thoroughly modern idioms. *Ulysses*, the first of those epics, makes the second, *Finnegans Wake*, possible. It does so when Joyce represents the artist and cultural consciousness not primarily in characters' thoughts but in the styles of the book itself. During the narration of *Ulysses* the thinking of characters transmitted through style becomes part of the work's context of the whole as representation of mind. The streams *of* consciousness become tributaries that merge into the stream *as* consciousness, whose final manifestation for Joyce is Anna Livia, the river as the artist's *Wake*. In his final works Joyce produces what Yeats in "The Tower" calls a "superhuman/Mirror-resembling dream," art built from past art, including "the proud stones of Greece." The artist wills the dream to his audience as legacy by enabling works of human culture to be thrust continually "back in the human mind again" ("Under Ben Bulben," st. 2).

Teller and Tale
in Joyce's Fiction

CHAPTER ONE

Twists of the Teller's Tale: *Finnegans Wake*

No longer the *artist*, he has himself become a *work of art*.
—Nietzsche, *The Birth of Tragedy*

Literature, in particular, is a mantic activity that is both intelligible and interrogating...: an answer to the one who consumes it yet always a question to nature, an answer which questions and a question which answers.
—Roland Barthes, "The Structuralist Activity"

THE TELLER IN THE TALE

Although *Finnegans Wake* marks the end, both the conclusion and the teleology, of Joyce's writing, for a variety of reasons critics have tended to treat the *Wake* as if it were relatively independent of his earlier works, even *Ulysses*. But this highly idiosyncratic narrative presents, at times in extravagantly extrapolated form, certain tendencies important in Joyce's earlier fiction, though not always as apparent there. The continuities involve Joyce's styles and his narrative structures, his representations of the artist and of consciousness, his metaphors of narration and of human experience, his linking of endings with origins. Joyce's concern with origins in the *Wake* and before it often takes the form of references to literary sources through allusion. I need hardly point out that Joyce's readers have long recognized him to be a master of allusion. James S. Atherton's commentary *The Books at the Wake: A Study of Literary Allusions in James Joyce's "Finnegans Wake,"* published a quarter of a century ago, persuasively demonstrates Joyce's reliance on allusion in his final work.[1] With good reason, Atherton stresses Joyce's attempt to subsume the texts of other authors in our literary tradition within his own writing. Disturbed by this attempt, Atherton refers to it gingerly in various ways but typically as "some odd idea."[2] In my discussion of the *Wake*, I shall explore that odd idea's rationale, effects, and implications. Inevitably, the numerous allusions suggest Joyce's intense self-consciousness about the artifice of literature, a self-consciousness that has become a critical cliché. Rather than being explanatory, the cliché points to what needs explaining, not through identifying Joyce's sources but by interpreting the technique of allusion itself. By interpreting that technique, we can define Joyce's conception of

1

the two activities most pertinent to the literary text as language: writing and reading.

Once we consider the *process* of alluding as well as the result of that process, the linking of writing with reading for Joyce becomes clear. No matter how often critics assert the symbolic nature of Joyce's works, his allusions are *not* symbolic in any easily defined way. Instead, they indicate the process of reading, which was a crucial component of Joyce's acts of writing. We encounter implicitly again and again in Joyce's tales the image of the artist actively engaged in reading and reusing the literary tradition. Sometimes that image emerges in curious ways. Among the most curious is Joyce's propensity to allude to his own earlier writing in *Finnegans Wake*.[3] The book is a veritable "Aludin's Cove" (108.27), in which the thieving author plunders himself. Even the phrase "Aludin's Cove," as Joyce uses it, reveals the tendency I have in mind. Here Joyce refers to *The Thousand and One Nights*, to Wyndham Lewis, and to *Ulysses*, for Lewis had said *Ulysses* was "an Aladdin's cave of incredible bricabrac."[4] Joyce's transforming of the phrase makes Lewis's remark and, indirectly, Joyce's own earlier work, part of the narrative's bric-a-brac.[5] In general, Joyce's allusions to *Ulysses* involve a similar layering of references. The complicated superimposing can occur because *Ulysses* itself contains the network of allusions to Homer's *Odyssey* that critics have explored so thoroughly. By including *Ulysses* in *Finnegans Wake* through allusion, Joyce indicates the Homeric aspect of his late writing and the connection to his own earlier work. To begin investigating the Homeric nature of aesthetic creation in Joyce's fiction, it will be helpful to look first at the artist as character in the *Wake*.*

Numerous passages of *Finnegans Wake* focus, though often not exclusively, on the process of artistic creation. Many of these passages concern either Shem the Penman or one of the letters that appear repeatedly during the narrative. In the *Wake*, Joyce adopts a protean narrating persona. This labile teller describes a character, Shem the Penman, who writes the real author's books. As several passages suggest, these texts are self-representations of Shem. Through this curious, pseudonymous, fictional presentation of the author as Shem and of Shem as an author in *Finnegans Wake*,

---

*Any discussion of *Finnegans Wake* will necessarily emphasize certain parts of that text at the expense of others. My commentary deals largely with the following sections and topics: the beginning (I.1) and ending (IV, especially 613.08–628.16), the section concerning Shem the Penman (I.7), the geometrical construction in the Schoolroom section (II.2), various allusions to *Ulysses* and to Homer, the tale of the Ondt and the Gracehoper (III.1), and several representations of Anna Livia's letter, especially the section about the "mamafesta" (I.5) and the elliptical version mentioned during the trial in I.4. For ease of reference, especially for those readers who have not studied the *Wake* at length, I have quoted longer passages that I treat extensively. The quoting makes for some congestion in the first half of this chapter, but that seems unavoidable given the nature of the text and this commentary.

Joyce's narrator manipulates the complicated relationships among author, teller, and tale with comic intensity. He does so by focusing on the doubling accompanying every act of narration, every adoption by an author of some persona as teller. We perceive the manipulation and doubling especially clearly in the *Wake* because Joyce incongruously assigns his own works to Shem. By implication, Joyce's texts, like Shem's, including the *Wake* itself, are self-representations of the character who is an author *and* of the real author. As autobiographical fiction, then, the *Wake* extends and distinguishes itself from Joyce's other autobiographical narratives by invoking them and their writer. We shall want to probe the nature of the connections between the *Wake* and the earlier fiction as we explore Joyce's presentation of the artist. For Joyce to assign his own published works openly to a character is a new departure. In *A Portrait* and in *Ulysses*, Stephen Dedalus writes a villanelle, keeps a journal, composes some verse on the strand, and tells stories, but Joyce never published any of these works separately under his own name. He did, however, occasionally use the pseudonym "Stephen Daedalus." As we shall see, allusions to Joyce's published works in passages dealing with Shem the Penman are unmistakable. In particular, Shem's writing, like at least one version of the recurring letter, resembles *Ulysses* in striking ways. Additionally, Joyce emphasizes his connection to the Penman through the name he assigns him. Joyce's persona as writer becomes linked to his character by the shared comparison with Jim the Penman, the notorious forger.[6]

While the tale presents characters, in this case as an author, it also constitutes a representation of the teller as the real author's narrating persona.[7] Because the artist's self-representation frames the character as artist, the reader can gauge the teller's own activities by comparison with the actions of the character. The interlocking configurations of teller with characters resemble the complicated framing and linking frequently presented in the *Wake*'s narration in passages reminiscent of "The House That Jack Built."[8] With respect to Shem the Penman, we can conclude the following about the relationship of author to teller and to character in *Finnegans Wake: Joyce wrote the book whose teller describes a writer who reads a book that resembles a book that Joyce wrote and who lives in a house that looks like a book and like the "jas jos" inside the house whose interior resembles the end of a book that Joyce wrote*. The warrant and the details for describing the relationship in this convoluted fashion occur in I.7, the chapter of the *Wake* that dwells at the greatest length on Shem, his life, and his works.

To complicate the situation, the reader can become enmeshed in something like these configurations. We tend to lose our distance from them, if only temporarily, and always in the midst of laughter, for at least two reasons. On the one hand, the language of the *Wake* forces us to collaborate with Joyce by rewriting his text as we read it through our actively re-creative response. But more to the point about the specific presentation of Shem in I.7, *he* is described as *both* reader and author. The text he reads and writes appears to be *Ulysses*: "It would have diverted, if ever seen, the shuddersome spectacle of this semidemented zany amid the inspissated grime of his glaucous den making believe to read his usylessly unreadable Blue Book of Eccles, *édition de ténèbres*" (179.24–27). As the writer of *Ulysses* or a book like it, for Shem to read that book would be for him to read "*the book of himself*" (*U* 187), to adopt a prominent phrase from "Scylla and Charybdis" alluding to Mallarmé. Both Shem's places of habitation—his den and the book he reads and writes—are blue. The den is glaucous, and the Book of Eccles is blue, as was the first Paris edition of *Ulysses*, an *édition de lux*, transmogrified here to an *édition de ténèbres*. Shem's book is also blue because of its supposed obscenity.

According to the narration in I.7, Shem has martyred himself: "(O, you were excruciated, in honor bound to the cross of your own cruelfiction!)" (192.17–19).[9] Some details of Shem's existence reiterate the self-destructive aspects of writing. More generally, repeatedly in the *Wake*, self-destruction characterizes the activity of aesthetic creation. It does so in part because artistic making, as a central element in the presentation of HCE and his family, becomes a metaphor embracing birth, sexuality, and death. For Joyce, writing is the copula as copulation linking birth and death. Specifically, it is a *felix culpa*, a fortunate fall that results in a creation like birth and in an expenditure of energies leading to death. The death and the birth are inseparable. Joyce indicates that inseparable quality in some of his many puns on *felix culpa*: "finixed coulpure" (311.26), "phaymix cupplerts" (331.2), "Colporal Phailinx" (346.36). The culpable, happy coupling of aesthetic creation as metaphor for life is corporeal, or nearly so. And it is a finish that is also a phoenix, an ending that marks a new beginning. I shall return later to the phoenix's complicated role in the *Wake* and in Joyce's conception of his own writing.

Shem's text, the site of his "cruelfiction," is "unreadable" because of its difficulty. As Anna Livia comments about her spouse, Shem's father, in the extended postscript to the long letter of IV, every text, "every letter[,] is a hard but yours sure is the hardest crux ever" (623.33–34). Here, in the typical fashion of the *Wake*, frame and tale, narration and narrative, are superimposed. Both fathers of the character-as-artist who writes difficult texts, the father in the narrative and the father of the narrative, create difficult texts. All these works spell in their sibylline leaves the name of the father, here HCE in "*h*ardest *c*rux *e*ver." Shem, the fictional author of *Ulysses*, is "bound" within the binding of the book itself. He *is* that book. In his act of creation Shem has made ink from his own urine and excrement in order to write on his body:[10] "[He] made synthetic ink and sensitive paper for his own end out of his wit's waste" (185.6–8). For Shem, the act of writing remakes and annihilates the artist, whose death and resurrection form the subject of the tale the artist writes. The dual process reveals itself in various ways in the language of the *Wake*. It resembles *"the abnihilisation of the etym"* (353.22) referred to in one of the bracketed interludes that occur during the skit by Butt and Taff in II.3, the Tavern chapter. The apparent destruction of the word and of truth (Gr. *etymos*, true; *etymon*, true sense of a word) is also the creation of them, seemingly *ex nihilo*.[11] In a passage I shall come back to later because it alludes to the printing of the text, the process of making attempts to sustain "the sameold gamebold adomic structure of our Finnius the old One" (615.6–7) in spite of decomposition, perhaps partly as a result of it. The atom, whether "etym" or Adam, maintains a recognizable integrity amid the detritus of experience.

Shem's aesthetic creations, like Joyce's books, emerge from detritus, from the waste of earlier creative acts. This is Joyce's law of the conservation of literary matter. The scraps include the unused portions of the author's previous attempts to create, parts of the earlier creations, and portions of works left behind by other writers. We know for instance that early in the writing of *Finnegans Wake* Joyce began collecting material in a notebook divided according to his own writings. This is the notebook published as *Scribbledehobble*.[12] We cannot be certain, of course, how much of the material collected was originally intended for the earlier works, how much was simply triggered by Joyce's retrospective reaction to those works, and how much was entered for other reasons unknown to us. But one rationale for the notebook is clear. Joyce was consciously connecting the new work to the previous ones, however obscurely, at the start of his process of writing. More important for readers of the *Wake*, whether or not they read the notebook, in the self-conscious activity of making art from leftovers, Joyce inscribes that activity within the tale he tells.

The following passage from I.7 describing at length Shem's excremental acts of creation presents the author's relation to his writings:

> . . . he shall produce nichthemerically from his unheavenly body a no uncertain quantity of obscene matter not protected by copriright in the United Stars of Ourania . . . with this double dye, brought to blood heat, gallic acid on iron ore, through the bowels of his misery . . . the first till last alshemist wrote over every square inch of the only foolscap available, his own body, till by its corrosive sublimation one continuous present tense integument slowly unfolded all marryvoising moodmoulded cyclewheeling history (thereby, he said, reflecting from his own individual person life unlivable, transaccidentated through the slow fires of consciousness into a dividual chaos, perilous, potent, common to all flesh, human only, mortal) but with each word that would not pass away the squidself which he had squirtscreened from the crystalline world waned chagreenold and doriangrayer in its dudhud. (185.28–186.8)[13]

The *édition de ténèbres* is a "nichthemeric," a night-Homeric and a non-Homeric, production simultaneously continuous with and different from its creator. The Greek word from which Joyce derived "nichthemerically" also means the duration of a night and a day, the span of time of *Ulysses*. The "usylessly unreadable" book reflects an "unlivable" life, a life that is fiction, a construction of words. It transforms the author's individual person into a "dividual," both a divided-dual and a more than *in*dividual, but still human form. The slow fires of consciousness effect the tranformation. These fires of imagination burn with sufficient intensity to temper and strengthen but not to weaken or destroy the metal being produced. They are the long-lasting, self-perpetuating, phoenixlike fires of the printed word. Consequently, they outlast the quickly burning, self-consuming fire of the author's process of doubling that is writing and narration. The references to acid and ore underscore the suggestion of tempering and refining, as in the production of metal. Refined by division of its elements, the product is rid of impurities, free of anything not "common to all flesh."

As a result of the transforming, creative act, the writer passes through a series of protean, allotropic states represented by, and sometimes *in*, the works he writes. The text is a continuous present-tense integument, like "Circe" and "Penelope" in *Ulysses* or like all works of art, which can be said to occupy an eternal present. The work's relation to time differs from the author's, for the artist grows old in the squidlike, reproductive activity of producing works that will not pass away. The word "dudhud" in the presentation of the squidself's waning "chagreenold and doriangrayer in its dudhud" as it creates, indicates the ambiguous activity (deedhood) in its creative nature (dadhood) and in its failure (dudhood) to preserve absolutely the self of the creator, except as language. As the writer becomes more wholly part of the past by expending energies in the act of creation, the text created becomes more completely and permanently present, as it preserves the author but fails to keep him from passing away. Like Wilde's Dorian Gray, the artist destroys himself in the act of creating a persona, or mask.[14] The writer contributes to his own demise by producing passages of language that defeat the passage of time.

The issue of beating time, in various senses, arises, among other places in *Finnegans Wake*, in the fable of the Ondt and the Gracehoper (414.16–419.11). Their confrontation suggests the contrast and connection between writer and reader by focusing on different relations to time. The Gracehoper, like Shem, is a "capsizer" (418.5), someone who rocks the boat and perhaps is mad as a hatter. After the Gracehoper "sekketh rede" (418.6) from the Ondt, the parable concludes with a lyric that poses a crucial question: "*Why can't you beat time?*" (419.8). In one frame of reference, the question implies that the Gracehoper's ability to make melodies, involving both keeping time to music and defeating time, distinguishes him as an artist from his brother creature, who only reads. While extreme, the contrast is not absolute, especially given the ambiguities of the statement and the Gracehoper's manner of living. In order to beat time by making music, he must expend himself to limits that threaten his annihilation. Consequently, he needs the Ondt as his helper, listener, reader, whatever the differences between them. As Shem's act of reading his own work indicates, the roles of writer and reader are not radically distinct. Rather, they coalesce into a composite, "dividual" form. The combination occurs because writing and reading are complementary.

Several other details of the parable suggest that its two figures are not entirely distinct. By the end, the Ondt has begun to cavort in the way the Gracehoper did previously (417.24–32; cf. 414.22–35). And the lyric itself emphasizes the possible reversal by suggesting the Ondt exchange roles with the Gracehoper by playing Jacob to his Esau (418.35). But the lyric is addressed to the Gracehoper as well as the Ondt in the final question about beating time, for he too suffers from "chronic's despair" (417.35–36). As so often in the *Wake*, apparent opposites coalesce. This particular merger is rendered as the Ondt's metaphorically coming to live in the Gracehoper's house when the Gracehoper actually comes to visit the Ondt's house. At the beginning of the parable, the Gracehoper lives in a house "cald fourmillierly Tingsomingenting" (414.34), while the Ondt lives in a house "cold antitopically Nixnixundnix" (415.29). But by the end, the Ondt is acting "like thingsumanything in formicolation" (417.26–27). Through various linguistic plays and repetitions, Joyce links each character with his antagonist's house. I mention these details about the houses because Shem and Glugg, one of his later incarnations, live in dwellings that merge the parable's two abodes. And in Joyce's earlier fiction, home, especially the act of leaving or returning home, is central. Shem's house is not only "the Haunted Inkbottle" but also "niggs, niggs and niggs . . . stinksome inkenstink" (183.5–6). Glugg's "shome" (231.4) is "a hovel not a havel. . . with a tingtumtingling and a next, next and next" (231.1–2). The houses are their inhabitants' books, in which characters can apparently become "*now one and the same person*" (354.8), as Butt, Taff, and many others do in the *Wake*.

The implications of these various representations of home are not limited to the narrative. They affect our understanding of the narration and of the way we read. They do so most obviously in the fable of the Ondt and the Gracehoper when we consider the possibilities for reversal or merger of roles with regard to the lyric's speaker. Because the song is not clearly assigned to either Gracehoper or Ondt, we are asked to treat both as the possible originators and performers of the song's words. Whichever character we choose provisionally to hear singing, the question about beating time turns out to apply to both singer (or teller) and listener, for it is a question about the failure of art to defeat death absolutely and about failures in the making of art, whether by the listener or the singer. Like the surrounding narration of the fable and the contents of the song, the dual, or "dividual," identity of the singer illustrates the roles in revolution so characteristic of

the *Wake*'s story and its storytelling. A double vision creates the oscillating perspective for the reader. Here, as elsewhere in the *Wake*, the only
definitive answer to the question "*Who is speaking*?" is the pragmatic
one: the *reader* speaks by taking on the role of the artist as teller. The
ambiguous status of the text's language not only allows but *requires* us to
mimic the teller in different voices that merge with one another.

In I.5, the chapter concerning the "untitled mamafesta" (104.4), reading
as textual inspection provides the means for coalescing to occur:

> Closer inspection of the *bordereau* would reveal a multiplicity of personali-
> ties inflicted on the documents or document. . . . In fact, under the closed eyes
> of the inspectors the traits featuring the *chiaroscuro* coalesce, their contrari-
> eties eliminated, in one stable somebody similarly as by the providential
> warring . . . our social something bowls along bumpily, experiencing a jolting
> series of prearranged disappointments, down the long lane of (it's as semper
> as oxhousehumper!) generations, more generations and still more genera-
> tions. (107.23–36).

The emergence of one somebody, which takes place because of reading as
investigation, happens in the readers' processes of mind during a state of
consciousness like dreaming, not in any scene fully accessible to the waking
senses. The "multiplicity of personalities" refers not only to the text's
numerous characters. It includes the author's changing personae and the
multitude of readers, whose minds may be as multiple and divisible as the
author's seems to be. Because the social process of communication
accomplished through writing and reading the book always fails in some
way, more generations are required in order to compensate for the
disappointments inherent in using language. The generations include the
further creations of the author and of other authors. But they are also later
generations of readers, some of them authors, who will inspect the text
anew. The coalescing and generating processes never reach an absolute
end. They are always with us and always only partially successful, like the
perpetual ("semper") nature of language, indicated by the reference to the
beginning of the Hebrew alphabet in "oxhousehumper."[15]

The shifting inherent to language itself helps generate the multiplicity of
protean characters in the *Wake* to be inspected and fused. Because the
fusion involves the processes as well as the products of aesthetic making,
reader fuses with writer and listener with teller as the acts of generating
approach a universal state. The author's self-consuming generating of texts
turns out to be a kind of burial giving rise to generations of readings as
resurrections. Tome as tomb to be opened becomes epitaph *and* progeny,
the writer's end and continuance. In I.5 the teller announces himself first to
be "a worker, a tombstone mason" (113.34), then a weaver of Oriental
carpets. The carpet's pattern is the teller's track as "proteiform graph"
(107.8), "tracing of a purely deliquescent recidivist" (107.10). This

habitual criminal's deliquescence is dual: both his melting away or dissolving in the book as river and his repeated acts of division to create networks, as in the veins of a leaf. His *Wake* is both the River Liffey speaking and the "leafy speafing" (619.20).

In his simultaneously defensive and self-revelatory act of writing, Shem devises a squirtscreen between his squidself and the world, a shield behind which he withdraws. But the passage quoted previously also suggests that the squidself is itself the squirtscreen that the author has produced spider-like using the materials of the world to write "the mystery of himsel in furniture" (184.9–10). This mystery, analogous to a religious mystery concerning the status of the divine creator, involves the simultaneous continuity and discontinuity between self and world, between teller and tale, and between reader and tale. The furniture mentioned is part of a pervasive group of references in the *Wake* to printing, the mechanical process that intervenes between author and book but also makes the book and the communication of reader and writer possible. In printing, furniture consists of wooden or metal pieces used to create both the blank spaces between type and the blank margins of the pages.[16] In both I.7 and at the conclusion of the *Wake*'s final monologue, the ambiguous use of the preposition "from" captures the paradoxical mysteries of writing and reading. *From* the materials of the world Shem makes himself as he screens himself from the world: "the squidself . . . he had squirtscreened from the crystalline world" (186.7–8). Later, Anna Livia addresses both her husband *and* the reader when she claims: "You're changing from me" (626.36). On the final page of the *Wake*, she informs those who are changing because of her and away from her: "My leaves have drifted from me" (628.6). At the "phoenish" (4.17) of the text, the artist leaves behind the book's leaves that have emanated from him. To reach that point of separation is the end for reader, writer, and character. The reader who is "phoenished" (130.11) has changed from (because of and away from) the experience of reading a text whose leaves and leavings are still in the reader's possession and in possession of the reader.

The statement about Shem's self-revelation in the furniture of printing occurs at the end of a long paragraph describing his house, "the House O'Shea or O'Shame . . . known as the Haunted Inkbottle" (182.30–31) or the "inkbattle house" (176.31). The description reiterates the intimate connection between teller and tale. As Stephen Dedalus suggests in his analysis of Shakespeare's relation to *Hamlet*, the author's text is haunted, because it contains the writer's ghostly voice (*U* 197). The exterior of the House O'Shame (Shame's House or James's House) resembles both the real author's eye-patched physiognomy and the cover of a book with a fictitious author's assumed name imprinted, "with his penname SHUT sepia scraped on the doorplate and a blind of black sailcloth over its wan phwinshogue" (182.32–34). The penname SHUT names Shame's Hut and alludes to the excremental nature of the writing.[17] The contents of the book as house, presented as an epic catalogue of miscellaneous litter, are the inky, personal, perhaps poisonous, puzzle of the writer: "For this was a stinksome inkenstink, quite puzzonal to the wrottel" (183.6–7). The word "inkenstink" fuses ink with instinct and continues the scatological references. The writer's ink-instinct to represent himself in language results in an inky end-stink. The smell may owe something to the traditional manner of storing leather appliances for inking type in handpress printing shops. The leather pelts were kept soft by soaking them in urine. The practice must have given the printing house something more than a faintly scented aroma.[18]

The prominent allusion to Molly Bloom's monologue at the end of the catalogue of the house's contents aligns Shame's house, Shem's book, and Joyce's *Ulysses*. The catalogue contains a string of monosyllablic equivalents for the English word "yes" (184.1–2). Two juxtaposed syllables, "jas jos," abbreviate the name of the real author, whose identity is always implicit in the text. We learn that in the house as book "one stands, given a grain of good will, a fair chance of actually seeing the whirling dervish . . . writing the mystery of himsel in furniture" (184.4–10). By entering the author's book as house, the reader can inspect the house that Jack built in order to discover the Jack who built the house.

THE SPIRIT BEHIND THE LETTER

The document that Shem, or any of his avatars, reportedly writes together with his mother ALP is a letter, whose various versions are quoted from time to time.[19] In III.1 the collaboration of mom and Shem, "mem and hem" (422.33), is mentioned specifically. One of the most engimatic representations of the letter helps explain both the author's abbreviated signature in the litter of Shem's house and the relation of signature and letter to the *Wake*'s overall structure. This version, only two lines long, is reported toward the end of the trial in I.4, between the conclusion of testimony ("And so it all ended" [93.22]) and the meandering deliberations of the four justices:

> What was it?
> A . . . . !
> ? . . . . O! (94.20–22)

These two elliptical lines evoke alpha and omega, which mark the letter's limits and its context. This is the letter in its barest possible form. In the beginning was the letter, then letters, then an epistle as simple as a, b, c.

The paragraph preceding the question links the lines with sea and river. "The letter! The litter!" (93.24) is echoed a few pages further on in "The latter! The latter!" (100.2), an even closer approximation to the Greek word for sea, *thalatta*. In III.1, immediately after the Gracehoper's poem and before a section concerning Shem's letter-writing, "the latter" is mentioned as part of the parable's closing: "In the name of the former and of the latter and of their holocaust. Allmen" (419.9–10). This conclusion suggests terms for describing aesthetic creation as *Finnegans Wake* presents it. The image of the former—that is, of the maker, whether divine or aesthetic—appears in the maker's creation, no matter if that creation be the divine son or an aesthetic letter composed of alphabetic letters. For Joyce, in the literary text "maker mates with made" (261.8), like dancer with dance in Yeats's "Among School Children." The mystery of the former's production of the letter and his continuity with it is indicated by the ghostly presence in "the latter." Although the aesthetic former precedes his creation temporally, the letter eventually displaces the former because of the work of art's peculiar temporal status. The forming spirit originally behind the letter finally takes up a position within it. Anna Livia as river, whose presence the motif immediately preceding the letter in I.4 announces, is apparently both behind and within her epistle: "Now tell me, tell me, tell me then!" (94.19). Because she is the writer *and* the subject of the letter, what the letter tells is "me." It always tells *now* of the writer's "me" that existed *then*. The river motif, together with a question followed by an "A" indicating an answer, connects the letter with the multitude of questions and answers that occurs in the *Wake*, and especially with the dialogue of the two washerwomen in I.8. Born by wave and retrieved by hen, the letter is told by the "elm that whimpers at the top . . . [to] the stone that moans when stricken" (94.4–5): "It was folded with cunning, sealed with crime, uptied by a harlot, undone by a child. It was life but was it fair? It was free but was it art?" (94.8–10).

Some of these descriptive details make sense if the letter is written out on a long sheet of paper to be cunningly folded, not in the conventional manner but in the way a sheet of paper is doubled over on itself to create a Möbius strip. The Möbean version of the letter mirrors the shape of the book that is its context (see figures 1, 2, and 3). The letter so represented is the winding sheet or twisted tale that defines the recirculation of the narration in *Finnegans Wake*. It is told by whimpering elm to stricken, moaning stone because the book containing the letter that stands for the book is a printed document, an inked impression like that made by pressing wood on stone in certain kinds of printing. In the last paragraph of this chapter, we learn of our relation to the river: "We have taken our sheet upon her stones" (103.9). The sheet here is laundry, but it is also a sheet of paper pressed on stone to print the leaves of the book.

As Clive Hart, among others, has noted, in general the letter in *Finnegans Wake* is the image of the book.[20] Several pieces of evidence suggest that this particularly enigmatic letter can stand for the whole text. The notion of synecdoche, part standing for whole and whole for part, is introduced early in the *Wake* through the assertion that "when a part so ptee

Recto

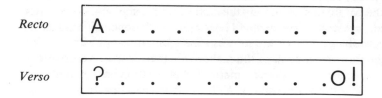

Verso

Figure 1

"The letter! The litter!" (93.24)

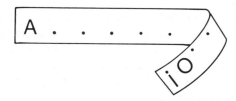

Figure 2

"furrowards, bagawards, like yoxen at the turnpaht" (18.32)

"by writing thithaways end to end and turning, turning and end to end hithaways writing" (114.16–17)

Recto = Verso

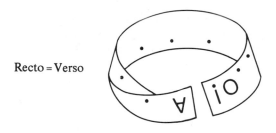

Figure 3

"an allforabit" (19.1–2)
"Doublends Jined" (20.16)
"thorough readable to intfrom and ... and this applies to its whole wholume" (48.17–18)

does duty for the holos we soon grow to use of an allforabit" (18.36–19.2). While suggesting the possible relationship of the petit, or small part, to the whole, of bit to all, this sentence presents the alphabet, or "allforabit," as that relationship itself. The alphabet implicit in the letter of I.4 defines one possible relation of part to whole, letter to text. *Finnegans Wake*, that "farced epistol to the hibruws" (228.33–34), contains letters that contain letters. By alluding to alpha and omega, first and last letters of the Greek alphabet, and to the connotations of those letters, especially their traditional connection with the all-pervasive presence of the divine creator, the letter reinforces some of the passages about Shem. Both small and large, contained and containing texts resemble sacred books with inscribed images of a creator. Consequently, we stand "a fair chance of actually seeing" the aesthetic creator whose mystery is contained in the mechanically printed book.

The implications of the two-line version, including the connections of letter with book, with sacred books, and with writing and printing, are not all immediately evident from the letter taken by itself, even though some of them are evoked by the context in I.4. They emerge more clearly when we take the letter as part of a network of passages dealing with Shem, the *Odyssey*, Joyce's texts, and the art of printing. In II.2, the passages following the failure of Glugg, as avatar of Shem, to guess "heliotrope" the first time in the guessing game illustrates the kind of repetition with variation that creates the network I have in mind. Many of the details of Shem's life are repeated but assigned to Glugg. When he leaves home, he writes "his farced epistol to the hibruws" (228.33–34). Either the exile or that epistle, probably both, is like *Ulysses*, the twelve middle episodes of which are alluded to in order (229.13–16). Glugg writes at his mother's dictation for "auditers" who include "Caxton" (229.31), the famous printer of Malory. The question the narrator puts about Glugg's activities, "Was liffe worth leaving," conflates several of the elements associated with writing in this and other sections of the *Wake*. Was it worth leaving Ireland, as the accused seems to do after the trial in I.4 and as the wandering writer inevitably does in Joyce's fiction? That leaving is also the turning of the River Liffey into printed leaves. And the production of leaves is death, our leaving this life. By reinforcing through repetition some of the perspectives presented in other parts of the narrative, this kind of reprise clarifies the basic aspects of the character-as-writer's life and brings a modicum of order to individual sections and finally to the work at large.

In the first and last chapters of the *Wake*, in its alpha and omega, some sense of the book's overarching order emerges, though briefly. If we take the elliptical letter as paradigm for the whole work, we expect to find connections between beginning and end amounting to more than just the continuation of the final words on the first page. As we shall see, passages near the book's beginning and its ending echo and complement one another.

Their placement and implications help explain the letter of I.4, just as *it* creates a structure in which their placement and implications make sense. Together with the elliptical letter, the early and late, former and latter sections tell us some important things about the small and large structures of the *Wake*, about its parts as separate but linked and as very nearly interchangeable.

BEGINNINGS AND ENDINGS/ COMPOSITION AND DECOMPOSITION (I.1 and IV)

Although the beginning and the ending of the *Wake* do not repeat one another in any slavish way, several repetitions do occur. We find the connecting links mostly between the ten pages or so following the tour of the "museyroom" (10–20) and those preceding ALP's final monologue (609–19). The *Wake*, then, has a postlude and a prelude consisting of its last and first few pages (619–28; 3–10). And the pages immediately preceding the postlude bear comparison with the section immediately following the prelude. These comparable sections contain the first and last full statements of the sentence Joyce borrowed from Edgar Quinet and transformed,[21] the first and last lengthy references to the letter, and the first and last dialogues between invader and native. For the most part, the order of presentation in I.1 reverses that of IV. If we treat the narrative as a continuous loop with ends joined, the repetition in reversed order forms a chiasmus, like the sequence of dates announced in I.1: "1132 A.D. . . . . 566 A.D. . . . (Silent.) 566 A.D. . . . 1132 A.D." (13.33–14.11). The two passages I explore here occur just after the dialogues. The earlier one (18.17–21.4) is placed between the dialogue of Mutt and Jute and the story of the prankquean. The later one (613.8–615.11) follows the dialogues of Muta and Juva and of Patrick with the druid, but precedes the final letter and monologue of ALP.

The passage in I.1 begins by inviting the reader to stop, "please stoop" (18.17), to experience the words of the printed text that the teller offers and to recognize the complex implications that make those words a world.[22] The reader who is "abcedminded" may be able to "rede" the world of "this claybook," with its "allaphbed" (18.18–19). The "abcedminded" can learn the book's "allforabit," the constituent elements of its language and the manner in which part and whole stand for one another. Often in the *Wake* the word "clay," as in "claybook," suggests the French word *clef* and its English equivalent "key." *Finnegans Wake* is like a *roman à clef*, because at least one character, Shem the Penman, can be associated with a real person, the author. The writer's inspiration, like that of the god of creation, provides the "human only, mortal" (186.4–5), claylike book with life. And the word "clay" connects the book with the four commentators, called "Mamalujo" after the names of the four Gospel writers: Matthew,

Mark, Luke, and John. These four, appearing frequently with their ass, who may narrate at times in Book III, are "claymen" (475.18). Shem is also a "keyman" (186.15). Especially in the context of other references to printing, the words "clay" and "ass," like "furniture," "sheet," and "leaf," indicate the making of the book. A "clayman" mixes clay, water, and dispersing agents for use in papermaking. Thus, the book that employs the paper so made and that inscribes within itself the process of making could be called a claybook.[23] This reading is confirmed when we learn that Shem the "keyman" did make his own "sensitive paper for his own end out of his wit's waste" (185.7-8). But that paper is Shem's own skin. The "only foolscap available" is "his own body" (185.35-36). Consequently, the artist makes *himself* from his own mortal clay when he writes the book of himself as the mystery in furniture. His book, like the narratives about Earwicker's naming, will inevitably be "andrewpaulmurphyc" (31.35), or anthropomorphic; they reveal the shape of a man and of humankind. It seems entirely likely that Joyce would have known the tradition of calling the compositor in a printing shop the "ass."[24] This early passage, then, links the history of writing explicitly to the making of books and to this book. We learn that even in an age with "as yet no lumpend papeer" (19.31), "the world . . .was and will be writing its own wrunes for ever" (19.35-36), just as it is now. While the world writes simultaneously its runes, or songs, and its ruins, we are asked to "rede" the world of the claybook produced by the writing.

Both within this printed book and in the history of humankind's development, printing announces itself as one aspect of the world "writing its own wrunes for ever":

> . . . and Gutenmorg with his cromagnom charter, tintingfast and great primer must once for omniboss step rubrickredd out of the wordpress else is there no virtue more in alcohoran. For that (the rapt one warns) is what papyr is meed of, made of, hides and hints and misses in prints. Till ye finally (though not yet endlike) meet with the acquaintance of Mister Typus, Mistress Tope and all the little typtopies. Fillstup. So you need hardly spell me how every word will be bound over to carry three score and ten toptypsical readings throughout the book of Doublends Jined (may his forehead be darkened with mud who would sunder!) till Daleth, mahomahouma, who oped it closeth thereof the. Dor. (20.7-18)

Gutenberg, the inventor of printing with movable type, appears as the morning "with his cromagnom charter . . . great primer," which is both the Magna Carta and a Cro-Magnon letter. Great primer also happens to be a size of printing type. The letter presumably resembles the earlier "meanderthalltale" (19.25), or Neanderthal story, which is the "meandertale" (18.22) of wanderings we are asked to "rede." As maker of the document, the printer is himself the "omniboss," hero and author of the story, who emerges from the press like a newborn child, "rubrickredd." A book may be embossed for decoration, but this "omniboss" is the context of the whole. (The English word "boss" derives from the French *bosse*, meaning "hump" or "hunch," the mark of HCE.) The printer is compositor and reader as well as hero and writer because printing involves composing and then reading the rubrics composed. The printing of rubrics—that is, passages in red—indicates the sacred nature of what emerges from the press: the religious books that Gutenberg actually printed; the book itself, like *Finnegans Wake*, as "wordpress," or storing place for words, from which Gutenberg emerges (in *A Portrait* Dante stores her brushes in a press); and Gutenberg himself as a booklike entity, the maker who has achieved some measure of identity with the books he produced (his book is not just the Bible, but the Gutenberg Bible). Gutenberg and the author who speaks here are "rapt," wrapped in the winding sheets of their own creations. The book of Gutenmorg seems Homeric because, like the Homeric mornings, this one is red, if not rosy-fingered (G., *Morgenröte*, dawn). One version of the recurring encounter in the *Wake* between the Russian General and Buckley occurs "on that redletter morning" (50.31–32), which among other times is the morning on which the letter is read. And the ballad at the end of I.2 written by Hosty about Earwicker is "privately printed at the rimepress of Delville" with a "red woodcut" (43.25–26). Gutenberg's stepping forth is associated with the power of "alcohoran."[25] Whatever else that word refers to, it includes the vowels "A" and "O" in a chiastic sequence, "a-o-o-a," indicating the presence of something like the divine alpha and omega in sacred books. Through the letters of language, that presence becomes disseminated into the human world generally, but specifically into this text. In alphabetical arrangements that are "allforabit," spelling creates chiastic sequences suggesting a presence in the words whose virtue allows Gutenmorg to step forth.

Chiasmus is illustrated two pages earlier in the first paragraph following the dialogue of Mutt and Jute: "furrowards, bagawards, like yoxen at the turnpaht. Here say figurines billycoose arming and mounting. Mounting and arming bellicose figurines see here" (18.32–34). The reader is to say and see what the teller sees and says the figurines say and see. The story is both chiastic and, like Martha Clifford's encoded address in "Ithaca" (*U* 706), boustrophedontic, taking the form of repetitions with a difference that resemble the back-and-forth movement of plowing. When ending and beginning are one, progress becomes a winding movement of the bag of words backwards down the furrow just made. The various plays on "backwards" in the *Wake* sometimes indicate the looking-glass perceptions of the compositor, who must reverse through "backwords" (100.28), "tantrist spellings" (571.7) the shapes and sequences of characters in the act of setting type. If the printer provides one analogue for the writer in *Finnegans Wake* because the work of printing involves letters and ink, then so does the actor in a theatrical troupe when its members are "players of Inkermann the mime" (48.10). The saga they perform is "readable to int from and," as would be a chiastic, continuous integument that could be started in the middle and read toward the introduction. When we read ALP's letter in IV, after "Dear," we begin *in medias res* with "And," then proceed toward the book's end and introduction. Of the persons in the saga, both characters and actors, as in a story whose double ends are joined, "no one end is known" (48.24).

Through the virtuoso and protean power of imaginative enactment and making associated with acting, writing, and printing, in *Finnegans Wake*, *homo ludens* as *homo faber* mimes, in comic Promethean fashion, the status traditionally associated with the godhead. Because human creations are full of the misprints, hints, and concealments (such as Shem's concealment behind his squirtscreen), for which paper is one medium, the words of "the book of Doublends Jined" (20.15–16) are bound, as are all words in books, to require multiple readings. These readings include the repeated perusals of the printer's proofs needed for making corrections and revisions, which may involve "tantrist spellings," such as those alluded to in the "Aeolus" episode of *Ulysses* (*U* 122). And they are the multiple meanings that proliferate until the person who opened the book "closeth thereof the" (20.17–18). The closing of the *Wake*, its final word, is, of course, "the." The distinction made between "finally" and "endlike" (20.11–12) in the passage about Gutenmorg indicates that "the" is not likely to be entirely final. Eventually, that is, finally but not absolutely finally, reader and author reach a state of repletion that is more a filling up ("fillstup" [20.13]) than a full stop. The book's last "the" lacks the punctuation of the full stop; the end is the "int."

Reader and author reach a provisionally final state when they "meet with the acquaintance of Mister Typus, Mistress Tope and all the little typtopies" (20.12–13) in such a way that the words can be bound over for closure, though not for ending in any categorical sense. When such closure takes place, the general, the myth, type, or archetype becomes incarnated in a specific place and at a specific occasion (in two senses of *topos*). Type as *model* then proliferates as "typtopies," both further incarnations of the myth and multiple copies in the typeface of printed books. In the making of the book, the typed copies of manuscripts are set in printing type to make passages (*topoi* again). In their complementary experiences with the text, reader and author meet with the acquaintance and make the acquaintance of type and *topos* as they become familiars of the text. The author meets with the printer, the person acquainted with types who is indispensable for publishing. And the author as teller meets with the reader, who must already be acquainted with printing type in order to experience the text. At the same time, the author makes the reader into a new acquaintance by creating the reader's persona. If the author chooses, as Joyce did, he can develop strategies for letting the reader perceive the continuity and overlap of reading, writing, and printing in the bookmaking process. Through the allusions to printing in the *Wake*, the reader can realize the experience of meeting author and printer, the acquaintances of type and *typos*. The writer, his book as epistle, and his printer concerned with letters, all together "once for omniboss step rubrickredd out of the wordpress," when the rubrics are read.

At this point it is worth pausing briefly to consider why Joyce decided to include printing terms in his book. Hugh Kenner has commented that *Ulysses* "was set in type the Gutenberg way, by hand": There had been typesetting machines for 30-odd years, but '*Ulysses*' was surely the biggest book of any importance to be set by hand since William Morris had set the Kelmscott Chaucer in 1893–96. . . . Moreover, the 'Ulysses' typesetters, of whom there were at least 26, lived in Dijon and knew no English whatsoever, which means they held strings of meaningless letters in their heads while swivelling back and forth between typescript and typecase."[26] This situation surely contributed to the statement in the *Wake* that the letter has "a multiplicity of personalities inflicted on" it (107.24–25). Given the problems Joyce had with publishers and printers prior to *Ulysses* and the difficulties in producing that book's first edition, by the time Joyce came to write *Finnegans Wake*, he must have largely integrated instructions to printers into his notions of writing and reading. Because his printers were his readers and, inevitably, he was theirs when he received proofs, Joyce must have considered the printer to be his collaborator and, frequently, his antagonist. In consequence, printing terms become primary metaphors as well as literal descriptions for the making of his books.

The printing terms have an advantage over other metaphors for literary creation. They can be rendered more immediately in the reader's experience of the book than other language describing writing because we have before us printed matter. There is always a large disparity inherent in any narration that tries to present the physical and imaginative acts of writing something down. In *A Portrait*, for example, we do not see Stephen's handwritten stanzas when he writes the villanelle on the rough surface of the cigarette packet. We cannot. Instead, we perceive the stanzas neatly printed in italic type. In the *Wake*, Joyce can create more immediate effects using printing terms and typography. In II.2, the Schoolroom chapter, one of Shem's avatars, Dolph, gives his brother, Kev, instructions for constructing a geometrical figure that represents ALP's gentials.[27] The procedure consists of first marking a point "A," or alpha, on the left, then a point "L," or lambda, on the right. These are the centers for drawing two intersecting circles of radius AL, one of whose intersections determines the point "P," which is marked last at the bottom of the diagram. On the page in which Dolph directs the connecting of the letters into a triangle, or delta, the lefthand margin contains the following comment in italics: "*Zweispaltung as Fundemaintalish of Wiederherstellung*" (296.L1). Next to that comment Dolph is instructing Kev "to mack a capital Pee for Pride down there on the batom[1]" (296.5–6). The marginal comment, which means "division into two is fundamental to restoration," resembles Stephen's statements in *Ulysses* about no reconciliation without sundering. But *zweispaltig* also happens to be a German typographical term that refers to printing in double columns. The marginal comment, then, resembles the author's direction to the printer to set a page with double columns. And that is how the pages of this chapter are set, with double columns of marginal comments flanking the central passages. While Kev is directed to make a capital "P" at the bottom of the diagram, we are told by the superscript indicating a footnote to look at the bottom of the page. There we find that the first word of the note begins with a capital "P." Dolph's instruction resembles the typical instruction a proofreader gives to a printer to make a letter a capital. Through his use of typography and a typographical term Joyce can align Dolph's instructions for constructing the diagram with the author's instructions to his printer for making the page and with his directions to his readers. All are involved in analogous activities. The literal directions of movement involved are from the left to the right and then down. And those are the directions along which writing and reading proceed.

Once the book has been opened, once it has become rubrics for reading, it can only be closed "finally (though not yet endlike)" in the middle. The reader of this text with joined ends is always in the midst of its language because of the invitation to participate actively in the telling of the tale. To "rede . . . its world" (18.18–19) is both to read the story and to utter it, for *Rede* in German means "speech." As the final paragraph of the section about Gutenberg in I.1 reports, this book is busily in motion for us. The narrator advises us to "look what you have in your handself": "The movibles are scrawling in motions, marching, all of them ago, in pitpat and zing-zang for every busy eerie whig's a bit of a torytale to tell" (20.21–23). The movable type of Gutenberg is alive and in motion in the hand of the person holding the book. This sentence, itself set in movable type, contains the alphabetical, synecdochic tale that it says movable type contains. That story, implicit in the letter, concerns the container that contains itself, in which the teller as "eerie" whig has and is a story to tell: "The movibles are scrawling . . . *all* . . . *for* . . . *a bit* . . . to tell" (my emphasis). And it concerns the past continuing into the present, where "ago" is still a-going.

The teller's vision of aesthetic processes, both creation and response, makes the realistic aspects of fiction, including his own, laughable. He suggests that "you can ask your ass if he believes" (20.26) this "one's upon a thyme" story that proliferates to "two's behind," then "three's among"

(20.23–24), and so on, to an infinite number of possible stories. However unbelievable the tale, the sustaining reality that involves teller with reader is written into it by the movables. This reality of the coalescing "multiplicity of personalities inflicted on the documents" (107.24–25) emerges in the use of pronouns in I.1 just before the story of the prankquean. After enjoining the reader to listen, "Lissom! lissom!" (21.2), the teller says ambiguously, "I am doing it" (21.3).[28] Here the teller speaks for himself, for the reader, and for ALP, who is confirming the teller's claim that "it's sure it was her not we" (20.36). Reader, teller, and character are doing "it" together. The specific nature of "it" matters much less than the parallel acts of "doing."

In *Finnegans Wake*, truth in art does not require verisimilitude, or it does so only incidentally. The wish the teller expresses at the end of I.2 concerning "the rann that Hosty made" (44.7–8) about Earwicker, a rann spoken by many, applies to this book to be "rede" by many: "May the treeth we tale of live in stoney" (44.9). When the wood of the engraving block meets the impressing stone, printed matter emerges as truth, having achieved a stonelike character. The stoney permanence resembles an epitaph carved by the "tombstone mason" (113.34): "Here line the refrains of " (44.10). This suspended sentence, truncated like the entire book, raises the question of exactly whose refrains and whose remains the lines of the ballad contain. The teller lists numerous possible names for the rann's subject, including an alphabetical sequence, but finally decides to "parse him Persse O'Reilly else he's called no name at all" (44.14). But the ballad is also the remains and the refrains of its writer, whose song shares the honor with its author of being "the king of all ranns" (44.16–17). Maker, again, mates with made. Hosty's composing the ballad matches the two acts that start and end I.2, the speaking of "Humphrey Chimpden's occupational agnomen" by the "sailor king" (31.11) at the beginning of the chapter and the teller's similar act of naming the subject of the ballad at the end. The speakers' actions and their subjects become intertwined when narration and narrative, speaking and utterance are parallel. The earwigger becomes Earwicker. And the parser names a Persse. *Finnegans Wake*, the ballad, and the various versions of Earwicker's naming are "andrewpaulmurphyc" (31.35) not just because they are shaped in the image of humankind, but because multiple voices speak them. The anthropomorphic form is that of "Mister Typus, Mistress Tope and all the little typtopies," the members of the human family transformed into type and into acquaintances of mythic types. All the contributing voices tell the story that includes them. In the welter of reading the "movibles" of the "meandertale" (18.22), the reader "finds the nameform ... that entails the ensuance of existentiality" (18.25–28), the form of the name that tells the story of life's continuity and in so telling sustains the name in the form of the tale that names teller and character. We shall return to this issue of naming when we examine the titles of Joyce's last two books.

The counterpart in Book IV for the passages in I.1 inviting us to "rede" and to "lissom" completes the earlier passages by revealing one goal of the tale and of its ending: "that the heroticisms, catastrophes and eccentricities transmitted by the ancient legacy of the past, type by tope, letter from litter, word at ward . . . may be there for you" (614.35–615.8). As the teller says earlier in IV, "what we have received, that we have transmitted" (604.30). When the past is transformed into a tale, the legacy may survive in the future as part of a continuous present-tense integument reflecting the "ensuance of existentiality." That ensuance involves the implied appearance of Gutenmorg at the end of *Finnegans Wake* in the arrival of the morning laundry, "mournenslaund" (614.8) in morning's land. Here, as elsewhere in the *Wake*, the laundry is linked with ALP and with the washing of sheets to be laid on the river's stones: "Mopsus or Gracchus, all your horodities will incessantlament be coming back from the Annone Wishwashwhose, Ormepierre Lodge, Doone of the Drumes, blanches bountifully and nightsend made up, every article lathering leaving several rinsings" (614.5). The penultimate title for the "mamafesta" given in I.5 contains the phrase "*So is My Washing Done by Night*" (107.1). Now, just before we read the letter, which begins with mention of dirt, the night's laundry arrives, "delivered as . . . Clean . . . Close" (614.10–13). The laundry consists of "horodities," ditties about heroes and whores as well as ancient histories such as those of Herodotus reporting heroic and erotic action ("heroticisms" [614.36]). But the "blanches" that have undergone "rinsings" are also clean sheets of paper that in handpress printing were always wetted and allowed to stand overnight.[29] These provide the "vergin page" (553.1) on which the hen can scrawl her "scribings" (615.10). Only clean sheets still damp from rinsing would take ink evenly. Without them, the work of printing could not proceed in the morning.

The "Close" of "the" that clothes the end is an "endnessnessessity" (613.27) setting "a marge [shore and margin] to the merge of unnotions" (614.17). Because it starts again the soiling and laundering, the marge of closing tranforms rather than truncates. Mookse and Gripes, two figures from a parable told earlier in the *Wake* (152.15–159.20), become "Mopsus or Gracchus" under the aspect of "Gudstruce" (613.12), a truth and truce in which the "crisscouple be so crosscomplimentary, little eggons, youlk and meelk, in a farbiger pancosmos" (613.10–12). The agon of you and me results in complementarity. The "laud of laurens" (613.15), the lord who tells the story that begins with a reference to "Laurens County's gorgios" (3.8), "now orielising benedictively when saint and sage have said their say" (613.15–16), along with all the other battling opposites of the book, announces the nature of the merging. That coalescence includes reader and teller as well as the various pairs of dialogists: "Yet is no body present here which was not there before. Only is order othered. Nought is nulled. *Fuitfiat!*" (613.13–14). The eggs cooked in the text as pan recall the ones Shem habitually prepares (184). And they are the completed book as "a homelet not a hothel" (586.18) for teller, characters, and readers, produced when the author "pits hen to paper and there's scribings scrawled on eggs" (615.10). The creation is not *ex nihilo*. Rather it is an affirmative act nullifying nought; that is, refusing to nullify anything, instead preserving what was and negating the concept of nothing. The order authored makes the old order into another order. *"Fuitfiat"* ("It was; let it be") places the dialogues of IV in relation to the initial one between Mutt and Jute by reversing the "Fiatfuit" (17.32) that occurs during that earlier colloquy. The aesthetic reordering takes the shape of chiasmus through reversal and repetition. The "pancosmos," the world we have "rede," is a "chaosmos" (118.21), or cosmos as chaos and chiasmus. In this world, described at length in I.5, we find "every person, place and thing . . . moving and changing every part of the time" (118.21–23) through the "continually more and less intermisunderstanding minds of anticollaborators" (118.24–26); that is, the minds of reader and writer.

The paragraph of IV immediately preceding the question that introduces the final version of the letter links the book to its printing, to the alphabetic structure of its types and myths, to the river, and to the readers.

> Our wholemole millwheeling vicociclometer, a tetradomational gazebo-croticon (the "Mamma Lujah" known to every schoolboy scandaller, be he Matty, Marky, Lukey or John-a-Donk), autokinatonetically preprovided with a clappercoupling smeltingworks exprogressive process, (for the farmer, his son and their homely codes, known as eggburst, eggblend, eggburial and hatch-as-hatch can) receives through a portal vein the dialytically separated elements of precedent decomposition for the verypetpurpose of subsequent recombination so that the heroticisms, catastrophes and eccentricities transmitted by the ancient legacy of the past, type by tope, letter from litter, word at ward, with sendence of sundance . . . in our mutter nation, all, anastomosically assimilated and preteridentified paraidiotically, in fact, the sameold gamebold adomic structure of our Finnius the old One, as highly charged with electrons as hophazards can effective it, may be there for you, Cockalooraloomenos, when cup, platter and pot come piping hot, as sure as herself pits hen to paper and there's scribings scrawled on eggs. (614.27–615.10)

Now known as "Mamma Lujah" (614.28), the "millwheeling vicociclometer" (614.27), presumably a mill on a river, has become identified with its own characters become readers: "every schoolboy scandaller, be he Matty, Marky, Lukey or John-a-Donk" (614.28–30). The book is self-moving, self-perpetuating, and self-consuming, "autokinatonetically preprovided with a clappercoupling smeltingworks exprogressive process" (614.30–31), which produces both fusion and purification by smelting. The "smeltingworks exprogressive process" is the end of the making of *Work in Progress* (the orginal, provisional title of the *Wake*) through a reversal identical with the first step in the production of new books. The "decomposition" mentioned in the paragraph includes the taking apart of composed type. This "endnessnessessity" (613.27) anticipates the process of composing and decomposing again.

In order for "heroticisms" to "be there for you," there must be available "the dialytically separated elements of precedent decomposition for the verypetpurpose of subsequent recombination" (614.33–35). The recombination occurs "anastomosically" (615.5) by the fitting together of preexisting parts, both of type and of "the ancient legacy of the past" recycled in each new work. Through anastomoses, the new text emerges "type by tope, letter from litter," out of the leavings of the literary tradition to express "the sameold gamebold adomic structure of our Finnius the old One" (615.6–7). At this finish of the text, the reader "finally (though not yet endlike)" makes the acquaintance of "Mister Typus, Mistress Tope and all the little typtopies" (20.12–13) announced in the first chapter. That acquaintance accompanies our perceiving of the book's "adomic structure." In that structure, the atom is an Adam within a "Finnius," a beginning within an end.

The reintroduction of the letter at the book's ending evokes the earlier representations of the letter, but especially the enigmatic one of I.4. By the time of its close the text has defined a perspective for recomposing the earlier version and fitting it into the pattern that version itself defines. If in no other way, the final, fullest letter is related to the earlier, shortest one because they begin and end similarly. The body of the longer letter begins with the "A" of "And" (615.12), and the postscript, if we read it as not continuing beyond one paragraph, concludes with the "O" of "too" (619.19). We might be able to discount the similarity except that this beginning and ending recur elsewhere in the text. For example, II.2 begins with the "A" of "As" (260.1) and ends with the "o" of "too" (308.25). *That* final "o" is also the last letter of a letter. Two other passages in II.2 provide further confirmation. The eighteen words of the first paragraph as prelude begin with "A" and end with "oo" (260.1–3), as does the following sequence of seven syllables in a paragraph devoted to letters: "ah eh oh, let me sigh too" (278.10–11). The numbers eighteen and seven will come up again.

One of the ostensible differences between the two letters concerns the passages following them. After the final letter, ALP's monologue leads into the beginning of the text, actually is the beginning except that the nature of this narrative does not allow for the illusion of an originating beginning. There is an obvious parallel here between the two letters, especially if ALP's monologue is read as continuing the postscript. Because the letter begins with "And," then merges with the introduction of the book, like the

saga mimed by Inkermann's players, it becomes "readable to int from and
. . . and this applies to its whole wholume" (48.17–18). The potentially
Möbean configuration of the letter in I.4 and the transforming of the whole
volume into an analogous, infinitely repeating narrative sequence through
the final letter point to the *Nachtrag* as a model for narration in *Finnegans
Wake*.[30] The shape of the telling in the *Wake* seems unusual not because it
is unique but because most writers devise a conventional screen to disguise
the aspects of narrative that characterize all Joyce's texts, the later ones
more explicitly. The continuity and mutual framing among elements in the
Möbean letter provide a principle for the narration voiced by one of the
washerwomen in I.8: "Never stop! Continuarration!" (205.14). Telling
informed by this principle, as Joyce's narration generally is, insures the
"ensuance of existentiality" through an entailing that turns each text into an
oroborus, a serpent biting its own tail.

The letter of I.4 is followed not by a monologue but by the wandering
deliberations of the four justices, the escape of the accused, and the story of
his later life and demise. Eventually, however, the chapter ends with
references to the babbling river, upon whose stones we have taken our sheet.
Before that ending, the network of implications associated with the letter—
including the defining presence of alpha and omega in the text, the allusions
to printing, and the doubling back caused by joined ends—all appears in the
tale of the escapee. Because the *a*'s and *o*'s are presented especially
prominently in the passage concerning the judges' deliberations, the reader
may become sensitized to the proliferation of these vowels. Within a few
lines of the letter appear the words "Somany Solans" (94.27), "a'duna
o'darnel" (94.31), and the "Ah ho" (94.33) that becomes a refrain
elsewhere in *Finnegans Wake*.[31] The repeated appearances of these
vowels in conjunction evoke the letter's form and its shapes as the text's
form and as the pervasive signs of aesthetic creation. Of course, we need to
be careful not to interpret the appearance of *a*'s and *o*'s in a monomaniacal,
indiscriminate way. Because there are only five vowels in English, and
because punning often depends on the substitution of one for another, the
narration of the *Wake* abounds with instances of these two vowels used in
curious ways. But the placement and clustering of *a*'s and *o*'s can lend them
some special significance. In the passages I have selected, though by no
means everywhere in the *Wake*, they indicate the omnipresence of the
book's creator. Rather than a divinity, he is simply the ordering force of a
work that, like Shem's creations, represents the author.

Within this frame of self-portrayal, the syllables "jas jos" in Shem's
inkbottle house say more than just yes twice. The author signs his texts not
only by affixing a name to a title page but by the mere act of writing. Like
Gutenberg as "Gutenmorg," the maker emerges from the book as wordpress by merging with it. Squirting out from the pressings comes the screen
that is the author's image. If "jas jos" abbreviates the real author's name,

the combinations of vowels here and in some other parts of the *Wake* abbreviate the abbreviation. Letter and house, with their similar alphabetical contents, bear analogous relationships to the whole tale. Not only do we find ourselves in the house that Jack built, but Jack turns out to have been an architect who kept models of all the houses he built. The author's name as signature is contained within book, house, and letter, composed of each in its entirety, and imprinted on the cover, which forms the "marge" between the book and its environs.

The Möbius strip works well as a model for our experience of reading the *Wake* for reasons that go beyond the obvious linking of end to beginning. It can help us describe the complicated network of repetitions with variations that, like the elliptical letter itself, often stand in some synecdochic relation to the book's larger structure. And it can help us grasp the reversal of roles we regularly encounter, since that reversal is related to a property of Möbean space. In exploring the analogy with the strip, we should remember that, like the surface of a sphere or an egg, it is finite but unbounded. Consequently, we can draw a line on a paper model of a Möbius strip that will be continuous with itself, like the equator. By following this line, it is possible to traverse the strip and return to the starting point. The line so traversed constitutes what mathematicians call a nonbounding cycle, because it does not form the boundary of a two-dimensional figure on the strip's surface.

The network of narratives in *Finnegans Wake* resembles a Möbius strip from which many other strips have been propagated. If a paper model of a Möbius strip is cut down its middle, not across its edges, the resulting geometrical entity is not two independent strips but one strip twice as long as the first, though narrower, containing two twists rather than one. Although this second strip is related to the original one geometrically, the properties are not identical. The original strip and its immediate offspring created by cutting differ in the relation of verso to recto. As the earlier drawings (figs. 1, 2, and 3) indicate, in the original Möbius strip, verso and recto are one and will both be traversed by any line drawn on the model's surface that is a nonbounding cycle. Consequently, the original strip has only one side. For the doubled strip and for any later strips made by cuttings, recto and verso are no longer one. The new strips have two sides. When cut in the manner described, the narrower lengths of joined recto and verso from the original form a new recto and new verso narrower than the first strip. The length of each new recto and each new verso is identical to that of the entire first strip. Although the sides both contain elements of the full length of the parent strip, they are not continuous with one another. Repeated cuttings create a convoluted mass of strips, connected like twisted links of a chain. All the strips are geometrically related because their lengths are all equal and because some of their edges fit together like the pieces of a jigsaw puzzle. Varying the widths and angles of cutting will produce a different shape for each strip (see figs. 4, 5, and 6).*

The mass of interlocking strips that can be generated gives us a non-Euclidean geometrical equivalent for the doublings, repetitions, and transformations in the narration of *Finnegans Wake*. The multiple strips originating from the one Möbius strip all tell versions of the same story contained in the source that they replicate with variations. Each new space of paper, though only part of the first strip, tells its own rendition of the whole story. As in the production of clones, the original entity is divided and doubled into simulacra of itself possessing related genetic structures. It seems hardly possible to reverse the process of multiplication (or division, depending on our perspective) by putting the fragments, like the parts of Humpty Dumpty, back together again into an original shape.

One of the unusual properties of the Möbius strip contributing to the analogy is what mathematicians call its nonorientable aspect. By that they mean that ordinary orientations of right and left are no longer relevant. An observer traveling along a closed curve, or nonbounding cycle, down the center of the strip cannot characterize points as consistently on the right or on the left. The difficulty arises because points on the right at the beginning of the journey are on the left when the observer returns to the origin. This is so because traversing the space back to the origin reverses the orientation. Because this reversal of orientation cannot be visualized from a conventional Euclidean perspective, we should imagine a transparent rather than an opaque paper model of the strip, and we should think of the traveler as *in* the strip rather than *on* it. By doing that, we can see the observer return to the starting point at a location that would appear in the opaque model to be on the opposite side of the paper from the starting point. In fact, the Möbean space has no opposite sides, though the usual paper model suggests that it does. Like Shem and Shaun or Mookse and Gripes, left and right change places. As in Möbean geometry, in reading the *Wake* our movement forward is always a moving back toward our origin, which we may reach unexpectedly, and the movement involves a fluctuation of orientations, an oscillating of perspectives.

---

* I must apologize for this complicated account of the strips. The properties of the Möbius strip do not conform to expectations deriving from Euclidean plane geometry. But this nonconformity is part of the point of the comparison, because Joyce's narratives do not function according to our traditional literary conventions. The Möbius strip and Joyce's late narratives take some getting used to. I suggest that anyone interested in pursuing the analogy obtain scissors, tape, and a section about four feet long from a roll of photocopy paper. For a fuller discussion of the strip's unusual properties, see Martin Gardner, "The World of the Möbius Strip," *Scientific American* 219 (December 1968): 112–15, and the material cited in that issue's bibliography, p. 144.

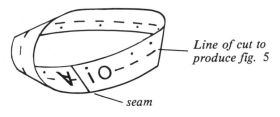

Line of cut to
produce fig. 5

seam

Figure 4

The strip to be cut

Figure 5

The strip after one cut, now twice as long with two twists

Figure 6

*The strip after two cuts;
each bisected strip contains two twists*

The cutting involved in transforming the single Möbius strip into its multifoliate offspring may remind us that the process of printing and binding books traditionally involves cutting and sewing cunningly folded papers. The importance of cutting and sewing in bookmaking probably has something to do with the recurring appearance of the tailor in the *Wake*. It also helps explain why ALP as Finnegan's widow is "the tailor's daughter" (28.7). This *"figlia del tuo figlio,"* child of the tailor and progeny of the author as teller, mother of Shem the writer and draper (421.25), is "sewing a dream together" (28.7). She produces the memorializing "mamafesta" standing for and within that other memorial, the book sewn together that we may unstitch and resew it. By reversing her activities, Penelope, we recall, was able to be an unraveler as well as a weaver.

A PURLOINED HOMERIC CORRESPONDENCE

In replying to the first question after the fable of the Ondt and the Gracehoper in III.1, Shaun castigates Shem as a writer.[32] His castigation alludes both to Homer and to Edgar Poe. According to Shaun, Shem exhibits criminal and literary aspirations, for which Shaun condemns "the strangewrote anaglyptics of those shemletters" (419.18–19) as "theodicy *re*'furloined notepaper . . . all about crime and libel" (419.29–33). Through the combination of the *Odyssey* with "The Purloined Letter," we can understand Joyce's use of Homer as a purloining. In his commentary on Poe's story, Jacques Lacan asserts that etymologically purloining means not only theft but a prolonging.[33] However fanciful that etymology, it captures precisely the literary process by which an auther borrows from a tradition of writing and extends its life. Lacan's essay and the response to it by Jacques Derrida yield some pertinent perspectives for the reader of *Finnegans Wake*, because both writers stress the place of the letter in our language and literature.[34] These interpreters of Poe see in his use of the letter the functioning of alphabetical characters in a structural play of difference producing meaning, and they perceive the working of the epistle as a primary image for communication. Even more emphatically than Poe, Joyce situates literature and life in relation to letters—alphabetical, typographical, epistolary, and belletristic. Of special concern here is the last of these, the literary tradition out of which Joyce's work stems. And that is where Homer, Poe, and the history of fiction come in. As he writes *Ulysses* and *Finnegans Wake*, Joyce establishes his relationship to the epic tradition represented by Homer. Along the way he also makes his place in the history of the novel, a history that begins in the eighteenth century with fictions disguised as other kinds of documents, including journals, collections of letters, and autobiographical accounts. So, Joyce includes various documents and examples of literary genres other than narrative in his fictions: newspaper articles, lyric poems, journals, dramatic episodes, and the letters of *Finnegans Wake*.

Together with the play on the purloined letter in *"re'*furloined notepaper," several other details concerning the letter in the *Wake*, especially the letter of I.4, suggest a comparison with the stolen letter of Poe's story. For instance, the letter in I.4 was "folded with cunning, sealed with crime" (94.8). And "hand tore" it (94.6). In Poe's story, the Minister of State, who first purloins the letter, hides it openly in his chambers by changing its appearance. He tears the letter nearly in half, soils and crumples it, refolds it until it has been "turned, as a glove, inside out," then reseals it and readdresses it to himself in a feminine hand.[35] The transforming of purloined to furloined in the *Wake* suggests the image of the glove through the association with fur lining. During ALP's final monologue a glove is mentioned again when she asks HCE to "draw back your glave" (621.24) to show his scarred hand. That hand has apparently been burned in punishment for his "taking a lifeness" (621.27), for committing murder and taking an aesthetic likeness. The two deeds merge in the artist's self-expenditures of aesthetic creation, in which a "suicidal murder" (100.10) occurs as the author produces an inscription for his own tomb. Just as the contents of the purloined letter are never revealed in the story, we never learn the exact nature or the entire story of the hand in the glove. By metonymy the word "hand" commonly takes on the meaning of handwriting (for example, in Poe's story). The exact details of the letters and of the writer's hand, that "unbrookable script" (123.32–33), as "a murderous mirrorhand" (177.30–31) reflecting the writer himself, are not fully accessible to us. The writer is behind and within the handwriting of the letter that forms a squirtscreen or a glove as protective covering. We know only that within the glove is "falskin" (621.25). Both hand and letter resemble the saga performed by the troupe of Inkermann, a saga described as "from tupp to buttom all falsetissues" (48.18–19).

In both *Finnegans Wake* and "The Purloined Letter," the indecipherable, perhaps unknowable, always false or stolen document within the tale represents the tale itself. In Poe's story, the title names both letter and tale. The relation of narration to narrative becomes especially clear at the end of "The Purloined Letter." When the detective Dupin retrieves the letter by repurloining it, he leaves a substitute. The contents of the substitute letter will reveal to Dupin's foe, the Minister, that Dupin has recovered the stolen letter. Because the message, a quotation about Atreus and his brother, Thyestes, alludes to another literary text, the purloining of letters takes on special significance. The curse on the house of Atreus, ensuing from a conflict between brothers, led to a proliferating chain of events, including the Trojan War. Consequently, the story's ending strongly suggests that the conflict in the narrative has not been resolved absolutely. By leaving his facsimile of the letter for the Minister as a calling card, Dupin insures that his purloining will prolong and intensify their antagonism.

Dupin's alluding also links the ending to the story's beginning with a quotation as epigraph. That beginning also suggests forgery. The epigraph purports to be from Seneca. Like the character's act of quoting, the author's involves theft. But alluding, an unauthorized borrowing, is actually *false* borrowing in Poe's story. His epigraph turns out to be a pretense, a forgery masquerading as an allusion, for the would-be quotation is not to be found in the works of Seneca.[36] If we assume that the quotation is not from a text by Seneca now lost, Poe has consciously forged Seneca's name to the epigraph, or he has inadvertently done so by misremembering, or he has borrowed the quotation from some other writer who has wrongly attributed it to Seneca. Whatever the case (and it seems part of the story's point that we cannot ignore the alternatives), the story contains doubly criminal acts of borrowing and forgery. The purloined quotation Dupin leaves for the Minister, the story's title, and the epigraph as forged allusion combine to suggest that every literary text involves purloining and forgery. No author can be absolutely original, and no text can be absolutely authentic. Every author copies in some way another's text. A work may even assert falsely its connection to a precursor. Joyce's allusions in the *Wake* to James Macpherson, the famous eighteenth-century forger of ancient Gaelic poetry, are to the point here.[37] Through allusion as copying and forgery, literary texts displace and replace precursors, just as Dupin's letter with its borrowed phrases replaces by substitution the letter the Minister has stolen and transformed.

The title of *Finnegans Wake* provides a similar perspective for understanding the tale, its letters, and literary texts in general. In the *Wake*, as in Poe's story, the title names the letter so important in the tale. The linking of Joyce's title (actually his titles, because *Ulysses* is involved as well) to letters emerges in a round-about fashion when Shaun castigates Shem's letter as "theodicy *re'*furloined notepaper" (419.29). As the title of *Ulysses* explicitly announces, one of the texts Joyce purloins repeatedly is the *Odyssey*. The word "theodicy" can refer as a metaphor rather than a pun to the letter, for the letter defends the father from the accusations brought against him. But Shaun's expostulation "Greek!" (419.20) in the same passage reinforces the pun. Both the reference to Greek and the ordinary meaning of theodicy link Shaun's comments to the letter of I.4, if we take "A" and "O" as alpha and omega, Greek letters and the attributes of God. The marks that make up that letter form a Homeric correspondence of a combined literary and epistolary sort referring to Joyce's previous purloining of Homer's text in and through *Ulysses*. Richard Ellmann has suggested that the letter of I.4 can be taken as a simulacrum of *Ulysses* because it contains the same number of periods as there are episodes in that work.[38] Although Ellmann has miscounted (there is one more period than he claims), the connection to *Ulysses* through Homer *is* implied. The total number of marks making up the letter (one "A," one "O," one question mark, two exclamation points, nineteen periods) is twenty-four, the same as the number of books in Homer's epic. Joyce was without doubt aware of the allusive potential of these numbers. For instance, in I.5 the teller describes the concluding element of Shem's work as "eighteenthly or twentyfourthly" (123.3). Various references, then, link the letter in the *Wake* to Greek letters, even to the whole Greek alphabet. Classical Greek contains twenty-four letters: eighteen simple ones and six compound additional letters.[39]

From the perspective of purloining, we can understand Joyce's title as referring to the book's relationship to its precursors and to letters of various sorts, some contained within *Finnegans Wake*. The "nameform" (18.25) that we "stoop" to "rede" "entails the ensuance of existentiality" (18.27–28) that links Joyce's writing to Homer's. That "nameform" is mirrored in the elliptical letter. The Homeric interpretation of the title depends on multilingual puns and on the technique of punning itself. The puns of the title developed in the narration derive in part from the theories of Victor Bérard concerning Homer. Joyce knew these theories well. As two critics have established beyond dispute, in his research on the Homeric epic Joyce became familiar with Bérard's notion that Odysseus was not a Greek but a Phoenician, whose travels in the Mediterranean would have included various islands, such as the Dodecanese in the Aegean.[40] Joyce, of course, knew Latin and ancient history, the "horodities" (614.2) "transmitted by the ancient legacy of the past" (614.36–615.1). He would have known the rationale for calling the wars between Rome and Carthage "Punic." The Carthaginians were Phoenicians, and in Latin *Punicus* means Phoenician.[41] An etymological pun links "phoenix" and "Phoenician," for the Greek word for Phoenician is *Phoinix*, or *Phoinikos*. The similarity in orthography between "Phoenician" and "Phoenix" and the similarity in their sounds to "Finn," the name of the Irish hero, and to the word "finish" enable Joyce to build interconnecting meanings out of his title and into his tale.

Like *Ulysses* before it, *Finnegans Wake* concerns, is, and exists in the phoenixlike wake of the Phoenician, whose tale is associated here with the finish of Finn. Both books are Homeric in spirit and in some of their letters, but belatedly so, for each comes in the wake of Homer and his Phoenician hero. Greek bard and epic hero wake again in Joyce's texts. Because Joyce wrote *Ulysses* before the *Wake*, the Phoenician hero's reawakening in the later narrative necessarily follows in the wake of that earlier resurrection. Joyce's sequence of purloinings and retellings, though more labyrinthine, resembles the convolutions of "The Purloined Letter." In its large features that sequence includes the alluding in *Finnegans Wake* to Joyce's own unauthorized borrowing of Homer's text, an earlier theft from an author who follows in the wake of the events he repeats, events concerning a hero who tells much of his own story and whose journey involves a return from the

dead. Because Homer's writing, like Shem's, is "not protected by copri-
right" (185.30), it is available for republication.

The process of reading *Finnegans Wake* involves learning what the title
means through the references to the etymological puns that emerge during
the narration. The question of the title is primary for the reader. As we learn
in the first query of I.6, "who guesse his title grabs his deeds" (137.10–11).
Joyce even made the title the subject of guessing among his friends when the
developing work was known only as *Work in Progress*.[42] The reader who
guesses that the title refers to *Ulysses* and Homer grasps the Homeric
nature of the author's deeds. Early on the phrase "as punical as finikin"
(32.06) gives the meaning away. Finnegan is not only a pun but Punic, as is
the "Punic admiralty report" (123.24) that Homer and perhaps Shem have
plagiarized. The Punic Wars of the *Wake* include both writing and Ireland.
They are "the penic walls" (156.03) and "Hirelings' puny wars" (270.30–
31). In III.4 both HCE and ALP are linked with the Phoenician as the
Phoenix, HCE as "Big Maester Finnykin with" ALP as "Phenicia Parkes"
(576.28–29), the Phoenix Park that is now Phoenician, as in its transformation to "Pynix Park" (534.12). HCE is "the gran Phenician rover"
(197.31) who "barqued it, the boat of life . . . till he spied the loom of his
landfall" (197.28–30), which would be, among other things, the loom of
Penelope as weaver. His travels are "the vaguum of the phoenix" (136.34–
35), the wandering (L., *vagus*) of the Phoenician, involving the "return to
the atlantic and Phenitia Proper" (85.20). The most explicit references
occur in IV, where we learn that "the Phoenician wakes" (608.32). And
ALP tells us in her monologue that "it's Phoenix, dear . . . and the book of
the depth is. Closed" (621.1–3).[43] When this book of the dead closes, "the
Phoenician wakes," and his *Wake* finishes and begins again. The work in
progress in this text is the waking of the Phoenician.

Joyce's title implies broadly that every act of writing reawakens earlier
texts, including the author's own. That reawakening occurs as the production of letters. Each author necessarily follows in the wake of earlier authors
and texts, and in his own wake. And that is why the name "Finnegan"
occurs as a plural as well as an implied possessive in Joyce's title. The
awakening involves many Finnegans, many Phoenicians and their avatars,
not just one, whom the author commands to arise. By displacing the earlier
work, the new one murders the old while awakening it, and in the process
murders itself. This "suicidal murder" (100.10), the "taking of a lifeness"
(621.27) that is one's own, is the "endnessnessessity" (613.27) of writing,
its endless necessity and its necessity to end.

To have its own seemingly independent life, the text must put an end to its
precursors. But by contributing to a sequence of new texts displacing old
ones, like the ongoing sequence of vengeance suggested by Dupin's
substituting a new letter for the purloined one, the new text prepares for its
own replacement by predicting its eventual role as a precursor. The

"empirative" of the author's "vendettative" (187.31), the piratical imperative of writing, prolongs the cycle of replacement. The book constitutes a wake for the dead, for itself, for its author, and for the literature it resurrects only to bury and buries only to resurrect from the midden of letters. The burial includes an intended temporal reversal, in which the earlier text rewritten in the later one is capsized in the wake, like that of a boat, produced by the new text.[44] What was once before is now behind. The *Odyssey* functions well in this conception of writing for the reasons I have already indicated, the Homeric hero's telling of his own story and his return from the world of the dead. By using Homer for the second time, Joyce tells, among other stories, the tale of himself as a writer and the tale of writing itself, in which the author wakes himself as he hosts his own wake.

In his title, then, Joyce combines two of the primary techniques from the narration in his late writing: allusion and the pun. As we have seen, the phrase "as punical as finikin" refers to the author and book's relationship to precursors. But through the play on the words "pun" and "Punic," it also indicates the most prominent recurring aspect of language in the *Wake*. Like the allusions, the puns all have specific implications that vary depending on context. As with Joyce's decision to allude, his use of the pun to develop extreme verbal elaborations has a functional relevance. The goal of langauge in the *Wake* is to be "as punical as finikin," to awake the Phoenician as the phoenix contained in every word. The technique of the book's language constantly illustrates the title, because puns are both "punical" and "finikin." By its name, punning is associated with the Phoenician as *Punicus*. By its effect, each pun enacts the title as a linguistic phoenix whose meaning arises from the capsizing in its wake of the word that it at once suggests and partially drowns out.

Like Joyce's selection of Homer as paradigm, his choice of the pun is a Viconian gesture. As Joyce employs the technique, punning reveals an essential operation in language that results in narrative. Here Joyce's kinship to Vico rivals his connection to Homer. In *The New Science* Vico chooses the pun, especially the etymological pun, as a central strategy for developing his arguments. Often the etymologies are Vico's own fictions. His use of puns, and Joyce's, can be understood as developments of the attitude toward metaphor expressed in *The New Science*. Vico's commentary on metaphor and on the other basic tropes of language suggests the close tie between language and history, and it indicates an important component of Joyce's generation of narrative in *Finnegans Wake*. According to Vico, metaphor—that is, naming—inevitably leads to metonymy, the essence of narrative.[45] Consequently, the mere act of naming engenders the actions, thoughts, and, especially, the language that compose humankind's history and its histories. Vico's use of imaginative etymology and Joyce's more extensive use of puns, including etymological ones, exhibit the transforming of word as trope into story. For Joyce, the pun contains a metaphor that is also a catachresis, a renaming of the original sign through an abuse of language. If metaphor always leads to metonymy and thereby to narrative, as Vico claims, the process of storytelling becomes almost unimaginably wide-ranging in its proliferations and eccentricities when the catachreses of multilingual and etymological puns dominate style. In the *Wake*, the subject matter of the narratives engendered out of the many puns includes the process of generating narratives, a process whose nature is implied by the work's title as pun. In such a text, each word becomes the grist for the "millwheeling vicociclometer" (614.27), as well as the force driving the mill wheel.

HOMERIC SELF-PORTRAITURE: REPETITIONS AND ORIGINS

So far, I have focused on several related aspects of narration and narrative in *Finnegans Wake*: the character-as-artist, his letters, beginnings and endings, the title's implications, and the making of texts through writing, printing, and reading. I have suggested that as readers we can compare our own activity to the author's because of the peculiar nature of the narration's structures and techniques. In the *Wake* the reader's engagement with the text is affected especially by the teller's linking of end to beginning, by his puns, and by his allusions. The effect of these elements, arising as it does from the large structure of the narrative, from the details of language, and from the rationale for the telling as mythic, can be nearly definitive for our experience as readers. By combining these aspects of his text in various ways, Joyce allows a complex kind of experiential order to emerge from the seemingly disparate details of his mannered prose. That order requires the reader's active engagement with the book, an engagement in which telling and reading involve one another. When we read *Finnegans Wake*, it is as if we are traveling with difficulty through a dark and brambly wood but encountering cleared areas regularly. These clearings reveal the teller's relationship to the character, and they make evident our role as comakers of the text. In all Joyce's mature fiction (and it is *all* mature), not just in the *Wake*, opening and closing are linked. But the details of language vary as Joyce experiments in each of his books with different ways of involving the reader through style. In *Ulysses*, the style and the involvement achieve particular prominence and vigor when Joyce portrays consciousness (his own, his characters', and his readers') as implicitly mythic. In the *Wake*, Joyce's earlier casting of minds in a mythic mold for the making of art itself becomes a crucial element in the structure and style for creating the mythic artifact. The making of that mythic artifact turns out to be the making of the mythic artificer as well.

Joyce projects an image of the artist as mythic teller and hero by presenting writing in general, and the *Wake* and *Ulysses* in particular, as the purloining of myth. The specifically Homeric aspects of *Finnegans Wake* and of its author are suggested in those passages, some of which we have already examined, concerning the act of writing and commenting on the letter. During the extended speculations about the letter (or "litter," both the catalogued contents of the artist's house as book and the midden from which documents can be retrieved for reuse), the teller in I.5 alludes prominently to *Ulysses* and to its Homeric forebear. The description of handwriting and of the letter's end makes the connection with Joyce's earlier book and refers to the *Wake* itself: "The toomuchness, the fartoomanyness of all those fourlegged ems: and why spell dear god with a big thick dhee (why, O why, O why?): the cut and dry aks and wise form of the semifinal; and, eighteenthly or twentyfourthly, but at least, thank Maurice, lastly when all is zed and done, the penelopean patience of its last paraphe, a colophon of no fewer than seven hundred and thirtytwo strokes tailed by a leaping lasso—" (122.36–123.6). As in the Minister's read-dressing of the purloined letter, the handwriting combines genders when a "male fist" (123.10) controls "feminine libido" (123.8). The *Odyssey*, *Ulysses*, and the *Wake* are mingled in the references to Penelope, to the number of episodes in *Ulysses* and in the *Odyssey*, to the number of pages of the first edition of *Ulysses*, and to the endings spoken by lasses. The allusions to *Ulysses* are especially dense here. The "Ithaca" episode would be the penultimate or "semifinal" one, the "x" and "y" rather than the "zed" of *Ulysses*, with "cut and dry" forms of asking why. The mention of the commentary by "Duff-Muggli" (123.11) after the description elaborates on texts and their originals by dealing specifically with Shem's stealing. In the chain of repeated actions, the thefts that have taken place are not entirely distinguishable from one another. While this portion of I.5 seems primarily concerned with the connection of *Ulysses* to the *Odyssey*, it presents as well the similar relationship of the *Wake* to both its precursors. And it suggests that Homer, too, indulged in borrowing.

Here, as elsewhere in the *Wake*, writing is a collaborative effort that amounts to a partnership. The teller in I.5 reports the name of "this kind of paddygoeasy partnership" to be "the ulykkhean or tetrachiric or quadrumane or ducks and drakes or debts and dishes perplex" (123.15–17). Several partnerships are implied: Shem the copyist with his mother the letter writer, HCE with ALP, the male author with the feminine telling voices that close *Ulysses* and *Finnegans Wake*, and Joyce with Homer. Writing and family life share for Joyce the relationship of parent to progeny. The later text is the offspring of its precursor, and both original and copy are the progeny of their authors. Writing, then, resembles reproduction. The sexual union of man with woman, and the artist's androgynous nature suggested here and in "Scylla and Charybdis," evoke the author's fathering and mothering of his books and of himself. In the partnership between author and precursor, the writer espouses the former's work in order to make his own. The espousal involves an antagonistic sibling rivalry informing the doubling that occurs in writing. The writer needs his brother, just as Stephen Dedalus needed Maurice and as Dupin needed the Minister. The brother becomes incarnated in language as the author's persona for narration, and the rivalry is presented within the narrative, most obviously in the *Wake* through the figures of Shem and Shaun. Another sibling and another possibility of four-handed, "tetrachiric or quadrumane," partnerships emerge when the reader makes the acquaintance of the writer and is made by that acquaintance through reading.

From the ink that is "double dye" (185.32) emerges a doubled dying, a doubled "I" and a doubled "ye." This is Joyce's "twinngling of an aye" (620.15), his doubling of "yes" into "jas jos." The "I" and the "you" of reader and writer are both doubled in the acts of aesthetic creation and response that generate personae. The writer disappears behind the mask of the teller, his double, in a first death that is the completion of the writing. Eventually, he experiences the literal death caused by expending life energies to make his aesthetic double, "the graven image of his squarer self as he was used to be" (429.13–14). The front and back paper covers of the first edition of *Ulysses*, that "book of craven images" (563.4), were in fact square. Joyce used the square as symbol for the title of the *Wake*, perhaps to indicate the connection between the title and the earlier text.[46]

By means of these doublings and fourhanded partnerships, the earlier text is rewritten:

> . . . in the case of the littleknown periplic bestteller popularly associated with the names of the wretched mariner . . . a Punic admiralty report . . . had been cleverly capsized and saucily republished as a dodecanesian baedeker (123.22–27). . . . The original document was in what is known as Hanno O'Nonhanno's unbrookable script, that is to say, it showed no signs of punctuation of any sort. Yet on holding the verso against a lit rush this new book of Morses responded most remarkably to the silent query. (123.31–36)

In I.7 Shem is associated with no-man Hanno when he is described stippling "endlessly inartistic portraits of himself in the act of reciting old Nichiabelli's monolook interyerear *Hanno, o Nonanno* . . . ser Autore" (182.18–21). Hanno, the Carthaginian explorer, appears in these passages about writing and repeating for several reasons. Not only does his name include the "A" and the "O," but Hanno was a navigator who wrote about his own explorations. Like Odysseus, he combines the roles of wanderer and teller. As a Carthaginian, and therefore a Phoenician, Hanno, along with the other Carthaginians mentioned in the *Wake*—including Hannibal, Hamilcar, and Hasdrubal—is an avatar of Odysseus as wandering Phoenician.[47] The book as stippled self-portrait of the artist is both periplic bestseller and the bestseller's "periplic bestteller." The nineteen periods of the Möbean letter represent the stippling and the stippler. As narratives, the *Odyssey* and *Ulysses* each includes a periplum, a voyage of discovery, such as the journeys undertaken by the historical Hanno.[48] Each book is its "periplic bestteller" because it gives us the author's image as literary explorer engaged in a voyage of self-discovery that is the act of narration. The Baedeker is "dodecanesian" in part because of the geographical location of those islands, but more importantly because there are *twelve* (Gr., *dōdeka*) islands, just as there are twelve episodes in the "Odyssey" portion of *Ulysses*.

A framing like the description of Shame's House occurs in these passages. In the *Wake* Joyce portrays an author like himself who makes portraits of himself as an artist reciting an earlier text, perhaps his own. Shem recites a "monolook interyerear," a narration characterized by an interior monologue that is like gazing into normally inaccessible orifices (of ear and rear). His text is the capsized, republished version of Homer's. Like his precursor, he writes a travelogue about the Dodecanese Islands, whose original is a Phoenician naval report. The interlocking perspectives also suggest, of course, that *Ulysses*, or the book like it Shem has written, is the model for the work we are reading. Like the closing of the described text, at once an original and a repetition, the end of *Ulysses* with its "unbrookable script . . . showed no signs of punctuation of any sort." The different texts alluded to are unbreakable: permanent as art; undecipherable as code; and unchangeable as currency or scrip. The sequence of meshed republishings presents within the narrative one meaning of the *Wake*'s title that the narration's language and structure continually illustrate. Not content merely to follow in the wake of his precursor, Shem as capsizer would reverse roles with the author he imitates by submerging the previous text in the billows of his own work's turbulent aftermath. The teller cites the letter's "cruciform postscript" (122.20–21) as proof of this temporal reversal. On that evidence, according to the narrator, Shem's work "plainly" inspired "the tenebrous *Tunc* page of the Book of Kells" (122.22–23). That page, then, imitates Shem's "Book of Eccles, *édition de ténèbres*" (179.27) and the letters, several of which contain either a capital "T" or tea stains. The suggestion is preposterous in the etymological sense of that word because it asserts the transposing of early and late. However odd the transposition may seem, it does not appear only in Joyce's final work. The writer's fathering himself aesthetically through such a reversal is an essential aspect of Joyce's portraiture of the artist long before *Finnegans Wake*.

The republishing is "repreaching" (29.25) and rapprochement, the saying again by the present author, who captures both himself and the past text in a single "monolook." This "repreaching" is ascribed to HCE when he arrives at the end of I.1 by ship to take the place of the fallen Finn. Usurpation by "repreaching" engenders the guilt of reproach because the act is criminal. But it leads as well to rapprochement with what has been displaced. Aesthetic making as thievery unites writer with model. For Joyce to become like Homer, he must appropriate his fatherly rival's offspring, which is also the father's spouse, in order to turn father into brother. To accomplish this improbable task of usurping as reconciliation, the artist studies, as does Shem, "various styles of signature so as one day to utter an epical forged cheque on the public" (181.15–16). The forgery is more general than an autobiographical self-portrait of the writer as teller, the persona forged in the smithy of the artist's soul along with the uncreated conscience of his race. This conscience manifests itself through the slow fires of consciousness inherent in the styles making up the work's representation of its teller as mythic, as both *typos* and *topos*.

By means of those slow fires, in *Ulysses* the teller forges his Bloom in two senses, for "bloom" refers to a mass of wrought iron fired in a furnace as well as to a flower. In I.7 and in IV we learn that the artist exorcises his instinct to write by forging metal and by smelting ore. Out of the author's workshop as bloomery emerges books that are himself, containing his mark that is and is not a signature:

> The teatimestained terminal . . . is a cosy little brown study all to oneself and, whether it be thumbprint, mademark or just a poor trait of the artless, its importance in establishing the identities in the writer complexus (for if the hand was one, the minds of active and agitated were more than so) will be best appreciated by never forgetting that both before and after the battle of the Boyne it was a habit not to sign letters always. . . . So why, pray, sign anything as long as every word, letter, penstroke, paperspace is a perfect signature of its own? (114.29–115.8)

Although the handwriting of the letter may be that of one person, at least two minds are engaged: the active one of the writer and the mind of the reader. The reader becomes agitated into perceiving the letter as the signature and portrait of the artist even if the work is anonymous or else impersonally narrated. "Signature," like "furniture," alludes to printing. The word refers to each large sheet of paper printed and folded to be cut and sewn into a book. And it refers to the letter of the alphabet placed at the bottom of the first page of each such large sheet to designate alphabetically the sequence for binding. Every printed book contains the artist's mark in the signatures composed of both letters and the paperspace of the text. Every volume is the "whole wholume" (48.19), the who-loom on which the author weaves the carpet and the pattern in the carpet that make up his signature as "proteiform graph[,] itself . . . a polyhedron of scripture" (107.08).

The kind of Homeric self-portraiture Joyce creates in *Finnegans Wake* and in *Ulysses* involves namings and renamings, origins and repetitions. Naming and repetition project us simultaneously toward and away from an origin represented by the text's precursors and by such metaphors as the river's source. The acts of writing these books start from the origins named in the titles and result in texts that are one with their origins. At its end, the *Wake* moves us out toward the sea in which the river ends at the same time as it represents the river's voice as the book's beginning. The unreachable origin, which among other things is the act of the mind in the midst of aesthetic creation, emerges through metaphor in many of the narrative's segments.

For instance, after the death of the escapee near the end of I.4, the narration shifts focus toward the origin of things by mentioning the river and ALP, the writer of the letter defending the accused. Then, at the beginning of I.5, we encounter an epic catalogue of the "many names" that "her un-titled mamafesta memorialising the Mosthighest has gone by" (104.4–5). These are the names it has passed by but by which it has been known. They are like the nets that Stephen Dedalus must try "to fly by" (*P* 203); that is, to avoid and to employ as vehicles for flying. The letter as posthumous memorial to the writer's spouse is not yet itself dead, though Shaun has tried unsuccessfully to deliver it to many addresses, including ones that were Joyce's (420.19–421.11). The letter as both epitaph and living name can only be spoken indirectly, by substitutions. As in "The Purloined Letter," the actual contents of the document are never fully revealed in any unambiguous way. In this regard, the link between the letters and the book containing them is particularly close. Just as we are never completely sure about the details of the narration in the *Wake*, we are never entirely certain of the contents of the letter's different versions. The teller as interpreter of the letter in I.5 draws the only possible conclusion from this textual indeterminacy: "[While] we . . . may have our irremovable doubts as to the whole sense of the lot, the interpretation of any phrase in the whole, the meaning of every word of a phrase. . . , we must vaunt no idle dubiosity as to its genuine authorship" (117.34–118.4). Although the conclusion is laughably obvious, it contains an important truth about the effect of the *Wake*'s narration. We know with certainty only that the text has genuinely been authored, only that an act of writing has occurred. In this regard, the *Wake* and its letters are similar in their effect to Eliot's "The Waste Land." We can spend our time investigating obscure details of such a text that may not carry any clear significance. Or we can take the obscurities as signs of the producing aesthetic process. As Joyce presents it, *that* is significant enough.

The godlike "Mosthighest" ALP memorializes merges the hero and author as teller. Like Finnegan, the teller is a mason, a "tombstone mason" (113.34) who creates lapidary memorials by marking the crypt through an encrypting. The combined burial and encoding produce the letter whose alpha and omega invoke the "Mosthighest" in the way a rosary does by directing the devotee's attention to the Holy Mother and the Holy Father.

In its Möbean configuration, the letter resembles the connected beads of the Catholic rosary, the use of which is always preceded by an "Our Father" and followed by a "Glory Be to the Father." The letter's marks as beads form a linguistic sequence like the ones Stephen Dedalus contemplates near the shore in "Proteus": "Monkwords, marybeads jabber on their girdles: roguewords, tough nuggets patter in their pockets" (*U* 48). The artist arranges the beadlike nuggets of language in varying configurations, like the ones Beckett's Molloy experiments with when he shifts his sucking stones from pocket to pocket. And the reader rearranges them partially and selectively.[49]

In the *Wake* the beads of the letter are the stones of the river, but stones in the lapidary sense, ones placed in a jeweler's setting or used in the movement of a timepiece that seems self-winding and self-regulating. The continuous motion and continuous creation of the text's wandering rocks receive their sustaining energy from the actions of readers. The nineteen dots of the letter suggest a document like the "Wandering Rocks" episode of *Ulysses*, one made up of nineteen parts arranged in a progressive, digressive sequence. Such arrangements indicate both simultaneity and parallelism of action along with a structure mirroring the shape of the entire book containing them. Letter and book are "anagrim[s]" (93.29), or Anna-grams, the messages of Anna as river, in which the anagrammatical relationship of "letter" and "teller" is spelled out as A's and O's. The letter is a "sexmosaic of . . . the eternal chimerahunter" (107.13–14), telling the story of the hero HCE's "existence as a tesseract" (100.35), a stonelike component of the design.

When the letter as brief (G., *Brief*, letter) is introduced at the trial, it becomes part of the story it tells. Generally, critics have associated the narrative of I.4 with the story of Parnell. James Atherton has identified John Macdonald's *The Diary of the Parnell Commission Revised from the "Daily News"* as an important source for some of the details. He points out that in this chapter "every paragraph contains some reference to Macdonald's book."[50] The fox hunt that takes place after the trial represents the hounding of Parnell from power. While the details of Parnell's fall provide some dominant motifs, the other elements we have been looking at also appear. Their cumulative effect allows the reader to create from the narration the peculiar sense of order we have seen in other sections focusing more exclusively on aesthetic processes. They function as do many of the Homeric allusions imbedded in the narration of *Ulysses*. Once we notice their presence, the narration takes on a supplementary coloration that does not subvert whatever order it may also have as narrative. As so often in the *Wake*, we find one story nesting within the language of another. The result of the superimposition resembles the relationship of figure to ground in some optical illusions or the seemingly double image in the drawing of duck and rabbit that E. H. Gombrich discusses in *Art and Illusion* (see fig. 7).[51]

Figure 7

Rabbit or duck?

As in the reversals of figure and ground, the reader achieves an oscillating perspective, like the one I have already mentioned with regard to the Ondt and the Gracehoper and the Möbius strip. In I.4, besides Parnell's tale, we have part of the story of the author's problems in finding a publisher. Like the tale of Moses, this one takes the protagonist up to and beyond his own imagined death that has become part of his own book. The narrative portrays the character's persecution, trial, escape, further life, and, finally, his afterlife *as a text*. And from time to time the narration includes references to the setting up of typographical characters in print.

After the trial we hear of the wanderer's life as an artist in exile, making and remaking the book of himself until his death completes the transfusion of his life into the memorializing works that survive in the continuous loop of letter as book and river. In the events following the trial, the accused escapes by "louping the loop" as an "ear canny hare for doubling" (97.8–9) during the fox hunt. The unsuccessful attack includes an attempt to "abridge" (97.22–23), or emasculate, him and his works. By "playing possum" (96.33–34) our "encestor" saved himself and in the process "saved . . . his posterity, you charming coparcenors, us, heirs of his tailsie" (96.35–36). The pronouns connect readers and teller as coparceners, or joint heirs, of their common ancestor. We and the teller are hairs of the writer's tail and inheritors of his tale that contains the "nameform" (18.25) of the narrative and its narrator. The letter dictated, written down, and delivered by the hero's survivors is the narrative of the inheritance he bequeaths to his heirs. And that narrative is the inheritance itself, which tells the tale of dictation, transcription, and delivery, and so on to infinity or to the recirculation of the text as never-ending "continuarration" (205.14).

Like the Crucifixion, the author's death is a martyring, a "suicidal murder" (100.10) announced by "an inked up name and title, inscribed in the national cursives" (99.17–18). The death, then, is announced by a sign very like the title page of a book. While in exile the artist has given of himself to produce this book, "his seventh generation" (98.8–9). The recurring number seven in *Finnegans Wake* can refer to a variety of groups, including the colors of the rainbow and the hills of Rome.[52] But in this case it designates the writer's seventh published volume. For Joyce *Finnegans Wake* was the last in a sequence including two volumes of poetry, a collection of short stories, a play, and two other long prose narratives. One of the abusive names Earwicker has been called confirms this interpretation. He is "*Hebdromadary Publocation*" (71.16). The hump of the dromedary merges with hebdomadary, meaning seventh, in this odd appellation. Apparently, as a pubkeeper Earwicker has had seven different locations; as an author, seven publications.

After reporting the exile's death, the teller anxiously asserts the expatriate's "lastingness" (100.18). Despite his demise, "his dode canal sammenlivers" (100.30), fellow wanderers among the Dodecanese Islands, including his readers, continue believing in "the canonicity of his existence as a tesseract" (100.34–35). The exiled author has been canonized in musical, religious, legal, literary, and typographical senses. As in the polyphonic composition of a musical canon, he has become an entity in which there will be exact repetitions of earlier parts of himself in various keys. Upon the writer's death, his life is transferred from the body become corpse to the corpus of his works become canon. As "tesseract" he is a "onestone parable" (100.26–27), both an epitaph on a tombstone and the essential medium of the "sexmosaic" (107.13) in which the tiny stone is at once a piece and the synecdochic "allforabit." As a stone within the mosaic of the literary canon, the author's corpus is an adjunct to the Muse's diadem. By his "suicidal murder," the writing of books, the author inscribes his ample "nameform" in the type of texts like the sacred, Mosaic one, which contains the canons of religious law. The largest size of type with a specific name happens to be the canon.[53]

The occasional stuttering of characters and teller, like the stuttering of Moses, indicates the Mosaic nature of book and characters. Like the letter, the exiled writer's works are composed of dots arranged into texts similar to Shem's stippled "inartistic portraits of himself " (182.19). These form a "new book of Morses" (123.35), "Morse nuisance noised" (99.6). The new Mosaic work would be a product of the "Stuttering Hand" (4.18) mentioned near the beginning of I.1. At the start of IV that hand is matched by another in language spelling HCE: "A hand from the cloud emerges, holding a chart expanded" (593.19). The hand emerging from a cloud together with a document recalls the emergence of "Gutenmorg" from his wordpress with a charter. And it prepares for the continuation of the author's writing as act and as text in the manner suggested metaphorically at the end of ALP's monologue.

Before the accusation and trial, the teller mentions two adversaries who "struggled apairently for some considerable time" (81.35–36). In this version of the recurring confrontation between the Cad and Earwicker, the Norwegian captain and the tailor, Buckley and the Russian general, Wellington and Napoleon, Shaun and Shem, the identities of these and other apparent opposites are disseminated into the narration: "The boarder incident prerepeated itself. The pair (whethertheywere Nippoluono engaging Wei-Ling-Taou or de Razzkias trying to reconnoistre the general Boukeleff, man may not say), struggled . . . under the All In rules around the booksafe" (81.32–82.2). This ur-enactment of the struggle that has "prerepeated itself" makes clearer than other versions that the confrontation occurs between author and publisher and centers "around the booksafe." When the more aggressive of the two raises as a stick the "oblong bar . . . with which he usually broke furnitures" (81.31–32), his weapon must be a shooting stick, the device used by compositors in letterpress printing to drive the furniture in the process of locking up or unlocking the type that has been prepared for imposing.[54] The incident is the prelude for the trial and exile of the accused. The narrative sequence resembles the story of Shem's problems with printers, and also Joyce's alluded to in I.7:

> . . . when Robber and Mumsell, the pulpic dictators, on the nudgment of their legal advisers, Messrs Codex and Podex, and under his own benefiction of their pastor Father Flammeus Falconer, boycotted him of all muttonsuet candles and romeruled stationery for any purpose, he winged away on a wild-goup's chase across the kathartic ocean and made synthetic ink and sensitive paper for his own end out of his wit's waste. (185.1–8).

George Roberts was managing editor of Maunsel and Company, one of the publishers involved in the infamous delays surrounding publication of *Dubliners*. John Falconer, the printer who burned the sheets and destroyed the type, is appropriately named "Flammeus."

During the encounter in I.4, as elsewhere in the *Wake*, the antagonists exhibit something like brotherly affection, as well as a rancour resembling sibling rivalry. The shooting stick raised in anger reflects the ambiguity because of its double purpose as an instrument for both setting up and dismantling printing type. It combines the "deathbone" (193.29) of Shaun as Justius with the "lifewand" (195.5) of Shem as Mercius mentioned toward the end of I.7. Like Justice and Mercy, the two staffs are mutually defining. When Justius points his deathbone, "the quick are still" (193.29). The living and the movable are stilled. But they also *still* exist; the deathbone represents life's continuity as well as its end. It, too, is a kind of lifewand.

Many of the details we have examined work together to suggest that the story of writer and printer is part of the more general story of artist and audience. The recurring encounters in the narrative provide an example. The more general implication of the assaults becomes clearest in I.3 during HCE's encounter with the Cad. On the one hand, the first-person plural pronouns align reader and teller, who together compose "us (the real Us!)" as "we seem . . . to be reading" (62.29). And the teller addresses the reader as "gentlewriter" (63.10) rather than "gentlereader." But there is antagonism between reader and writer as well. Like the assailant with the shooting stick, the Cad assaults his victim with a weapon, in this case "a barkiss revolver" (62.31). Considering the recondite nature of *Finnegans Wake*, the reader may see himself as a Cad's victim. Like HCE, we are accosted "by an unknowable assailant (masked)" (62.32–33); that is, by the artist in persona. Like the roles of Ondt and Gracehoper, Justius and Mercius,

Shaun and Shem, the roles of reader and writer in this text are in revolution. The violence of the revolving resembles the pummeling that may occur during a mugging. In the author's engagement with the printer and other readers, each party may sustain some injuries.

According to the narrator in I.4, such injuries leave the victim not "a whit whorse for her whacking. Her who?" (84.27). The shift to the feminine pronoun effects that other revolution of roles by which male becomes female in Joyce's narrative. Here the shift introduces ALP and the hen, the representatives of the feminine principle that produces the letter. It presages the emergence of the mother's voice later: at the end of the dialogue between Mercius and Justius in I.7, and in the letter and monologue after the final dialogues in IV. The immediate gloss of "her" in I.4 indicates the movement toward an origin that defines the text's progress toward Anna Livia's voice at its ending and toward the continuity of that voice with its beginning. We are told we are "wurming along gradually for our savings backtowards motherwaters so many miles from bank and Dublin stone" (84.30–31). We reach our salvation as "salvocean" (623.24) at the conclusion of the quest both for the river as mother and for the source of the river itself. Although those saving waters are suggested by the washerwomen's dialogue in I.8, we reach them more fully in IV. We arrive briefly at the river's source as metaphor for the writing that is the book-as-river's origin. Anna Livia in the role of the River Liffey spawns the entire text by beginning it again at its ending. "Reverend" (615.12) and river's end become the "riverrun" of the first page. Her final monologue presents the meeting of river and sea and predicts the appearance of ALP's young replacement, "a daughterwife from the hills again" (627.2). The new waters will come, as ALP once did, from the "great blue bedroom, the air so quiet, scarce a cloud" (627.9), blue like Shem's book, like his den, and like *Ulysses*.

The "daughterwife" that will rain down is "Nuvoletta," the daughter as the "lass" (159.5) who tries to attract the Mookse and the Gripes in I.6. "Nuvoletta" is both a new letter and the title of the Italian translation of Joyce's story "A Little Cloud" from *Dubliners*. The word could even be translated loosely back into English as "scarce a cloud" (627.9). The narrative in I.6 merges elements from I.8 and IV. Nuvoletta observes the two washerwomen who pluck Mookse and Gripes as laundry from their places on the banks. When they are picked up, like the other antagonists in the *Wake*, they have switched positions, in this case banks (158.25–32; cf. 153.9–11). The reversal resembles the exchange of tone between right and left marginalia mid-way through II.2, the Schoolroom chapter. And it foreshadows the transforming of the book's conclusion into an introduction when ALP announces the arrival of her replacement. Once Mookse and Gripes have been gathered, Nuvoletta decides to descend from the sky in order to become the river, as ALP suggests she will during the final monologue. Giving a "cloudy cry" (159.9), Nuvoletta becomes "Missis-liffi" (159.12–13). When she makes up "all her myriads of drifting minds in one" (159.7), she is like "myriadminded" (*U* 205) Shakespeare, the model for the artist in Stephen's aesthetic theory. And, by extension, she is like the *polytropos* Odysseus.

In the monologue predicting Nuvoletta's future hegemony, the reader and ALP as the river's voice perceive the stream's sourceless origin to be a dynamic process rather than a place only: the natural cycle that transfers water between sea, cloud, and river. The little cloud rejuvenates the book as a new letter prolonging the old one that is Joyce's earlier work, including the stories containing "A Little Cloud."[55] Implicit in the book's ending is the process of imagination leading to the aesthetic continuous creation of a literary universe constantly in flux. Like the rising vapor and the Abyssinian clouds in Wordsworth's *The Prelude* (Book VI, 592–616), the cloud represents the discovery of the Nile's source and the writer's contact with the distant waters within the mind and within texts already written.

In *Finnegans Wake* Joyce regularly directs our attention to origins, especially to the sources for his own text. Those sources include the various works and authors to which he alludes and the mechanical process of printing by which the book is made. As we read the *Wake*, we experience in mediated ways how the text was produced. And we encounter characters involved in producing documents. Joyce cannot give us in unmediated form the experience of his mental processes that result in writing. Instead, he provides a finished document that becomes the raw material for us to undergo analogous experiences. By waking the Phoenician, he provides his readers with the opportunity to wake the Phoenician. But for us, Joyce himself has become an avatar of the figure to be roused.

Joyce represents himself in his writing through characters-as-artists and through styles of language. But this self-representation is not a purely egocentric venture. It includes Joyce's vision of the artist not just as a special person or even as a general type *among* humankind but as the general type *of* humankind. Joyce's portraits of the artist, especially in the *Wake* and in *Ulysses*, tend toward the portrayal or the evocation of universal mental and social experiences. I make this assertion despite the mannered eccentricities of style in his late works. We cannot separate the large historical and cultural dimensions from the more narrowly aesthetic ones in his fiction. Joyce's writing makes available an "*ancient legacy of the past*" (614.36–615.1; my emphasis) that combines history with ALP as the source in human consciousness for humankind's story as history. As James Atherton has said, *Finnegans Wake* is "everyone's dream, the dream of all the living and the dead," emanating from Joyce's persona, the universal mind to which we all contribute.[56]

Although many of the details of Joyce's fictions concern a specifically Irish past, the trajectory of his writings is toward the telling of an Irish narrative that cannot be distinguished from the story of humanity. The attempt to write an Irish tale of universal relevance about sources leads Joyce to adopt the Homer of Victor Bérard's interpretation as his primary model. For Joyce, combining Homeric and Irish material meant writing about the inseminating source of the culture he knew best and about the well-spring of Western culture generally. In his Triestine lecture, "Ireland, Island of Saints and Sages" (1907), Joyce refers at length to the theories about the Irish language put forward by the scholar Charles Vallancey (1721–1812):

> This language is oriental in origin, and has been identified by many philologists with the ancient language of the Phoenicians, the originators of trade and navigation, according to historians. This adventurous people, who had a monopoly of the sea, established in Ireland a civilization that had decayed and almost disappeared before the first Greek historian took his pen in hand. It jealously preserved the secrets of its knowledge, and the first mention of the island of Ireland in foreign literature is found in a Greek poem of the fifth century before Christ, where the historian repeats the Phoenician tradition. The language that the Latin writer of comedy, Plautus, put in the mouth of Phoenicians in his comedy *Poenulus* is almost the same language that the Irish peasants speak today, according to the critic Vallancey. The religion and civilization of this ancient people, later known by the name of Druidism, were Egyptian. The Druid priests had their temples in the open, and worshipped the sun and moon in groves of oak trees. In the crude state of knowledge of those times, the Irish priests were considered very learned, and when Plutarch mentions Ireland, he says that it was the dwelling place of holy men. (*CW* 156)

As the editors of Joyce's lecture point out, Vallancey's speculations are no longer accepted. Joyce probably knew they had been discredited. But the connection of the Irish with the Phoenicians was one his imagination could use. What he does with the imagined relationship matters more than its scholarly accuracy. Together with Victor Bérard's theories, Vallancey's ideas allow Joyce to forge the link between Homer and Ireland.[57] When Joyce creates and explores that link in his writing, like the Greek historian he mentions in his lecture, he "repeats the Phoenician tradition." According to Vallancey, from that tradition Western civilization itself sprang through trade, navigation, and the practice of secret wisdom.

Joyce does not employ the theories of Bérard and Vallancey about Homer, the Irish, and the Phoenicians in any mechanical way as an exoskeleton for *Finnegans Wake*. Instead, their infusion into the metaphors, narrative situations, and styles contributes to the internal dynamic process of a narration that yields the "sameold gamebold adomic structure" of recurring human experiences. As we encounter that structure, that process, and those experiences, we discover what all Joyce's fictions provide in their various ways through style: links between the artist and the reader composed of related processes of mind, language, and narrative that make the beginning and the end, the writing and the reading of Joyce's texts continuous.

CHAPTER TWO

The Preposterous Shape of Portraiture:
A Portrait of the Artist as a Young Man

Formally the novel is close to the dream; both can be defined by consideration of this curious property: *all their deviations form part of them.*
—Paul Valéry

The genius in the act of creation . . . resembles the uncanny fairy tale image which is able to see itself by turning its eyes. He is at once subject and object, poet, actor, and audience.
—Nietzsche, *The Birth of Tragedy*

OSCILLATING PERSPECTIVE

In my commentary on *Finnegans Wake*, I explain how Joyce provides the reader in various ways with the means for achieving an oscillating perspective. That perspective is a viewpoint for reading that vacillates between mutually defining poles, just as our perception of the relation between figure and ground in some optical illusions may shift. The vacillating viewpoint is available in Joyce's writing much earlier than the *Wake*, as early, in fact, as *A Portrait of the Artist as a Young Man*. Joyce creates it through style in the continuing refinement of his techniques for rendering consciousness that he develops during the writing of *Dubliners* and *Stephen Hero*. The subtle intermingling of third- and first-person perspectives that Joyce effects in *A Portrait* is the most significant change in the style of his autobiographical work, one that differentiates it clearly from *Stephen Hero*. The mixing of narrator's and character's views and voices in *A Portrait*, which is prepared for by aspects of *Dubliners*, will become the *donnée* of *Ulysses*, the stylistic element the later work starts with, deviates from, then returns to in "Penelope." It is also an early step toward the radical superimposing of voices in *Finnegans Wake*.

In addition, Joyce encourages the oscillating perspective in *A Portrait* by constructing his narrative to avoid the pretense that his narration is a transparent vehicle for plot. He eschews that pretense through subverting the conventions of realism. Generally speaking, in fiction those conventions, including a single telling voice or style and a coherent chronological presentation, are undercut when the narration includes apparently heterogeneous material: diagrams, documents, or stories-within-the-text. Joyce achieves some of his most arresting and puzzling effects in *A Portrait* by injecting heterogeneous elements into the narrative. By disrupting the semblance of a continuous flow of narrative, these elements draw attention to the book's artifice, to its status as art, and to themselves as relatively independent of the text containing them. These aspects of narrative can function similarly to the epic similes in *Paradise Lost* as Geoffrey Hartman has described them.[1] They set up countermovements in the reading process that may engender an oscillating perspective on the totality of the work's details.

In this regard, Joyce's autobiographical fiction resembles another eccentric work, a fictional autobiography, Laurence Sterne's *Tristram Shandy*. Sterne's book is one of the most famous heterogeneous instances in the history of fiction, in part because the narrator's divagations distract the reader repeatedly from any passive response to the text based on unquestioned assumptions about what a novel should be and what its implications may legitimately include. Sterne's book contains blank, black, and marbled pages, as well as ellipses, diagrams, and a musical score. The narrator quotes at length from documents such as his parents' marriage contract. He prints *en face* an English translation of a story written in Latin by Hafen Slawkenbergius, a fictitious author. Because of their styles and structures these divergences from what Tristram calls the straight line of the narrative encourage the reader to reflect on the various styles and structures of the larger work providing their context. Text as whole and internal segment as part become mutually defining. The part differs radically from its context, but both part and context contribute to the whole that is the narrative.

Such elements as the title and the epigraphs in *Tristram Shandy* tend to create perspectives for the reader that raise problems about how to understand the novel in its parts and in its totality. The full title, *The Life and Opinions of Tristram Shandy, Gentleman*, indicates that within the covers of the book can be found the central character's life and opinions. But the title is at odds with the narrative, for much of the novel presents material from before the time Tristram and his opinions supposedly come into existence. By trying to fill in background and past history, Tristram as narrator is hardly ever able to present himself as character, is almost never able to write about the present or the recent past relative to the time of his act of writing. That act of writing itself, as well as the subjects being written about, becomes an important focus of the reader's attention and of Tristram's. Of the various epigraphs affixed to the volumes of *Tristram Shandy*, the one ascribed to Pliny the Younger at the head of volume seven suggests most clearly a possible interpretation for the form of the narration with its numerous digressions and embellishments. Even though volume seven swerves from the narrative immediately preceding it by presenting unexpected subject matter, the epigraph states in Latin that "this is not an excursion from it, but is the work itself."[2] The oddities of the narration can create an essential frame of reference for interpreting the text containing them.

Although Joyce's *A Portrait of the Artist as a Young Man* is neither as obviously idiosyncratic as *Tristram Shandy* nor as unusual as Joyce's later fictions, like them, it is only marginally a *novel*, if by that term we mean a prose narration that abides by the canons of realism. These works include elements of form revealing disequilibria in the conventions of the telling that are startling and, at times, disquieting. In *A Portrait* the disturbing elements that raise the question of the book's marginal status are most prominent at the beginning and the ending. These are the locations of the text's margins, its borders with a world not delimited by the language of the story. Title, epigraph, and journal are the gates into and out of Joyce's work. They provide for the reader portals of discovery, margins to be negotiated and filled during the reading process.

These parts of *A Portrait* and many of the anomalies that characterize similar texts are analogous to an element Freud claims is present in every dream. In what must be the most unusual footnote in *The Interpretation of Dreams*, a book full of curiosities, Freud asserts that "there is at least one spot in every dream at which it is unplumbable—a navel, as it were, that is its point of contact with the unknown."[3] The navel is the point at which the umbilical cord has been cut. It suggests simultaneously the connection and the severing of the connection between parent and child, or, in aesthetic terms, between creator and artifact. It is both the mark or signature of the creator's activity and the sign of the creation's autonomy. As point of contact with the unknown, the navel of the dream cannot be completely apprehended through the logic of propositions either because evidence is insufficient for a determinate conclusion or because some paradox pre-empts the efficacy of conventional logic. The navel is the mark of the conundrum, of what can be known only marginally, not fully or directly. Both Freud's essay and Joyce's book depend on pretexts—on ruses and on previously existing works. Through its form, each announces itself to be a revision of prior texts, particularly ones by the writer, which are either displaced or included within the text we read. In Freud's essay the process of revision is indicated by multiple references to previous editions, parts of which have been reprinted, others deleted, still others recast in the production of subsequent versions. Freud's pretext for writing his volume, to illuminate the nature of dreams and dreaming, disguises a book that is not primarily about the originating process of dreaming but instead focuses on the belated process of interpretation.

A Portrait also contains numerous references to other texts, including poems, stories, novels, and diaries, that exist earlier than itself either in actuality or in the fiction of the narrative's chronology. The book is the revision of these previous texts contained either wholly or partially within it. Here Joyce anticipates the procedure of his later works. As in the *Wake*, in

A Portrait, the artist's activity is essentially rewriting. Joyce indicates within the text the task performed by every serious writer: the act of revision that is at once the author's writing and reading (as interpretation) of his self-made image in language. Like the narrator of Proust's *Remembrance of Things Past*, who touches up his earlier work before including it in the novel, Joyce as teller engages in the continuing work of revising the book of himself.[4] Both Proust and Joyce include in their narrations infinitely regressive paradoxes about the relations of life and art. With regard to *A Portrait*, the act of revision, for which the book is evidence, is a crucial but unstated implication of the story's form.

Joyce responds to texts that already exist by rewriting his own earlier work, whether or not published, the work of his predecessors, and occasionally the work of his contemporaries. In the *Wake*, Joyce alludes to and transforms numerous texts by other writers of his period. These include, most prominently, Wyndham Lewis and T. S. Eliot, both of whom had responded in print to *Ulysses*.[5] Lewis's negative comments are well-known. Eliot reacted to *Ulysses* by writing his famous review "*Ulysses*, Order, and Myth" and (in Joyce's opinion) "The Waste Land." Although Joyce's allusions of this kind are, in one sense, autobiographical, their peculiar literary nature makes them something other than simple contributions to our vision of the author's life. Instead, they give us aspects of a general image of both the artist and the creative process, a process that includes within its products responses to its own earlier incarnations.

Many critics who have written on *A Portrait* interpret that work autobiographically, claiming that it is based on details of Joyce's youth. Generally, they adduce the title as evidence for the link between the life and the work of art: the portrait is of the artist who writes the book. Unquestionably, strong evidence supports this kind of autobiographical reading. But an autobiographical interpretation of a different sort is also possible, one that sees Stephen Dedalus as the teller of his own story.[6] When we read Freud on dreams, we learn that the fulfillment of the process of dreaming, another kind of retelling of stories, occurs in the interpretation of dreams, a belated activity in which the dreamer and the analyst may be one. In *A Portrait*, we discover that the fulfillment of the process of becoming an author occurs in the act of writing, a belated activity in which character and narrator may be one. Implicit in the story of Stephen Dedalus's growth to maturity is the process by which his book emerges from previously existing texts that Stephen knows, some of which he has written himself. *A Portrait* is both the author's autobiographical fiction and the autobiography of the fictional character. It provides the portrait of both artists.

Any interpretation that suggests Stephen may be the narrator will take exception to most readings that dwell on the problem of irony, or aesthetic distance, and on the impersonality of the narration.[7] By emphasizing the narrator's invisibility and the would-be dramatic or objective presentation of Stephen, those readings generally fail to account adequately for at least two crucial aspects of *A Portrait*: the narrator's recurring presentation of Stephen's consciousness and the various paradoxes of the narration that make describing the details of the story and its form so difficult.[8] Although there can still be disagreements concerning the precise mix of the narrator's attitudes toward the central character at any given moment in the story, if Stephen narrates, the large problem of his future as an artist can no longer be at issue. If he writes his own tale, the story itself as text provides the strongest possible indication that his choice of vocation will yield more valuable work than the writing he produces within the narrative. And the narration indicates exactly what kind of artist Stephen has become. The teller in *A Portrait*, like the purloined letter of Poe's story, is well-hidden out in the open, where anyone who cares to look can find him.

DISLOCATIONS IN STYLE AND STORY

A Portrait of the Artist contains displacements in both narrative and narration, story and telling. The literal displacements include the moves of the Dedalus family from one residence to the next always less attractive abode, compounded with Stephen's displacements from school to school, from Clongowes to Belvedere to University College. "Still another removal" (*P* 163), Stephen exclaims to himself during the scene in the kitchen with his siblings at the end of IV.2. In Stephen's boyhood and adolescence, sex and religion replace one another in mutually modifying and mutually defining alternation, until their ultimate displacement through coalescence in Stephen's choice of art as vocation. In the future projected by the book's ending, this last development will be last in the sense of previous. That future may bring a series of further developments, each transforming the last from final to merely previous. Stephen's choice of vocation is accompanied by suggestions of the next physical displacement, his planned departure from Ireland, which will take him eventually not just to Paris, but to Trieste.

Displacements in *A Portrait* are temporal as well as spatial and stylistic as well as literal. The ending indicates that Stephen may be entering a period of more mature adulthood, which will replace his young adulthood, the most recent in a series of states stretching back through adolescence to childhood and infancy. The displacements of style are both those of Stephen as developing artist and of the narrator as mature artist. As William M. Schutte has pointed out, "*Portrait*, like *Ulysses* and *Finnegans Wake*, has no one style."[9] By entwining strands of language into a narrative, the teller of the story reaches back through the past to the origins of Stephen's development as an artist. The reaching back by weaving a thread of narrative is like the process of gazing "in your omphalos" practiced by "mystic monks" (U 38) on which Stephen muses jokingly in "Proteus." There he imagines placing a phone call to "Edenville," his place of origin, along the "strandentwining cable of all flesh," the navel cord that links us all to the past. By transforming the relatively homogeneous style of *Stephen Hero* into the varying, fluctuating styles of *A Portrait*, Joyce manages to produce a "strandentwining cable" of words linking both writer and character to a literary past as origin.

Although they are less emphatically stressed in Joyce's text, the juxtaposed styles in *A Portrait* function essentially as do the shifting voices of Eliot's "The Waste Land." They exhibit the individual talent of author and character encountering, fracturing, and reusing the resources of the tradition, simultaneously creating a new voice and revivifying the voices of dead authors. In this way the book anticipates the more flamboyant multiplication of styles in *Ulysses*, especially the chronological replication of styles contained in "Oxen of the Sun." In *A Portrait*, by shifting styles Joyce meets a special challenge: to present a wide variety of stylistic exercises that would simultaneously mark the development of a young character's aesthetic sensibilities and form the basis for the writer's exhibition of his own technical mastery. In the various styles of portraiture we have proof of both the character's aesthetic sensitivity and the narrator's virtuosity. The same language serves two purposes.[10] From time to time Joyce directs his adventure in styles toward culminating passages of discovery and self-revelation in which the heightened language vividly calls attention to the relationship of narrator's skill to character's state of mind. The writing of the villanelle in part V will be especially important in this regard for our consideration of the teller's merging with character in *A Portrait*.

During the displacing of earlier parts of the narrative by later parts, the teller modulates among his different styles of narration, including a "vague, nineteenth-century romanticism," "exalted, almost hysterical lyricism," "workaday prose," and the language of Pater and the decadents.[11] In general, the narration consists of anonymous representations of scene, action, and dialogue in the third person together with the report of Stephen's thoughts, also in the third person. The thoughts of other characters are not reported. This sort of presentation allows Joyce a great deal of flexibility. Modulation from one style to another can be smoothly executed as a shift in the character's thinking within the often relatively unobtrusive framework of third-person narration. Some of the more violent, jarring shifts of style occur at the breaks between typographically demarcated segments of the narrative, between the five parts, and between the nineteen smaller sections making up those parts.*

---

*I discuss some aspects of the relations among the book's parts and section in Appendix 1: "The Parts and the Structural Rhythm of *A Portrait*."

There are so many modulations of style in *A Portrait* that any endeavor to characterize generally the details of narration will prove inadequate in some respects. Part of the work's richness and appeal is a verbal texture so variable that it defeats all attempts at reduction to a simple pattern. But the fluctuations do develop in a general direction as the narrative proceeds. In broad terms, the style shifts from psycho-narration narrowly conceived toward narrated monologue; that is, it moves from the narrator's discourse concerning the character's mind to a presentation that also includes the character's mental discourse rendered as the narrator's language. Occasionally, the narrator employs the technique of quoted monologue, language that we understand as the character's supposedly unmediated mental discourse because it employs first person and present tense. The general distinctions between psycho-narration, quoted monologue, and narrated monologue will emerge as we examine specific passages in *A Portrait*.[12] Each technique affects our stance toward character and teller and our sense of the teller's relationship to the tale. All three occur in the context of third-person narration. While we may want to distinguish between them for the purposes of analysis, they hardly ever occur in complete isolation from one another.

Of the three, the most problematic is the narrated monologue, also known as *erlebte Rede* and as *le style indirect libre*, a technique Joyce would have found in Flaubert. This device involves the rendering of the characer's consciousness in the third person and the past tense. Although there may be no explicit announcement of mental process in the narrator's language, we understand the passages as thoughts occurring to the character in the first person and in the present tense. The present time of the action, as opposed to the past time indicated by the narration, is often emphasized by deictic adjectives and adverbs and by demonstrative pronouns, which create a sense of immediacy. Here arises the crucial complication that Joyce develops with such subtlety in both *A Portrait* and *Ulysses*. The reader translates the third person into "I" during the reading process. We speak the character's subjectivity, as do narrator and character in their different ways. The use of third person and past tense indicates a tendency toward a fusion of character's voice with teller's voice. The ambiguous merger of voices makes it difficult, even impossible, for the reader to distinguish between the cunningly combined voices of character and narrator. Because the technique requires the reader to translate third person into first and to attempt discriminations, however difficult, between the merged voices, it necessitates the reader's active recreative rendering of the narration. The reader *performs* the text of narrated monologue with a special kind of involvement because of the device's unusual nature.

Quite frequently, the narrator in *A Portrait* summarizes Stephen's thoughts as psycho-narration employing verbs of consiousness prominently either in the past tense or as infinitives. There are numerous examples from the book's early pages: "felt" (*P* 8), "wondered" (*P* 10), "to remember" (*P* 11), "knew" (*P* 29). Occasionally several verbs indicating thought are clustered together. In one paragraph early in I.2 (*P* 12), there are six instances of such verbs. In general, in this portion of the narrative, there is little emphasis on the complex combination of voices that appears later.* The reader can easily distinguish the narrator's discourse about Stephen's thoughts from the presentation of scene and dialogue; for instance, in the alternation between these two complementary aspects of the narration in I.3, the Christmas dinner. As Stephen grows older, the narrator's techniques for presenting his thoughts change. Verbs denoting mental process still occur but less frequently, and other words connoting thought supplement them. Predicates less directly evocative of consciousness, often together with a prepositional phrase, become the reminders that we have access to Stephen's mind.

In II.2, when Stephen begins wandering the streets of Dublin alone, the passages describing his adventures contain just as many indicators of thought as do some earlier passages, but the indications are of a different order. Stephen makes a map of the city "in his mind." As he follows physically the routes of this internal map, the verb "to wonder," used before in the past tense, now occurs as a present participle, "wondering." While an explicit reference to mental process is still provided, the transformation of the verb denoting thought from a predicate to a modifier makes the reference less obtrusive. Instead of telling us that Stephen thought, felt, or remembered, the narrator presents Stephen's impressions as they "suggested to him," "wakened again in him," or "grew up within him" (*P* 66). As before, the references to thought are clustered together, though they are more muted now. These last three predicates and the two preceding quotations are all from a single paragraph. And the predications of thought, even these muted ones, begin to be supplemented or replaced by a new affective vocabulary presenting mood, as in the phrases "mood of embittered silence" and "angry with himself" (*P* 67). Or nouns and verbs not necessarily denoting mental activity, such as "vision" and "chronicled," take on connotations that suggest consciousness because of their use in context.

There are two distinctions implicit in the alternation between scene and psyche that occurs in the work's first sections: the distinction between an external world and the character's mind and between narrator and character. Starting in part II both begin to be blurred in various ways. The alternation becomes overlap when the narrator quotes Stephen's thoughts in II.2 using the same typographical indicator, the dash, that previously identified only direct discourse: "—She too wants me to catch hold of her,

---

*Some exceptions to this general description are I.1 and such passages as the paragraph in I.3 beginning "Why did Mr. Barrett . . ." (*P* 30).

he thought. That's why she came with me to the tram. I could easily catch hold of her when she comes up to my step: nobody is looking. I could hold her and kiss her" (*P* 70). The character's interior speech is utilized here as the equivalent of a stage monologue or aside in drama. It has the form of direct discourse but a different effect. In II.3 the narrator carries his modifications further during Stephen's encounter with his schoolmate Heron just before the play. We are given the narrative of Stephen's heretical essay and the drubbing it leads to as scene, dialogue, and action (*P* 78–82). But this narrative occurs in Stephen's mind. His memory now is rendered in nearly the same way as the narrator's presentation of the external world. The growing resemblance between the two modes of narration prepares for the more radical alignment of teller and character that occurs later.

The more striking fusion of inner and outer and of character and teller begins emerging in the next part, when the teller adopts the narrated monologue while presenting the retreat in III.2. As in the narration of the Christmas dinner, the telling alternates between an external scene (the sermons) and Stephen's reaction to the outer world. Although the narrator continues to employ techniques introduced in previous sections, there are some crucial modifications. These changes suggest, among other things, the intensity of Stephen's reaction to events. Section III.2 consists of an introductory talk and three sermons that take place on consecutive days. The initial, prominent use of narrated monologue occurs in the passage presenting Stephen's walk home the first evening after the introductory talk: "So he had sunk to the state of a beast that licks his chaps after meat. This was the end; . . . And that was life" (*P* 111). The device is especially manifest because Joyce uses demonstrative pronouns in a paragraph otherwise relatively free of them. The statements can be easily transformed into the character's speech to himself in first person and present tense. In the paragraph that follows, the narrator presents the initial sermon, on death and judgment (*P* 112–15), in a curious way. He renders it not as direct discourse, the technique he uses to report the two subsequent sermons on hell, but as speech mediated by Stephen's consciousness. The brief passage of narrated monologue acts as the preparation for this odd filtering of Father Arnall's words through Stephen's mind. The narration of the sermon begins in the past tense with a series of verbs and phrases indicating Stephen's consciousness is being rendered: "stirring his soul," "fear," "terror," "into his soul," "he suffered," "he felt" (*P* 112). In the middle of the sermon, although the dashes of direct discourse are absent, the past tense is replaced with a mixture of tenses, including present and future, much closer to the quotation of the later sermons as speech.

After this lengthy report of Stephen's consciousness during the first sermon, the alternation of passages focusing on psyche with those focusing on scene is again established, but now the narrated monologue has become a recurring feature of the narration. The narrator employs it briefly but regularly throughout the remainder of III (instances occur on 115, 117, 125, 126, 138, 143, 145).* In III.3 Stephen's thoughts are quoted directly, once with a dash indicating direct discourse when he hears voices (*P* 136), but at other times without the dash as apparently unmediated interior exclamations: "Confess! Confess!" (*P* 139). While this last exclamation can be read as a direct presentation of Stephen's thought, the similar one, "For him! For him!" (*P* 138), that occurs only a page earlier is an instance of narrated monologue. We read "For him" as "For *me*," understanding the third person as applying to the character.

With a device as problematic as narrated monologue, there will almost certainly be some disagreement among readers concerning the application of the term to specific passages. Whatever the differing judgments about the particular passages I have identified as narrated monologue, the general point concerning the sudden, recurring appearance of the technique in the narration is irrefragable: these numerous possible instances of narrated monologue grouped together in part III mark a significant shift in the style. The shift is increasingly toward renderings of Stephen's intensely felt thoughts that create an ambiguity concerning the relationship of the style to the character's language. In the two remaining parts the narrator freely employs in combination the various techniques he has used to present Stephen's mind. Once the reader has grown accustomed to the different modes for representing consciousnenss that have been introduced seriatim over the course of nearly 150 pages, the teller can rely on the reader's newly created capacity for responding to the salmagundi of techniques that will now be employed in the narration.

The narrator has been making a persona for the reader as well as for himself in his portrayal of Stephen. The reader has learned the conventions of the literary techniques that the author uses to compose his own self-representation as teller and to present Stephen's gradually developing sensibilities. Only after all the techniques have become thoroughly established as conventions of the fiction can the narrator begin to shift rapidly from one to another. The swift alternation of devices evoking the hard, gemlike flame of Stephen's mind occurs in the book's two climactic segments: at the end of IV.3 when Stephen is on the strand, and during Stephen's composing of his villanelle in V.2.† At the end of IV.3, the narrator gives us Stephen's interior exclamations, "Yes! Yes! Yes!" (*P* 170), combined with possible instances of narrated monologue (*P* 170, 172) and with Stephen's thoughts quoted as if they were direct discourse: "—Heavenly God! cried Stephen's soul, in an outburst of profane joy" (*P*

---

*This and the following lists provided parenthetically are meant to be indicative only, not exhaustive.

† See Appendix 1 for a description of the place of these two segments in the narrative's overall structural rhythm.

171). Near the end of my discussion of *A Portrait*, I shall deal with the implications of the similar combination in V.2

In V.1 and V.3 there are numerous instances of narrated monologue (177, 179, 228, 232, 234, 245). The narrator also employs at great length the technique he used in II.3 by presenting Stephen's memories while he is walking to the university as scene, action, and dialogue (as in the long recollection of Davin's story about his walk in the country and his encounter with the peasant woman [*P* 181–83]). The ambiguity about the source of the narration's language is particularly pronounced throughout V. Repeatedly the narrator introduces long passages of Stephen's thoughts by asserting first that Stephen "watched" (*P* 185), "saw" (*P* 186), "looked at" (*P* 189), or "had heard" (*P* 191) something, then that someone or something "seemed" (185, 186, 189, 191) a certain way. These passages omit the phrase "to him" or "to Stephen," which would identify explicitly the language to follow as Stephen's rather than the narrator's. The narrator will introduce a long paragraph of revery with only a brief reference to "Stephen's mind" (*P* 192), which the reader may tend to forget, or he will conclude rather than introduce such a long paragraph with a phrase indicating the passage was Stephen's "thought" (*P* 228). As in so many other late passages, the effect is to align the teller's voice and the character's, if only temporarily. The residual and cumulative sense of merger created by such alignments molds the reader's stance toward the narration with particular force. While *some* distinctions can be made between teller and character (this discussion would not have been possible without them), the passages ask us again and again to consider the relationship of the two voices that are so complexly mixed.

The subtly mingled but counterpointed language of teller and character emerges vividly in the book's second half, primarily because the narrated monologues together with the related techniques appear frequently beginning in III.2. Along with the seemingly intimate presentation of Stephen's thoughts, in part V the reader encounters longer and more elaborate statements to his companions than Stephen has made earlier. His voices, both internal and public, are thrust to the foreground. At the book's ending, it is primarily these voices that determine the reader's overall judgment of Stephen's potential.

JOURNAL AND EPIGRAPH:
BEGINNING AND HOMEWARD GLANCE

The representations of Stephen's consciousness that occur in part V are particularly relevant for understanding the relationship of narrative to narration in *A Portrait*. The following paragraph, in which Stephen comments silently on Cranly's remark about a fellow student, is typical of the last section:

> It was his [Cranly's] epitaph for all dead friendships and Stephen won-
> dered whether it would ever be spoken in the same tone over his memory. The
> heavy lumpish phrase sank slowly out of hearing like a stone through a quag-
> mire. Stephen saw it sink as he had seen many another, feeling its heaviness
> depress his heart. Cranly's speech, unlike that of Davin, had neither rare
> phrases of Elizabethan English nor quaintly turned versions of Irish idioms.
> Its drawl was an echo of the quays of Dublin given back by a bleak decaying
> seaport, its energy an echo of the sacred eloquence of Dublin given back flatly
> by a Wicklow pulpit. (*P* 195)

Such insertions, made by the narrator during his report of conversations,
amount to brief digressions. As part of a commentary on time in fiction,
Jean Ricardou remarks on the effect passages like this one can have in a
narrative. Because of their length, they disrupt any illusion of a continuous
flow of time in the plot by calling attention to the time of the narration. As
Ricardou says, they emphasize "the writing (habitually concealed by the
story)."[13] When their prominence begins to define the mode of narration, as
it does in *A Portrait*, in Ricardou's formulation the work "ceases to be the
writing of a story to become the story of a writing."[14] The passage
emphasizes writing in two senses, as process of narration and as style of
language. The teller's activity of narrating is emphasized in ways it cannot
be through the quotation of dialogue. And attention is drawn to the specific
kind of language employed, particularly in this passage, in which Stephen
explicitly makes contrasts between various styles.

As narration, *A Portrait* includes all the styles mentioned in the
paragraph and many more. They are the literary styles the character has
heard or read (and sometimes spoken) and that the narrator has adopted in
his written mimicry of the character's mind and the character's world. At
times we understand them primarily as styles within the narrative; at other
times, as styles of the narration. When the styles characterize Stephen's
thoughts intimately presented, distinguishing narrative from narration is
often no longer possible. At issue in such a passage is the question of the
nature of narrative as mimetic or as diegetic, a question treated at length by
Gérard Genette.[15] The narration of *A Portrait* supports Genette's conclusion that all narrative is essentially diegetic and that pure mimesis is not
possible. The speaking voice of the discourse is always evident. Narration is
never simply a purely transparent vehicle for narrative. The language of
narration is opaque. We see *it* as well as the story communicated, just as
Stephen sees the phrase Cranly speaks. Stephen understands the semantic
meaning of Cranly's words and the implication of Cranly's style. And the
reader understands the implications of the narration, including the recurring
reports of Stephen's thoughts.

Through an energetic echo that gives back Stephen's eloquence, the narrator fuses inextricably with character. There is no means for disentangling Stephen's attitudes from the voice of the narrator who speaks them. The two voices are linked by the author's act of writing, a mediating process we become aware of through the style of narration but can never experience directly. We know the product and its implications but not the process itself. Instead, we experience the analogous mediating process of the act of reading, which aligns *our* activities of mind with those of character and teller. As Wayne Booth has said, "any sustained inside view, of whatever depth, temporarily turns the character whose mind is shown into a narrator."[16] The narrator's reiterated shifts between internal and external views make *A Portrait* a work about the transforming of a character into an artist in which style regularly turns the character into a teller. When the style includes narrated monologue, the reader shares the role of teller with the character by speaking the character's mind.

The final style adopted by the narrator, one especially pertinent to the present inquiry, is that of the journal, from which the entries of 20 March through 27 April are apparently only an excerpt. In the narrative's fictive chronology, as distinct from the chronology of narration, the journal is the last example of Stephen's styles as well. The potential ambiguity of the word "last" is the crux of the difference between the narrative and the narration. The style of the journal displaces the villanelle, the aesthetic theory, and the other examples of Stephen's expression—written, spoken, and internal—that are either directly presented or alluded to earlier. In its turn, the styles of the entire book displace that of the journal. The dual, interlocking process of feedback points to the problem of the ending and the end toward which the narrative tends. Two styles, the teller's and the character's, not just one, are brought to conclusion, or at least partial closure, in the one document that can be read as two documents. The journal kept by a character is also a portion of a narrative reported by the teller.

There is an acute disequilibrium between process and product, between Stephen's activity of keeping a journal and the portion excised by the narrator through an act of quotation that resembles the reporting of dialogue. The reader of *Ulysses* faces an analogous situation, for the language of "Penelope" presents two discourses simultaneously: the character's internal one, which is a process of mind, and the narrator's more public one, which is a style of language. The shifting focus becomes particularly evident for the reader of *A Portrait* who attempts to reconcile the journal in its fictional and textual contexts (of story and of narration) with the title and the epigraph of the title page and with the dates and places noted on the final page. All these parts of the book are relatively independent of what falls between them. Their implications do not appear at first to be wholly integrated with the remainder of the book as coherent aspects of style and story. This apparent failure of integration provides grounds for interpreting *A*

Portrait as preposterous in that word's etymological sense.

Before and after, pre- and post-, are made to exchange places and to interact reciprocally. The exchange and interaction are manifest in the ending, from the perspective of which the reader revises the provisional interpretations generated up to that state of the reading.[17] At the end of any narrative the reader engaged in an interpretive process experiences the preposterous aspect of reading. The reader's new perspective for scrutinizing the text's details allows a look backward that sees the text in retrospective arrangement. That arrangement modifies and displaces provisional readings, which are now seen anew in revision. The reading process flows temporally from the present to the past as the reader experiences portions of the text becoming parts of new contexts that are the bases for reinterpretations. Prospective and retrospective, provisional and revisionary judgments merge as the reader encounters and assimilates the conceptual implications of the narrative's form. The reader's experience of retrospective rearrangements shifting places through time duplicates the character's experience when he becomes the teller of his own tale in retrospect.

The closing of both book and journal with the notation of dates and places, "Dublin 1904/Trieste 1914," presents in small the problematic, preposterous quality of the entire work. The reader must decide whether the references are part of the story or part of the writing, whether they are appropriate to the product or to the process of creation. Like the title, they refer at once to both product and process, to both character and author as artists. The autobiographical bases of the dates and places are well known. They point to the time and locations at which the author initiates and completes the writing of the book. Joyce finished *A Portrait* in Trieste just over ten years after leaving Dublin. Serial publication began in 1914.[18] The authorial, autobiographical significance in no way diminishes the relevance the references possess for Stephen Dedalus's story. There is a complicated, uncanny doubling lurking within and behind the apparently innocent closing that is a *post scriptum*. This doubling that occurs through the telling of the story is more radical than most interpretations have allowed. Its precedent in Joyce's earlier fiction is found in "A Painful Case." In that story the central character, James Duffy, "had an odd autobiographical habit which led him to compose in his mind from time to time a short sentence about himself containing a subject in the third person and a predicate in the past tense" (*D* 108).

The strange duplication becomes apparent once dates and times are both understood as referring to Joyce's process of writing *and* to the story of Stephen Dedalus as it appears to develop beyond the time of the excerpt printed from the journal. Although no exact dates are ever provided for Stephen's activities earlier in the narrative, Dublin is obviously the place appropriate to the journal and to much of the action, and 1904 is within the limits of probability suggested in the fiction. Nineteen fourteen would be the year and Trieste the place in which Stephen completes the transforming of the journal into a book that is the simulacrum of Joyce's. The last portion of *A Portrait* presents what comes first with respect to the remainder of the text. In Stephen Dedalus's fictional life, which includes his life as a writer of fiction, the keeping of the journal precedes the completing of the book. The last—that is, the most recent—stage of Stephen's development as an artist is presented through the narration, not in the narrative. The dates and places that stand both inside and outside the story are the signatures of author and character as writers, their superimposed self-portraits painted in the corner of the finished canvas. They are the equivalent of the closing that Stanislaus Joyce reports his brother intended to append to *Stephen Hero*, "the signature, *Stephanus Daedalus Pinxit.*"[19]

In Ovid's *Metamorphoses* the line quoted as epigraph to *A Portrait* refers to the mythic artist Daedalus, the "old father, old artificer" (*P* 253) mentioned at the end of Stephen's journal. Ovid presents Daedalus setting his mind to work upon unknown arts. As with the notations at the book's end, the question of the epigraph's meaning concerns its referent. Like the journal, the epigraph is presented as a fragment quoted out of its original context. For the epigraph, but not for the journal, the original context is available to be examined. There is no evidence that the fragmentary journal actually has an origin in the same way as the epigraph does. In the *Metamorphoses* the epigraph's context indicates Daedalus's longing for home:

> Homesick for homeland, Daedalus hated Crete
> And his long exile there, but the sea held him.
> . . . He turned his thinking
> Toward unknown arts, changing the laws of nature.[20]

In the case of Ovid's Daedalus, the act of turning the mind to work on obscure arts has an explicit cause and an explicit effect. Daedalus fashions wings for himself and for Icarus in order to escape from a prison and return home. Daedalus's work violates the laws of nature through the accomplishment of a feat seemingly beyond human possibility. The result also includes the death of Icarus, an apparently unavoidable concomitant of the mature artist's act of making in order to escape.

At the beginning of *A Portrait* as well as at its end, Joyce challenges the laws of conventional narrative by turning his own mind to intricate arts that result in a death and a doubling through the creation of a ghostly presence for the artist in a voice that repeats itself. Like the designations of place and time, the epigraph refers to the Dedalian character as well as to the Daedalian author. When the character's role as son is over after the final page, his fatherly role as teller is born phoenixlike to return home on the first page. Character transforms himself into artist as the son becomes his own father. Essential to the transformation is the importance of home in both Ovid's work and Joyce's. The act of producing the portrait combines the longing for home with the homecoming itself. *A Portrait* is the *nostos* whose end is continuous with its beginning, a beginning to which it returns the reader and the character in a way that anticipates the recirculating structure of *Finnegans Wake*.

As in *Ulysses* and *Finnegans Wake*, in *A Portrait* Joyce presents both fathers and sons in analogous relationships to mythic figures: HCE with Shem and Shaun, Ulysses with Telemachus, Daedalus with Icarus. The doubling in all these texts is accompanied by the unity of parent with child. Both roles are associated with a single character and with the special figure who tells the tale. According to one of the washerwomen in the ALP section of *Finnegans Wake*, "every telling has a taling and that's the he and the she of it" (*FW* 213.12). In the production of literary texts, the artist achieves a state comparable to androgyny, in which a procreative act occurs that results in the literary progeny. The washerwoman's later statement, "We'll meet again, we'll part once more" (*FW* 215.5), indicates the nature of the process and product of creation. Author and text are one in a unity in separation like that of parent and child or of husband and wife. This strange but familiar unity is reflected in the relationships of teller to character, teller to tale, and teller to reader in all Joyce's longer fiction. Such a unity finds an appropriate stylistic expression in the narrated monologue.

In *A Portrait* the mutually self-engendering relationships of teller to character come close to being explicitly presented. The author's persona as narrator tells the story of a young man developing into a writer. The journal Stephen Dedalus produces is part of the workshop from which issues the story of a young man developing into a writer, and so on. The nature of the journal in *A Portrait*, along with the elliptical letter in the *Wake*, suggests that the Möbius strip provides the nearest structural analogue for the relation of narrative to narration in Joyce's fiction after *Dubliners*. Because some of the large movements of Joyce's narratives are finite but unbounded, they are capable of a precise definition that is a description of the perpetual circulation called "continuarration" (*FW* 205.14) in *Finnegans Wake*. The recirculation can be described through Möbean geometry because father and son, teller and tale, teller and character are one. For Ovid, Daedalus and Icarus are separate. For Joyce they are not. Stephen as character and as narrator is both the immature and the mature artist, both Icarus and Daedalus. Because of the narrative's peculiar form, Stephen's destiny, like the fate of the mythic figures behind and within Joyce's fiction, is to be read as dual. According to Tiresias, Odysseus will return home but also continue wandering. In *Ulysses* Odysseus's double destiny is split between Stephen Dedalus and Leopold Bloom at the narrative's end when the former decides to wander and the latter chooses to remain at home. The two fates are combined for the narrator of *Ulysses*, whose stylistic divagations bring him home and redefine home.

In *A Portrait,* because Stephen exhibits the antithetical traits of Daedalus and Icarus in his two manifestations, the Daedalian narrator can present the young protagonist in the guise of an Icarus transforming himself into a Daedalus. Both Odysseus and Daedalus are homesick and homeward bound in their myths. At the end of *A Portrait* Stephen is outward bound, having determined to serve no longer. Stephen's decision to leave is necessarily connected for the reader to his act of keeping a journal, for the presentation of the journal signals Stephen's departure. But the keeping of the journal, which indicates the decision to write as well as to leave, is glossed by the epigraph. In order to write Stephen turns his mind to obscure arts, arts that lead him far from home, as Daedalus is lead far from home, but these arts inevitably bring him back to a home, not literally but literarily. The subject of the journal that ostensibly announces departure from home, like the subject of the book containing the journal, is home, as well as the displacements of wandering. For Joyce, to turn the mind toward intricate arts is to look homeward. In the act of refusing to serve the home, the artist makes it possible for the home to serve him as the primary material for his art. Daedalus and Icarus, Sicily and Crete, Trieste and Dublin, 1914 and 1904, Stephen as teller and Stephen as character all merge in the book's oscillating focus. In *A Portrait* and later, the homeward look, no matter how intricately expressed in and as wanderings of style, involves a merging of citizen and artist that occurs in the encounters of reader and teller and of reader and character. In Joyce's fiction the two encounters are not necessarily distinct.

The language of the one book casts two shadows, projects two images related by superimposition as in a palimpsest. The character who tells his own tale never writes on a tabula rasa. He always and inevitably displaces the past by erasing it and writing over the erasure, even when the writing constitutes a recapturing of the past as well as a displacing of it. Like *Tristram Shandy* and every other teller, Stephen Dedalus as writer can never capture himself or his own process of writing. He can only suggest the nature of the activity of writing as self-portrayal, as self-representation. The pretext for the narration given in the title, to portray a young, developing artist, precedes the reader's experience of the story. But the prior text for the character, the writing that precedes the text temporally in the character's experience, is the journal that is part of the book as well as prior to it. That journal allows the reader to redefine the narrative in a new frame of reference. By experiencing the earlier text as both behind the later one and within it, the reader can see through, as well as by means of, the story's pretense.

PRELUDES

After Stephen has been offered the chance to be a priest in IV.2, his voice becomes increasingly prominent. The verbal evidence for Stephen's developing vocation includes his internal reaction to the offer, his articulation of an alternative, the aesthetic theory, the villanelle, and the journal. He begins to fulfill the necessary conditions for becoming a writer interested less in serving any institution than in preserving his freedom of thought. Stephen's preservation is grounded in his actions prior to his acts of writing that occur within the narrative and after its closing. The last two parts present some of Stephen's aesthetic attitudes and abilities in contrast with the inimical environment in which he strives to develop them. The details of the contrast illuminate the narrative's paradox, especially through the various references to tales, preludes, prophecies, precursors, and the workings of aesthetic response and creation.

As at the narrative's beginning, in his interview with the director, Stephen is the listener to a tale told by a father, though this father is of a different order from Stephen's biological one: "The grave and cordial voice went on easily with its tale, and in the pauses Stephen felt bound to set it on again with respectful questions. He knew that the tale was a prelude and his mind waited for the sequel" (*P* 154). The terms *tale, prelude*, and *sequel* suggest the relationships that the work transforms in its large structure. All of the documents and tales within the tale, including the story of baby tuckoo, the director's tale, and Stephen's journal, are preludes to which the narration of *A Portrait* is the sequel. In this section, the director's story contrasts sharply with its context. The goal of the priest's tale is to "assign to [Stephen] . . . [a] clear and final . . . office" (*P* 158), to locate Stephen in a definitive way, "to end for ever, in time and in eternity, his freedom" (*P* 161-62) through Stephen's "definite and irrevocable act" (*P* 161). The goal of the larger story is to locate Stephen through dislocations, to assign him a role that is protean rather than static, dynamic and alive rather than official and dead, a role in a prelude that is at one with the sequel it anticipates.

Stephen's decision to reject the priesthood transforms the director's sequel by reversal into the static entity that the director would have Stephen become: "He knew now that the exhortation he had listened to had already fallen into an idle formal tale" (*P* 162). The use of the past participle "fallen" indicates Stephen's relegation of the tale to a past severed from his present and his future. In the midst of his interview with the director, Stephen feels as though the church is becoming past, "as though he were slowly passing out of an accustomed world and were hearing its language for the last time" (*P* 156). From the perspective of the book at large, even this feeling is too categorical, for the effect of the narration is to show the relevance of the passing out not to what is past but to what is in the process of becoming. The language of Stephen's decision, especially the use of the present and past participles in a future context, captures the temporal paradox of Stephen's life and Stephen's book: "He would fall. He had not yet fallen but he would fall silently, in an instant. Not to fall was too hard, too hard: and he felt the silent lapse of his soul, as it would be at some instant to come, falling, falling but not yet fallen, still unfallen but about to fall" (*P* 162). In V.3 we find an explicit reference to a similar complexity of temporal relations when Dixon uses the phrase *"paulo post futurum"* (*P* 230), indicating the relation of the present to what will follow in the future. In its suggestion of something resulting from a future act, the phrase is the herald of the book itself as sequel to the prelude that it contains. The scenes in IV.3 following Stephen's rejection of the priesthood present Stephen's perception of "an elfin prelude" (*P* 165). The sequel to that prelude, including the narration of *A Portrait*, is Stephen's attempt to grasp "the end he had been born to serve yet did not see [that] had led him to escape by an unseen path" (*P* 165). The book becomes the translation into narrative of Stephen's climactic vision at the end of part IV, a vision of a world in process "spread in endless succession to itself" (*P* 172). During his experience on the beach, Stephen realizes, "as never before, his strange name . . . [to be] a prophecy" (*P* 168) spoken in a prediction.

Stephen's intense experience on the beach is predictive but also merely provisional. At the end of part IV Stephen sleeps only to wake to a world less satisfying than the "glimmering and trembling, trembling and unfolding" (*P* 172) one of his vision. Part V brings him to the verge of the experience he will have after the events recorded in the narrative, the evidence for which is the linguistic trace those events and that experience leave as the narration. Stephen's final encounters and statements as prolepses indicate the nature of the narration. The remarks Stephen makes at the beginning and end of the brief discourse on aesthetics addressed to Lynch express his dual role. Toward the beginning of his ruminations, Stephen asserts that "Aristotle's entire system of philosophy rests upon his book of psychology and that . . . rests on his statement that the same attribute cannot at the same time and in the same connection belong to and not belong to the same subject" (*P* 208). His closing remark is the famous description of the artist, who, "like the God of the creation, remains within or behind or beyond or above his handiwork, invisible, refined out of existence, indifferent, paring his fingernails" (*P* 215). This description, of course, derives from Flaubert, as does the narrated monologue, which provides a technique of narration that makes possible the translation of this attitude toward the artist into the form of the telling.[21] If Aristotle's principle of non-contradiction is valid, the artist cannot be both within and not within his handiwork. He cannot be within "at the same time and in the same connection" as he is "behind or beyond or above" it. A double temporal perspective makes possible Stephen's dual status as within and behind, as character and as narrator, in *A Portrait*. By the end of the narrative Stephen is becoming both the augur and, as "hawklike man" (*P* 225), the augur's birds, both predictor and portent. No longer part of a story his fathers tell, he becomes his own foretelling. His augury is that he will, like the birds, be "ever going and coming, building ever an unlasting home . . . and ever leaving the homes . . . to wander" (*P* 225).

The duality implicit in the book's form is repeated in a minor key in various passages toward the end. Besides Dixon's reference to "a *paulo post futurum*," there is Stephen's play on the ambiguity of temporal terms that also have spatial connotations in his repartee with Cranly after his declaration not to serve: "—I will not serve, answered Stephen. —That remark was made before, Cranly said calmly. —It is made behind now, said Stephen hotly" (*P* 239). In this same conversation Stephen asserts the protean nature of his own identity changing through time, which is one of his concerns in the "Proteus" and the "Scylla and Charybdis" episodes of *Ulysses*. Speaking of his past, he says, "I was someone else then. . . . I was not myself as I am now, as I had to become" (*P* 240). A conception of identity as allotropic makes possible the narration's form here and in Joyce's later works. It underlies the doubling of self that enables an older Stephen to assume the posture of partial detachment necessary to write anonymously in the third person about his past. Some of the entries in the journal suggest in a jocoserious way both Stephen's situation in the story and the text's paradoxical nature. When Stephen casts Cranly as John the Baptist because of Cranly's role as precursor, Stephen is in the process of writing the journal that makes him his own precursor. Stephen reveals the enjoyment of conundrums that he shares with Cranly when he records Cranly's story about the crocodile: "A mother let her child fall into the Nile. . . . A crocodile seized the child. Mother asked it back. Crocodile said all right if she told him what he was going to do with the child, eat it or not eat it" (*P* 250). As if to illustrate the shared propensity, Stephen reports his own remark made to Davin that he is leaving Ireland because "the shortest way to Tara was via Holyhead" (*P* 250). To find Ireland, he must leave Ireland. Stephen's desire, gushingly stated, "to press in my arms the loveliness which has not yet come into the world" (*P* 251), recalls his search in part II for someone elusive. In his continuing wanderings he will tell a story that "has not yet come into the world" at the time he writes his journal, a story contained in the future book the reader holds.

BETWEEN THE ACTS

In *A Portrait* Joyce goes the Flaubert of *Bouvard et Pécuchet* one better. At the end of the first volume of Flaubert's unfinished novel, the two central characters are to resume their original roles as scribes. They will apparently transcribe a version of Flaubert's "Dictionary of Received Ideas," a compilation of the kind of nonsense that informs their story throughout the novel's first part. But the text they intend to compile will not be identical with the one the reader has already read. Flaubert's work concludes with writing but not with its own beginning. Stephen's work as a writer is unfinished at the end of *A Portrait* in a different sense than Flaubert's. Stephen finishes in his telling what is yet to be done at the end of the narrative. When Joyce has Stephen take up his pen at the end of *A Portrait*, he suspends the narrative between two acts of journal writing that are both the work's beginning and its end. The one act is Stephen's writing in his journal as a character in the narrative. The second act is his representing the journal in his role as narrator. The constant displacement of Stephen through time from the role of character to that of teller locates him as the primary element of the narration as well as the focus of the narrative. In the past of the story, the present of the telling, and, by implication, the recent past of the writing, Stephen Dedalus is the central figure. His centrality is a multiple one, like the multiple location of Christ during the simultaneous celebrations of the Mass that Stephen thinks of in the "Proteus" episode of *Ulysses*. Because telling and tale, process and product, are both suggested to the reader at once, there are always two Stephens to be experienced and judged. A fathering occurs during the period of gestation indicated by the dates 1904/1914; Stephen fathers himself in language. The last stroke of the pen finishes the portrait, completes the process of creation by cutting the umbilical cord. That last stroke resembles its precursors in the narrative in a sequence stretching back to the first paragraph. The narrative begins, as it ends, with references to precursors: prior texts, previous tellers, fathers, and other forebears.

The first paragraph of *A Portrait* is just as preposterous in its temporal placement in the narrative as is the journal that follows it in the reading of the text but that it follows in the writing. While the journal as an origin is the book's beginning, the first paragraph, another kind of prior text, indicates its teleology. The book achieves its end and what follows its ending almost before it begins for the reader, though the full implications of this beginning as end are not evident at the start. The initial paragraph is the first prior fiction presented in the narrative and the first story that Stephen remembers hearing as a child: "Once upon a time and a very good time it was there was a moocow coming down along the road and this moocow that was coming down along the road met a nicens little boy named baby tuckoo" (*P* 7). This fragmentary beginning of a tale-within-the-tale at the inception of the narrative is spoken, like the journal, by two tellers. The one teller is Stephen's "father [who] told him that story . . .[,] looked at him through a glass . . . [, and] had a hairy face." Stephen is both inside and outside the father's story, just as he is one with his parent and separate from him in the consubstantial mystery of the family. He is at once his father's listener and part of his father's tale. The tale is told to him, but in the third paragraph, the reader learns that "he was baby tuckoo." Stephen's naive, childlike reaction to his father's tale illustrates comically an extreme version of Stephen's aesthetic theory, for the listener experiences in a lyric mode and in immediate relation to himself the image placed between his mind and the teller's mind.

The other teller is Stephen's aesthetic father, the writer as Daedalus, the image of the author in the language constituting the story as a tale in the midst of being told. Here we find the essential large implication for the telling in both *A Portrait* and *Ulysses*: the teller enacts implicitly through the narration's devices and its structure a mythic identity that links him to his central characters and to their mythic precursors. In *Ulysses* as well, the narrator achieves heroic stature through style as the mythic, aesthetic father of Stephen in the role of Telemachus, the writer's fictional creation as mythic progeny and as progeny of myth. In *A Portrait*, the repetition of Stephen's father's words by the teller is part of a new tale building on the old one but containing and transforming it. The words are the same but meaning and audience are different. As listener, the reader becomes the double for Stephen, just as the narrator is the double for Stephen's father in the role of teller. While listening to the same story as Stephen, the reader, like the teller, also observes Stephen as listener.[22] The narrator tells the same story as Stephen's father, but only initially and only as part of the larger story that includes the father's act of telling. If the older Stephen narrates, he is both his father's listener and the teller of his father's tale. While as child Stephen becomes part of his own father's story, as adult he becomes the teller of a tale in which his father plays a part. To become this kind of teller is the teleology of Stephen's development as portrayed later in the narrative. Stephen as teller fathers himself aesthetically by fathering his own father, by producing an image of himself in language in which he inscribes the image of his own progenitor.[23] At the end of his beginning as a writer at the close of the journal and the book, Stephen asks his mythic "old father, old artificer" to stand him "now and ever in good stead." At the beginning of achieving his end as a writer at the opening of the book in which he presents himself first as a listener, through artifice Stephen stands in the stead of his old father.

Although the narrative begins with the story told by Stephen's father, that story is not primordial in any absolute sense. Nor are Stephen's journal and Ovid's *Metamorphoses*. All of these are origins. No single tale or writing is *the* origin, just as the book is not *the* portrait but *a* portrait. The home that Stephen longs for as a child is no more easily located than the origin of the text. In part I, Stephen desires a home that is imaginary, one that has never existed for him in the past and does not exist in the present of his desire but that he hopes will come to be in the future. The home, or, more precisely, *a* home, does exist as a fictional text in a future relative to the past of

Stephen's development. That development results in the construction of an aesthetic domicile, the permanent residence of the artist in his persona as teller. The end of homesickness, its cessation and its outcome, is the production of an image of leaving home that becomes itself the future habitation of the artist's image, for which he has searched in the past and which he has searched the past for. As we have seen, Joyce develops the metaphor of the book as the writer's dwelling more explicitly in *Finnegans Wake* in the description of Shem the Penman's "inkbattle house" (*FW* 176.31) filled with "chambermade music" (*FW* 184.4). In *Ulysses*, the beginning and ending of the book are the teller's stylistic home ports.

Stephen carries on his search throughout the portion of his life presented in the narrative, but at certain points the elusive quality of the quest and the aesthetic activity to which it tends become manifest. Soon after the family moves from Blackrock to Dublin near the opening of II.1, Stephen begins not only to wander, as he has before, but to note with acuity his surroundings and his situation, as he will again:

> He passed unchallenged among the docks and along the quays. . . . The vastness and strangeness of his life . . . wakened again in him the unrest which had sent him wandering in the evening from garden to garden in search of Mercedes. And amid this new bustling life he might have fancied himself in another Marseilles but that he missed the bright sky and the sunwarmed trellisses of the wineshops. A vague dissatisfaction grew up within him as he looked on the quays and on the river and on the lowering skies and yet he continued to wander up and down day after day as if he really sought someone that eluded him. (*P* 66)

Stephen's reading of *The Count of Monte Cristo*, the book that informs his thoughts in this passage, leads to his frustrated attempt to reconcile art with experience. His failure to do so contributes to the process of maturing that will lead eventually to his transforming of experience into art. The reader's own encounter with a text, this one, is related to Stephen's. The critical controversy over aesthetic distance indicates that readers of *A Portrait* also search for someone who eludes them, the real Stephen Dedalus, artist or esthete. Just as Stephen is unable to find that someone in the external world, the reader does not find Stephen in the narrative. Reader and character can locate the elusive presence only in the narration through the analogous activities of reading and writing. Stephen seeks an identity available to him only in the act of writing a book about his search that is itself the provisional end of that search.

The paragraph immediately following the description of Stephen's wanderings and his search suggests that Stephen's character is developing toward a stance compatible with that of the narrator. Stephen responds to Dublin as he and his mother visit relatives at Christmas. As so often in *A Portrait*, the narration modulates from the presentation of an external scene to the rendering of Stephen's thoughts, all in the anonymous third-person style of much of the telling, the journal aside. The colon in mid-sentence indicates the entry into Stephen's mind that follows. In the passage we can distinguish two components of Stephen's response that correspond to the narration's two dominant aspects:

> He went once or twice with his mother to visit their relatives: and, though they passed a jovial array of shops lit up and adorned for Christmas, his mood of embittered silence did not leave him. . . . He was angry with himself for being young and the prey of restless foolish impulses, angry also with the change of fortune which was reshaping the world about him into a vision of squalor and insincerity. Yet his anger lent nothing to the vision. He chronicled with patience what he saw, detaching himself from it and testing its mortifying flavour in secret. (*P* 67)

Stephen's internal reaction includes both strong emotion and chronicle, the correlatives for the reports of thought and those of scene typical in the narration early in the book. The verb "chronicle" introduces the act of writing even though no writing is presented yet. Stephen's visions, his reshapings of "the world about him," are cast as vignettes, the precursors of stories. The narrator provides three brief sketches, presumably renderings of Stephen's chronicles, in the next few pages. They are indicated as Stephen's internal chronicles only by the repeated use of introductory sentences beginning "He was sitting." The focus of each succeeding vignette becomes increasingly psychological until the narrator transforms the final one into his own recurring idiom of narration. This last and longest vignette begins with the children's party at Harold's Cross and ends with Stephen's attempt the next day to write a poem about his experience on the tram with Emma after the party. The description of this poem, which is not quoted, presents it as antithetical to Stephen's interior chronicling. The poem is all vague emotion with no precise delineation of scene and situation: "There remained no trace of the tram itself nor of the trammen nor of the horses: nor did he and she appear vividly. . . . Some undefined sorrow was hidden in the hearts of the protagonists as they stood in silence" (*P* 70–71). The elements Stephen separates in the interior chronicles and in the poem coalesce in the narration.

While the young Stephen's manner, especially his inability to coordinate internal reaction with external scene, contrasts with the narrator's amalgamation of them in techniques such as narrated monologue, it also anticipates the combination Stephen will eventually achieve. Despite the differences, there are indications both here and later that Stephen has the potential to develop into an artist capable of narrating in the way the teller narrates his story. The vignettes, which are similar to passages from *Dubliners* in their intense focus on the realistic details of a fictional world, indicate that the young boy possesses the powers of observation necessary to write fiction with the precise attention to nuances of scene and language exhibited in this book and in *Dubliners*. He is becoming more like the narrator, "seemingly a tranquil watcher of the scene before him" (*P* 69). The difference, though, is still a large one, for the narrator in both *Dubliners* and *A Portrait* "watches" scenes that include psyche. The vignettes anticipate most directly not *Dubliners* but "*A Pisgah Sight of Palestine or the Parable of the Plums*," the story Stephen tells in the "Aeolus" episode of *Ulysses*. There, as well as in *A Portrait*, Stephen as character is still more detached from his chronicles than even the teller of *Dubliners*. He has yet to achieve the literary forms for which his poem and journal provide a distant sight.

In the second part of *A Portrait*, both Stephen's emotional reactions and his chronicles are private and largely unwritten. Later he begins to express himself, at times eloquently, in public and in writing. Especially during his time at University College, Stephen is willing to reveal some of his anger and grievance to others, to express his ideas in a systematic way, and to write a chronicle different in kind from the detached vignettes, one that combines an emotional response with representation of scene, action, and speech. The journal as chronicle is the section in which the earlier contrast between young Stephen and the narrator becomes attenuated as it takes a new shape. Now Stephen rather than the narrator acts as reporter, not from an anonymous third-person perspective but from a personal, involved position that combines first with third person. The journal is the arena in which both Stephen and the teller can move away from their habitual stances. For Stephen the act of repositioning is his preamble for adopting a partially detached persona as a voice for telling his story. For the narrator, the journal is the abandoning of his persona of partial detachment. It is both the teller's unmasking and the author's total masking at the text's margin. The mimetic and diegetic elements merge as the narrator presents the surprising capstone of his artifice. Like the scenes the narrator has presented with seeming objectivity, the journal is presented as fact, as a document within the world of the story narrated anonymously by the teller. Here the teller appears to achieve an absolute mimesis when he withdraws wholly behind his persona, the apparently transparent medium for presenting the story.

But the mimesis is still implicitly and explicitly diegetical; the narrator has not disappeared entirely. He is still present at the least in the act of selection implied by the presenting of only an excerpt from the diary.* More importantly, the diegetic function of narrating has been largely transferred to the character, who now speaks with apparent autonomy. The resem-

---

*Of course, I assume here that we are to think of the journal as excerpted, not as the whole of Stephen's diary. Other assumptions are possible.

blance to "Penelope" is evident. The transference of the teller's role to the character in both works manifests what is the case in many instances of narrated monologue as Joyce employs it. At the ends of his longer narratives, Joyce vividly renders the paradox of telling as an ambiguous relationship between mind and language, between process and product of writing. The ambiguity is rendered repeatedly by the narrated monologue. The ends of the two books reveal in special ways the nature of the literary text as a mimesis of a speaker's mind that can be the presentation of two minds at once. Because the mimesis is always mediated, it can never be transparent. It cannot provide for the reader a direct experience of the teller's mind, whether we think of a separate narrator or the character as teller. The ineluctable mediation occurs through the language, which places every representation of mind—that is, every text—at some distinct remove from the processes of consciousness themselves.

In *A Portrait* the passages concerning Stephen's villanelle suggest clearly the different yet inextricably conjoined natures of writing as process and writing as text. The journal points to this same conundrum in a less fully elaborated way that effects the narrative's closure. That closure is possible because the journal, unlike passages of narrated monologue, has a determinate source within the narrative. By enacting the interpenetration of character's and teller's roles, the journal exposes the implication of the narrated monologue: the narrator's presentation of the character's turning thought into language is the displaced equivalent for his own storytelling. As report of the character's thought, the journal seems as direct as the narrator's other such reports, but Stephen is himself now the mediator turning mental process into style of language. If the narrator is an older Stephen, the journal is not withdrawal behind a wholly anonymous persona. Instead, it is the emergence of the teller from behind his mask of detachment into the more fully personalized narrating voice that has been withheld. The journal achieves simultaneously the teller's beginning and his goal in the presentation of the book's two central voices as indistinguishable from each other.

THE VILLANELLE AND THE SOURCE OF WRITING

The combining of sexuality with aesthetic creation in Stephen's statement of his desire in the journal forms part of the recurring emphasis in Joyce's fiction on the connection between lovemaking and writing. Joyce has already adumbrated the connection in "The Dead" when Gabriel Conroy associates the touch of his wife's hand with the love letters he exchanged with her. He caresses each as if it were the other. Through metonymy and sentiment the letter written in the sender's hand is identified with the hand that stands for the writer. Writing and reading in Joyce's works become strongly associated with touching. Toward the beginning of part V of *A Portrait*, Stephen meditates, albeit sentimentally, on the living warmth of his well-used copy of Horace: "The pages of his timeworn Horace never felt cold to the touch even when his own fingers were cold: they were human pages: and fifty years before they had been turned by . . . [other] human fingers" (*P* 179). While he is writing his villanelle of the temptress, Stephen calls up in memory "the image of the young priest" who is his rival for the affections of Emma. He remembers the moment when she looks at the priest "out of dove's eyes," while either the priest or Emma (the syntax obscures which one) is fondling a book, "toying with the pages of her Irish phrasebook" (*P* 220). In the very short II.5, the narrator has already juxtaposed Stephen's writing a prize-winning essay with his discovery of nighttown.

The desire Stephen mentions in his journal, at once sexual and textual, anticipates some of his comments about aesthetic creation in the "Scylla and Charybdis" episode of *Ulysses*. In the conclusion to his dialogue on Shakespeare, Stephen characterizes God as an artist, specifically as a playwright. He wishes to portray the curious status of the artist in general, based on his previous comments about that human playwright William Shakespeare. For Stephen, the artist attains, like the God of creation, an idealized manifestation as "glorified man, an androgynous angel, being a wife unto himself" (*U* 213). It appears that the artist can make the beast with two backs alone by a process of aesthetic creation that is androgynous and self-espousing. The book, the child of the artist's self-marrying activity, is literally the beast with two backs. In his exploration of the possibilities for language in fiction, Joyce discovered that the process of aesthetic creation can be represented through styles and merged with story by means of a sexual metaphor. Lovemaking and poesis become figures for one another. As in the title of Robert Frost's famous essay "The Figure a Poem Makes," figure can suggest both language as figuration and the shape of the sensual body. Aspects of life and aspects of art stand for and imply one another. And the style of writing, linguistic product of the artist's androgynous poesis, can be an image of the process of creation. Joyce actualizes for the reader the reciprocal relationship between text and creative process when Stephen Dedalus writes his poem in the last part of *A Portrait*. By having Stephen write this poem, Joyce gives us a vivid and sustained linking of sexuality with aesthetic processes. Through this linkage, Stephen achieves partial satisfaction of his desire to possess an uncreated loveliness, a satisfaction that anticipates the concluding monologue of *Ulysses*.

Stephen's act of writing in V.2 indicates an important change in his attitude toward himself and his world. Joyce points to the nature of that change by framing this self-contained segment of the narrative (*P* 217-24) between two scenes in which Stephen stands on the steps outside the library. In the earlier scene, Stephen thinks about Emma as if she were a bird. Her life may be "simple and strange as a bird's life" (*P* 216). In the later scene, "leaning wearily on his ashplant" (*P* 224), Stephen looks at the birds that are now the augury of his own future, which will consist of migrations and the interminable building and abandoning of nests. His meditation on the birds in this later scene is a response to the weariness he has expressed while writing the poem and expressed in the poem itself. Through the act of writing and its aftermath, he begins to identify with the birds and with Daedalus, "the hawklike man whose name he bore soaring out of his captivity on osierwovenwings" (*P* 225). The creation of the poem marks the union within Stephen's mind of the hawklike man and the girl Stephen saw on the beach as "the likeness of a strange and beautiful seabird" (*P* 171). The goal, as well as the indication, of the union is the production of song, lyric poetry. During the brief respite Stephen takes in the middle of his composing, he recalls his own earlier singing for Emma at her house (*P* 219). Through writing as singing the artist begins to become the artificer he always wanted to be by merging with his own Muse as interior paramour. As a central character who writes, and in writing sings, Stephen is the precursor for Molly Bloom, the character as singer whose interior performance eventually becomes the narration in *Ulysses*, and for Anna Livia Plurabelle, the "gnarlybird"[24] (*FW* 10.32, 10.34) as bard, bawd, and bride in *Finnegans Wake*, who writes a letter that is the text itself.

My concern is less with the product of Stephen's writing than with the process by which he writes and the means the narrator uses to present the act of writing. This portion of the book calls attention to itself with particular force because it provides us with a finished text written by the character, something we are given nowhere else in *A Portrait* and only rarely in other narratives. Even in *Ulysses* we find nothing quite like the villanelle. Most surprising is the narrator's attempt to present the process by which Stephen writes the poem. Here is the extreme application of the narrated monologue and related techniques in fiction: to reveal the process of mind that is aesthetic creation itself in the ambiguous relationship between the speaker's act of mind and what he speaks. Because that revelation must always be indirect, Joyce's single extended attempt to present it in *A Portrait* takes extremely odd turns, some of which suggest that the section on the villanelle presents in little a version of the relationship of the teller to his tale.

The attempt to present the producing of a literary text within a literary text is a highly unusual procedure that here directs attention to the dual status of writing as simultaneously product and process. The section presenting the villanelle is Joyce's astonishing and successful attempt to make thought, speech, writing, aesthetic response, and sexual fulfillment all appear to commingle in the language and the processes of a single text. That text is the book, not just the poem. The reader's judgment about the poem's value is less important than the role it plays as indicator for the fusion of writing as act with the text that is written and with the response to that text, both ours and the character's. The important value is not in the poem as something signified, as part of the narrative, but in the poem's place as signifier, as part of the style of narration. We encounter Stephen Dedalus waking early in the morning after a night of dreams, inspired to write. As Stephen composes his poem stanza by stanza, the emerging parts are presented to us in sequence until finally the entire poem is printed at the end of the section. In the hiatus in the middle of this writing Stephen remembers some of his past encounters with the woman for whom he writes. The narration that presents the stanzas can be read in two ways. It gives us the process Stephen follows in the act of composing, and it provides an elliptical explication of the poem's obscurities.[25] As it gives us the text, the narration suggests both a process of mind that is aesthetic creation and an interpretation that is an aesthetic response. The two become inextricably conjoined in the narrator's report and mimicry of the character's interior language as both writing and reading.

That conjunction occurs for the reader as well as in the narrative. It occurs for us, for the character, and for the narrator because of the style. The teller uses narrated monologue together with the techniques with which it overlaps to render Stephen's thoughts throughout the section. At times these thoughts are evoked in a nearly unmediated fashion as quoted monologue. At other times, the narrator's mediation is particularly evident in the report of thought as a psycho-narration.[26] But generally we have the two voices superimposed as in narrated monologue. We understand the narrator's use of third person and past tense as the partially transparent equivalent of the character's first person and present tense. Stephen is immediately involved in composing and explicating his own text, while the narrator, the mediator and explicator for Stephen's mind and Stephen's poem, is also producing *his* text. We perceive Stephen's actions, then, through the narrator's mediations, through his attempts to evoke the process of creation while explicating the poem. The reader is necessarily involved actively in the style and the story because the ambiguities of the teller's relation to his character define our relation to teller and to character. We see our activities meshed with theirs because style and story call up our reading of the text both as experience and as the interpretation of that experience. We share with character and teller the readings and writings of the narrative and the narration.

The subtleties of the narration are particularly evident at the beginning and the end of the section and in the presentation of the poem's stanzas one or two at a time. We respond to these fragments as parts of two documents that are not separable: the poem and the book. But the poem, even as fragments, has literally *yet to be written* when we reach the first printed stanza. Immediately after reporting this stanza, the narrator comments that "the verses passed from his mind to his lips and, murmuring them over, he

felt the rhythmic movement of a villanelle pass through them" (*P* 217–18).
Shortly, we are given a second, then a third, stanza taking shape in
Stephen's thoughts and perhaps in his speech. Only several paragraphs
later does the narrator present Stephen writing down the first half of his
poem in the making, which he then recites to himself:

> Fearing to lose all, he raised himself suddenly on his elbow to look for paper
> and pencil. . . . His fingers found a pencil and then a cigarette packet. He lay
> back and, tearing open the packet, placed the last cigarette on the window-
> ledge and began to write out the stanzas of the villanelle in small neat letters
> on the rough cardboard surface.
> Having written them out he lay back on the lumpy pillow, murmuring them
> again. (*P* 218–19)

At this point Stephen thinks of having sung "a dainty song of the
Elizabethans" to Emma. After his thoughts wander for several pages, he
composes a fourth and a fifth stanza, which he also recites and then writes
down:

> He spoke the verses aloud from the first lines till the music and rhythm suf-
> fused his mind, turning it to quiet indulgence; then copied them painfully to
> feel them the better by seeing them; then lay back on his bolster. (*P* 221)

He speaks and writes down his speech in order to experience tactilely the
medium of his art.

The origin and the end, as well as the start and the finish, of Stephen's act
of writing the poem are explicitly sexual. Before the narrator presents the
first stanza, he reports Stephen's interior ejaculation: "O! In the virgin
womb of the imagination the word was made flesh" (*P* 217). While
Stephen's thoughts present the process of aesthetic creation, they also
identify the woman of the poem, the "Lure of the fallen seraphim," with the
Virgin Mary. Throughout this section, the process and the product of
Stephen's act of writing are presented in vivid sexual terms, but nowhere
more explicitly or at greater length than at the end:

> A glow of desire kindled again his soul and fired and fulfilled all his body.
> Conscious of his desire she was waking from odorous sleep, the temptress of
> his villanelle. Her eyes, dark and with a look of languor, were opening to his
> eyes. Her nakedness yielded to him, radiant, warm, odorous and lavish-
> limbed, enfolded him like a shining cloud, enfolded him like water with a
> liquid life: and like a cloud of vapor or like water circumfluent in space the
> liquid letters of speech, symbols of the element of mystery, flowed forth over
> his brain. (*P* 223)

Following this paragraph, the narrator presents the entire poem in its six—
not five—stanzas without indicating directly Stephen's act of copying out
the final quatrain. The reader must fill in this gap. The metaphorical
language presenting Stephen's state of mind carries the force of the acts of

speaking and writing, which the narrator has presented more explicitly earlier: "The liquid letters of speech . . . flowed forth over his brain."

Thought, speech, and writing all merge in Stephen's climactic act of completing his poem, in which he achieves an extreme relationship like physical intimacy with the character in his own text, with the figure he makes of his poem, a figure that incarnates the androgynous coupling of artist with interior paramour. In the final paragraph and in the presentation of the poem in its entirety (that is, all the stanzas, their interpretation, and their process of gestation), teller and reader as well as character reach a culmination. The printing of all the poem's stanzas at the end of the section indicates that the teller attains an intimacy with the character in his text like the one Stephen himself experiences. The reader shares that intimacy because of the style, especially when the style's implications are laid bare through the printing of the poem. Here is the extreme penetration by the narrator of the character's mind and one limit of narration at which a character's thoughts and words, his thoughts *as* words, take over the job of the telling. The poem is the narrator's purely mimetic report of a document, an object composed of material signifiers that can be rendered transparently through language by means of quotation. But it is also a report of character's thought, a report of character's speech, and a report of the character's physical act of writing down the final stanza. As rendering of thought, the printed poem suggests both the character's memory of the stanzas he has written and his act of creating the last of them. It may also represent Stephen's reading of the poem to himself silently or in murmurs. Mimesis now becomes indistinguishable from diegesis; representation fuses with discourse; and mediation approaches the status of the immediate. By reciting what he has already written down and is in the act of writing down, the character reads the "small neat letters on the rough cardboard surface" of the cigarette packet while the reader perceives them in the italics on the smooth white page. Despite the failure of the medium to give us the material reality of the holograph, reading, writing, speech, memory, mediation, immediacy, creation, and response are jointly available to the reader in the narrative, in the narration, and in the act of reading.

During the discussion with Lynch that occurs in V.1, the section preceding the writing of the villanelle, Stephen distinguishes between "three forms progressing from one to the next" into which "art necessarily divides itself": the lyrical, the epical, and the dramatic (*P* 214). Stephen rejects Lessing's *Laocoon* because it is based on sculpture, an art that he considers inferior, and focuses his attention on literature. Even there, he claims, "the forms are often confused" (*P* 214). At first, Stephen's distinctions seem to apply to literary genres, but they have other implications relevant to the composing of the poem. Stephen draws his distinctions among forms essentially for analytic purposes. While they refer to genres, they also suggest the phases of a writer's career, the stages of aesthetic creation, and the modalities that are combined in varying proportions in every literary text, regardless of genre. We see those phases, stages, and modalities evoked in the writing of the poem.

Stephen's conception suggests that the writer develops expertise in one form and then moves on to another, from the lyric poem to the epic narrative and then to the drama. But Stephen is also tracing the stages of artistic composition when he says that "the personality of the artist, at first a cry or a cadence or a mood and then a fluid and lambent narrative, finally refines itself out of existence, impersonalises itself, so to speak" (*P* 215). The stages occur during the writing of the poem when the "rhythmic movement" (*P* 217) Stephen feels eventually leads to the fluidity of the final paragraph and then to the withdrawal that is the completion of the poem, its separation from the poet. While Stephen discusses the three forms as if distinct from one another, the narration combines them as a fusion of modalities. By including Stephen's composing of the poem, Joyce initiates the fusion by placing the lyrical within the narrative form. He carries the merger even further and achieves the dramatic phase by quoting the entire poem at the end of the section. At that point the "rhythmic movement" of the lyric as a cry within the liquid, enfolding lambency of narrative combines with the impersonalizing that occurs when the process of creation results in a document. Lyrical has become epical and dramatic when mimesis and diegesis, representation and discourse, are one.

It would seem excessive to claim an absolute identification of teller with character and of character with reader for any literary text. But Joyce's texts tend toward excess on their road to the palace of wisdom. In *A Portrait*, the style enables the narrator to suggest arrestingly in language a process in the character's mind that can be described and interpreted with direct reference to writing and reading. In V.2 itself we are given an example of the identification between writer and character against which to gauge our own experience as readers. Because of its place in the narrative, the writing of the poem presents in little, as I have already mentioned, the relationship of the teller to his tale. That relationship emerges through the network of connections linking Stephen's act of writing with earlier and later sections of the narrative. While there are close connections to many other sections, the most important links join the poem to Stephen's earlier and later writing: his previous attempt to write a poem for Emma in II.2 (*P* 70-71) and his later writing in the journal punctuated by references to dates and places. Stephen's actions and the language of his thoughts make the connection with the earlier effort to write. Just before he writes the villanelle's final stanza, Stephen "turned towards the wall, making a cowl of the blanket" (*P* 221). Here he is imitating Emma's much earlier act of throwing a shawl over her head to form a cowl as they walk toward the tram together (*P* 69). Stephen's act suggests his attempt to *become* the figure from his past about whom he writes. The poet acts out physically his move toward merger with his own character.

The narrator insures that Stephen's gesture will be understood as a re-enactment of the earlier scene by reminding us that Emma "had worn her shawl cowlwise about her head" (*P* 222) and then by mentioning the details of the scene at length. The numerous echoes of the language of II.2 are unmistakable (cf. *P* 69 and 222). In general, the later passages are less adjectival and adverbial, but at some points the narrator's language dupli-cates almost exactly the earlier passages. The following sentences of V.2 are quoted verbatim from II.2 except for the substitution of a semi-colon for a period: "It was the last tram; the lank brown horses knew it and shook their bells to the clear night in admonition. The conductor talked with the driver, both nodding often in the green light of the lamp" (*P* 222). This kind of exact recall of the previous scene invites the reader to ponder both the source of the language in teller or character and the relationship between the two attempts to write poetry. We are given the material for acts of recollecting and reconstituting similar to those Stephen undertakes when he composes his poem. In II.2 much of the language repeated in the section on the villanelle appears to be the narrator's depiction of scene. But when the words are repeated, they become allusions that we recollect as the narrator's previous language at the same time as we understand them as Stephen's memories. It seems exceedingly odd that the narrator's public language of narration should have become the character's interior language 150 pages later. Such oddities, of course, are more obvious and numerous in *Ulysses*, a work in which the teller alludes to his own earlier narration, as in the reference to the beginning of "Calypso" that occurs in "Sirens."[27] In *A Portrait* the quotations are the most explicit indications that the whole section concerning the villanelle gives us *both* the narrator's rewriting of the earlier scene (a repetition with some crucial differences) *and* Stephen's transforming reenactment of it. The product of Stephen's reenactment is the poem, while the product of the narrator's rewriting is the entire section. But narration and narrative are so closely bound together here that it is impossible to distinguish the narrator's act completely from the character's. Like the narrator, Stephen is involved in the rewriting of his own earlier text, the poem that the narrator describes but does not quote in II.2. The various activities of reader, writer, and character have become complexly inter-woven as strands in analogous processes of recollection and revision.

There are clear parallels in Stephen's sequences of actions in II.2 and in V.2. In II.2, as Stephen watches Emma moving up and down the steps of the tram, he remembers another girl, Eileen, and feels listless, "seemingly a tranquil watcher of the scene before him" (*P* 69). After failing to take the initiative and missing his chance to kiss Emma, he tears up his ticket in frustration. The next day he writes a poem at the end of which he achieves in imagination the desired kiss. At the end of V.1, Stephen has failed to salute Emma standing on other steps, those in front of the library. As he writes the poem his frustrated desires now become anger, which leads to memories of other girls. Stephen feels weariness and languor matching his earlier listlessness. But at the conclusion of his writing, he is no longer a tranquil watcher, having become an active participant in an interior drama that is translated into the narration's vivid language. He achieves not a kiss but an emotion and a release expressed by the figurative language of lovemaking.

The narrator presents Stephen's anger in V.2 in a rather curious way that is essentially chiastic, for it involves repetition and reversal.[28] The structure of chiasmus is implicit in the following sentences: "Rude brutal anger routed the last lingering instant of ecstasy from his soul. It broke up violently her fair image and flung the fragments on all sides. On all sides distorted reflections of her image started from his memory: the flowergirl" (*P* 220). The reflections are rendered as a list of the girls Stephen associates with Emma through memory. The elements of the chiasmus can be simplified to the following scheme: anger routs ecstasy, breaks image, and flings fragments on all sides; on all sides, reflections of image emerge from memory. We are given the statement in the middle of Stephen's writing, between his composing of the third and fourth stanzas. The configuration represents the workings of the creative process by which Stephen is writing the poem and, presumably, by which the artist has written the book. This representation resembles the passage in Book IV of *Finnegans Wake*, just prior to ALP's letter, that announces the end of one cycle to be the beginning of the next. According to that passage, the text as "wholemole millwheeling vicociclometer . . ., autokinatonetically preprovided with a clappercoupling smeltingworks exprogressive process, . . . receives . . . the dialytically separated elements of precedent decomposition for the verypetpurpose of subsequent recombination so that the heroticisms, catastrophes and eccentricities transmitted by the ancient legacy of the past . . . may be there for you" (*FW* 614.27–615.8). As we saw in the last chapter, the statement asserts, among other things, that the literary text consists of a self-moving process of decomposings and recombinings by which past is transformed into present and made available for the reader. The past includes the literary tradition, earlier parts of the text, and the author's past life. All three aspects of the past are involved in *A Portrait* as Stephen rewrites by imitation poems in the literary tradition (including Shelley's "To the Moon," which he thinks of at the end of II.4), tries again to write the poem he wrote years before, and draws on his past experience for material. The chiastic passage suggests that strong emotion decomposes an image from the writer's past life. But that decomposition includes a proliferation of related images out of memory. And these images enable Stephen to return to the production of a reconstituted image in his poem. The transforming process of writing always includes the decomposing and recomposing of the past. The product of this process is a repetition of the past with a difference, a repeating in speech of the author's thought that reverses, like the pattern of chiasmus, what happened earlier, while it is also continuous with that past. In this case, Stephen's anger and his refusal to salute Emma in front of the library are transformed in the poem, by a reversal, into the homage of the speaker's address to the woman.[29]

The transforming process of writing, which is like a chiastic repetition with a difference, helps account for the detailed evocation of the earlier scene during the writing of the villanelle. By placing the repetitions just before Stephen's final inspiration to write the last stanza, the narrator implicates the memories in the composing process. For Stephen's writing to continue he must go back to something he already knows and attempt to make it new. His past, then, is the cause of the writing as well as what is to be transformed by it. (I make no claim here that the poem is particularly successful. While a turning to pasts of various kinds may be a necessary condition for successful writing, it is not a sufficient condition.) In this regard, the chiastic passage clarifies the details of the process. The strong emotion of anger that routs the ecstasy of writing is not wholly distinguishable from the acts of memory. The memories caused by anger are the means the writer uses to restore the ecstasy of writing temporarily abated because of anger. There is an apparent imbalance in the chiastic construction because this restoring of ecstasy is not mentioned at the end of the final sentence to balance the routing of ecstasy at the beginning of the first. Instead, Stephen's subsequent return to the poem indicates the restoration. There is a systole and a diastole in this process of writing, each to be understood with reference to the other. Stephen's intense achievement of ecstasy again at the end of the section completes the chiasmus and effects the large reversal that makes this repeating of an earlier scene significantly different. As Stephen reaches into his own past, the poem expresses his former listless attitude as languor by transferring it to the woman. During the writing of the poem, an ecstasy that goes well beyond the earlier imagined kiss replaces his *present* weariness.

When Stephen's memory and the narration's language call forth at such length and in such detail an earlier scene, we are likely to look back to the passages we have heard before. By confirming the similarity in details of language and the parallel sequences of action that link the two sections, we undergo an experience analogous to Stephen's. The similarity is emphasized for anyone who, referring back to II.2, encounters the following sentences: "He heard what her eyes said to him from beneath their cowl and knew that in some dim past, whether in life or in revery, he had heard their tale before. He saw her urge her vanities, her fine dress and sash and long black stockings, and knew that he had yielded to them a thousand times" (*P* 69). These sentences about recurrence create the basis of a parallelism in which the reader becomes involved in the character's experience. In II.2 Stephen hears a tale he has heard before from someone whose head is cowled. In V.2, we hear as the interior language of Stephen's cowled head the tale we have heard before in II.2. And we hear elements of the story we and the character will hear again in the book's continuing series of transformations that are repetitions, each with a difference.

Stephen's reiterated reaction to experience contributes to a self-constituted, self-moving tale that is always the same but always different. The scenes in II.2 and V.2 provide the pattern of Stephen's recurring response to life by writing. When Stephen sits down to compose his poem "To E— C—" in II.2, the narrator reports his memory of unsuccessfully "trying to write a poem about Parnell on the back of one of his father's second moiety notices" "after the discussion at the Christmas dinnertable" (*P* 70). This memory fills a gap in the narrative in a way that emphasizes a design in Stephen's life. From our retrospective point of vantage in V.2, we look back to Stephen responding to the world repeatedly with verse: from under the table in I.1 by chanting a playground verse; abortively after the Christmas dinner of I.3 (the result of his effort is an alphabetical list of several classmates); vaguely in the poem written after the tram ride in II.2; now from under his blanket as he completes the villanelle. The two poems Stephen actually writes point forward to future writings by Stephen and by Joyce, as well as back to previous ones. They direct us beyond the villanelle to Stephen's journal, to the writing of the book itself, and, ultimately, from the perspective of *Ulysses*, to Molly Bloom's monologue.

The poems and the end of the journal are linked in various ways as repetitions of similar scenes and processes. When the narrator says in II.2 not only that Stephen "had heard their tale before" but that "he had yielded . . . a thousand times" (*P* 69), a connection to the villanelle *and* to the journal is included in the scene. I have in mind, of course, Stephen's announced intention to encounter the reality of experience as repetition "for the millionth time" (*P* 253). The specific lapse of time between Stephen's attempts to write poetry emphasizes the connection of poems to journal (and finally to the book). As he composes the villanelle he says twice that it had been "ten years" since "he had written verses for her," "ten years from that wisdom of children to his folly" (*P* 222). At the end of ten years, the process of writing as the repeating and transforming of earlier texts and experiences can yield a new work. This span of time is a prolepsis within the narrative for its own gestation. At the end of the similar period of time indicated at the journal's conclusion (1904–14), the villanelle will have been rewritten as part of a later work, and the tale heard before will have been told again in the repetitions of the book itself. As part of the larger text to come in a decade, the villanelle in its new literary context will achieve the status of the dramatic as purely mimetic, as a work separated from its writer. It will become what Stephen describes in his aesthetic theory. And it will provide the direction of Joyce's development toward "Penelope."

MASKING AND UNMASKING/WEAVING AND UNWEAVING

A Portrait fulfills both journal and aesthetic theory. It does so by indirection, through the pretext of an anonymous narration in the third person when Stephen becomes the kind of artist his aesthetic theory predicts. Stephen as teller reaches back to reconstitute the earlier self that can come into being only through the simultaneous and indistinguishable acts of masking and unmasking. Stephen as character reaches forward to become in the act of reaching the kind of artist he will be once he can reach back to reconstitute an earlier self. That self will come into being only through the presentation in image of the simultaneous and indistinguishable acts of reaching forward and reaching back. The image is the aesthetic mirror image of the author's visage as reflected in the book. Joyce transcends the temporal boundaries of what he calls "the adolescent portrait" (*WD* 60) in his early narrative essay "A Portrait of the Artist" (1904). He does so by including both the prelude to adolescence *and* its aftermath. In addition to "the features of infancy not commonly reproduced" (*WD* 60), we are given the artist's mature work as the portrait of the artist itself, without which such a portrayal must be incomplete.

Between character and teller, journal and narrative, prior text and final version, both linking and separating them, are the book's navels, the evidence of a presence that hides and reveals itself in the vertiginous forms of the narration. Through the process of unfolding the panoply of implications inherent in the tale, the reader subscribes simultaneously to initial and ultimate pretexts appropriate to *A Portrait*. In the reader's fulfilled engagement with the fiction, the ultimate pretense that Stephen Dedalus tells his own story merges with the announcement on the title page that precedes the narrative, the ascription of the story to the writer, James Joyce. Like the Catholicism from which Stephen is and is not liberated, the work is founded upon "an absurdity which is logical and coherent" (*P* 244), an absurdity revealed in the heterogeneous elements that are not excursions from it, but are the work itself.

Joyce will return in his later writings to the kind of paradox that animates his *Portrait*, most prominently in the "Scylla and Charybdis" episode of *Ulysses*. There, during Stephen's further ruminations on the artist's relationship to his work, he presents Shakespeare as equivalent to Sabellius's God: "The Father was Himself His Own Son" (*U* 208). As Buck Mulligan says, he was "Himself his own father" (*U* 208). In his meditation on *Hamlet*, Stephen implicitly contemplates writing its equivalent, a work about a brooding young man in which the artist becomes anonymous because multiple and in so doing fathers himself and his own race, not in nature but in art: "When Rutlandbaconsouthamptonshakespeare or another poet of the same name in the comedy of errors wrote *Hamlet* he was not the father of his own son merely but, being no more a son, he was and felt himself the father of all his race, the father of his own grandfather, the father of his unborn grandson who, by the same token, never was born for nature. . . abhors perfection" (*U* 208). By following his own injunction to "see this" and to "remember" (*U* 192), Stephen prepares for the future in which he will narrate his present as a past: "One day in the national library we had a discussion. Shakes. After his lub back I followed. I gall his kibe" (*U* 215). And he projects that future in relation to which the present has become past, a future that captures the complexity of *A Portrait*'s narration: "In the intense instant of imagination, when the mind, Shelley says, is a fading coal that which I was is that which I am and that which in possibility I may come to be. So in the future, the sister of the past, I may see myself as I sit here now but by reflection from that which then I shall be" (*U* 194). The allusion to Shelley suggests the connection to Stephen's writing of the villanelle and to his other acts of writing in *A Portrait*. Through wandering, the artist encounters his own image: "His image, wandering, he met" (*U* 200). And he finds "in the world without as actual what was in his world within as possible" (*U* 213). When the artist is able, Penelope-like, to "weave and unweave his image" (*U* 194), through his creative actions "His own image" becomes "the standard of all experience" (*U* 195). That standard, like the artist's image in *Ulysses* and *Finnegans Wake*, is the myth of wanderings, weavings, and maskings by which the artist knows himself and represents the nature of human experience as telling.[30]

CHAPTER THREE

Precursors of Portraiture/
Preludes for Myth:
Stephen Hero and *Dubliners*

The physician Alkmeon observed, with Aristotle's approval, that men die because they cannot join the beginning and the end. . . . fictions, whose ends are consonant with origins, and in concord, however unexpected, with their precedents, satisfy our needs.

—Frank Kermode, *The Sense of an Ending*

FEATURES OF INFANCY

In *A Portrait of the Artist*, we see and hear about only fragments of Stephen Dedalus's literary production as he begins his apprenticeship for writing. Of James Joyce's apprenticeship during the decade indicated by the dates at the book's end, we know much more, though by no means everything. Between 1904 and 1907, he wrote the autobiographical sketch "A Portrait of the Artist" (1904), parts of the projected novel *Stephen Hero*, and the fifteen stories that became *Dubliners*. With the completion of those stories in the writing of "The Dead" (1907), Joyce reached a turning point after which he was able to begin transforming *Stephen Hero* into *A Portrait*.[1] The exact details of this revision, which began in 1907 and may not have been finished until 1915, are unclear. We know that the first three parts of *A Portrait* had been written in some form by February 1909, for at that time Joyce's pupil Ettore Schmitz (Italo Svevo) mentions their existence in a letter to Joyce (*Letters* II, 226–27). We still do not know precisely how Joyce then proceeded in his work on the manuscript during the next six years. While some critics claim Joyce abandoned the manuscript for the most part during this time, others find evidence for his continuing work toward finishing the book. We need to be cautious in our speculations about a process of composition for which firm evidence is not abundant.[2]

As we have seen, in *A Portrait*, Joyce himself faces the problem of representing the necessarily hidden nature of the act of writing in Stephen's villanelle. He gives us an equivalent for the features of his own book's infancy by including Stephen's poem and journal in the completed *Portrait*. But the journal and the section presenting the villanelle are mediations, not unmediated portrayals of the artist's process of producing his book. As such, they pose for readers a question like the one contained in the final line of W. B. Yeats's "Among School Children": "How can we know the dancer from the dance?" Because this question is amphibolic, it provides one version of the oscillating perspective.[3] It suggests two questions, each nesting within the other: How can we know the teller independently of the tale, and how can we know the teller by means of the tale? The reader can never know exactly or experience with immediacy what transpired between 1904 and 1914 in Dublin and Trieste. We possess only the artist's *Portrait* and his character's, not the act of portrayal. Whatever the exact course of Joyce's composing of his book, by means of the tale we *can* chart the changes that the hidden process of revision effects. Based on changes in structure and style, we can draw some conclusions from the tales concerning the writer's course of development as teller, especially his development as a stylist. Those conclusions will always reflect primarily our belated processes of response, which become our closest approach to the author's past act of writing.

In Joyce's writing of *A Portrait* and *Ulysses*, revision was surely an essential mode of discovery.[4] Joyce's revision of both works over a long period of time involved a self-reflective process that included the mastering of various styles. As his styles developed in overlapping succession, Joyce saw the potential for leaving traces of an earlier style within a later one and for gradually anticipating a style's full emergence in his narration. He learned to inscribe within his fiction representations of its own genesis by modulating between drastically different styles in a single work. These representations include more than just sections like V.2 and V.4 of *A Portrait*, in which the character writes. In a more arresting way, through the large configurations of narration in *A Portrait* and in *Ulysses* Joyce gives the reader a means of knowing the text's coming into being for its author. From the perspective of the author's experience, and the reader's, the narration reveals the writer's self-reflective process of discovery by evoking it in the reader. Through their shifting sequence, the styles build on previous styles and, by transforming them, lead to later ones.

According to Richard Ellmann, Joyce once urged one of his friends not to plan all the details of a literary text in advance of the writing, because "in the writing the good things will come" (*JJ* 370). Various good things develop in the writing of *Dubliners* and *A Portrait*, including Joyce's new skill with the various techniques for presenting consciousness in fiction that we have already surveyed briefly. Joyce developed much firmer control of the possibilities for presenting minds with apparent immediacy between the writing of *Stephen Hero* and the final revisions of *A Portrait* a decade later. By describing the techniques of narration presenting mental activity in Joyce's early fiction, we gain a sense of his movement toward the arrangement of those techniques in *A Portrait*. Joyce gave his manuscript a shape in a bold way. Once the later parts began to take on a different aspect from the earlier ones because of new elements of style, Joyce decided *not* to revise the early sections in ways that would make the entire narration relatively homogeneous stylistically. This procedure resulted in a special effect: the revisions create an ambiguous relationship between teller and character by leaving within the text an image of the author's process of discovery resembling the character's process of development. The reader experiences the equivalent of both processes in the gradual shift from psycho-narration to narrated monologue. Together with the segmenting of the narrative into juxtaposed units, the modulations of style help make *A Portrait* a writerly text (to use Roland Barthes's term), one in which the reader's active response resembles the act of writing.[5] By segmenting his narrative and varying his style, Joyce gives the reader lessons in the teller's techniques. When the writer's finished work becomes the reader's raw material for an active aesthetic re-creation, the act of reading mimics the writer's transforming of texts *he* has read, including his own finished and drafted works, by producing another work. Through reading we forge the link between artist and citizen by performing and discovering the interacting roles of teller, character, and reader evoked by style. When the reader takes on the role of writer temporarily, the oscillating perspective achieves one of its most compelling forms.

PORTALS OF DISCOVERY

Joyce does not begin his writing career by creating texts that are obviously writerly. The style of *Stephen Hero* and the style of the stories in *Dubliners* are, each in its own way, more nearly homogeneous than the later writing. They are portals of discovery through which Joyce had to pass. Despite the near contemporaneity of *Dubliners* and *Stephen Hero*, both of which were written primarily between 1904 and 1906, the final versions of the short stories stand in a closer stylistic relationship to *A Portrait* than they do to *Stephen Hero*. This is the case largely because *Stephen Hero*, which we possess only in fragments, is unfinished and unpolished. Comparisons will inevitably be lopsided and disadvantageous to *Stephen Hero*. As originally conceived and executed, the book could hardly have succeeded. It needed the radical alteration Joyce eventually undertook.

Remembering the relatively premature and fragmented condition of our *Stephen Hero*, we can say that its style varies relatively little compared with the narration of *A Portrait*. But the style is not *consistent* in the sense in which finished works, like a novel by Hemingway or Joyce's own short stories, are generally internally consistent. Its homogeneity is unsophisticated; its shifts of language are not of the controlled, purposive kind that we find in *A Portrait* and in *Ulysses*. The style of *Stephen Hero* possesses virtually no structural design or coherent complexity of implication. The narrator's relationship to his character, for instance, does not develop significantly with changes in the register of the language. While *Dubliners* and *Stephen Hero* share a focus on details of scene, action, and speech, in the novel Joyce has yet to move with assurance toward the intimate presentation of mind that characterizes the later works, including the stories. As in *A Portrait*, in *Stephen Hero* the teller presents the central character's thoughts, apparently with full knowledge of them. But in this early version the style places the reader at a greater remove from the character as the source of thinking. The feeling of distance arises from frequent obtrusive interventions between reader and character as the teller presents Stephen's attitudes. These intrusions create the narration's dominant effect.

At times, the posturing in some of the convoluted sentences of *Stephen Hero* anticipates unintentionally the carefully crafted, comic meanderings of "Eumaeus": "A metaphor is a vice that attracts the dull mind by reason of its aptness and repels the too serious mind by reason of its falsity and danger so that, after all, there is something to be said, nothing voluminous perhaps, but at least a word of concession for that class of society which in literature as in everything else goes always with its four feet on the ground. Mr. Daedalus, anyhow. . . ." (*SH* 88). This passage may be Joyce's early attempt to reflect a character's idiolect in the narration; in this case, that of Stephen's father. If so, he has not yet managed to make clear either the act of reflection or its implications. At other times, the teller employs crudely manipulative strategies to guide the reader's sense of the character, including occasional addresses in second person: "The fifty-mile journey is made by the train in about two hours and you are therefore to conceive Stephen Daedalus packed in the corner of a third-class carriage and contributing the thin fumes of his cigarettes to the already reeking atmosphere" (*SH* 237–38). Such awkward disruptions of the narration's texture preclude smooth transitions to intimate renderings of mind. The mixture of obtrusive techniques of telling with the presentation of Stephen's thoughts results in our constant awareness of the narrator as a mediating presence often judging the character.

The narration in *Stephen Hero* incorporates Joyce's attitude toward himself and his world mentioned in the narrative essay "A Portrait of the Artist" (1904). The rejection of this essay by the editor of *Dana* spurred Joyce to begin writing the autobiographical novel.[6] There the essayist presents the artist having forged, like Shem the Penman, a defensive persona as protection against the unattractive environment he inhabits but scorns. Behind that "indurating shield," "the sensitive" provides judgments about his world that are "exquisite, deliberate, sharp," delivered in "sculptural" prose (*WD* 61). Only in *A Portrait*, not in *Stephen Hero*, are we actually given lengthy passages of flamboyantly stylized, if not sculptural, prose that we can read as both the narrator's and the character's language. Like the adolescent artist's image of himself expressed in the essay, the narration in *Stephen Hero* contains both evident flattery and "a danger of complacence" (*WD* 61). The teller in *Stephen Hero* refuses, as does the artist in the essay, to expose what lies behind the repelling and repellant shield of style.

According to the narrator in *Stephen Hero*, Stephen's style as essayist contributes to his defensive "enigma of a manner" : "Stephen's style of writing, . . . though it was over affectionate towards the antique and even the obsolete and too easily rhetorical, was remarkable for a certain crude originality of expression. He gave himself no great trouble to sustain the boldnesses which were expressed or implied in his essays. He threw them out as sudden defence-works while he was busy constructing the enigma of a manner" (*SH* 27; the phrase "enigma of a manner" also occurs in the essay of 1904, *WD* 57). The description applies as well to the teller's overblown and decorative language, as in his description of Stephen, "this heaven-ascending essayist" (*SH* 80), and of Stephen's brother Maurice, "the shrewd young heathen" (*SH* 147). Such phrases carry the force of judgments, some of which we may be tempted to ascribe to Stephen himself. But any determinate ascription of them to Stephen's consciousness is prevented because the narrator has not firmly established narrating conventions clearly differentiating and merging his perspective and his character's. That deficiency is corrected later in *Dubliners*, whose style presents more coherently the character's attitudes in relation to the act of telling. The added control often enables both the recognizable merger of teller's and character's attitudes and their separation.

Expatiating on the impact of Stephen's enigmatic manner, the narrator creates his own fruitless enigma when he comments that Stephen "came to be regarded as a very unequilibrated . . . young man" (*SH* 27). The word "unequilibrated" is especially puzzling. The context does not make clear that Stephen's contemporaries would have referred to him with such an ungainly adjective. Nor are there strong indications that the word reflects Stephen's judgment of his own position or that it either agrees with the narrator's view or diverges from it. We may well suspect that a transfer has taken place, that a word from Stephen's thoughts has been injected into the narrator's diction to reveal Stephen's self-posturing judgment concerning the attitudes of others toward him. Leo Spitzer calls such transferences the "stylistic contagion" of a narrator's language by a character's voice.[7] This type of contagion is typical of fictional styles employing narrated monologue. But Joyce has yet to develop the subtleties of that device. In this case, other aspects of style and statement never confirm our suspicion. The narration's vagaries constantly create this kind of quandary for the reader, which is never exploited to any manifest purpose.

The puzzling use of the adjective contrasts with the more careful choice of diction in "The Sisters" when the narrator there employs the equally unattractive word "inefficacious" (*D* 12). The adjective describes Father Flynn's attempts to brush away grains of snuff from his priestly garb. This word, which Joyce added during revision of the story, has a definite impact, particularly because the narrator is sparing in his use of a sophisticated adult vocabulary.[8] "Inefficacious" stands out as would an oddly colored tessera strategically placed in a largely monochromatic mosaic. In contrast to "unequilibrated," the word is *not* an example of inflated vocabulary reflecting ironically the character's pretensions. Instead, it functions coherently to remind us that the details of the story, like the details of Pip's childhood in *Great Expectations*, are presented by an adult narrator. This adult teller has sufficient control of the narration's language to move easily from remembered boyhood visions to his own present perspective.

There are, of course, ambiguities in the interlacing of character's and narrator's views in Joyce's writings after *Stephen Hero*. But by the time he revises the stories of *Dubliners*, Joyce can avoid the kind of *frustrating* ambiguity that mars the earlier work. In *Dubliners*, the recurring ambiguities of voice and presence are *not* confusions of perspective but deliberate, purposive mergings and divergings. As we have already seen, in *A Portrait* the mergers can evoke the process of writing itself by suggesting that the character's activities of mind are similar to the storytelling. The famous ostensible disappearance of the narrator in Joyce's supposedly impersonal fiction is no disappearance at all, simply a careful alignment of style with story, narration with narrative. Psycho-narration, narrated monologue, and quoted interior monologue in the later fiction give the reader stronger indices than does *Stephen Hero*'s style for attributing specific passages to the character, to the narrator, or to both at once. In such techniques the narrator is implicated in the fiction's dynamics in ways the obtrusive narrator of *Stephen Hero* cannot be. But these later developments take us away from that draft, into the stories of *Dubliners* and beyond them.

In *Dubliners* Joyce overcomes the weakness of *Stephen Hero*'s style in several ways, primarily by evoking two voices rather than one: a voice for the narrator and a different one for the character, which we may often treat as a definable element of the narrator's language. Frequently, we can identify the two voices through contrasts of diction, as in the case of the word "inefficacious." Similar contrasts in diction are also our guide regularly in the early portions of *A Portrait*. There, the contrast between the narrator's unobtrusive presentation of scene, action, or dialogue, and the character's simple language of thought usually makes the distinction clear. In the *Dubliners'* stories told in the first person, the determinate gap between the mind of the character and that of the narrator is greater than it is in the surviving portions of *Stephen Hero*, in part because the stories concern a child rather than a young adult. But even in the stories told in third person, disparities arise when the narrator presents the relatively simple thoughts of many of the central characters.[9] Through its conventions, the narration regularly gives the reader the impression of hearing the narrator's voice in alternation with the character's. Joyce's great strength here, as later, is his ability to shift from style to style and to amalgamate styles. The teller's modulation among various voices inevitably creates some ambiguity concerning the language's source. Later, we shall examine more closely the spectacular stylistic configurations Joyce achieves at the start and the close of *Dubliners* that stress this ambiguity.

The following passage from "Eveline" is typical in certain ways of the narration in the middle stories:

> She had consented to go away, to leave her home. Was that wise? She tried to weigh each side of the question. In her home anyway she had shelter and food; she had those whom she had known all her life about her. Of course she had to work hard both in the house and at business. What would they say of her in the Stores when they found out that she had run away with a fellow? Say she was a fool, perhaps; and her place would be filled up by advertisement. Miss Gavan would be glad. (*D* 37)

Rather than calling attention to the act of narrating, the teller uses the verb "weigh" to introduce thought and to present it as a logical procedure. Together with the contrasting statements about Eveline's situation, the questions that precede and follow the indicator of thought emphasize the character's interior colloquy rather than the narrator's mediating voice. The phrases "of course," "anyway," and "perhaps" present the certain and the tentative qualities of her thinking. By keeping the statements short and the diction simple, the teller maintains his difference and the reader's distance from these thoughts. The lack of deictic adjectives and adverbs helps to limit the degree of our involvement with Eveline's ruminations. The passage is followed by Eveline's memories of Miss Gavan's corrective comments, although the dashes indicating direct discourse distract us from dwelling on the character's mental process of remembering. Many of the statements in the next paragraph and later in the story, like those in the passage above, move toward the narrated monologue, but of a simple kind.[10] We can easily transform third person and past tense into first person and present tense, yet no exclamations, or emotional phrases, or deictic phrases encourage us to undertake that transformation. The sensibility represented by this language is clearly distinct from the sensibilities of teller and reader.

The following passage presenting the thoughts of Lenehan in "Two Gallants" is constructed differently:

> His mind became active again. He wondered had Corley managed it successfully. He wondered. . . . He suffered. . . . But the memory of Corley's slowly revolving head calmed him somewhat: he was sure Corley would pull it off all right. All at once the idea struck him that perhaps Corley had seen her home by another way and given him the slip. His eyes searched the street: there was no sign of them. Yet it was surely half-an-hour. . . . Would

Corley do a thing like that? He lit his last cigarette and began to smoke it nervously. He strained his eyes as each tram stopped at the far corner of the square. They must have gone home by another way. The paper of his cigarette broke and he flung it into the road with a curse. (*D* 59)

Although there are not two absolutely distinct voices in this passage, we have the impression of two different speech patterns. Joyce is already starting, however distantly, to move toward the kind of problematic narration we find in episodes of *Ulysses* like "Cyclops." There too, we have the clear impression of two voices that merge as well as diverge. In "Two Gallants" we sense two voices, in part because of the reiterated words indicating mental activity. In addition, the colon introduces expressions of Lenehan's attitudes in language approximating his own. As in the passage from "Eveline," the internal colloquy and the certainty and conjecture of thinking are rendered by the question and by phrases like "he was sure," "perhaps," "surely," and "they must have." The narrator's expression at the beginning of the paragraph, "had Corley managed it successfully," contrasts with Lenehan's more colloquial statement, "Corely would pull it off all right." Corely could conceivably think "managed it" but never "managed it successfully." The colloquialisms are more prevalent than in "Eveline."

Several other elements of the story make the passage notably different from the presentation of Eveline's mind. The narrator alternates several times between describing actions and reporting thoughts. This alternation is closer than the narration of "Eveline" to the first parts of *A Portrait*. As in *A Portrait*, Joyce has begun to stress our proximity to the character's perspective by having him remember previous thoughts or perceptions. Because Lenehan has perceived the head earlier turning "like a big ball revolving on a pivot" (*D* 56), the reader can accept his "memory of Corley's slowly revolving head." The situation of the passage in the later story's general context makes a difference as well. In "Two Gallants," the narrator asserts his presence briefly but vividly in the first paragraph before presenting any of the characters: "Like illumined pearls the lamps shone from the summits of their tall poles upon the living texture below which, changing shape and hue unceasingly, sent up into the warm grey evening air an unchanging unceasing murmur" (*D* 49). No reader will confuse the mind of Lenehan with the narrating sensibility revealed in this sentence's rhythmical, highly adjectival language. In "Eveline," the narrator's less ostentatious assertion of presence through a similitude comes only at the story's end, not its beginning. Despite the use of third person in both stories and in *Stephen Hero*, the narration in *Dubliners* creates none of the muddles that plague the novel. The narrator is *not* invisible. Instead the kind of presence he chooses gives the reader some definite guides for distinguishing his language and mind from the character's words and consciousness.

In producing his stories' final versions, Joyce learns to manipulate skillfully, within the limited scope of their literary form, determinate fluctuations of distance between narrator and character and clear alternations between description and thought. We have already encountered his use of these variations in *A Portrait*. The transforming of *Stephen Hero* into *A Portrait*'s narration through the crucible of *Dubliners* involves recasting "Stephen's style of writing" (*SH* 27) into a style of thought. We understand that style as the character's private mode of consciousness, not immediately, as in *Stephen Hero*, as the narrator's ambiguous public mode of telling. We can trace the shift in the details of narration. The ambiguous mediations of Stephen's thoughts in *Stephen Hero* are replaced in *A Portrait* by renderings of his mind in a new kind of language. That language exhibits his "originality of expression" not because the narrator merely asserts that originality, but because of the rhythm and eloquence of Stephen's interior voice, even when it includes "the antique . . . the obsolete and too easily rhetorical" (*SH* 27), the stylized and the sentimental.

In *Stephen Hero*, the narrator reports that Stephen has committed to memory a moving story by W. B. Yeats, "The Tables of the Law," which he recites to his companions and to himself in his walks around Dublin (*SH* 176–78). In the narration of *A Portrait*, we encounter an interiorized, fragmented equivalent of such recitations when Stephen walks across Dublin associating aspects of scene with styles of writing in V.1 (*P* 176) and when we hear the varying styles of Stephen's internal voice, especially late in the narrative. In the surviving portions of *Stephen Hero*, there are no examples of Stephen's writing in the antique style the narrator refers to or in any other vivid style. Besides the fleeting references to his verses (*SH* 214, 226), we are given only two stanzas imitating Yeats's work of the 1890's (*SH* 37). The narrator summarizes Stephen's essay on aesthetics (*SH* 77–81), but he quotes little of it, and he describes Stephen's public reading rather than presenting the details of the talk (*SH* 100–101). In *A Portrait*, by contrast, Stephen's interior styles, along with the villanelle and the journal, are important components of the narration. By either displacing or merging with the teller's voice, the interior styles become the voice of Stephen's telling, which he has yet to write at the time he begins his journal. Without the development through *Dubliners* of a viable style for presenting consciousness, one that avoids unnecessary confusions of voice, the style of Stephen's mind as traced in his *Portrait* would have remained unwritten.

ELEMENTS OF A SCRUPULOUSLY MEAN ENIGMA

So far, I have suggested we can generally distinguish narrator from character in the narration of *Dubliners* in ways that *Stephen Hero*'s style prevents because of its muddles. We have seen that stylistic distinctions in the stories create a distance from character for both narrator and reader. However, some aspects of the narration attenuate the distance almost to the vanishing point. The stylistic vacillations create an unavoidable contradiction for any comprehensive analysis of the stories' narration. This is the engaging enigma of Joyce's mature manner of telling, which requires our reading to include oscillating perspectives. In order to characterize the narration of *Dubliners* precisely and to chart the shift in narration from *Stephen Hero* to *A Portrait* and beyond, we must look closely at a wider range of stylistic elements in the stories than we have so far. Along with outlining the relative prominence of reports of thought in the different tales, we shall consider the shift from first- to third-person narration after the third story, the subtle connection between "The Sisters" and "The Dead," and the special place of "The Dead" in the volume.

Barbara Hardy has suggested in a tentative way that at the end of *A Portrait* Stephen Dedalus is preparing to write the stories of *Dubliners*.[11] We can think of these stories, along with *Ulysses*, as a continuation of Stephen's story, albeit one that does not mention him directly. We know that Joyce used the pseudonym "Stephen Daedalus" when early versions of some of the stories were published in the *Irish Homestead* (*JJ* 170). Like Joyce's later fiction, these tales are as much about their teller as their characters. The arrangement of narrative segments and styles in *A Portrait* nurtures our expectation that Stephen's aspirations, expressed in flamboyant, eloquent language, will inevitably yield to styles expressing the grim limitations of experience. The hyperbolic language and intensely felt attitudes of the final entries in Stephen's journal, like his intensely presented experiences at the end of each earlier part, may well be the prelude for something quite different. Insofar as *Dubliners* represents the sober realization of Stephen's vaguely stated aspirations, *it* is that something different. Rather than presenting in a high style the narrator's soaring, impalpable, imperishable being, *Dubliners* depicts the unpleasant but honest physical, social, and mental realities of a less than ideal world. That world is the teller's world, from which he cannot withdraw absolutely. The stories' narration composes his literary self-image, as different from the end of the journal as the beginning of V.1 is from the end of IV.3 in *A Portrait*.

Dubliners fulfills the soberer version of Stephen's aspiration to "forge in the smithy of my soul the uncreated conscience of my race." Joyce outlines that soberer aspiration in the oft-quoted letter to one of his recalcitrant publishers, Grant Richards:

> My intention was to write a chapter of the moral history of my country and I chose Dublin for the scene because that city seemed to be the centre of paralysis. I have tried to present it to the indifferent public under four of its aspects: childhood, adolescence, maturity and public life. The stories are arranged in this order. I have written it for the most part in a style of scrupulous meanness and with the conviction that he is a very bold man who dares to alter

in the presentment, still more to deform, whatever he has seen and heard. I cannot do any more than this. (*Letters* II, 134)

I quote this well-known and *polemical* passage as much for what it leaves out as for what it includes. It necessarily omits mention of "The Dead," a story yet to be written, whose style deviates in distinct ways from one of "scrupulous meanness." And it leaves out what Joyce communicated to his brother Stanislaus in an earlier letter: that the childhood represented is the author's (*Letters* II, 111). The uncreated conscience being incarnated in a moral history of a special sort includes the consciousness of the moral historian meeting itself as it forges an aesthetic counterpart in language.

Joyce can and boldly does dare do more than he claims in this letter. He can represent consciousness, his own as teller and the minds of his characters, in a style not adequately described as scrupulously mean. His project involves an act of self-observation that becomes part of the image he creates as a fictional world. Both style and story vividly suggest self-scrutiny at the end of *A Portrait* and at the beginning of *Dubliners*. Stephen's ironic remarks in his journal, some directed at himself; the vacillating viewpoint of the narrated monologue; and the oscillations of *A Portrait*'s narrating situation are matched in the first stories. Their counterparts include the boy's self-conscious realizations within the narratives and his later self-reflective narration in the first person. The switch to third-person narration in *Dubliners* occurs only *after* the boy makes a painful but honest self-conscious judgment about himself in the narrative. And it occurs only *after* the boy's older self presents his own previous actions as others might see them and as he sees the actions of others.

The self-scrutiny and the shift of grammatical person in the narration give us a frame for describing the collection's overall structure. Early in *Dubliners* the stories told in first-person reach a point of self-consciousness in style and story that becomes the hinge for a turn toward a third-person narration that can view character from both inside and out. Within broad limits, the stories that follow, up until those of public life, maintain this combination of inner and outer views in a third-person perspective. In those stories, the three following "A Painful Case," the external view predominates.[12] But late in *Dubliners*, in a coda as *post scriptum*, "The Dead" reestablishes the internal view and its dominance. This complex and powerful story holds a special place in Joyce's early writing in part because it repeats and reverses the previous shift from first person to third person. The reversal occurs in the final pages, when Gabriel Conroy's voice and the narrator's third-person voice become virtually indistinguishable. We come to understand the narrator's voice as the character's first-person, internal speech. When the style provokes this understanding, it reverses and completes the earlier shift. It completes what that shift marks: the narrator's penetration of the character's mind (Eveline's) rather than his withdrawal from it. The penetration of mind and the merger of voices at the volume's conclusion links "The Dead" closely with the opening of "The Sisters." As with Joyce's other narratives, when the volume of stories reaches its ending, it turns back to its beginning. Joyce surely realized what we eventually understand: that the titles of the first and the last stories are interchangeable.

In the general scheme I have just outlined, I take the stories as one volume, part of one project, rather than as individual, autonomous works. There is good cause to speak of them in this way. Besides mentioning a coherent order of arrangement in his letters, Joyce remarked after having written only one story, "The Sisters," that the stories would be "a series of epicleti—ten—for a paper" to be called "*Dubliners*" (*Letters* I, 55). However, because the stories were written individually, neither in the published order we have nor as part of a continuous narrative, we must be careful not to ascribe too rigid a pattern to them. As for Joyce's quadripartite division of the stories, it is less useful for defining any superficially coherent development of subject matter than for investigating the shifts of style. As in *A Portrait*, techniques for representing consciousness are coherently arrayed among the stories. The order of the stories as we presently have it, rather than the chronological order of their production, provides a basis for describing the style's general orientation. Our sense of closure when we examine the stories' language collectively arises primarily from the placement of the tales early and late, especially the first three and the last four. The eight stories in the middle, from "Eveline" through "A Painful Case," reveal various arrangements and employments of techniques for rendering mind in third person, but without the same sharply distinguishing features of the stories preceding and following them. The language of these middle stories creates the impression of stylistic homogeneity for the collection. But in "The Dead," Joyce moves sharply away from that relative homogeneity to a narration that repeats in small compass the gradual introduction and arrayal of the techniques for presenting mind.

The stories of *Dubliners* are in part stylistic exercises enabling the author to explore different, though generally not wildly different, orientations toward tale and character. These exercises contribute to Joyce's developing an intimate narration of mind employing the third person rather than the first. And they allow him to practice the arrangement of narrative segments. When we look at *Dubliners* structurally as a sequence of varying but linked styles and stances of narration grouped either according to Joyce's four rubrics or according to style, the family resemblances between the collection and the three later narratives become clear. The writing of fifteen stories loosely related by overlapping elements of style furthers Joyce's eventual production of longer narratives composed of relatively discontinuous but connected segments: the nineteen sections of *A Portrait*, the eighteen episodes of *Ulysses*, and the seventeen chapters of *Finnegans Wake*. All four books are made up of between fifteen and twenty segments of narrative arranged into three, four, or five parts. The segments and parts are generally demarcated by some combination of typographical indicators: titles, roman numerals, asterisks, or changes in typeface. But other groupings of tales and episodes according to style rather than story are possible, at least for *Ulysses* and for *Dubliners*. In "The Dead," in *Ulysses*, and, more emphatically, in *Finnegans Wake*, Joyce began to lengthen the segments and to subdivide some of them into parts. The nineteen sections of "Wandering Rocks," the questions and answers of "Ithaca," and the eight paragraphs of "Penelope" anticipate the chapters of the *Wake* divided into questions and answers or into unmarked segments, whose enigmatic boundaries the reader must discover.

THE PRELUDE: MEMORIES OF BOYHOOD

It is one of the principles of this study that the first and last narrative segments in Joyce's writings are of special importance, that they provide frames for his works by presenting boundaries of style and story and by representing the text's origin. We find a striking validation for that principle at the beginning and at the end of *Dubliners*, most surprisingly at the beginning. At the start of the first story and at the end of the last we encounter the primary stylistic points of contact between *Dubliners* and *A Portrait*. In "The Sisters" and "The Dead," Joyce exhibits his mastery of the complicated mixture of techniques that makes the narration of *A Portrait* and the initial style of *Ulysses* possible.

In general, the narration of "The Sisters" alternates between self-narration and the first-person presentation of scene and dialogue. Self-narration is the first-person equivalent of the psycho-narration so prominent in the third-person telling of *A Portrait*. The self-narration of thoughts in all three of the stories told in first person is primarily consonant rather than dissonant; that is, the narrator does not frequently allow his adult consciousness to intrude as he evokes his earlier thoughts.[13] I do not mean to suggest that we have no evidence for distinguishing between the teller's past and present. As I have already argued, the inclusion of adult vocabulary, such as the word "inefficacious," helps maintain the distinction. Even though the teller at times expresses attitudes toward his past thoughts and actions (but not analytic judgments about them), numerous commentators have assumed that the young boy is the narrator.[14] That assumption must overlook both the adult vocabulary and the use of the past perfect as well as the past tense.

Like the psycho-narration in *A Portrait*, the consonant self-narration in

"The Sisters," combined with brief direct presentations of the character's thoughts, creates a sense of intimacy between reader and character. The brief self-quoted monologues of "The Sisters" anticipate the snatches of quoted monologue in *A Portrait*. In them, direct representation of thought indicates intensity of feeling, as in the boy's interior exclamations about old Cotter: "Tiresome old fool!" (*D* 10) and "Tiresome old red-nosed imbecile!" (*D* 11). Just as psycho-narration employed together with quoted monologue resembles the narrated monologue's fusion of voices, the consonant self-narration of "The Sisters" combined with self-quoted monologue sometimes moves the narration close to self-narrated monologue. To insure these proliferating terms do not obscure our sense of the style's impact, we shall need to examine some of the effects Joyce creates in "The Sisters."

The potential for a merger of voices is generally held in check in the story in various ways. The self-quoted monologues are too short and occur too infrequently to provide the reader with any strong feeling of sustained, unmediated contact with the character's mind. And much of the story is devoted to representations of dialogue, which move us out of the character's thoughts by interrupting the mimesis of consciousness. In the self-narration, the narrator employs the same repertoire of words and phrases evoking thought and affect that he uses in *A Portrait*. Sometimes this vocabulary of thought appears so frequently that these mediations hinder our sense of contact with the character's consciousness, even though there are no explicit commentaries. For instance, in one paragraph, eight such words and phrases occur in nine sentences: "angry," "puzzled my head," "imagined," "think," "felt" (occurs twice), "wondered," and "remembered" (*D* 11). The teller varies his techniques but always moves us skillfully into and out of his own earlier thoughts. If his strategies for presenting those thoughts, past and present, were invariably the same, we might become so habituated to the narration's conventions that the teller *would* seem invisible. Because the strategies change, even in this first story, the representation of mind subtly draws our attention to its language in ways that mix immediacy and mediation.

As the stylistic prelude for story and volume, the opening paragraph of "The Sisters," especially the first sentence, operates according to different principles from the rest of the story: "There was no hope for him this time: it was the third stroke" (*D* 9).[15] We have grown to know the stories of *Dubliners* so well that we may tend to overlook the lack of overt specificity concerning voice and referent in this initial sentence. From one perspective, there is no radical, no permanent, ambiguity, because our uncertainty about speaker and referent can be resolved if we are willing to adopt some straightforward assumptions about the narration. The reader soon understands that the third-person pronoun refers to the priest dying on the other side of the window at which the boy regularly gazed. And, if we assume that the boy is the narrator, there is no ambiguity of speaker—until we ask *when exactly* the boy speaks, or thinks, this sentence. As I have already suggested, the ascription of the narration as a whole to the boy is untenable. The irresolvable ambiguity placed at the beginning of the first story announces a central element of the entire volume's stylistic exploration: the varying, and sometimes unstable, relationship between the reporting self and the experiencing self in narration. This sentence is the precursor for the two most significant shifts in the volume's style, the one involving the change to third-person narration, and the more complicated shift that takes place in the final pages of "The Dead." As we shall see, in those last pages, third-person narration approaches the status of first-person narration asymptotically without any explicit shift of person. Similarly, at the start of "The Sisters," with no shift of grammatical, speaking person, a sentence in a first-person narration creates the impression of third-person narration before the telling becomes for us the first-person narration that we shall soon know it is.

The complications can be put more simply. We cannot read the first sentence of *Dubliners* as part of a first-person narration when we encounter it initially unless we already have preconceptions about the voice. We can only do so retrospectively, once we have situated ourselves within the narrating perspective of a teller who was a participant in the story's action. The sentence would seem at first to be part of a third-person narration. Because the opening is only briefly unconventional, as educated readers and rereaders of stories, we tend to rationalize this most curious beginning, to transform it into something much simpler than it is. The reduction is ours, not Joyce's. Like the brief first section of *A Portrait*, the entire first paragraph of "The Sisters" is a stylistic tour de force, though less overtly so than its counterpart in the later work. In spite of our habitual accommodation of the story's beginning, the first sentence, with its two impersonal constructions, its third-person pronoun, its deictic reference to time, and its colon, is a distinctly odd start for a story told by a participant and filled with unambiguous circumstantial details. There would be no question about the source and implied person of the sentence if it occurred later in the story. Or, if the order of the story's first two sentences were simply reversed, much of the uncertainty would not arise. But the teller has refused these easier options.

Although the purely referential ambiguity concerning the pronoun "him" is soon clarified, the other ambiguity, stylistic in nature, cannot be explained away entirely. It emerges from the story's essential situation: the relationship between narration and narrative, telling and experiencing. In its own way, this sentence is as anomalous as the presentation of Stephen Dedalus's act of writing the villanelle in *A Portrait*. This combination of what appears to be a third-person stance with the representation of the character's mind in a context of first-person narration is an example of the device I suggested earlier the narration of "The Sisters" tends toward: the highly unusual technique of self-narrated interior monologue.[16] As its name suggests, this device is the first-person equivalent of the better known (because more widely employed) narrated monologue. As in the third-person technique, the sentence is in past tense, but a demonstrative pronoun ("this") creates a sense of the character's immediate situation rather than the teller's. Our understanding of that past tense, however, depends upon its context; specifically, on the contrast with the past perfect later in the paragraph.

The narrator employs the past perfect to describe his repeated actions as a boy prior to the time of the narrative. In this regard, the paragraph resembles the opening of what C. K. Scott Moncrieff calls the overture to *Remembrance of Things Past*. There the first person narrator employs, in French, the imperfect tense to evoke retrospectively his customary actions of the past. In "The Sisters" the repetition of related phrases lends an itera-tive coloration to the past perfect: "night after night" (used twice), "often," "every night," and "always." By contrast, the past tense referring to actions and attitudes occurring at the time of the narrative's action is linked to deictic references; besides "this" in the first sentence, "now" is used twice. The first sentence, however, cannot be accommodated com-pletely to the other sentences of the paragraph that employ the past tense and deictic expressions. Although "this time" often carries "now" as one of its implications (as in the phrase "at this time"), in context, it refers to the culmination of a sequence of repeated actions. The deictic expression carries an iterative implication that the second clause of the sentence emphasizes. While the rest of the paragraph is built on the contrast be-tween repeated acts on one hand and singular ones that can be distin-guished on grammatical grounds on the other, the first sentence combines repetition with the narrative's specific "now." By waivering on the cusp between the definite and the frequentative without being wholly one or the other, it includes the story's generating conflation of two temporal modes that alternate in the narration to follow. The conflation is originating, as well as initial, because it *requires* the continuing act of narration to explain the relevance of past repetition to determinate present actions of two kinds: the present action of the narrative and the present act of narration.

We can understand, retrospectively at least, the past tense in the first clause as the narrator's transforming of the original present tense of his own past thought. The first explicit reference to thinking occurs in the phrase "I thought" in the third sentence. As in some of the passages of part V in *A Portrait*, the phrase ascribes the language to the character's mental activity only belatedly. But this reading limits the sentence too severely. It could simply be indirect discourse; that is, it could be the boy's memory of what the adults around him have said about the priest's situation shortly before the time of the action in the narrative. Neither the action nor the boy's character as presented later in the narration allows us to eliminate one of these alternatives. We could usually discount the first reading in a story about childhood, because a small child might not understand about strokes. But this precocious child, who thinks about paralysis, simony, and gnomon, might well understand.

Both the source of the memories and the specific context of the remembering are *unlocalized*, even though they largely deal with action at a specific location: gazing up at the window from in front of the priest's house. We are told neither where the boy is nor what he is doing when he has these thoughts. Like the narrator's language, the boy's thoughts emerge from an indeterminate place and time. He *may* have had them upstairs before supper. But as they are presented, the thoughts are not clearly linked to the scene and time introduced in the next paragraph. Such a passage full of uncertainties places us in a position resembling that of the letter's interpreter in *Finnegans Wake*, who can say only that "somehow and somewhere . . . somebody . . . wrote it, wrote it all, wrote it all down, and there you are" (118.3–14). What we say about the time and location of the passage's origin in the narrative must always be relative to the act of narrating. It occurs as memory at the time of the narration in the narrator's mind. That is all we know and all we need to know for the telling to become part of the passage's referential content. Narrative is discourse, discourse narrative, even in the first story of *Dubliners*.

In interpreting the story's initial sentence, it will be helpful to discriminate between the first and second clauses. Joyce gives us some guidance by providing the second sentence for contrast: "Night after night I had passed the house (it was vacation time) and studied the lighted square of window: and night after night I had found it lighted in the same way, faintly and evenly." Taken together the sentences provide perspectives by incongruity. They turn out to be both antithetical and similar. The shift from the first to the second involves repetition of structure and reversal of implication. Consequently, the second sentence sheds light on the first by counterpoint. In each we have two independent clauses linked by a colon. But the second sentence is spoken in first person. And its colon could just as well be a comma, for the "and" together with the logical parallelism of clauses makes the sentence a compound construction. The first sentence lacks the conjunction, and its clauses, while constructed in parallel, are not entirely parallel logically. Here the significance of the first sentence's iterative implication emerges. That sentence's first clause, with its demonstrative pronoun, refers to a definite past situation. The second clause does as well, but it begins to call up emphatically the sequence of actions standing behind the speaking of the sentence.

Lurking within and behind that initial statement's impersonal, definite construction is an iterative sequence requiring the explanation that starts in the next sentence. The second sentence reverses the imbalance between the clauses in two ways. There the clauses not only look parallel, they *are* parallel both in construction and in their references to iterative actions. A strong impression of repetition dominates the entire sentence. Despite that impression, inserted into the first clause weakly and parenthetically, is the statement of a definite past situation: "(it was vacation time)." The parentheses complete the reversal and repetition linking the sentences, each composed of two primary clauses, while they complicate the clauses' reflective relationship. The first sentence refers ostensibly to a definite past situation, but its second clause introduces an iterative implication. The second sentence refers ostensibly to reiterated past actions, but its first clause includes a reference to a definite past situation. All this contributes to the highly ambiguous nature of the story's narration at its outset.

The narrator deliberately knocks the reader off balance at the start by raising questions that do not admit of easy answers. By assaulting us in this way, he emphasizes his own place, and ours, in the telling. At the same time, he points the direction his narration will eventually take later in *Dubliners*. He does so by accomplishing the subtle reversal and counterpoint in the story's, and the book's, first sentences. It is as if he were taking his style and, like a glove, turning it inside out for wear on the other hand. It becomes its own opposite and is yet the same. This turning, indicated only briefly at the beginning of "The Sisters," occurs again in a more extended form at the end of "The Dead." There, the apparent contradiction of grammatical and temporal relationships projected at the beginning of *Dubliners* realizes itself as a conjunction of minds. The teller's speech and the character's interior voice combine again to a new purpose: to evoke the cultural and the mythic within the yoked sensibilities, psychological and aesthetic, of character and narrator. The double evocation of the cultural within the mental and the mythic within the aesthetic that leads to both *Ulysses* and *Finnegans Wake* begins to emerge, albeit tentatively and sketchily, as the interpenetration of iterative and definite in the first sentences of *Dubliners*.

The crux of the ambiguity is a matter of voices and tenses. Joyce is able to create for the reader an oscillating perspective in an extremely brief compass by conflating the narrator's past and present voices. A sentence that seems initially to be third-person narration turns out to be part of a first-person narration that can be read in at least these three ways: as the character's thoughts presented in self-narrated monologue—that is, in the guise of his own later utterances as a narrator speaking in the past tense; as the character's thoughts presented first in that guise (initial clause) followed by his straightforward report of the past situation; and, finally, as the character's thoughts presented in that guise followed by a second clause in which no absolute distinction can be made between the narrator's past and present voices. This last alternative, which includes the other two readings and anticipates later developments in Joyce's styles, is the most revealing of the three. Like the retelling of Simon Dedalus's story of the moocow at the beginning of *A Portrait*, even though it comes first in the telling, the beginning of "The Sisters" indicates fleetingly the *goal* of the style.

The reader reaches that goal again only after experiencing the modulations of style to follow. We can think of the series of styles in *Dubliners* as analogous to a transformational sequence of rhetorical tropes.[17] The stories begin with a puzzling identification, like that of metaphor, between telling and experiencing selves in the self-narrated monologue. That uneasy fusion is followed metonymically by styles in which the fusion has been transformed into an alternation of voices. These are past and present voices in the case of the first-person stories, character's and teller's in the case of the third-person tales. In the three stories of public life, the dominance of the teller's voice replaces the alternation. That voice manifests itself, like synecdoche, as context of the whole. In the last story, the narrator subverts and transforms the dominance by a doubling, in the mode of irony, when he has recourse to narrated monologue. This recourse, like the end of *Finnegans Wake*, brings us back to the beginning.

The contrast between iterative and singular action that informs so thoroughly the first paragraph of "The Sisters" gives us a way to define one aspect of the relation between teller and tale, narrator and character, in the first three stories. As in *Remembrance of Things Past*, the customary action of the past results in the definite, present act of storytelling. In the first-person tales of *Dubliners*, the definite act of telling reverses the customary action of the narrative. In each story, the boy is an observer who tends to mask his feelings behind a protective façade of silence and detachment. In "The Sisters," the narrator claims he tried to show no reaction whenever he was aware of being observed: "I continued eating as if the news had not interested me" (*D* 10); "I crammed my mouth with stirabout for fear I might give utterance to my anger. Tiresome old red-nosed imbecile!" (*D* 11). With its presentation not only of action but of motivation, restraint of speech, and thought directly reported as self-quoted monologue, this latter example captures especially well the reversal that the narration enables. The boy's habitual acts in the past result in a present action that is their opposite, just as speech is the opposite of silence.

The explicit mention of silence and its implied contrast with the telling occur in the next two stories as well. In "An Encounter," the narrator asserts that he was careful "lest I should betray my agitation" (*D* 27). And in "Araby" he observes the object of his desire, his playmate's sister, long before he finally speaks to her briefly, when *she* initiates the conversation with a question about the bazaar (*D* 31). The reversal of the tale's action in the telling anticipates *A Portrait*. Through the telling, habitual inhibition is exhibited and transformed into the public speech of narration. As we shall see, the narration of "The Dead" provides a different perspective on the relation of public speech to private. To achieve closure for the volume, the narrator moves from the character's public speaking to focus on an interior speech that eventually defines the form of the teller's own public narration.

We can approach the rationale for narration in Joyce's fiction and articulate the contrast between the first stories and the last one through Joyce's use of the word "encounter" and the act it suggests. The story of that name resembles aspects of part II of *A Portrait*, in which Stephen recalls his reading of *The Count of Monte Cristo*. Although the boy in "An Encounter" has been reading other stories—"the literature of the Wild West" and "some American detective stories" that include "beautiful girls" (*D* 20)—like Stephen he discovers the lack of congruence between stories and life. The incongruity becomes part of the generating motive for the telling of a different kind of story when the boy grows up, one that seems closer to the realites of life, truer to their frustrations. In that different story, which we have, the teller inscribes the contrast between literature and life that gives rise to the process by which experience is turned into art. In this process, the contemporaneous encounters with literature and with the old man are combined as prelude for the later encounter of the narrator with himself and with his own past as he writes in the first person. The trace of the later encounter is the written story, the evidence that the narrator has combined and interpreted the earlier encounters.

Joyce's writing develops toward an expansive kind of fiction, one that employs the subjectivity of the individual character without being limited by solipsistic boundaries. That expansive quality is clear in the frequently quoted penultimate entry of Stephen's journal, in which he describes his quest using "encounter" prominently as a verb: "I go to encounter for the millionth time the reality of experience" (*P* 252–53). In "Scylla and Charybdis," a slightly older Stephen articulates a less ecstatic, more realistic version of the artist's recurring encounter with the world and with subjectivity. In his peroration, he says of Shakespeare: "He found in the world without as actual what was in his world within as possible. . . . We walk through ourselves . . . always meeting ourselves" (*U* 213). The first-person stories of *Dubliners* present explicitly what the narration in all Joyce's narratives traces: the encounter of the teller with himself. Out of that encounter will be forged not only the consciousness of an individual but the consciousness of the race, the lineaments of humankind, as the recurring shape of myth and as the teller's counterpart in language. A new kind of iteration emerges from the transforming of recurring silence into acts of storytelling. In "The Dead" that new iteration is social, physical, and, at the end, mythic, though briefly and implicitly so. When Joyce has Stephen say in *A Portrait* that he intends to forge "the uncreated conscience of my race," Joyce himself has already written the volume of stories that prepares directly for the presentation of mind as myth in *Ulysses*.

Before having his teller achieve a close approach to the mythic at the end of "The Dead," Joyce prepares his readers for that approach by presenting the minds of his characters in various related ways in the stories that intervene between "The Sisters" and "The Dead." The first sentence of "The Sisters" aside, the techniques of narration in all three stories told in first person are essentially the same. But there are some important distinctions to be made. The most significant of these concerns the teller's changing distance from his earlier self. That distance increases as we proceed. While the style in all three is self-narration, it shifts gradually from a thoroughly consonant self-narration in "The Sisters" toward a style that occasionally approaches dissonant self-narration in "Araby." In this shift we find an early example of Joyce's coordinating of style and story. The style of "An Encounter" acts as the transition from consonance toward dissonance. Assuming that each story concerns the same boy and that he is slightly older in each than in the last, we have a fragmented autobiography. As the boy grows older, his experience is of a wider sort than previously, and his sense of himself changes. As in *A Portrait*, the varying mix of elements in the teller's style indicates the character's changing sensibility. The changes the boy undergoes, like the developments Stephen experiences, prepare for his greater critical distance from his own past. While the teller's language implies such a distance, it only develops for the boy as he moves toward a position of judgment that will enable him eventually to tell his own story.

In "An Encounter," the teller presents thought less directly and intimately than in "The Sisters." There is no self-quoted monologue. Instead, we are given the attitudes of the group of friends to their common experiences and of the boy and his companion to their adventures. The narration includes many fewer words indicating thought than in the previous story. They are different in kind from the earlier ones and tend to be clustered in the last four pages. The affective diction of narration gives us the boy's reactions, impressions, consideration, surprise, and motivation, but not his thinking, feeling, wondering, imagining, and remembering as in "The Sisters." Although the narration in these final pages communicates the boy's sense of disquiet, his agitation per se is secondary. The narrator is less concerned than in "The Sisters" with the specific fluctuation of the boy's emotions and his thoughts. Instead, he emphasizes the scene causing the emotions and the boy's own provisional judgment about his feelings at the end.

In "Araby," the narrator continues to increase our distance and his own from his boyhood perspective. I have claimed that the style nearly becomes dissonant self-narration because the teller expresses judgments about his own earlier state of mind. He refers to that state metaphorically; for instance, as "all my foolish blood" (*D* 30). The introduction of metaphors is an important distancing factor that draws our attention to the teller's language as well as to the boy's interior speech. The style here moves toward those passages in *A Portrait* in which rhythmic language and flowing syntax evoke the character's romantic and sexually charged thoughts:

"These noises converged in a single sensation of life for me: I imagined that I bore my chalice safely through a throng of foes. Her name sprang to my lips at moments in strange prayers and praises. . . . My eyes were often full of tears . . . and at times a flood from my heart seemed to pour itself out into my bosom. I thought little of the future. . . . But my body was like a harp and her words and gestures were like fingers running upon the wires" (*D* 31). I stress the similarity to the rhythmically eloquent presentations of Stephen's adolescent thoughts in *A Portrait* because style in both the story and the longer work indicates the narrator's presence. We even have an alliterative series embedded in the passage: "Single sensation . . . through a throng . . . prayers and praises." And the language is more highly metaphorical than the narration anywhere in the two preceding stories. While the narration ascribes the metaphor of the chalice explicitly to the boy's imagination, the metaphor of an emotional "flood" may originate in the teller's past thoughts or his present ones. And the sentence about the future seems the narrator's judgment rendered *in* the future, relative to the time of the narrative, about his past. For reader and teller, what the character does *not* think about—his future—is at least as important as the teller's past. With that sentence and the following simile of the harp, which is surely the teller's, not the character's, the narrator stresses his distance from the earlier feelings he presents.

I have intentionally left out some important phrases and statements in this passage that occur during the indicated ellipses. Even before the simile at the end of the passage, the narrator reminds us of his mediating presence by providing a commentary on his earlier state of mind. These obtrusive statements create a counterpoint to the boy's thoughts in the midst of their representation: "Praises which I myself did not understand. . . . (I could not tell why). . . . I thought little of the future. I did not know whether. . . ." (*D* 31). On the next page the narrator renders overtly his judgment of his own childish thoughts: "What innumerable follies laid waste my waking and sleeping thoughts after that evening!" The exclamations in "The Sisters" are always examples of self quoted interior monologue. In "Araby" they can be the teller's commentary. Toward the end of the story, the narrator's language and the character's are more closely merged through the teller's subtle infusion of the boy's attitudes into his descriptions, as in the following report about action and scene: "After an intolerable delay the train moved out of the station slowly. . . . In front of me was a large building which displayed the magical name" (*D* 34). The delay would be "intolerable" and the name "magical" only to the boy's consciousness. And a merger of views occurs by implication in the story's final paragraph when the narrator tells us that he saw himself "as a creature driven and derided by vanity" (*D* 35). Here the merger does *not* occur primarily through style but through a temporal dove-tailing. The attitude the boy achieves in the experiences recounted as the narrative of "Araby" meshes with the attitude toward himself he later expresses through the sometimes dissonant style of narration he employs as an adult writing about those experiences.

METAPHORS OF THE NARRATION/METAPHORS IN THE NARRATION: "EVELINE"

Joyce continues to employ metaphors once he shifts to narration in the third person after "Araby." Consequently, use of figurative language provides a thread linking different tales. While the origin of the figures in character's or teller's mind is not always indicated, generally the metaphoric language marks the narrator's presence. In the commentary on "Eveline," we shall examine Joyce's strategic placing of a simile in the story's final paragraph. I mention that placement now because it helps establish the continuity of the telling, despite the change in the grammatical person of the narrator. That continuity arises *not* from an invisible, impersonal narrator but from one willing to create similitudes. The narration's consistency, though, emerges not just through the continuing use of metaphorical language. Rather, it emerges because the metaphors create similar stances for narration, whether the narration is first- or third-person. Metaphor in "Araby" contributes substantially to the dissonant quality of the telling by emphasizing the difference between narrator and character. That dissonance and differentiation make the shift to third person less jarring than it might otherwise be. Like the simile at the end of "Eveline" and the later simile of the pearls at the beginning of "Two Gallants," the other metaphorical language in the middle stories tends to keep the narrator in the reader's view.

Metaphor in Joyce's fiction can also function structurally by giving the reader access to large rationales for the narration. Generally, the title rather than the language of narration contains this kind of structural metaphor. We have already seen the implications of the title of *Finnegans Wake* when treated as figures, both pun and metaphor. As I have interpreted it, that title focuses the reader's attention on the act of writing as telling but also suggests the possibility that the storytelling bears a determinate relationship to the narrative's action. Although I would not overemphasize the larger implications of Joyce's titles in *Dubliners*, several of them are suggestive, particularly in their interaction. We have already formulated some of the relationships between narration and narrative using the title of the second story. The encounter is the narrator's with himself and ours with both narrator and character, as well as the boy's encounter with the old man, with literature, and with his own feelings about his companion. Robert Scholes has suggested that the title "Counterparts" can be taken in a similar way when he argues that through style Joyce has offered us "the opportunity— and the challenge— . . . of becoming . . . Joyce's counterparts." Scholes speaks of the reader's "complicity" "in the creative process," and he claims that by "entering the world of *Dubliners* we all acknowledge our Irishness."[18] It is worth adding that in *Dubliners* Joyce is still only developing styles for creating the reader's complicity. The reader's active re-creative dialectical relationship with the text emerges more fully from the works following *Dubliners*.

While Scholes quite correctly stresses the sense of similarity implied in the word "counterpart," that word can also refer to something complementary that functions to complete. In this sense the reader is the teller's counterpart not only because the reading and the telling of Joyce's fiction are similar creative processes but also because the reader completes the teller's work. In these stories the teller is the counterpart of his characters sometimes because of a resemblance between them but more often because the teller's representations of consciousness complete in some way the characters' acts of mind. We have seen the teller's acts of completion already in the stories told in the first person, in which the character's silence has been transformed into the narration presenting it. A related, though not identical, transformation occurs in the later stories whenever the narrator presents the character's mind in the narration's language. I shall deal further with the difference and the similarity between these two types of transformation in my commentary on the end of "Eveline." In "The Dead" the act of speaking *for* the silent and the inarticulate is inscribed in the narrative as well as in the narration when Gabriel Conroy speaks, however inadequately, *for* as well as *to* the people who attend his aunts' party. With regard to this story especially, Scholes is right to mention the relevance of the volume's title to the reader's involvement. By creating the possibility of that involvement, in "The Dead" Joyce begins to express, and allows us to recognize, the cultural consciousness linking past and present that we encounter repeatedly in the later fiction. Teller, reader, and characters of these tales are *all* Dubliners, and they are all related in various ways to the dead. We become members of an extended family created by the book. In his after-dinner speech Conroy speaks for and about the dead, with whom he ultimately associates himself. In their analogous acts of speaking, Conroy and the teller of his story are counterparts. But the titles of these stories, while significant as metaphors for the teller's and the reader's stance toward the narratives, do not call attention to themselves in the way Joyce's later titles do. Those later names point more obviously to structural principles of narration, as in *A Portrait*, where the structural principle involves the dual reference to both portrayer and portrait.

In "Eveline," the simile at the story's end depends for its effect on preceding strategies for presenting Eveline's thoughts. The story's style consists essentially of psycho-narration together with some brief instances of quoted monologue that are identified through the use of the exclamation point ("Home!" *D* 37) or the colon (*D* 36). The narrated monologue, toward which these other techniques, especially in combination, tend, also occurs here occasionally. In the example of narrated monologue in "Eveline" quoted earlier, the lack of deictic references and exclamations belies the feeling of immediacy and of alignment between character and teller that is possible with this technique. Overall, early in the story we have the impression of Eveline in meditation and of her process of mind as a logical, orderly procedure, though not a sophisticated one. But toward the end of the story, narrated monologue occurs more often, and the language of Eveline's thoughts becomes heightened. The teller renders one climax of Eveline's agitation in a particularly intense, comparatively extended passage of narrated monologue:

> She stood up in a sudden impulse of terror. Escape! She must escape! Frank would save her. He would give her life, perhaps love, too. But she wanted to live. Why should she be unhappy? She had a right to happiness. Frank would take her in his arms, fold her in his arms. He would save her. (*D* 40)

After presenting Eveline's act of standing in affective terms, the narrator shifts first to an interior exclamation as quoted monologue and then to the narrated monologue. The remainder of the paragraph can be understood as the character's interior speech in first person and a combination of present and future tenses that have been translated into the third person, the past tense, and conditional expressions.

After this climax of style and story, a row of periods intervenes before the brief conclusion, which is narrated differently. In the conclusion, the narrator alternates, as earlier, between presenting scene and presenting Eveline's thoughts. But now those thoughts exhibit the emotional agitation of the climactic passage of narrated monologue. The narrator closes the story with a short paragraph in which he seems to withdraw completely from the character's perspective:

> He rushed beyond the barrier and called to her to follow. He was shouted at to go on but he still called to her. She set her white face to him, passive, like a helpless animal. Her eyes gave him no sign of love or farewell or recognition. (*D* 41)

While the focus on action and on description in this paragraph might suggest impersonality, objectivity, and the withholding of judgment, the narrator's stance is *not* entirely impersonal. In his simile the narrator is not simply recording facts. Through the comparison, he expresses a judgment about Eveline's state of mind: that she has been reduced by her situation and by her own reaction to a helpless, passive condition. By comparing her to an animal, the teller does not suggest by any means that she is subhuman, simply that her condition is one of severe, paralyzing fear. The comparison takes on this *affective* connotation as the conclusion of an accumulating series of words and phrases indicating fear that fills the story's last two pages (*D* 40-41), not as a complete withdrawal from an affective presentation: "trembled," "terror," "distress" (used twice), "nausea," "frenzy," "anguish." Rather than withdrawing from the character's mind absolutely, the narrator has chosen to represent it in a new way that builds on and completes the earlier representations of her mind at the same time as it brings the story to closure.

The language of narration manages to work in at least two ways at once. While it expresses what the character's actions and feeling mean, it also announces through figuration its difference from any mode of thinking or speaking available to the character either in the narrative action or as a result of that action. We can read the shift in style as the narrator's demarcation of one limit for his own techniques in this story. Once he has brought the character gradually to a climactic state of frenzy, he can render that agitation only metaphorically, not by any seemingly more direct representation. As an admission that Eveline's state of mind is beyond the reach of referential language, the act of shifting styles *itself* represents that state of mind which cannot be rendered adequately through psycho-narration, quoted monologue, and narrated monologue. This structural representation involves the two meanings of counterparts as both resemblance and completion. As a means of closure, the shift in style is appropriate in two ways. Structurally, it mirrors the change the character undergoes when she breaks off her previous communication with Frank and within herself. She indicates that change through the physical gestures of clutching the railing, setting her face to (that is, both toward and against) him, and showing no recognition. Since Eveline's turning her face toward Frank is also her rejection of him by setting the features of her face against him, Joyce can include the psychological within a physical description. (He does this again when he describes Gabriel's tears at the end of "The Dead.") The stylistic change also enacts the difference between character and narrator in a more definite way than do other aspects of the story. The difference recalls the contrast in the tales told in first person between the teller and the reticent character that is his earlier self. The act of representing in the final paragraph counters Eveline's refusal to give any "sign of love or farewell or recognition" (*D* 41). The teller's stylistic farewell recognizes her state. But the resemblance to the narrating situation in the preceding stories is just that, a resemblance, not an equivalence. The boy's development is toward speech. Eveline's is toward silence.

PAINFUL CASES

The narration of "Eveline" sets the mode for the eight stories of adolescence and adult life. In all these tales, besides frequently evoking the character's thoughts, the narrator always asserts his presence and his difference from the characters, but not obtrusively. He creates two effects at once: one of intimacy, the other of withdrawal. At the end of "Eveline" he assumes his last ambiguous position in the narration with particular subtlety and concluding force. Neither the representation of consciousness nor the narrator's separation from his characters is particularly surprising. But the combination can be, for it results in a strong tension and contrast within the narration. The narrator generally controls that tension by translating it into an orderly fluctuation of perspective, a modulation emphasizing now the character's view, now the narrator's, depending on the exact mix of techniques and diction. But the tension is always there. It emerges most strongly when we feel in the modulations, as we regularly do, the narrator's dominance. We are dealing not simply with an antithesis between two wholly separate poles. Each position in the contrast possesses the potential for becoming the other view or at least for moving closer to that view, and, in so doing, for establishing a dialectical relationship. That relationship is our oscillating perspective.

We can put this potential in another way: the inner and the outer views are not absolutely segregated between the character and the narrator respectively. The overcoming of separation can develop out of either the narrator's or the character's pole of the contrast. In *Dubliners* the development of the character's view toward the narrator's occurs for the most part in the stories told in the first person. As we have seen, the boy's sense of himself moves toward coincidence with his own later judgment about himself, based, of course, on his earlier experience. In the middle stories, although some of the characters may come to realizations about themselves that narrator and reader share, a wide gap of sensibility predominates. The mergers of inner and outer views that seem possible in the third-person tales develop from the narrator's perspective. The simile in "Eveline" is a good example. The narrator's language allows the inner view so prominent in the story to nest within what seems ostensibly to be his outer view. This use of style does not yet achieve fully the oscillating perspective of *A Portrait*, with its radically ambiguous relationship between teller and character. But it is that perspective's immediate percursor, a crucial stage on the road to its development.

Without the curious first sentence of "The Sisters," there would seem little possibility that the superimposing of views in these stories could be developed further than the style of "Eveline." The creation of an oscillating perspective in third-person narration seems especially unlikely. Joyce's ability to achieve it nevertheless is one of his great strengths as a writer. He presents it more fully than in "The Sisters" once he combines the two movements that have been largely separated in the first- and third-person stories: the shift of the character's perspective toward that of the narrator and the shift of the narrator's style toward one embodying the character's perspective together with his own. The narration of the middle stories never reaches that combination. Instead, by reiterating the narrator's difference from his characters, it prepares us for the change to tales of public life.

The particular combinations of techniques and choices of language in these middle stories deserve careful analysis. Because our primary concern is the overall development of the style toward techniques and visions enabling Joyce to write *A Portrait* and *Ulysses*, I shall limit myself, for the most part, to brief comments about the remaining stories. I shall treat in greater detail only "A Painful Case," the transition to the stories of public life. In general, the narrator maintains his distance by presenting the character's thoughts in ways that mark them as indisputably the character's attitudes. A number of the strategies from "Eveline" reappear, at times in slightly exaggerated ways. In "The Boarding House," although Mrs. Mooney's thoughts are presented at some length, we have little sense of immediacy in the presentation. While Eveline's mental processes are generally logical, though unsophisticated, Mrs. Mooney's are cold and calculating, essentially devoid of emotion except as a mask for self-interest. The colloquial, conventional, or cliché quality of the character's internal speech is often more extreme in the stories after "Eveline." For example, when Jimmy Doyle comments to himself that his companions are "devils of fellows" (*D* 48) and that "this was seeing life, at least," no matter what techniques may be used for presenting thought with seeming immediacy, we feel strongly our own and the teller's difference from the character. In this story, the narrator reports the wonderfully muddled metaphors Doyle uses to characterize his own experience: "The journey laid a magical finger on the genuine pulse of life and gallantly the machinery of human nerves strove to answer the bounding courses of the swift blue animal" (*D* 45). Doyle may be trying to fuse his body and mind with the car in which he is riding, but the teller is clearly not merging with his character's mind, the ungainly vehicle for his narration. "Clay" is the extreme case of thought evoked in conventional language in *Dubliners*. Often the ostensible representation of mind in that story would better be called a report of attitudes. The evocations of Maria's perspective are so flat and unelaborated that they seem little more than sense perceptions couched in vague, stilted language.

In the more complicated stories, "A Little Cloud" and "Two Gallants," both written late and inserted into the already formed collection, the metaphorical elements of the narrator's style differentiate his statements clearly from the character's internal ones. Like the simile of the pearls at the beginning of "Two Gallants," the narrator's language in "A Little Cloud" calls attention to itself vividly though not at great length. As Little Chandler walks the streets of Dublin on his way to meet Ignatius Gallaher for a drink, he passes through an area in which "a horde of grimy children populated the street": "They stood or ran in the roadway or crawled up the steps before the gaping doors or squatted like mice upon the thresholds. Little Chandler gave them no thought. He picked his way deftly through all that minute vermin-like life and under the shadow of the gaunt spectral mansions in which the old nobility of Dublin had roistered. No memory of the past touched him, for his mind was full of a present joy" (*D* 71-72). This passage bears comparison with Stephen's walk across Dublin on the way to the university (*P* 176), in which he associates what he sees with styles of language. By contrast, in "A Little Cloud" the interest of the walk for the reader is not what passes through the character's mind but the narrator's style for presenting what does *not* occur to the character. Here is one of those brilliant passages in these middle stories exhibiting sharply the opposition between teller and character. While Little Chandler ignores his present physical surroundings and their past, the narrator turns them both into striking, rhythmical language. The juxtaposition of high and low styles, the one evoking a possibly noble past, the other a grimy present, anticipates directly the contrasts of style and focus in *A Portrait*. The energy of this story is not in Little Chandler's mind, however immediately or distantly rendered, but in the mediations the teller employs to present the life that Little Chandler gives "no thought."

Another kind of contrast between teller and character emerges at the end of "Counterparts" in a conclusion resembling in certain ways the end of "Eveline." As in the earlier story, the concluding two pages are separated from the rest of the narration. The conclusion in both stories begins with a presentation of the character's thoughts followed by a focus on scene and action. But the shift is of different proportions and more extreme in "Counterparts." The presentation of thought is briefer; that of scene, action, and speech, longer. As in "Eveline," the character reaches a pitch of agitation (for Farrington a compound of frustration and anger, not fear) that accompanies a break in communication, this time as the father confronts and terrorizes his helpless son. But there are no similes or metaphors to announce and possibly to bridge the gap between inner and outer views, to modify the starkness of the shift to an external perspective. While the narrator's change in mode reflects again the failure of communication between characters, now it represents as well a more resolute turning away from the character's mind and a harsher judgment. The narrator can speak for the character's interior silence or turmoil in these stories, when he wishes to, but here he allows the character's actions to speak virtually for themselves.

In the symmetrical arrangement of the stories in *Dubliners*, "A Painful Case" provides the transition to the stories of public life, just as "Araby" and "Eveline" act jointly as the transition from first- to third-person narration. If we leave aside "The Dead" temporarily and consider the volume's shape before that story was added to the sequence, the large features of the symmetry are evident. What were originally the last three stories balance and, in certain ways, counter the first triad. "A Painful

Case" carries the burden of transition by reversing some and duplicating other features of the earlier shift separating the first triad from the rest. As we have seen, "Eveline" ends with a change in style indicating the narrator's relative withdrawal from the character's mind, which the narration has prepared us for since early in the story. Her thoughts are largely a response to a situation she has not encountered previously, one that holds out the possibility of escape from Dublin. In Duffy's story, the movement of the narration is different. There is little report of thought at the start, much less than in the first pages of "Eveline." Within the story, the style develops gradually toward the intimate techniques of narrated and quoted monologue, which the narrator employs, then abandons, then employs again in a sustained way for the story's conclusion. Although the narrator does draw away partially from the character's perspective and from these techniques in the final paragraph, the swerve is not nearly as extreme as at the ends of "Eveline" and "Counterparts."

The increasing intimacy of narration within "A Painful Case" reflects the character's changing perspectives, ones that make the placement of this story as the last of the middle sequence appropriate. What little report of thought the narrator includes at first consists of a few references to the character's attitudes. The handling of these brief references suggests that Duffy no longer needs to think actively about the way he feels and lives. His life has become a routine that he controls rigidly. Consequently, at first the narrator has little fluctuation of habitual behavior and mental processes to report. Some of Duffy's attitudes and actions make the story a preamble for the ones to follow. We learn immediately that he lives in Chapelizod because he wishes to withdraw from Dublin. He desires to live as if he were not an inhabitant of either the city or its "mean, modern and pretentious suburbs" (*D* 107). His disdain for the city prepares us for the teller's decision in the next three stories to adopt a distanced, ironic stance in relation to his characters and their world. Through another detail of Duffy's habitual thoughts mentioned early in the story, the narrator emphasizes the correlation between the character's withdrawal and a perspective for narration: "He lived at a little distance from his body, regarding his own acts with doubtful side-glances. He had an odd autobiographical habit which led him to compose in his mind from time to time a short sentence about himself containing a subject in the third person and a predicate in the past tense" (*D* 108). Duffy's habit is reminiscent of *The Life of Giambattista Vico Written by Himself*, an autobiography in third person and past tense that Joyce would have known.[19]

The mention of autobiography and the implied contrast between first- and third-person narration make the comparison between this story, the first three, and "Eveline" almost inevitable. While Eveline's final agitation is not amenable to direct presentation in referential language, the conclusion Duffy arrives at subsequent to his disturbing experiences consists of a self-conscious judgment that the narrator can report directly. The kind of judgment Duffy makes and even the act of judging contribute to the transition to the next stories. The contrast I am suggesting between Eveline and Duffy and between their stories concerns the characters' responses to crises. By the time Eveline fails to board the boat with Frank, she has been virtually agitated out of thinking rationally. Duffy's crises do not affect him in precisely that way, though they do finally undermine his habitual modes of thought. Ultimately, Duffy begins to consider his own actions and thoughts critically when forced to by personal distress, arising because his familiar attitudes cannot cope adequately with his experiences. Inadequate, inept, familiar behavior and attitudes will be the narrator's continuing focus of judgment in the stories to come.

After sketching the regularities of Duffy's life in the first few paragraphs of the story, the narrator presents the character's mind more frequently and with increasing specificity. This increase corresponds to Duffy's growing tendency to be communicative as his relationship with Mrs. Sinico develops toward intimacy. As "little by little he entangled his thoughts with hers" (*D* 110), the narrator gives us more of Duffy's thoughts. The narrator emphasizes Mrs. Sinico's role as catalyst for Duffy's thinking by first repeating nearly verbatim this statement about the entangling of their thoughts and then comparing the couple to a sensitive plant and its soil: "Little by little, as their thoughts entangled, they spoke of subjects less remote. Her companionship was like a warm soil about an exotic. . . . This union exalted him, wore away the rough edges of his character, emotional-ised his mental life" (*D* 111). In the paragraph in which this passage occurs, the narrator places himself temporarily at some remove from the details of his characters' attitudes by summarizing, in a series of iterative statements, the history of the private encounters between them. The actions and thoughts presented occur "often" (used twice), "little by little," "many times," "sometimes," and "more and more." Within the context of these iterations the teller inserts the similitude of soil and plant along with his judgment about the effect the relationship gradually works on Duffy's harshness.

At the end of the paragraph, the narrator punctuates the summary by shifting briefly to a more direct rendering of thought in the present tense, as if the statement by Duffy's interior voice were direct discourse: "We cannot give ourselves, it said: we are our own." This more direct rendering marks a moment of intensity in the characters' relationship. Although the sentence is the narrator's report of what Duffy hears his "strange impersonal" interior voice say, it also tells us what Duffy says to Mrs. Sinico just prior to her singular act that will end their affair. The narrator achieves the jointure between iterative and singular skillfully by allowing this specific example of Duffy's inner, and perhaps audible, speech to emerge from the otherwise sketchily presented discourses. The ambiguity in the narration by which the inner voice can be read as becoming audible during the characters' talks pinpoints the immediate context and the provocation for Mrs. Sinico's action. Her emotions, like his, are finally manifested as perceivable gestures. The interplay between man and woman, thought and speech, emotion and gesture, language and sexuality introduced in this paragraph only to be abruptly truncated is developed more fully, as we have seen, in Stephen's act of writing his villanelle in *A Portrait*.

As in several of the earlier stories, but unlike the presentation of the villanelle, in "A Painful Case" the narrator's act of storytelling stands in clear contrast to the character's actions. Like the boy in the first stories, Duffy usually keeps his thoughts to himself. During their conversations, Mrs. Sinico asks him why he does "not write out his thoughts" (*D* 111). He responds, in effect, that he does not wish to expose himself to misconstrual. Instead of writing, he speaks his thoughts to her, only, in his opinion, to be wildly misunderstood. For Duffy, the experience confirms his general propensity not to try communicating and his specific one not to write. The narrator, however, does write out Duffy's thinking, including even his abandoning any significant, self-reflective mental activity. It is clear from those thoughts and from Duffy's actions that *he* and not his listener misunderstands the implications of his own statements. The remainder of the story concerns how Duffy comes to realize the meaning and effects his attitudes can have when he acts upon them, as he does with Mrs. Sinico. He finally discovers, too late to mend his error, that *he* has misunderstood himself and his companion.

Once Duffy "break[s] off their intercourse," he returns to the "even way of life" he established before meeting Mrs. Sinico. He maintains his interests in music and philosophy, but he writes "seldom" and avoids "concerts lest he should meet her" (*D* 112). Stylistically, the narration also regresses. The movement of style in the story's second half parallels that of the first half: from little or no report of thought to a great deal of it. But in the latter half the shifts and contrasts of style are more exaggerated. As at the story's beginning, the narrator starts with a mediated presentation of Duffy's mind. Only now the references to thought are so attenuated as to be almost absent. It would be hard to call the style here psycho-narration, because the narrator does not present the character's attitudes explicitly. He can do without them, having previously established for the reader the nature of Duffy's mind. He merely mentions a few details of Duffy's life in summary together with a comment about "the orderliness of his mind." This phrase contains the only direct reference to consciousness in the narration concerned with Duffy's reestablished routine prior to his chance reading of the newspaper article. This segment of the narration suggests even more emphatically than before that Duffy's life has become so routine that he has to think hardly at all in order to continue his normal round of living. It also intensifies by counterpoint the effect of the greatly agitated thinking that occurs after Duffy reads the article. In Duffy's reaction to the article, the narrator presents the character's thoughts more directly and at greater length than earlier.

Like the thought reported as if speech that destroys the affair with Mrs. Sinico, the more direct presentation of consciousness in the story's last pages indicates a period of intensity in the character's emotional life. The length of the representation of mind and the prominence of narrated and quoted interior monologue, as well as psycho-narration in the conclusion, set it apart as special not only in this story but in the entire volume. Except for the final pages of "The Dead," Duffy's response to the article is the longest intense evocation of thought in *Dubliners*. The narrator interrupts the flow of thinking at length only once, to describe the scene at the pub Duffy visits in order to meditate. This description, like the presentation of Duffy's routine, increases by contrast our sense of the character's interior turmoil. By presenting Duffy's thoughts the teller reaches an extreme of style, after which he switches to another kind of narration for the next three stories. The switch that occurs between stories here is reminiscent of the change in "Eveline" when the narrator shifts his mode of narration in the final paragraph. And the change resembles the more extreme shifts of style in *A Portrait*. There is a strong irony at work in the style at the end of "A Painful Case" that makes the change appropriate. The longest, most vivid evocations of Duffy's interior voice present his growing realization that he has lost the voice he might have had. That realization silences even the voice he does possess. The interior voices of characters will be almost completely silent in the three stories that follow.

Momentarily, Duffy thinks he hears and feels Mrs. Sinico again: "At moments he seemed to feel her voice touch his ear, her hand touch his. He stood still to listen" (*D* 117). This act of listening is the beginning of the end for Duffy's interior life, which has temporarily reached a pitch of sustained intensity before its demise. Besides presenting Duffy's thoughts as narrated and quoted monologue, the narrator renders that intensity in its final moments as the character's mind turning to metaphors in order to grasp its own plight. With these metaphors the narrator begins drawing away slightly from Duffy's perspective. Duffy thinks of himself twice in the penultimate paragraph as "outcast from life's feast." Then, as his interior colloquy stops, his perceptions begin to be largely metaphorical and symbolical. The "goods train" he sees in the distance looks "like a worm with a fiery head." He hears the "drone of the engine reiterating the syllables of her name." Once Duffy has associated the instrument of Mrs. Sinico's death with an infernal worm, which also suggests the decay of the body in the grave, the sound reminding him of her violent end displaces the interior voice that was his memory of Mrs. Sinico. After the locomotive moves out of hearing he can discover only a silence that is both external and internal: "He could not feel her near him in the darkness nor her voice touch his ear. He waited for some minutes listening. He could hear nothing: the night was perfectly silent. He listened again: perfectly silent. He felt that he was alone" (*D* 117). As in the earlier climactic report of thought as if speech, this passage fuses inner and outer but with a reversal of implication, because the external silence replaces speech and indicates an interior silencing.

The earlier statement, "we are our own," resembles both grammatically and rhythmically the story's final clause, "he was alone." But that final clause must be read differently from the earlier one. To end the story, the narrator chooses the mediation of psycho-narration rather than the more direct techniques of either quoted or narrated monologue he has used frequently in the preceding paragraphs.[20] He moves sufficiently away from the character's perspective to provide another frame of reference. Because the statement occurs in the past tense rather than the present, we cannot read it as a gnomic expression or as audible speech, as we could the earlier remark. And it does not appear to indicate the character's clearly formulated interior speech. Instead, through psycho-narration, the narrator translates an unverbalized or partially verbalized feeling. Unlike the earlier statement, this one is singular, not plural. It applies specifically to the character *only* rather than to a couple or to the generality of humankind. There is no need now for the statement to be plural, or audible, or even verbalized: the character communes only with himself. The irony of the story's last sentence is vivid and startling: we can read it as an example and as the result of Duffy's "odd autobiographical habit" of mind, which expresses the essence of his habits.

Like the boy at the end of "Araby," Duffy reaches a state of mind that includes a self-conscious, negative judgment about himself. The boy's insight, however, concerns his connection to a social world populated by people similar to himself, no matter how unattractive he might find those people and the world he shares with them. In his antithetical perception, Duffy realizes with pain and guilt that his habitual decision to withdraw from intercourse of emotional and sexual kinds has resulted in his permanent isolation from others. The intensity of this realization overcomes the disdain that has always protected him from honest self-reflection. The boy's new insight prepares for the outward turn that occurs in "Eveline" with the shift to a third-person narration representing consciousness. Together with his cynical and pessimistic attitudes about the relations among people, Duffy's self-consciously perceived alienation provides an apt place in the volume for a shift to a narration in which consciousness seems hardly to be an element of character. In the conclusions of both "Eveline" and "A Painful Case," the style includes its own internal countermovement. In "Eveline," the concluding paragraph incorporates as a kind of parenthesis a representation of the character's state of mind when the narrator inserts a simile into his otherwise external view. In "A Painful Case," although the inner view dominates the later portions of the story, it

turns into its own opposite when the character's thoughts become a judgment rendered by the character about his own status as an outsider. Like the
boy of "Araby," Duffy has learned to see himself as others might see him
but without the boy's possibility of developing a mature style of writing as
compensatory intercourse for the communication he has destroyed.

THE POSTLUDE: WITHIN AND BEYOND PUBLIC LIFE

It seems unlikely that the characters in "Ivy Day in the Committee
Room," "A Mother," or "Grace" could ever come to any clear judgment
about their own lives. They certainly do not achieve such insights in these
stories. With only a few exceptions, the narrator maintains a resolutely
external perspective in this triad. He concerns himself primarily with the
characters' behavior, not their thoughts. Consequently, these tales stand
manifestly apart from the preceding eleven, in all of which the narrator
presents mind as well as manners. Of the three stories, "Ivy Day" eschews
the presentation of consciousness most completely. The contrast with "A
Painful Case" is particularly acute. We move from the story in *Dubliners*
with the fewest instances of speech quoted as direct discourse to the one
story in the collection composed almost entirely of quoted dialogue.
Although Hynes is apparently strongly moved after his recitation, the
narrator does not present his feelings. Like the boy in the first stories,
O'Connor is careful "to hide his emotion" (*D* 135), but we never learn the
nature of that emotion. In the teller's single report of a character's attitude,
he tells us only that Crofton, like James Duffy, is condescending: "He
considered his companions beneath him" (*D* 131). The teller employs none
of the techniques for presenting mind that characterize the narration of
earlier stories. Instead, he sets rigorous limits on his language in a stylistic
exercise that produces one of the volume's extremes. The new restrictions
create a shift in style as evident as the earlier change from first to third
person, though without any manifest change in the grammatical person of
the telling.

The focus of narration in both "A Mother" and "Grace" is still largely
external, but less extremely so than in "Ivy Day." Despite some limited
report of thought in these stories, we are never given any sense of a process
of thinking. We know only a few attitudes held by selected characters. None
of these tales of public life has a central character in the way the other stories
do. Even Mrs. Kearney, while nominally the central figure of "A Mother,"
is more the social role named by the story's title than a psychologically
realized character. Each of these stories concerns a *group* of persons
interacting in public, rather than private, ways. Although some of the earlier
stories also concern groups—for instance, "The Boarding House"—in
them private processes of mind are always vividly presented. When the

interior life of a character does emerge briefly in these late stories, it generally turns out to be dominated by restrictive social conventions and inflections. Although we hear occasionally what Mrs. Kearney "perceived" or "determined" (*D* 137), "wondered" or "noticed" (*D* 139), "knew" or "thought" (*D* 141), her attitudes are always presented fleetingly, often as clichés. The psycho-narration providing the character's attitude never approaches the teller's perspective. The only possible instance of quoted monologue in the story conveys Mrs. Kearney's conventional view in a present tense that we read as gnomic: "It cost a pretty penny; but there are occasions when a little expense is justifiable" (*D* 138). She apparently has no intensely held, privately formulated beliefs. The only hint of a mind with values different from Mrs. Kearney's occurs in Mr. Hendrick's mildly sensual response to Miss Healy's polite attentions (*D* 145).

In both "Eveline" and "A Painful Case," the narration reaches a climax in passages of narrated monologue that occur near the tale's conclusion. In "A Mother," the narration's climax occurs not as interior dialogue, but as its external equivalent, the indirect discourse used to present the "hive of excitement" (*D* 147) in the dressing room just before the Kearneys leave. The mother's talk is the loudest, most insistent buzz in this hive. In Mrs. Kearney's indirectly reported speech—as presumably in her thoughts—the clichés tumble over one another in an ecstasy of verbal fumbling starting with her representation of her antagonists' thinking: "They thought they had only a girl to deal with and that, therefore, they could ride roughshod over her. But she would show them their mistake. They wouldn't have dared to have treated her like that if she had been a man. But she would see that her daughter got her rights: she wouldn't be fooled. If they didn't pay her to the last farthing she would make Dublin ring" (*D* 148). By presenting Mrs. Kearney's version of society's conventional wisdom as her cliché speech and thought, her speech as thought, the narrator prepares directly for the more complicated narration he uses at the beginning of "The Dead."

The individual minds in "Grace" are represented as no less superficial than those of the two preceding stories. Mentioned regularly, though not often, in the story's second half, Mr. Kiernan's impressions and feelings give us no sense of any significant interior life. His wife's attitude of resignation toward their marriage, while presented at greater length (*D* 156–58) than any of her husband's reactions, is not one she is in the process of formulating. Rather, she has drawn her conclusions long before the events of the narrative, and they play no dynamic role in those events. In the few instances of psycho-narration in "Grace," the narrator does not create any impression that the character's interior language has infiltrated his diction.

Through a variety of the stylistic contagion withheld in "Grace," Joyce achieves one of the transformations in style that make "The Dead" a coda for the other stories. Homer Obed Brown has this transformation in view when he claims that in the first pages of "The Dead," "the narrator's voice represents the . . . group mind of the occasion," or "the spirit of the occasion as experienced by the chief participants."[21] As Brown suggests, the narrator evokes first the thoughts of the maid, Lily, who greets visitors, then shifts to the thoughts of the hostesses, the Misses Morkan. The style provides a sublation by combining aspects of narration the teller has segregated in the groups of preceding tales. This sublation foreshadows the fusion that occurs in the final episodes of *Ulysses*. In the stories of public life, from an external view the narrator has presented groups interacting in public situations, either working in concert or at cross-purposes. But he has largely withheld the interior voices of characters, which, in earlier stories, have been incorporated into the narration's diction. Now the two modes of telling are brought together when the mingled voices of characters acting in concert emerge as narration.

The medley of voices in the first three paragraphs of "The Dead" is not, however, characteristic of the story. The narrator does not return to it explicitly during the remainder of the first part or in the two subsequent parts. In the brief coda that follows Gretta's falling asleep at the end of the third part, another related interplay of voices defines the narration. As in "Two Gallants," the teller begins in one style, only to modify it when he introduces the two central characters. The emergence of a central figure as a strong psychological presence sets "The Dead" clearly apart from the three preceding stories. Again, there is a fusion of modes, for "The Dead" is the story of *both* the group and the individual, the story of *both* public and adult life. The curious medley of voices in the story's prelude, like the first sentence of "The Sisters," focuses attention on the teller's role, especially on his relationships to the group his characters compose and to the character that emerges from among them as central.

Because of the opening, the act of telling bears a close structural relationship to Gabriel Conroy's actions and thoughts. We first encounter the narrator in the initial paragraphs making his voice out of the speech, interior and audible, of his characters. Their voices, thoroughly embedded in his narration, cannot be distinguished categorically from the narrator's voice. The story concerns a man who speaks for that same group of characters, to which he belongs. Among other things, Conroy discovers his necessary connection to people he has taken for granted and even disdained. By the end of the story, he understands his inextricable relationship to a community, a relationship that is implied as well by the teller's stance in the fusion of voices. Because of that stance, the style of narration communicates Conroy's attitude in ways that take us back to the beginning of "The Sisters."

As part of the process of making the character's insight available to the reader through style, the narrator exposes us to Conroy's mind gradually as the narrative develops. The introduction of techniques one by one and the strategic use of them once they have been established resembles Joyce's method in *A Portrait*. "The Dead" is clearly the stylistic proving ground that makes possible the configuration of techniques in the later work. By the end of the first part, the narrator has used all the basic devices for presenting consciousness in a third-person narration. In the second part (186–206), he employs those devices more frequently, at greater length, and with numerous variations, and he begins to place them strategically with respect to the rest of the narration. At the end of this part, we encounter one of the story's two climaxes, one not rendered as a presentation of mind. In the third part (206–24), the longest sustained presentation of consciousness in *Dubliners* provides the second climax as coda and conclusion of "The Dead."

The teller accomplishes the transition from the story's introductory paragraphs by involving Lily and the Misses Morkan, whose voices we have heard indirectly already, centrally in the initial dialogue with Gabriel. Lily, the first to speak, even tells Gabriel what her mistresses "thought" about his tardiness. And we hear the voices of Kate and Julia Morkan not directly, but as indirect discourse (*D* 177), filtered through stylistic devices like those used in the first paragraphs. Before presenting Gabriel's thoughts as psycho-narration, the narrator describes Lily and what Gabriel knows of her unambiguously from Gabriel's perspective. The style's direct quality depends on his being alone with her in the pantry. Next, by interpreting a change in Gabriel's features psychologically, the narrator adopts a device that is almost psycho-narration. When Gabriel blunders by mentioning the subject of marriage to Lily, he "coloured *as if* he felt he had made a mistake" (*D* 178; my emphasis). While Conroy waits alone outside the drawing room, the narrator begins the psycho-narration in a paragraph containing numerous references to thought: "discomposed," "cast a gloom over him," "undecided," "feared," "reminded" (*D* 179). The paragraph ends with several sentences of narrated monologue: "He would only make himself ridiculous by quoting poetry to them which they could not understand. They would think that he was airing his superior education. He would fail with them just as he had failed with the girl in the pantry. He had taken up a wrong tone. His whole speech was a mistake from first to last, an utter failure." But, as in the narrated monologue toward the beginning of "Eveline," no deictic references, exclamations, or vivid phrases encourage us strongly to read the sentences as originating in the character's first-person, present-tense ruminations, though they do appear to originate there. In the remainder of the first part, we do not encounter Gabriel's thoughts again. We do hear of an intention he does not fulfill, to ask his aunt some questions about Lily (*D* 181). But otherwise he engages in conversation or leaves the room to take care of Freddy Malins and escort his Aunt Kate.

The second part of "The Dead" begins with a lengthy presentation of Gabriel's thoughts during Mary Jane's performance (*D* 186–87). Here the teller's psycho-narration becomes narrated monologues that are more manifestly and vividly the character's voice than the earlier brief narrated monologue. Much of the language seems to come directly from the character's interior speech: "Probably," "It was strange," "Thanks to her," "and that was not true . . . at all." In Gabriel's confrontation with Miss Ivors, the narrator uses the device similarly. And for the first time he employs the colon to introduce a brief passage of narrated monologue, then as part of Miss Ivors' speech rendered as indirect discourse. The shared use of the typographical indicator helps the narrator shift from one technique to the other unobtrusively. Typically, in this middle section of the story, Gabriel does not listen to what goes on around him, and the narrator presents Gabriel's thoughts as narrated monologue. As in the scene with Miss Ivors, often the teller juxtaposes Gabriel's indirectly rendered inner speech with indirectly rendered audible speech. Shortly, while we hear Mrs. Malins's talk as indirect discourse, "Gabriel hardly heard what she said" (*D* 191), and we hear *his* thoughts as narrated monologue. But now the interior diction emerges in a more concentrated and ejaculatory way in his monologue: "Of course the girl or woman, or whatever she was, was an enthusiast but there was a time for all things. Perhaps he ought not to have answered her like that. But she had no right to call him a West Briton before people, even in joke. She had tried to make him ridiculous before people, heckling him and staring at him with her rabbit's eyes" (*D* 190). The series of nouns, the partial qualifications indicated by "but," the present participles, and the metaphor all contribute to present thought in a diction and rhythm that seem closer to internal expostulations than previously.

Finally, when Gabriel, alone in the window embrasure, looks out at the snow, his thoughts occur in the present tense and as conditional statements. The series of exclamations composes a passage of quoted interior monologue: "How cool it must be outside! How pleasant it would be to walk out alone, first along the river and then through the park! The snow would be lying on the branches of the trees and forming a bright cap on the top of the Wellington Monument. How much more pleasant it would be there than at the supper table!" (*D* 192). Then, in the process of reformulating his speech, Gabriel quotes to himself from his own published book review and from the talk he has yet to give. At this point, the narrator makes free, vivid use of various techniques to which he has accustomed us by punctuating Gabriel's thoughts with some heated inner remarks in a combination of narrated and quoted interior monologue: "Very good: that was one for Miss Ivors. What did he care that his aunts were only two ignorant old women?" (*D* 192).

In the next ten pages (192–202), the teller refers only twice briefly to Gabriel's thoughts and feelings (196–97) as Conroy listens to Aunt Julia sing and to conversations in which he is not involved, then busies himself carving the goose and eating. The narrator has referred with increasing frequency to Gabriel's thoughts and then abruptly withheld them as preparation for the long speech at the section's end. Just before Gabriel delivers his encomium to the party's hostesses, in an important passage the narrator alludes unmistakably to the previous sustained presentation of Gabriel's thoughts, his meditation on his speech in the window embrasure. The teller mentions again the "trembling fingers" (*D* 202), which Gabriel now leans against the tablecloth but previously had used to tap the cold windowpane (*D* 192). Then the narrator evokes the scene outside the window that Gabriel had thought about as the pleasant alternative to the supper table: "People, perhaps, were standing in the snow on the quay outside, gazing up at the lighted windows and listening to the waltz music. The air was pure there. In the distance lay the park where the trees were weighted with snow. The Wellington Monument wore a gleaming cap of snow that flashed westward over the whole field of Fifteen Acres" (*D* 202).

I quote this passage in its entirety because it foreshadows the other climax of the story in the final pages. The teller does not indicate explicitly in the narration that these statements occur in Gabriel's mind as he is about to speak. They could conceivably be the narrator's speculation about the scene outside the house. But by this point in the narration, we have become familiar enough with Gabriel's interior voice and with the narrator's techniques for presenting that voice to recognize the character's thoughts without any words or phrases explicitly pointing them out. The tentativeness of "perhaps" and the resemblance to the earlier passage that was clearly Gabriel's thought make the ascription to his mind entirely plausible. But the narrator leaves the voice ambiguous, as he will again more emphatically in the conclusion of "The Dead," and as the narrator of *A Portrait* does in the villanelle section (V.2). We can read the statements as both the narrator's speculations and the character's recollection transformed by imagination. The conclusion of the story will balance the ending of this part by reversing the proportions of Gabriel's audible speech to his ambiguously narrated thought. Here, a short passage of the character's thought, which is also the narrator's statement, precedes a long speech. There Gabriel's brief questions to his wife precede a long passage in which his interior voice and the narrator's voice are superimposed.

As in the late sections of *A Portrait*, we reach one kind of conclusion in the narration when the public voice of the character becomes especially prominent. For several pages, Gabriel's public speaking is interrupted only infrequently by the audience's comments and applause and by his own silent reflection. His speaking enables the singing "in unison, with Mr. Browne as leader" (*D* 205) and "Freddy Malins acting as officer with his fork on high" (*D* 206) that closes the section. The laudatory communal singing in honor of the hostesses is certainly comic, at least in part. And Gabriel has been reduced both by the infelicities of his speech and by the association with the besotted Malins and the boisterous Browne. But the group's celebratory activity is not wholly unattractive, regardless of what we know about the specific qualities of those individuals involved. And the singing in unison prepares us for the other verbalizing in unison to come.

In the third part, as the final guests prepare to depart, there is no presentation of thought until Gabriel begins to reflect on his wife's pose as she stands listening to Bartell D'Arcy's singing. The narrator mixes quoted and narrated monologue using the present tense, the subjunctive, and conditional expressions in a way that would not be possible without the earlier gradual introduction of those devices: "He asked himself what is a woman standing on the stairs in the shadow, listening to distant music, a symbol of. If he were a painter he would paint her in that attitude. Her blue felt hat would show off the bronze of her hair against the darkness and the dark panels of her skirt would show off the light ones. *Distant Music* he would call the picture if he were a painter" (*D* 210). Besides reinitiating the intimate presentation of Gabriel's mind, the scene contains a cluster of aesthetic references. We now have works within works and one medium transformed into another: the song, "The Lass of Aughrim," is transformed into an imaginary painting, which represents music within a fictional narrative. Through this interlocking configuration, performers and listeners, tellers and characters participate in overlapping relationships that point to the alignment of teller and character in the concluding style. One result of D'Arcy's singing becomes especially important. It leads to the conversation about the snow containing Mary Jane's statement that will be taken up in the story's ending: "I read this morning in the newspapers that the snow is general all over Ireland" (*D* 211).

The style of narration begins to enact the alignment of narrator and character when the teller presents Gabriel's sentimental memories in a past tense of recollection hardly distinguishable from the past tense used to narrate Gabriel's act of recollecting (*D* 213). But the alignment is not absolute at this point. Instead, Gabriel's interior storytelling, which the events following will undercut, replaces his recollections: "Perhaps she would not hear at once: she would be undressing. Then something in his voice would strike her. She would turn and look at him" (*D* 214). But instead, she turns to break "loose from him" (*D* 218), and Gabriel does the looking—at his own puzzled expression in the cheval glass. Gabriel had hoped for an intimate equivalent of the singing in unison of the party; he hoped "her thoughts had been running with his" (*D* 217). Instead of achieving easily a communion of thought, Gretta and Gabriel engage in a dialogue in which their attitudes differ markedly.

The narrator creates a counterpoint to the dialogue by interjecting Gabriel's interior response to Gretta's words, as Gabriel tries feverishly to understand his wife's unexpected behavior. The interjections include numerous instances of narrated monologue interspersed with the dialogue. Once Gretta has broken away from the embrace and thrown herself on the bed, psycho-narration replaces the narrated monologue. Gradually the dialogue begins to predominate as Gretta tells her story about Michael Furey. Finally, the dialogue becomes virtually a monologue, and even the psycho-narration of Gabriel's thinking ceases as Gretta narrates the details of her young lover's death (*D* 220–21). Gabriel adopts a curious role here that bears comparison to the narrator's role in the narration of consciousness. He limits his part in the dialogue to the asking of questions that will assist Gretta in completing her story. His role is maieutic as he helps her verbalize her thoughts as speech.

As I mentioned earlier, the story's conclusion as climax provides a contrast and balance to the earlier climax of the dinner speech and singing. Gretta's brief tale becomes the catalyst not for an audible singing in unison but for the merger of the character's interior speech with the narrator's storytelling. Gabriel's meditations continue once his wife is asleep, having been rechanneled by his failure and disappointment. Following the typographical break after Gretta's emotions overcome her, the narration becomes almost entirely affective. The few sentences describing the scene all refer to Gabriel's thoughts and perceptions or else carry an affective meaning in context. At times the affective connotation of adjectives and adverbs focuses our attention on the ambiguous relationship between teller and character in these final paragraphs. When the teller reports that "generous tears filled Gabriel's eyes" (*D* 223), the adjective is both the narrator's physical description of the size of Gabriel's tears and an assertion that those tears are caused by Gabriel's generosity.[22] We are given an external and an internal view simultaneously and without contradiction.

Even the initial, and seemingly straightforward, statement "She was fast asleep" depends on our having learned that in "The Dead" the third-person singular feminine pronoun in all its grammatical cases usually refers to Mrs. Conroy *in her husband's thoughts*. Gabriel may address her as Gretta, but he thinks of her as "she," just as Molly Bloom thinks of her husband and her other lovers as "he." We are more aware of Molly's use of "he" as interior speech because the referent is sometimes ambiguous. Because of Gabriel's consistency of reference, we are hardly aware that the pronouns suggest he is thinking. If the teller said "Gretta" or "Gabriel's wife" instead of "she," we would know that the perspective is not primarily Gabriel's. During the dinner, while Gabriel's thoughts are withheld, the narrator actually does call Gretta "Gabriel's wife" (*D* 200) as she serves dessert. The narration at the end of "The Dead" reverses the disorienting effect of the volume's beginning. Now we know the character's interior speech and his references so well that we can take them almost completely for granted. Joyce's character, not only his narrator, has become nearly invisible. Teller's voice and character's are the virtually transparent media *for each other*.

In the final paragraph the remarkable, symbiotic relationship of narrator and character is unmistakable. After several paragraphs composed mostly of psycho-narration, narrated monologue, and quoted monologue, the last paragraph consists almost entirely of narrated monologue of the sort that tends to be radically ambiguous. With its focus on the snow, the passage resembles the brief ambiguous rendering of Gabriel's thoughts just before his speech, but now the ambiguity is more pronounced. As at the beginning of "The Sisters," several impersonal constructions complicate our assigning the language to teller or to character. Although metaphors in *Dubliners* can usually be attributed to the narrator, the highly metaphorical and vividly imagistic language of this paragraph is as much the character's as the teller's. The shared attribution is possible in part because of the complex interplay of metaphor, image, and simile, whose effect recalls the earlier presentation of aesthetic objects within aesthetic objects. The simple comparison would be of death to snow. But here death, the metaphor from the teller's title, is not like the snow; rather, the snow, an image the character has held in consciousness several times, resembles death, which the metaphor of descent represents. The accumulated comparisons prevent us from identifying categorically a source for the similitudes in either the character's mind only or the narrator's.

The narrator has returned implicitly to the narration of the story's beginning. He does so in two ways. The more obvious way, and the one that seals the alignment between narrator and character beyond question, involves the character's interior voice. Among the sentences in the story's final paragraph, this one is indisputably Gabriel's thought presented as narrated monologue: "Yes, the newspapers were right: snow was general all over Ireland." The colon, the assertion, and the tense are all characteristic of Joyce's use of the technique. In the first paragraphs of "The Dead," we hear in the medley of voices Lily, Kate, and Julia, but we do not hear Mary Jane's inflections, though she is centrally involved in the occasion. Gabriel has been the group's spokesman in the narrative, just as the narrator has been the spokesman in the narration. Now Gabriel's interior voice has become the counterpart of the narrator's voice, whose action it completes by taking Mary Jane's earlier statement as its own.

The narrator returns in another way to a narration that represents a cultural consciousness. This way also involves an allusion, not to a character's voice within the story but to the voice of another artist and to a literary tradition manifestly associated with the west of Ireland. The voice belongs to W. B. Yeats, some of whose short stories Joyce, like Stephen in *Stephen Hero*, admired inordinately (*JJ* 85). Many of Yeats's stories have their origin in a specifically Irish folk tradition for which he was an articulate literary spokesman. As Joyce brings his own volume of Irish tales to closure, even though they are not drawn overtly from the folk tradition, Joyce takes that tradition and Yeats's stories as his own implied heritage, as part of the origin of his own voice. He does so by basing many of the concluding details of "The Dead" on Yeats's *Stories of Red Hanrahan*

(1904–5),[23] especially on "Red Hanrahan," "The Twisting of the Rope," "Hanrahan's Vision," and "The Death of Hanrahan."

The conclusion of "The Twisting of the Rope" includes references to waves "beating on the strand," to "grey shapes," and to death, especially in the closing words. In "Hanrahan's Vision," the poet encounters a "grey mist" that turns out to be what Joyce in "The Dead" calls "that region where dwell the vast hosts of the dead." After Hanrahan thinks of lovers "that were awakened from the sleep of the grave itself by the strength of one another's love," he has a vision in the grey wavelike mist. His vision includes a procession of the dead. In "Red Hanrahan," he has another visionary experience, which he recalls just before his death near the end of "The Death of Hanrahan." In that vision he saw old women holding four symbols: cauldron, stone, spear, and sword. To his despair, "he could not think of the right words to bring out" to ask the meaning of those symbols. Old women, the inadequacy of Gabriel's "lame and useless" words, and finally, at least two of the four symbols, stone and spear, are mentioned in the final paragraphs of "The Dead": "It lay thickly drifted on the crooked crosses and headstones, on the spears of the little gate, on the barren thorns." Joyce replaces cauldron and sword with Christian crosses and thorns to include in his story's closing yet another tradition about the relations between the living and the dead.

TOWARD MYTHIC ARTIFICE

In the style and allusions at the end of "The Dead," Joyce moves firmly toward achieving the mythic, virtuosic stature as artificer that Stephen Dedalus longs for in his journal, one of whose entries alludes to Yeats's Michael Robartes. This is the entry in which Stephen mentions his desire to hold and, by implication, to produce future loveliness: "6 *April, later*: Michael Robartes remembers forgotten beauty and, when his arms wrap her round, he presses in his arms the loveliness which has long faded from the world. Not this. Not at all. I desire to press in my arms the loveliness which has not yet come into the world" (*P* 251). Usually, Stephen records his impressions only once a day in his journal. For this day, as for only one other (21 March), he makes two entries. The earlier one for 6 April, for which the one about Robartes is an afterthought, presents Emma as a creature of memories: "Certainly she remembers the past. Lynch says all women do. Then she remembers the time of her childhood—and mine if I was ever a child. The past is consumed in the present and the present is living only because it brings forth the future. Statues of women, if Lynch be right, should always be fully draped, one hand of the woman feeling regretfully her own hinder parts" (*P* 251).

These passages in Stephen's journal provide another arrangement of the concluding elements of "The Dead." In both tales the character's voice has become, in different ways, the primary vehicle of the telling. Each character-become-teller meditates on a woman cherishing an idealized past. And each thinks of a man named Michael who has become nearly a legend, in one story through the woman's idealizing memories, in the other through a poet's imaginative vision. The poet's act of mind and the woman's do not differ substantially. Stephen's attitudes and Stephen's style in these entries resemble Conroy's sentimental passion and his fantasies of receiving Gretta's love gratuitously. But the narration's perspective at the end of "The Dead" allows us to judge the character's earlier inadequacies because he begins to perceive them clearly. When the narrator closes "The Dead" in the way we have seen, we discover Gabriel beginning to share the teller's perspective, which Stephen has yet to develop fully in his journal. Through style, the teller communicates Gabriel's link with his wife, who, like Emma, Molly Bloom, and Anna Livia, remembers the past. And he communicates a link with the generality of humankind. By contrast, Stephen has yet to reconcile himself to Emma, to Michael Robartes, to Robartes' poetic creator, or to his race.

At the end of "The Dead," Joyce as teller has moved beyond the Stephen of the journal. At the same time as he revivifies a seemingly dead and deadening Irish world, allowing it to live and to speak, he bridges the apparently uncrossable chasm between first- and third-person narration. In "The Dead," closing that gap involves re-creating the conscience of his race. And it makes the end of Joyce's stories meet their beginning by expressing a cultural origin and an ineluctable human ending in a representation of mind. Neither an idealized past nor a vaguely imagined future rules that representation. Instead, past and present, death and life have merged to define possibilities for living and for writing that may be actualized in a future that allows the mergers to repeat themselves. Iterative and singular, mythic and individual, cultural and mental have come to nest within one another as permanent features of Joyce's fiction.

CHAPTER FOUR

Styles of Mythic Wandering: *Ulysses*

Leonardo . . . has noted the tendency of the mind to impress its own likeness
upon that which it creates.
    —"Mr. Mason's Novels," *The Critical Writings of James Joyce*

. . . every word of literature is impregnated with the mind of the one who wrote
it. As he makes us read it, he awakens in us the analogue of what he thought or
felt. To understand a literary work, then, is to let the individual who wrote it
reveal himself to us *in* us. It is not the biography which explicates the work,
but rather the work which sometimes enables us to understand the biography.
    —Georges Poulet, "Phenomenology of Reading"

THE MYTH OF JOYCE'S IMPERSONAL NARRATION

Critics of Joyce's fiction have been living with a myth, the myth of the
teller's impersonality. That impersonality is an illusion; it can fool us, yet
we know it is not real. The narrator's ambiguous status depends on "genuine
forgeries" of the sort Bloom mentions in his talk with Stephen about "the
existence of a supernatural God": "it's the big question of our national poet
over again, who precisely wrote them, like *Hamlet* and Bacon." (*U* 634)
However strongly we may be tempted to assert the impersonality of
narration in Joyce's fiction, we cannot discard the notion of a narrator
completely. This is so because the term *narrator* names a problem for
literary criticism. It points to the mediation of a consciousness, the author's,
through language, a mediation that occurs in every narration. When we
assert the effacing of the narrator, we do not thereby efface the conundrum
at the base of storytelling. Impersonality is simply one among many possible disguises, or personae, in narration. And it is one necessary element in
every persona as the product of writing permanently separated from its
author. As a persona, it can be neither wholly personal nor wholly
impersonal, and never absolutely invisible. The difficulty in discussing
Joyce's narrator arises in part from the notion itself of a narrator as persona,
for that notion is self-contradictory. We can easily, and do necessarily,
oversimplify the complications of narration in any assertions about a teller's
presence or absence. We mean at least two things when we speak of a
narrator. We are giving a name to the writer's consciousness inscribed in the
tale's language, whatever specific forms that language may take. And we
are naming the effect of the tale's language on the reader, an effect that will

at times exclude the writer's presence as a personal consciousness. The two possibilities create the potential for an oscillating perspective, one that sees double by perceiving the teller as both the author and the author's fictional double. We can sense *both* a seemingly real consciousness as creating or reporting presence *and* a fictive presence, of a different order from the author, that is the language of fiction. In all fiction, the language indicates at once the author's previous, ineluctable presence during the writing and his necessary absence during the reading. We designate that presence and that absence by a single term: *narrator*.

We have strong grounds for probing the odd aspects of Joyce's fiction, grounds for asking in what sense there is a narrator at all in any traditional way. Does the narrator disappear? Can the narrator become invisible, be refined out of existence, like the artist of *A Portrait*'s aesthetic theory as many critics have interpreted it? While I would not ascribe to Joyce's narrator a full, fictive personality of the sort we might claim for Stephen Dedalus or Leopold Bloom, I am just as skeptical about an absent or disappearing narrator. As Wayne Booth has remarked, "though the author can to some extent choose his disguises, he can never choose to disappear."[1] A teller disappears only when the page becomes blank, once the book is complete. Although the teller in *Ulysses* does not appear in conventional ways, for instance, as a commentator in the manner of many nineteenth-century English novels, he does appear in other forms. In the case of *Ulysses*, the narrator's supposed disappearance is also his presence everywhere. Like Poe's purloined letter, and like the narrator of *A Portrait*, the teller of *Ulysses* is hidden in the open where anyone who looks can discover him. Joyce's narrator in *Ulysses* is like gravity. We do not see gravity, but we do perceive its manifestations. It would be as wrong-headed to deny a narrator's presence as to deny gravity. Although neither is directly visible to us, both exist. We could not get along without them.

In his aesthetic theory in *A Portrait*, Stephen's comments on the artist's impersonality echo similar ones of Flaubert. But Flaubert claims that the artist resembles God in *two* ways, not just as invisible but also as all-powerful (*tout-puissant*).[2] For Joyce's all-powerful narrator, the choice of invisibility and the acts of withdrawing mark his presence. The narrating situation is especially complicated, arrestingly so, in the final episode of *Ulysses*. Does no one besides Molly Bloom narrate "Penelope"? Even the stream of consciousness needs banks, in this case provided implicitly by the chameleonic narrator of the preceding seventeen episodes. His change of state reveals him. The paradox here may make us uncomfortable, but it seems unavoidable and indisputable: the author's persona makes itself felt through its apparent invisibility. Like the boy from the pantomime "Turko the Terrible" alluded to several times in *Ulysses*, the narrator announces that he *enjoys* invisibility. He enjoys it in two senses of that verb: he *possesses* the power to efface himself, and he *relishes* the role of invisibility, at least sufficiently to choose it as his ultimate narrating stance. Insofar as we perceive the teller's ability and his enjoyment of his role, the act of effacing becomes an indication of presence.

Besides invisibility, Joyce gives us other metaphors *in* and *of* the narration that reflect the curious, compelling nature of his persona in *Ulysses*.[3] Like Macintosh, the unknown man at Paddy Dignam's funeral, he earns a name, attains a status as present because of the apparently anonymous garment he wears. But anonymous narration becomes, as in *Finnegans Wake*, "Anonymoses" (*FW* 47), a mythic figure. As in Yeats's "A Coat," style is the garment the author has made for his work as song or tale, and that tale is the coat he wears. Through his choice of styles, Joyce emphasizes attitudes similar to Yeats's. We can never see the writer actually walking naked, never know the dancer solely from the evidence of the dance, or the author on the evidence of the tale. While we may not be able to see the figure *of* the writer, we have figures *for* the writer: his figurative language, the figures who speak for him as personae, and the figure woven and unwoven, Penelope-like, by styles.

The narrator's presence is of a structural sort, and that is an odd kind of presence indeed. It reveals itself through difference: through the difference between the character's interior voice and the surrounding narration and through the differences between styles as the narration proceeds from episode to episode. Through these differences, these shifts of language, in the interstices between the different styles, the narrator's structural presence emerges as the rationale for the book's arrangement. That rationale is the pattern in the carpet, the spectrum of a coat of many colors, by which the teller as tailor and wearer, like "myriadminded" Shakespeare in "Scylla and Charybdis," seems a "man all hues." The pattern is polytropic and Odyssean. Like the hero of the *Odyssey* in Homer's opening invocation to the Muse, the heroic teller of *Ulysses* is not named. We know him only by his actions and by the figure left behind as the linguistic trace of his acts of telling. In this regard, the book's title becomes the structural metaphor for the narration as well as for the narrative. Through wanderings of style, Joyce as teller attains a mythic status different in kind from the critical myth of invisibility. He earns his title as mythic artificer, an agnomen that happens also to be the title of his mythic artifice. As in the case of Shem the Penman's house as book, we find the author's pen name on the cover (*FW* 182.32–34). The styles of *Ulysses* are the styles of its teller as Ulysses, as *polytropos*. For Joyce, the heroic teller, *–tropos* means trope.[4] As I mentioned in the chapter on *Finnegans Wake*, the choice of Homer as model is a Viconian gesture. In *The New Science*, Vico devotes one of his five books to Homer, whom he treats as the paradigm of the artist. In order to achieve Homeric status as an artist who creates the conscience of his race, Joyce compares himself as teller with Ulysses. In part, he does so because Homer often allows his hero to tell his own tale in the *Odyssey*.

Odysseus's heroics are verbal as well as martial. His heroism includes narration.

We have already seen Joyce using titles metaphorically early in his career and employing myth openly by giving Stephen the surname Dedalus. In *Ulysses* the mythic name designates the work. And, as in *A Portrait*, it applies both to characters and to the teller. The epical fiction provides the local habitation and the name for its informing spirit. The situation resembles that of Ezra Pound's first Canto. The writer defines his persona at the work's beginning by alluding prominently to the text of an epic precursor in translation. The modern artist's identification with his precursors, both Homer and Odysseus, is not, of course, absolute. Joyce indicates the inevitable mediation and temporal dislocation by choosing the Roman rather than the Greek name. He is on the way to the sort of title he chooses for *Finnegans Wake*: one that alludes to the epic precursors of artist and character, provides a metaphor for the narrative's action and for the act of narration, and links the myth to a specifically Irish culture. Only that final linkage is missing in the title *Ulysses*, though the interaction between title and narrative makes the connection clear.

When asked as a schoolboy to write on the topic "My Favorite Hero," Joyce wrote about Odysseus.[5] When, as an adult, Joyce decided to make actual in the world without what was possible in his world within, the steps of the aesthetic journey by which he met and made himself tended toward those of Odysseus. Those steps are the wanderings of *Ulysses* as narrative and as narration. The supposedly impersonal narration is the making of a personal image. That image emerges in the movement from an initial style, a Rock of Ithaca, dominated by narrated and quoted interior monologue, through various styles as adventures, to the final styles of the *nostos* that bring the artist home to Ithaca and Penelope. The final style of the concluding episode brings the teller home at the same time as it carries him to the limit of the implications for interior monologue as stylistic technique. At that limit teller's voice fuses with character's. In the apparently unmediated style of Molly Bloom's soliloquy, the teller, like his favorite hero, cohabits with Penelope in a climactic homecoming. The multiple Homeric correspondences within *Ulysses* that have been so thoroughly discussed by critics point to the nature of this narrative as mythic epistle. Joyce's *Ulysses*, Joyce *as* Ulysses, is a Homeric *correspondance* from author to reader and between teller and character. When we read *Ulysses* we hear the ghost not of Hamlet's father but of Stephen Dedalus's aesthetic father, the father of Telemachus. As we explore the lineaments of that aesthetic forebear, we will be concerned with the multiple *relations* of the tale and the telling: the text's relatives, especially Homer's *Odyssey* and Joyce's other texts, the teller's acts of relating the tale, the structural relations within the telling and of telling (as style) to tale, and the relations among teller, character, and reader.

"CIRCE": THE PLAY OF CONSCIOUSNESS

I begin with "Circe" for reasons similar to the ones that led me to introduce this study with a chapter on *Finnegans Wake*: the episode brings several elements important in *Ulysses* and in Joyce's fiction generally into a special kind of focus. The episode's placement, length, density of language, and odd typographical form mark it as a section apart from the others, one that draws attention to itself for its virtuosity and for its difficulty. To read "Circe" critically requires referring backward and forward in *Ulysses*, just as reading *Ulysses* critically requires placing it firmly in the context of Joyce's earlier and later writings. As in *A Portrait*, Joyce as teller continues to move beyond the attitudes and limited achievements of Stephen Dedalus, without leaving them completely behind, while presenting Stephen moving toward the future writing he, like his author, will produce. As in "The Dead," Joyce brings the deadening world of Dublin to life by giving it the power of speech. In so doing he overcomes the ostensible disparities between first- and third-person narration, between lyric, epic, and dramatic genres, and between cultural present and cultural past even more vividly than in "The Dead" and in the fifth part of *A Portrait*. Joyce's flamboyant syntheses of linguistic and literary forms and of past and present build on the earlier works by carrying their directions forward, although *Ulysses* is in some respects wildly different from the works preceding it. At the same time, Joyce's strategies point toward the final ones of the *Wake*.

"Circe" and "Penelope": Lyrical, Epical, or Dramatic?

As in Joyce's other works, in *Ulysses* endings are of crucial importance: ends of episodes, the episodes ending each of the three parts, and "Scylla and Charybdis" as unmarked end of the first half. Like the aesthetic theory of *A Portrait* that precedes villanelle and journal, "Scylla and Charybdis" suggests attitudes that we find at work in the other episodes, especially the later ones. "Proteus," "Circe," and "Penelope," the three episodes that conclude the major divisions, are all reminiscent in various ways of Stephen's villanelle and his journal. In them we encounter again a mix of genres, minglings of voice that indicate the merging and diverging of character and teller, a movement toward formal closure through the character's seemingly autonomous speech, a pushing of mimetic form to its limits in fiction, and, perhaps most important for our inquiry, a return to origins.

In "Proteus" Joyce displays and extends his mastery of techniques for presenting consciousness and for mingling ambiguously character's and narrator's voices. Joyce presents again the act of writing, though less elaborately than Stephen's villanelle, and the lyric intensity of the character's consciousness emerges within the genre of narrative. Both "Circe" and "Penelope" raise prominently through style the question of the narrator's presence. And each provides an end point, a limit, for the book and its styles by evoking an oscillating perspective in wide frames of reference. Those contexts include literary genres and the status of fictional language as mimetic or self-referential. The two episodes provide the most intense version in *Ulysses*, perhaps in all Joyce's fiction, of the dramatic and the lyrical within the epical. By placement, function, and implication, like villanelle and journal in *A Portrait*, they act as a climax and a *post scriptum* for the narration.

While all the episodes contribute to the narration's epical pattern, "Circe" and "Penelope" punctuate the stylistic wanderings. And each stands at the crossroads of narrative. In and between them, we understand the narration as an interaction of lyrical and dramatic. While "Circe" is dramatic in its formal aspects, "Penelope," like a dramatic monologue, is dramatic in its referential implications. "Penelope" as lyrical is the character's act of the mind presented with immediacy and apparently available for virtually unmediated apprehension. "Circe," however, through mediations continually evokes the act of the mind by which the episode has come into being. Despite the trappings of drama in "Circe" and a referential immediacy in "Penelope," the would-be withdrawn artist continually reveals himself as all in all.

Through narration Joyce combines two different kinds of source as his end and his ending. The one source, literary and mythic, involves the texts and mythical patterns on which he draws in composing his fiction. The other involves the characters' acts of mind embedded in a referential reality like the Ireland Joyce knew. By combining them through style Joyce achieves a representation of himself as artist that is one with literary and mythic sources and with the character's consciousness. In "Penelope" as return to origins, the mental processes not only of writer or character as artist but of humankind in general emerge as the origin of aesthetic creation and as evidence for a shared humanity. Joyce represents that common bond as the end and the source of his writing. His act of writing begins with the interaction between the literary tradition and the creating consciousness. It achieves its end when that merger produces alignments between artist and citizen, including writer and reader. The merger and alignments contribute to the large polytropic, Odyssean pattern in the narration. The pattern's power depends on details of narration in various episodes as well as on large shifts in style that those details frequently serve. To define the pattern, we must examine the styles' characteristics, and arrangements in and of the styles.

The Cracked Looking Glass of Joyce's Art

Those styles actively invite the reader's re-creative dialectical involvement. In the reflective and self-reflexive styles of Joyce's late texts, the writer inscribes and the reader recognizes their composite image in the looking glass of art. That looking glass is always visible because cracked. I use Stephen's metaphor from "Telemachus" (U 6–7), purloined from Oscar Wilde, to draw attention to the verbal texture of "Circe." That verbal texture provides the most accessible, convincing evidence for the narrator's place in the episode. Along with the ordering patterns of allusion embedded in the narration, the various styles of language and conventions of presentation evoke the artist's actions. I have in mind those aspects of "Circe" that every reader grapples with, the astonishing swerves from one kind of language to another during the narration. We are placed by these swerves in a position like that of the letter's interpreter in the *Wake*: "[While] we . . . may have our irremovable doubts as to the whole sense of the lot, the interpretation of any phrase in the whole, the meaning of every word of a phrase . . . , we must vaunt no idle dubiosity as to its genuine authorship" (*FW* 117.34–118.4). We may not know "who in hallhagal wrote the durn thing anyhow" (*FW* 107.36–108.1), but we know emphatically that it was authored. As cracked looking glass, the language of "Circe" never pretends to be a transparent vehicle for plot. It is not a window but a mirror. We see it as a mirror because of the oddities in the episode's form. The shifts and contrasts constantly fracture any sense of conventional coherence and continuity, throwing us off balance rather than encouraging us to make easy assumptions about what and how we are reading.

Those assumptions are referential ones, which simply do not apply to "Circe" in any consistent way. Interpretations of "Circe" that explain the vagaries of its language as a mimesis of action fail to deal convincingly with the episode's implications. Generally, the referential view asserts some mingling of thoughts and action in the presentation but slights form and style. The emphasis in such a view can fall on a fictive physical action as the focus of the language. It might interpret the language as a report of characters' actions and speech, while maintaining that many other things, including the thoughts of some characters, are presented as well. Or it might give more prominence to the mimesis of consciousness by describing an alternation between characters' thoughts and actions. Finally, it might emphasize the primacy of characters' thoughts, interpreting the language as regularly reflecting one or more than one character's perceptions of the action.

None of these views satisfies completely, because "Circe" is not organized like a conventional realistic narrative with seemingly real characters in a recognizable setting acting and thinking in believable ways. I would not deny the referential component completely. Without it, the episode would give no impression of action; it would not be part of a narrative. However, the realistic action in this lengthy episode is minimal. We can summarize it briefly by a division into four parts. In the first section (U 429–33), before Bloom arrives in the brothel district, the stage directions and the characters' unusual language introduce the scene. Then Stephen Dedalus appears with

Lynch on their way to Bella Cohen's brothel. In the much longer second section (*U* 433–502), Bloom wanders in Nighttown as he follows Stephen, about whose welfare he is concerned. In the third and longest section (*U* 502–86), Stephen and Bloom are both in the brothel. During this part, Bloom encounters the dominating whoremistress. Although Bloom appears in danger of losing his self-control in the brothel, he asserts himself shortly before Stephen drunkenly smashes the chandelier. And he prevents Bella Cohen from calling the police. In the final section (*U* 586–609), which takes place outside in the street, after Stephen fights with a soldier, Bloom rescues him from the watch with the help of an acquaintance.

While such a summary can be useful for organizing our impression of events occurring, it minimizes the effect of the language and the importance of what may seem to be characters' thoughts. We can try attributing these elements not accounted for by a summary of external action to the fantasizing consciousness of whichever character appears most prominent in the plot at any particular point. In the first six episodes of *Ulysses*, as in Joyce's earlier fiction, the reader has learned to distinguish between presentations of action in a fictive external world and presentations of characters' thoughts. Such distinctions are not always easy to make in those early episodes, and they largely disappear during the middle ones. They are impossible to make in the final episode of Part II.

Of the various discussions of "Circe," Hugh Kenner's comes closest to dealing adequately with the narration's complexities. As he points out, the principle of assigning bizarre aspects of the episode to a character's mind, which seems to work at times early in "Circe," quickly breaks down:

> Joyce does establish in a way calculated to catch the reader's eye, a workable convention, clearly discriminating two planes of reality, which he is then careful seldom to follow again; the reader who learns the convention at this point will be misled wholly. This is Bloom's fantasy of becoming Lord Mayor, Messiah, and martyr. We can tell exactly where it begins and ends; it is cleanly spliced in between Zoe's "Go on. Make a stump speech out of it" (478.6) and her "Talk away till you're black in the face" (499.9). . . . We may have recourse, in short, to the myth of the stimulus-response psychology, its comfortable, "real" world whence stimuli are emitted, its plasticized "fantasy" world in which they are responded to. . . . We shall find we are wrong almost immediately.[6]

The convention of distinguishing between internal and external action is undermined as soon as Bloom begins to talk away. The voice attributed to him is that of the Irish peasants in J. M. Synge's plays (*U* 499). Even in those parts at first appearing to present the characters' actions and speech rather than their fantasies, what they do and say cannot be explained as realistic. When language and action in a literary work are so unusual, the reader attends *not* to a referential world but to style and to the act of narrating.

Kenner's metaphor of splicing in is important for understanding how the narration works, for it suggests interpolation. Bloom's language and his specific remarks about his father's suicide in his apparent response to Zoe are interpolated between representations of more believable actions and thoughts apparently occurring in a fictive physical world. That world reasserts itself briefly, for instance, at the end of Bloom's speech, when Zoe responds as if he had said something straightforward, which we have not heard because the interpolation may have displaced it. The digressions in part V of *A Portrait* anticipate this sort of narration. These are also sometimes seemingly spliced into the conversations, though the digressions there are neither so long nor so extravagant as in "Circe." And they do not disturb the narration's texture so severely by appearing to displace more ordinary action. Instead, digressions in *A Portrait* generally present Stephen's consciousness through the narrated monologue and related techniques. The presentation of consciousness frames and may even suspend temporarily the dialogue or other action. But for examples of such interpolations we need not turn as far back in Joyce's writing as Stephen's rumination about Cranly's speaking as style (*P* 195). We have only to look to the early episodes of *Ulysses*. Near the start of "Telemachus," Stephen's brief thoughts ("Cranly's arm. His arm" [*U* 8]) begin to be inserted between passages of Mulligan's direct discourse. During the same conversation, longer passages of Stephen's thoughts sometimes intervene between the report of Mulligan's speech and the report of Stephen's spoken response (*U* 8).

There is a crucial difference between the early and late episodes, for "Circe" has no basic third-person referential style marked by direct discourse. Consequently, the narrator returns to no base from the digressions. The episode only *appears* to have its ground in the presentation of would-be speech and of scene and action as in drama. Without a consistent referential base, we simply move from one stylistic digression to another. In such a text, meaning becomes almost wholly connotative, because the language is largely lacking in denotative limits. The realistic style that includes direct discourse has now become one among many styles in a proliferating sequence of contrasts and modulations. Through contrast and complementarity, "Circe" as a whole digresses in form from the beginning style of *Ulysses* and from all the other styles. In so doing it makes digression the core of the work itself.

Some of the shifts within "Circe" appear to duplicate the earlier shifts from presenting action to presenting thought. They may even remind us of the earlier stylistic shift characteristic of the initial style. Despite the recall, the nature of the shift is entirely different, for it produces a different effect. The narrator repeats himself with a crucial modification. This is so because, like the allusions to earlier details of the narrative, which I shall outline shortly, the stylistic shift has been broken away from its original context and function to serve in another kind of narration. In "Circe" we have only the *ghost* of the initial style. Joyce presses the issue of the narrator's impersonality by evoking contradictory implications. He emphasizes the possibility of a transparent, or objective, presentation independent of the author by casting the episode in the trappings of drama, with typography suggesting direct discourse. But the details of style, especially the changes in register, suggest instead the narrator's presence by stressing the act of narrating.

Despite his reservations about the stimulus-response principle as a key for understanding "Circe," Hugh Kenner has devised a chart entitled "The Principal Fantasies."[7] Instead of dividing the episode into parts reflecting the presentation of scene and external action, he partitions it into an inner world of seven major fantasies dispersed among actions occurring in an outer world. While his division accounts for much of the shifting between thought and action, it is finally only a sophisticated summary of plot in which action, broadly defined, includes the character's mental activities. Like my own schematic plot summary emphasizing external action, Kenner's chart of fantasies does not clarify the self-consciously literary aspects of "Circe"; that can be done only by taking into account the stylistic shifting and the patterns of allusion that order the episode. As critics of "Circe," we find ourselves in a position like Freud's when he describes the mental apparatus. The complications of the phenomena being scrutinized are so numerous that we need several models to account for them, no one of which satisfies fully.

Like *Finnegans Wake* and "The Waste Land," "Circe" is a writerly text. It enables us to reconfigure its language in various ways that depend on our assumptions about narrative, literary style, and consciousness. And whatever our attitudes, it always defies them. Kenner has made one kind of good order and good sense out of the episode by focusing on the principal fantasies he identifies as embedded in its dense texture. But the order is too orderly, even taking into account the enjoinders to caution included in his interpretation. Kenner assumes, albeit tentatively, that the episode has a large referential component, that Bloom's consciousness colors its narrative in a controlling way, that the narrative concerns psychic purgation, that the purgation occurs, and that the characters either do or can change. Because of these presuppositions, "Circe" becomes for him a narrative of psychic cleansing in which the exorcising of demons in Bloom's consciousness enables a final transformation. In the scene of transformation, Bloom has a vision of his dead son as a young boy, a vision marking his newly gained ability to reconcile himself to the death and possibly to Molly. In this reading, Stephen is secondary, though Kenner cites Stephen's vision of his mother as the only "genuine hallucination." All the principal fantasies are Bloom's.

Such a mimetically oriented reading is not just possible, it is necessary. But it is *not* definitive. Other mimetic interpretations are equally possible, ones not stressing so emphatically either Bloom's point of view or the purgation. But more importantly, all referential readings provide only one moment in our response to a text like "Circe." There is release, but not just for the characters from their internal restraints. Release occurs for teller and reader in various ways, though the release is *to* as well as *from* attitudes and styles that are not ultimate in any categorical sense. We can hold other than mimetic attitudes about how the episode functions, ones that do not displace entirely the referential ones but instead inhabit and generate the same structure, just as conscious and unconscious are both part of the mental apparatus in Freud's various descriptions of it. Those other presuppositions place the mimetic reading in a frame of reference that makes possible the reader's oscillating perspective. That perspective is more uneasy about the mimesis in "Circe" than Kenner's chart, helpful as it is, can be.

Unlike Kenner, I would not attempt to distinguish between action and thought by focusing primarily on specific fantasies, because the distinction between inner and outer is impossible to maintain. Nor can we accept the more complicated convention according to which the bizarre action and language reflect Stephen's, Bloom's, or some other character's strange thoughts, even when those thoughts are not obviously being presented. Although we may read some parts of the episode this way, the principle is not wholly applicable. No one would argue that either Bloom or Zoe, the only two characters involved in the scene Kenner mentions, are capable of the kind of parody presented in Bloom's Syngean speech. Even if they were, that ability would not account for the stage direction presenting Bloom in peasant garb. While the parody may indicate the fleeting thoughts of either Bloom or Zoe about stage Irish during their conversation, the language primarily draws attention to itself as parody, rather than reflecting characters' thoughts and actions.

Many other portions of the episode—for example, the first pages—are not amenable to interpretations stressing the reflection of characters' thoughts. In those initial pages, though Stephen and Bloom have not yet arrived in nighttown, the language presents a scene as bizarre as many that follow later when the contents of their fictive minds might possibly be influencing the presentation. Even before any important characters appear, the first stage direction, which begins as apparently referential description, presents aspects of a scene that are fantastic and not clearly attributable to any character's mind.

Although it does not call attention to itself as language in the way some later passages do, that first stage direction raises the question of the text's relation to any possible referential world, whether physical or mental. The referential view in any of its versions cannot explain satisfactorily this stage direction, Bloom's speech, the other instances of bizarre action and language, or the episode's dramatic form. It cannot because it tends to ignore the most important action relevant to the entire episode: the narrator's implicit act of narration that becomes explicit through parody, linguistic play, and the presenting of fantastic actions. We learn the nature of this narrative by understanding that it might have been a realistic drama or even a highly psychological drama but that it is *not* either of those because it is not primarily referential. The liberties taken with style and narrative in "Circe" make sense only in context, by contrast with earlier and later styles, once we have become familiar with their techniques and implications through the reading process. The primary fantasy of the episode is the episode itself. Its organizing principles, rather than referential ones, are self-referential. They involve several patterns of allusion, which, together with the shifting texture of the language, give us the means to understand our own act of reading as well as the nature of the narration and the narrative.

The Circe Episode's Homeric Descent

Like Buck Mulligan in "Telemachus" (*U* 18), John Eglinton in "Scylla and Charybdis" remarks that Stephen thinks "*Hamlet* is a ghoststory" (*U* 187). So, too, is "Circe," for the descent into the underworld is the organizing metaphor for narrative and narration. The episode's equivalents in the *Odyssey* are *both* Odysseus's two visits to Circe's island, Aeaea, *and* his trip to the underworld. Many commentators on this episode have mentioned the correspondences between "Circe" and the events of *Odyssey* X, in which Odysseus and his crew land on Circe's island. The episode's animal imagery originates in the sorceress' transforming half of Odysseus's crew into swine. Joyce's modern counterpart for Circe is the whoremistress called both Bella and Bello Cohen.

Along with these obvious parallels between "Circe" and the *Odyssey*, there are subtler, more complicated relationships. One key to these is Tiresias, whose androgyny the names of the masculine, dominating whoremistress suggest. In the *Odyssey* Odysseus actually visits Aeaea twice, once in Book X and again in Book X̄II. Between these two visits, in Book XI, he descends into the underworld to consult with Tiresias. Even though there has already been a "Hades" episode earlier in the day of *Ulysses*, "Circe" repeats the trip to the underworld by conflating it with the two visits to Aeaea. Occurring exactly twelve hours apart according to the information Joyce gave Carlo Linati, "Hades" and "Circe" are counterparts, one a daytime version, the other a nighttime version of the descent.[8] As Marx says of repetition in the opening of *The Eighteenth Brumaire*, the first occurrence is as tragedy, the second as farce. The repetition of "Hades" in "Circe" recalls, if only distantly, the relationship between V.2 and II.2 in *A Portrait*. In *Ulysses* the congruence of parts even includes the two episodes' stylistic functions within the large pattern of styles. In "Hades" the narrator finishes with his initial style; in "Circe," he finishes with the second major grouping of styles.

Bloom's encounter with his mother, Ellen Higgins Bloom (*U* 438), provides the first significant hint of a visit to the underworld in "Circe." Like Odysseus, Bloom sees his dead mother. After Odysseus's dialogue with his mother, the Greek hero witnesses a procession of famous Greek women, including Tyro, Antiope, Alcmene, and Epicaste. This procession explains Bloom's encounter with women who have been important in his past and his present subsequent to his vision of his mother. After he sees Molly in Turkish garb (*U* 439–41), then a young woman named Bridie Kelly from his youth, then Gerty McDowell (*U* 441–42), and finally Josie Powell Breen (*U* 442–49), a stage direction describes Bloom as walking on toward *"hellsgates"* (*U* 449).

His comment about Stephen's staying ahead of him, that drunks "cover distance double quick" (*U* 452), corresponds to two events, one reported in "Hades," the other in the *Odyssey*. Here, as elsewhere in "Circe," the details evoke our multiple perceptions by alluding to more than one earlier narrative situation in this and other texts. In "Hades" Bloom says of Dignam: "Got here before us, dead as he is" (*U* 101). This comment and the one about Stephen's speediness allude to Odysseus's statement to Elpenor in *Odyssey* XI. When Odysseus first enters the pit providing access to the underworld, he remarks with surprise that Elpenor has beaten him there on foot, even though Odysseus has traveled by ship. In their haste to leave Aeaea, the crew had abandoned Elpenor's body when he broke his neck in a drunken fall from the roof of Circe's pavillion. Later in "Circe," a stage direction mentions that *"several paupers fall from a ladder"* (*U* 485). As in "Hades," in "Circe" the besotted Dignam corresponds to the young man who is the first of the crew to arrive. In the sequence after the procession of women, Bloom, who has just fed a dog that follows him, is accused, put on trial, and finally vindicated when the dog becomes Dignam, who confirms Bloom's alibi (*U* 453–73). Like Elpenor in the underworld of the *Odyssey*, Paddy Dignam speaks out in "Circe." The details of the trial refer both to "Hades" and to the Homeric descent. John O'Connell, the caretaker of the cemetery where Dignam is buried, appears, as does the attorney J. J. O'Molloy, who swears "by Hades" (*U* 464). Bloom's feeding of the dog recalls Odysseus's feeding the shades to enable them to speak. But, in fact, Odysseus does not need to feed Elpenor, who can still talk because he has not been buried. Bloom's feeding the dog-Dignam, then, may echo as well Odysseus's providing food for his crew at the start of their adventure on Aeaea.

Details later in "Circe" emphasize the correspondences between Stephen, Elpenor, and Paddy Dignam. Stephen, another drunken young man, also suffers a fall and travels quickly. At the episode's end he seems about to be buried. Corny Kelleher, who works for the funeral home that supervised Dignam's burial in "Hades," helps Bloom save Stephen from the watch (*U* 603–8). According to a stage direction, Corny, appearing with wreath in hand prepared for a funeral, tells the watch that Stephen has only been celebrating after winning his bet on a horse race, the "Gold Cup." Elpenor, of course, drank from Circe's golden cup. In his speech to Odysseus, Elpenor requests that the crew return to Aeaea to provide him a proper burial. When entreating Odysseus for burial, the young man evokes Odysseus's feelings for the family left behind in Ithaca by reminding him of his wife, his father, and his son, Telemachus. Although Stephen does not ask Bloom for help in "Circe," Bloom's actions in this episode and in the next two are like Odysseus's concerned response to Elpenor's request. The paternal attitude toward an unfortunate young man that links Bloom with Odysseus and Stephen with Elpenor emerges again in the episode's last scene when Bloom remembers his own dead son, Rudy, who appears to him as he gazes at the fallen Stephen.

In the episode's middle, when Bloom and Stephen are in the brothel, there are many allusions to all three relevant books of the *Odyssey*. The animal imagery is particularly prominent in this part. Like Circe, Bello Cohen knows of a libation that can provide access to the underworld: "I can give you a rare old wine that'll send you skipping to hell and back" (*U* 543–44). In the dialogue between Bloom and his grandfather (*U* 511–23), Lipoti Virag describes another libation that sounds Homeric: "I presume you shall have remembered what I will have taught you on that head? Wheatenmeal with honey and nutmeg" (*U* 514). Like Tiresias, Virag is an old man who dispenses advice. Although, unlike the prophet, he cannot see both past and future, at least the muddled syntax of his immigrant's English suggests comically a confusion of them. His statement about dealing with the whores echoes Circe's advice to Odysseus in Book XII about avoiding the sirens, while it may refer as well to Tiresias's advice in Book XI about the oxen of the sun.

Among the various allusions to the whole of Odysseus's adventure with Circe, from the initial landing on Aeaea until the final, second departure, the correspondences between Stephen and Elpenor are balanced by ones between Stephen and Odysseus. Toward the episode's end, Stephen hails Lynch as "Sisyphus" (*U* 587), one of the shades Odysseus sees in the underworld. Like Odysseus and Bloom, Stephen speaks with his dead mother. His dream of her, which he remembered in the morning (*U* 5, 10) is enacted at length in "Circe" (*U* 579–83) just before he and Bloom leave the brothel. Since numerous allusions to Odysseus's actions focus on Bloom, the inclusion of ones focusing on Stephen emphasizes the parallels between the central characters. Stephen, then, is compared through allusion with both Elpenor *and* Odysseus. Together with his connection to Telemachus early in *Ulysses*, the correspondences in "Circe" recall Stephen's association in *A Portrait* with both Icarus and Daedalus. And they foreshadow the multiple, shifting roles that permeate the narrative of the *Wake*. As with the complex, mythic relationships in Joyce's earlier and later works, in *Ulysses* the Homeric correspondences are multiple and cannot be reduced to simple one-to-one parallels. Neither Stephen nor Bloom can be identified with only one or another character in the *Odyssey*. This is the case for them because, like Odysseus and the narrator, they enjoy the power of imagination enabling them to play many roles, to become all in all. Although critics have usually associated Bloom with Odysseus, in "Circe" he resembles as well the crew, a shade in the underworld, and Tiresias. The scenes showing him dominated by Bello suggest his resemblance to the crew, who are transformed by Circe, while his hunger links him with both the hungry crew on their arrival at Aeaea and the shades, eager for the blood Odysseus offers. Like Tiresias, he appears to experience feelings appropriate to *both* sexes. Although Stephen and Bloom may be heroic in some respects, their heroism is not idealized through unequivocal, symbolic correspondences. And our response to them is always vacillating.

The situation of characters linked through multiple, partially overlapping parallels is evoked within the episode when a stage direction describes Bloom and Stephen looking into a mirror. They see there the face of William Shakespeare, whom Stephen's theory has identified as both father and son:

LYNCH
(Points.) The mirror up to nature. *(He laughs.)* Hu hu hu hu hu hu.

(Stephen and Bloom gaze in the mirror. The face of William Shakespeare, beardless, appears there, rigid in facial paralysis, crowned by the reflection of the reindeer antlered hatrack in the hall.) *(U* 567)

They share a common visage, though that visage does not define them completely. Each resembles the artist sufficiently for reader and teller to link them. The exchange and coalescence of roles in "Circe" recalls the links between Butt and Taff, Ondt and Gracehoper, Shem and Shaun, among many others, in the *Wake*. The relationship is like that of the Yin and Yang, which Rudolf Arnheim describes as parts of a model of interaction.[9] The supposed opposites appear to change places and switch valences and in so doing call up a virtual third term constituted by their interaction. In *Ulysses* the virtual third can be Shakespeare, the artist as narrator, and, at a different level of generality, narrative itself as interaction between lyrical and dramatic and this narrative as the interaction among elements revealed in patterns of allusion.

The details of the links among "Circe," "Hades," "Scylla and Charybdis," and *Odyssey* XI suggest that the descent is a controlling metaphor of the narrative not just in a single episode but in *Ulysses* at large. Like Hamlet and Odysseus, the characters encounter the ghosts of their pasts. And the metaphor encompasses the narration as well. It applies to both the narrator's act of telling and our acts of reading. As readers we encounter the writer's ghostly voice defeating the passage of time, the voice of the aesthetic father become consubstantial with its literary offspring. On his way to becoming like Odysseus, the writer becomes like Shakespeare, a dramatist, though only for an episode. When he becomes a dramatist, he descends into an underworld in his act of telling. Before considering further the descent into the underworld as metaphor for the narration, I shall describe briefly two patterns of allusion to texts and traditions other than the Homeric one. These involve Christian history and the narrative and styles of *Ulysses* as a whole. The episode's extravagant proliferations sometimes obscure their presence, though it is pervasive. For ease of reference, I have included as Appendix 2: "Patterns of Allusion in 'Circe' " a chart presenting the details of the patterns by ranging them in relation to one another. I indicate there as well my division of the episode into four parts.

Allusions to Christian History

The vivid enactment of Stephen's dream of his mother, which alludes to Odysseus's encounter with his mother's shade, introduces the apocalyptic portion of "Circe." Some of the details of this section (*U* 583–600) suggest a correspondence to the apocalypse of Christian history. Along with several earlier references, these compose a second major pattern of allusion within the narration. The mingling of the Christian with the Homeric in *Ulysses* begins on the book's first pages when Buck's reference to the Mass becomes the substitute for the epic invocation to the Muse. In "Circe," the allusion to that beginning in "Telemachus" when Stephen speaks phrases from the Mass at paschal time (*U* 431–32) initiates a sequence reflecting the chronology of major events in Christian history. References to the creation are followed by ones to the life of Christ and to the apocalypse. Early on in the episode, two acts of creation are suggested. First, Stephen appears to create light by shattering "*light over the world*" (*U* 432). Then, a newly created sun rises from the east when Bloom points in that direction: "*A cake of new clean lemon soap arises, diffusing light and perfume*" (*U* 440). The order of the two creations recalls Stephen's remarks in "Scylla and Charybdis." There he contemplates briefly the preposterous notion that the creating of light preceded the creating of the source of light: "The playwright who wrote the folio of this world and wrote it badly (He gave us light first and the sun two days later), the lord of things as they are . . . is doubtless all in all in all of us" (*U* 213). Later in "Circe," Bloom's imagined public career (*U* 478–99) alludes to Christ's ministry and crucifixion. Like Christ at the start of his vocation, Bloom is "thirty one" (*U* 481) at the beginning of his career. After Bloom's genealogy identifies him with the Emmanuel of Isaiah (*U* 496), Reuben J. Dodd's appearance as a "*blackbearded Iscariot*" (*U* 497) suggests the betrayal of Christ. During his martyrdom Bloom is clothed in "*a seamless garment marked I.H.S.*"

(*U* 498), recalling Christ's seamless tunic mentioned in the Gospel of St. John. After his burning Bloom exhibits his wounds.

When Stephen and Bloom are together in the brothel (*U* 502–86), the coming of the apocalypse is indicated in a number of ways. Florry tells the others that "the last day is coming this summer" (*U* 505). Then Reuben J. Antichrist appears (*U* 506), followed by a Hobgoblin that destroys tiny roulette planets and cries out in French (*U* 506). Enacting the language of the handbill Bloom has seen earlier in the day, Elijah now arrives and admonishes all those present to acknowledge their sins (*U* 507–8). Toward the end of his dialogue with Bloom (*U* 511–23), Lipoti Virag cries out "Apocalypse" (*U* 520). Stephen's smashing the chandelier with his ashplant at the end of his encounter with his mother also evokes destruction. This destroying of light matches Stephen's creation of light earlier. After Stephen leaves the brothel, the allusions to Christian history reach culmination when the springing up of brimstone fires, the resurrection of the dead, and the performance of a Black Mass (*U* 598–600) represent the apocalypse. These details, of course, also present this underworld as hellish and Satanic, though always comically so.

Allusions to Ulysses *Itself*

As my description of the patterns has already begun to suggest, "Circe" includes allusions to other episodes, especially to earlier ones. The reference is at times to a specific action, at times to thoughts a character has had, including memories of past events. These allusions, some occurring in the order of the original referents, are not limited to recalls of "Hades." In the chart of Appendix 2, under "Events of the Day," are references to other episodes, which are alluded to in many cases either in their original sequence or as part of the Homeric or Christian schemes. At the beginning and end, the order of the episode's details resembles most obviously the order of presentation in the corresponding parts of *Ulysses*. Stephen's entry with Lynch and the words from the Mass Stephen speaks are the midnight transformation of Stephen and Mulligan in the morning, when Mulligan mockingly intones other words from the Mass. The disappearance of Stephen and the arrival of Bloom alone in nighttown recapitulate the shift from "Proteus" to "Calypso." Toward the beginning of Bloom's nighttime wanderings in "Circe," details from the first three episodes of his daytime wanderings are repeated, largely in their original order. Starting with the allusions to "Hades," Homeric and Christian rationales and a more random sequence of references to various episodes replace the orderly repetition of the day's events. Finally, the order of presentation defined by other parts of the narrative reasserts itself at the end, for the concluding tableau anticipates the book's ending. In its order of presentation, then, "Circe" recapitulates the large structure of *Ulysses*. The episodes written in the relatively accessible initial and final styles are alluded to most explicitly at the beginning and end of "Circe." Between the early and the late allusions, the order is more problematic, just as the episodes between "Hades" and the "Nostos" are, in general, more extravagant than the ones surrounding them. Even if the reader does not perceive the specificity with which "Circe" reflects the shape of the entire work, the contrast between the relative simplicity of the episode's beginning and end and the greater obscurity of the middle portion suggests the general correspondence between part and whole. In both, the middle of the way is errant.

The Drama of Descent as Figure of Thought

These patterns of allusion can help us establish connections between "Circe" and Joyce's other writings and describe the narration as evoking a descent into the underworld. As we have seen, the effect of visiting the dead, their resurrection through memory and through the enabling power of speech, is important in Joyce's fiction as early as "The Dead." In that story, however limited we may judge him to be, Gabriel Conroy, one of Dublin's dead, enjoys the power to speak both in public and to himself. Through style the narrator allows the dead of Dublin and their cultural past to speak and thereby to live. He re-creates the consciousness of their race by putting it into words. And in *Finnegans Wake*, the title, the narrative, and the act of writing all involve waking the dead, including the author's forebears. In "Circe," through allusion Joyce enables his fathers to speak. His precursors include Homer, God, and Joyce, "Himself his own father" (*U* 208), as Mulligan quips. It is to their texts, the *Odyssey*, the Bible as Christian history, and *Ulysses* itself, that Joyce's drama owes its structure.

As I have described it, "Circe" becomes the equivalent of the *Wake*'s elliptical letter. Besides bearing a synecdochic relationship to the work containing it, like that letter the episode alludes to the wanderings of Odysseus, to God, and to the author's own work. The design in choosing these specific elements for building interlocking patterns of allusion seems clear enough. Within the framework of this dramatic episode, whose form suggests the parallel between the teller and Shakespeare, Joyce aligns three things: (1) his mythic precursor, Odysseus in the underworld, as paradigm for the artist; (2) the analogy between the artist and God, the story of whose works from beginning to end the episode includes within itself; and (3) his own work of writing together with his own literary works, whose details as internal allusions form both a third pattern and aspects of the other two. The last of these patterns projects *Ulysses* as a context of the whole for understanding the others. We apprehend that context by means of the interaction among patterns of allusion, though we may well not grasp fully the nature of the patterns or their interaction as we read.

Here Joyce moves toward what becomes more explicit in the *Wake*: the use of allusions to his own work and to the works of other writers to suggest, among other things, the nature of aesthetic creation as a rewriting that includes the writer's representation of himself. He creates after his own image. In *A Portrait* Joyce had already begun this movement by presenting Stephen writing his poem, another internal segment of narrative that can stand in some ways, as does the letter, for its own context. In "Circe" the teller repeats parts of his own work, just as the teller in V.2 of *A Portrait* repeats phrases from II.2. The crucial difference, of course, is that the repetitions in *Ulysses* are not verbatim. They are repetitions with a difference. They have undergone the sort of process that occurs in Stephen's consciousness when he transforms the images gleaned from earlier experiences, including his reading, into a poem separable from himself, a text that is dramatic as he uses that word. That transforming process explicitly evoked in *A Portrait* is only implied when the teller of "Circe" reuses his own story.

Through reuse, Joyce treats his own writing as part of the tradition out of which it emerges. By doing so, as in the *Wake*, he implies that his book is potentially inexhaustible and self-engendering: "autokinatonetically pre-provided with a clappercoupling smeltingworks exprogressive process" (*FW* 614.30–31). It becomes a phoenixlike work whose decompositions result in resurrections. When the author perceives the "canonicity of his existence as a tesseract" (*FW* 100.34–35), his work has become part of the canon from which he can take tesserae to add to and extend that very canon as mosaic. The resulting seemingly self-engendering proliferations contribute to the book's appearing to achieve a status like consciousness itself, as if it had a memory and a transforming imagination whose gyrating play defies simple explanation.

The tendency of *Ulysses* toward that status, most evident in "Circe," prepares us for the concluding style of "Penelope." That style suggests a metaphor for the entire text as a consciousness. The metaphor applies to both "Circe" and *Finnegans Wake*, because consciousness, through memory and imagination, enables the resurrecting of the dead, the revivifying of pasts, be they personal, aesthetic, or cultural. The "slow fires of consciousness" (*FW* 186.5), the self-feeding fires of imagination, produce images and texts that are "perilous, potent, common to allflesh, human only, mortal" (*FW* 186.6–7). These are fires and images like those in Yeats's "Byzantium," flames begotten from flame and "images that yet/Fresh images beget." Together they provide the writer's "thumbprint, mademark or just a poor trait of the artless" (*FW* 114.31–32), both the portrait of the artist and the trait shared even by the would-be artless, including Molly Bloom and the reader. In their different ways, both "Circe" and "Penelope" point toward the geometrical construction that stands for the mother's genitals in the middle of the *Wake* (*FW* 293). Diagram and episodes are composed of "those fickers which are returnally reprodictive of themselves. Which is unpassible" (*FW* 298.17–18). These are figures of speech and figures who speak that return seemingly eternally to reproduce and to speak of themselves. And as "fickers," by analogy with lovemaking, they figure the process of aesthetic creation that is their origin. They are no more "unpassible," or impossible, than the "logical and coherent" (*P* 244) absurdities of narration and narrative that occur in *A Portrait*. And they will not pass away.

When I suggest that "Penelope" and "Circe" taken together anticipate the *Wake* by providing a textual metaphor, a metaphor *for* textuality, in mental processes, I am not asserting that every literary text is a consciousness. I mean something more specific about Joyce's late works, and about the nature of mind they project. The sort of consciousness these books evoke is not an empiricist one that functions primarily metonymically by association. That is part of the reason Umberto Eco's recent work on Joyce from a semiotic perspective is unconvincing—in fact, wrong-headed.[10] His theory of mind simply cannot deal adequately with Joyce. Although Eco provides in some ways an extreme example, I mention him not as an exception. Rather, he illustrates what is often the case when critics try to deal with Joyce's fiction, including his representations of mind, by making simplistic assumptions about consciousness as part of their unstated interpretive frames of reference. We require a more supple theory of mind, one that includes some recognition of the unconscious, of memory, of imagination, of what is sometimes called the imaginary than any empiricist view can muster.[11] I am not suggesting that a Freudian notion of the unconscious operates in Joyce's writings or that a Freudian critical perspective is necessary for explaining Joyce's work. But repression, repetition, forgetting, and the return to or return of the repressed are helpful notions in describing the complicated representations of mind in Joyce's fiction, including his representation of consciousness as fiction and fiction as consciousness yoked to an unconscious. These related notions, especially repression as Freud used it, express the complications of an ambivalence that may include remembering and forgetting, forgetting as prelude to remembering and to working through or acting out.[12]

As *Finnegans Wake* approaches its beginning near its end, the teller mentions explicitly the work of memory that Joyce's late writing expresses so emphatically:

> Begin to forget it. It will remember itself from every sides, with all gestures, in each our word. . . .
> Forget, remember!
> . . . .
> Forget! (*FW* 614.20–26)

To balance this last command, instead of another explicit enjoinder to remember at the text's end as beginning, we have the equivalent in the book's title read as an imperative: through memory and imagination in writing and reading the Finnegans are to awake. By announcing that his own text is an awakening, Joyce begins his final work by turning back implicitly to his first publication, his review of Ibsen's last play, "When We Dead Awaken."[13] That title would not be inappropriate to Joyce's own play "Circe." The resurrection of the dead, or descent into the underworld, of Joyce's fiction endeavors to give the dead speech. As it does so, it releases what had been largely omitted by the tradition of English fiction and what has often gone unacknowledged because suppressed by much literary criticism through its canons of coherence, organic unity, and mimetic form. It involves the achieving of a liberated literary form through a multiplicity of styles. In my commentary on the multiple styles of *Ulysses*, we shall explore the context within which "Circe," "Penelope," and *Finnegans Wake* are possible, a context that includes the representing of the conscience of the race.

"Circe" and the Form of Ulysses' Forms

Because of the careful arranging of references into patterns within "Circe" to evoke the correspondences between parts of the episode and other portions of the narrative, Hugh Kenner's comment that "as *Ulysses* is the *Odyssey* transposed and rearranged, 'Circe' is *Ulysses* transposed and rearranged"[14] takes on a more specific meaning and a greater importance than Kenner himself suggests. The transposing and rearranging help account for some of the particular interpretative connections we may make as we read the episode. As in the *Wake*, we perceive the teller fracturing, transforming, and recombining elements from the literary past, here through the numerous shifts in style, through the large patterns of allusion in the narration, and through the dramatic form. Because of these aspects of form, we can treat "Circe" as a synecdoche for the entire book. These broad aspects of the episode reflect Joyce's related combinations in *Ulysses* at large that forge its overall pattern. In general the shifts in style between episodes amount to a structural pattern of allusion by which the teller achieves the status of his precursors. We already have the nature of that pattern in sight from our reading of "Circe," whose formal elements in context encourage us to compare the artist with Shakespeare as paternal ghost and with Odysseus as adventurer. To elucidate the overall scheme we shall need to move back to the book's beginning, then forward through the various styles to their end in the "Nostos."

Our voyage of discovery and the teller's is a drama of mimesis with "Circe" as the climax and "Penelope" the denouement. Joyce departs from the mimesis of consciousness of the early episodes in order to make that mimetic style one of many stylistic ports of call during his and our wanderings.[15] That kind of mimesis is finally subsidiary to another sort of literary imitation and representation. The other representation takes the referential style as part of its encompassing design by stretching mimetic implications and forms to their limits. Those boundaries define the most extreme wandering and the home port of the book as voyage. Both "Circe" as descent into the underworld and "Penelope" as return to mimesis of mind represent the mental underworld that lives within us and is the origin of writing. Each episode contributes to the narration as a sequence of styles presenting a mythic pattern of action as narrative. Both the stylistic sequence and the pattern of narrative originate in the wanderings of Odysseus and terminate in Molly Bloom's monologue. They begin in a process of mind like that represented by Molly's style, and they end in the last of a sequence of representations resembling the mythic hero's wanderings. Mimesis of consciousness involves more than just the characters' minds in *Ulysses*. The mimesis of mind that emerges through the styles presents and evokes the teller's own highly literate, heroic consciousness by engaging ours.

THE INITIAL STYLE: "TELEMACHUS"—"HADES" —ROCK OF ITHACA

. . . for the interest of everything is all that it is *his* vision, *his* conception, *his* interpretation: at the window of his wide, quite sufficiently wide, consciousness we are seated, from that admirable position we "assist." He therefore supremely matters; all the rest matters only as he feels it, treats it, meets it. A beautiful infatuation this, always, I think, the intensity of the creative effort to get into the skin of the creature; the act of personal possession of one being by another at its completest.

—Henry James, "Preface to *The American*"

In "Circe" and throughout *Ulysses*, the reader encounters two elements that constantly require interpretation: style and the allusions to Homer initiated by the title. In August 1919, while at work on "Cyclops," Joyce wrote to his friend and patron Harriet Shaw Weaver, apparently responding to her complaints about "Sirens." In that letter Joyce speaks about both these aspects of *Ulysses* in a way that connects them: "I understand that you may begin to regard the various styles of the episodes with dismay and prefer the initial style much as the wanderer did who longed for the rock of Ithaca. But in the compass of one day to compress all these wanderings and clothe them in the form of this day is for me only possible by such variation which, I beg you to believe, is not capricious" (*Letters* I, 129). Besides designating, albeit offhandedly, the early and middle styles of *Ulysses* as the "initial" and the "various styles," Joyce makes two comparisions that illuminate each other.[16] He compares the initial style to "the rock of Ithaca," and he draws an analogy between the reader and Odysseus. There is also an implied link between himself as artist and both the wanderer and Homer, for by stylistic variation Joyce claims to be compressing and representing Odysseus's wanderings.

In "Circe" we have already seen the multiple parallels in *Ulysses* between teller, characters, reader, and their precursors, both aesthetic and mythic. But that intricate parallelism begins much earlier than "Circe" in the reading process. As this letter hints, it was part of Joyce's conception of his own process of writing well before he reached "Circe." For the artist as teller, each episode is an adventure in style as well as part of the characters' wanderings. The early styles of the first episodes are the narrator's rock of Ithaca, to which he will return at the end of the telling as journey, as does Odysseus to his rock, though he may seem greatly changed by his wanderings.

Hero and bard hold special places of honor in the world of Homer's epic, as Homer does in Vico's philosophy. Homer connects martial arts and poesis at a crucial point in the narrative of Odysseus's homecoming when he describes Odysseus's stringing the bow he will use to slay the suitors:

> So spoke the wooers, but Odysseus of many wiles, as soon as he had lifted the great bow and scanned it on every side—even as when a man well-skilled in the lyre and in song easily stretches the string about a new peg, making fast at either end the twisted sheep-gut—so without effort did Odysseus string the great bow. And he held it in his right hand, and tried the string, which sang sweetly beneath his touch, like to a swallow in tone. (Book XXI, ll. 404–10)[17]

For Homer, Odysseus, the heroic wanderer, resembles an artist, "one well-skilled in the lyre and in song." By reversing the terms of the comparison, Joyce creates the epical simile informing his book. For Joyce, the artist, one well-skilled in writing and telling, resembles a heroic wanderer. Through stylistic variation he translates this simile into epical narration.

But within the structural scheme for his book, Joyce uses Homer's comparison in other ways that help account for some of the details of both his narration and his narrative. In the narrative, the parallels between Stephen Dedalus and Leopold Bloom actualize the Homeric comparison of bard to wanderer. That comparison, clearly at work in "Circe," has already been established in the six episodes narrated in the initial style, three presenting Stephen on the morning of 16 June in counterpoint with three presenting Bloom. In the narration, Joyce realizes Homer's comparison in another way by embodying it in the relationship between the central characters as wandering heroes and the artist as teller of their tale. The similitude is identical to Homer's but shifted to a different conceptual level, one that guides both the overall stylistic context and many of the stylistic details for the parallels between Bloom and Stephen in the narrative. In this way the metaphor *in* Homer's narration becomes the metaphor *for* Joyce's. The simile works structurally by linking both teller and central characters to the same mythic precursor. It functions in details of style through the alignments between teller and central characters that occur in the first six episodes. To explore those alignments we shall need to identify the elements of the initial style and describe how Joyce uses that style to create the effects he begins with as preparation for the various and ultimate styles to come.

The narration of the first six episodes is consistent enough, within certain broad limits, to be treated as one style rather than several. This is not to deny the distinctions between the narration in different episodes. What I am calling a single style actually involves a range of techniques, including most prominently the ones clustering around narrated monologue that Joyce mastered in his earlier fiction. There, the most sophisticated and flexible uses of those techniques tend to occur near the end of each narrative—in the conclusion of "The Dead" and in part V of *A Portrait*. Part of the difficulty at the start for the reader of *Ulysses* is Joyce's use of the whole range of techniques early in the narration. Although he introduces them gradually, he does so more quickly than in either "The Dead" or *A Portrait*. And in *Ulysses* he exploits both the quoted monologue and the narrator's use of the character's ideolect in third person more frequently and more eccentrically than before.

Joyce uses the narrated monologue and related techniques in complicated ways virtually from the beginning because this is *not* to be the style toward which the work develops. Instead, he begins with it and uses it just long enough for the reader to learn its conventions and to start comparing artist and citizen in the narrative. He does so to create a home from which he departs in the stylistic divagations of the book's middle, divagations that take him beyond the mimetic tradition. It is not just the similarities among specific techniques of narration, then, that allow us to speak of this mode of writing as a single style. The initial style is single because the narrator uses the techniques that compose it primarily for referential purposes. Our conventional literary critical ideal of stylistic consistency in narration assumes this mimetic purpose of style in fiction. Joyce could expect that it would. Consequently, we can treat the initial style as the basic style not just in *Ulysses*; it represents the mimetic tradition of English fiction.

The mixture of techniques in the first six episodes limits the narrator's prominence. Even in "Telemachus," where the third-person passages greatly overshadow the slim presentation of Stephen's thoughts, the narrator's language, although sometimes remarkable, is not especially obtrusive. In later episodes other techniques draw more attention to the teller. Once the representation of consciousness becomes dominant, the narrator's limited visibility places a great deal of the narration's burden on the character and, because of the style's characteristics, on the reader. Through the frequent direct renderings of thought, we feel we know the fictive personality of the character more thoroughly than we know the anonymous third-person narrator, who tends to have little impact early in the book except as a reflector of action and thought. It seems from time to time almost as if the character can speak without the narrator. But the narrator makes it clear he cannot in these early episodes by injecting himself explicitly into the narration. The frequent inclusion of short statements in the third person reminds the reader of the narrator's continuing presence, though that presence seems to provide only brief descriptions of action. The narrator often avoids calling attention to himself by adopting diction similar to the character's thoughts spoken in the first person. Joyce employs extensively the psycho-narration slipping into narrated and quoted interior monologue and filled with the character's ideolect that he uses so effectively in presenting Stephen's villanelle and in other sections near the end of *A Portrait*.

Henry James's comments on *The American* capture the relations among teller, character, and reader in the initial style of *Ulysses*.[18] Through the commingling of two voices in the narration, narrator and reader penetrate the character's mind. In that penetration, the character begins to take over the teller's role, as so often in the presenting of consciousness in fiction.[19] And the reader begins to assume the character's part. We take over the character's role by saying "I," by translating he or she into "I" and the past tense into the present. Narrated monologue as Joyce employs it emphasizes the ambiguous status of speaker and of addressee. It does so by superimposing two discourses: that of the character, addressed to himself, and that of the teller, addressed to the reader. In this mixing of discourses, the reader says "I" and is also addressed. We share the teller's perspective, because we listen to his report of the character's interior voice, a voice for which we sometimes provide the "I," at the same time as we listen to the character. We are asked to be in two places at once. Consequently, we oscillate in our readings.

Henry James expresses these ambiguities by introducing a sexual metaphor. James suggests the sexual nature of the relationship between the artist as teller and his character when he says "a beautiful infatuation this, always, I think, the intensity of the creative effort to get into the skin of the creature; the act of personal possession of one being by another at its completest." He continues by asserting "that it is, by the same stroke, the effort of the artist to preserve for his subject that unity, and for his use of it (in other words for the interest he desires to excite) that effect of a *centre* which most economise its value."[20] The intimate relationship between teller and character is also one between artist and tale, which the character as "*centre*" stands for. The teller's penetration of the character is the most economical means for the artist to satisfy his desire to excite the reader's interest.

In the metaphor of the window of the character's consciousness at which "*we* are seated," James links reader to writer and both to character. His "we" is *both* an authorial "we" *and* the indication that the reader possesses the writer's perspective. The reader shares the writer's maieutic role as midwife for the character's thoughts: "From that admirable position we 'assist.'" Reader and writer are on both sides of the window, proscenium, or looking glass simultaneously. Because of its ambiguities, the initial style as window is also a looking glass in which the reader observes the roles assumed during reading. We are seated with the author looking in at the window of the character's mind, in which we see the story's action. And along with the character, reader and author look out of the character's mind as window at the scene of external action. As both voyeurs of and participants in activities of narrative and narration, we are at once inside and outside the house of fiction. We achieve the double perspective through the vacillation between first and third person inherent in the initial style.

"Telemachiad": "Telemachus"—"Proteus"

Joyce actualizes and, at times, counters the great potential in the initial style for alignments between teller, characters, and reader on his way toward the abrupt shift in focus that occurs with "Aeolus." He does so by developing the range of techniques he uses in ways that create varying effects. Joyce's flexible handling of the techniques anticipates his more extreme use of contrasting stylistic conventions in "Circe." Within the initial style there are two conventions at work. On the one hand, the teller *alternates* between the mimesis of scene and action in the third person and the mimesis of consciousness in the first person. But that straightforward alternation, like the impression at times of separate external and internal worlds in "Circe," does not account adequately for the narration. The more complicated convention that operates early in *Ulysses* includes the mixing of third- with first-person perspectives in psycho-narration and narrated monologue.

By employing the quoted monologue frequently together with these other techniques, Joyce creates the impressions of both alternating and mixed voices. Although with each convention we have access to the characters' thoughts, in combination they produce a fluctuating perspective that we experience as our own and the teller's variable proximity to the character's mind. When Joyce employs the quoted monologue, we may often feel we can distinguish between teller's voice and character's voice, perhaps because some typographical device, such as the colon, indicates a distinction. Or the narrator's completely formed syntactical constructions will differ from the grammatically elliptical language full of odd paratactic juxtapositions suggesting the flow of the character's thoughts. But regularly and increasingly in the first six episodes, the style tends to mix voices in radically ambiguous ways. The reader becomes actively engaged in trying to distinguish between the voices and in responding to the difficulty, even at times to the impossibility, of making a determination.

We can chart two tendencies in Joyce's use of the initial style by comparing the beginnings of the first episodes. In the "Telemachiad," those beginnings mark the shift toward the evoking of thought as unmediated that characterizes the developing narration. But with the openings of "Proteus" and, in a different way, "Calypso," the ambiguous mingling of voices begins to dominate the style. As we move from episode to episode in the "Telemachiad," the stylistic emphasis shifts to create the impression of the narrator's increasing proximity to the character's thoughts. "Telemachus" begins with a description of Buck Mulligan's appearance and actions in third person without any explicitly identified renderings of thought. "Nestor" opens with a stichomythic dialogue between Stephen and Cochrane, one of his students, followed immediately by the direct rendering of Stephen's thoughts indicated explicitly by the use of first person: "I hear the ruin of all space, shattered glass and toppling masonry, and time one livid final flame" (U 24). As the dialogue resumes, the narrator reasserts his presence by identifying the speakers and describing their actions in third person: "—Asculum, Stephen said, glancing at the name and date in the gorescarred book" (U 24). Even in this sentence, the vividly metaphorical adjective "gorescarred" carries some resonance of the linguistic vigor of Stephen's thoughts. There may even be a mental association here between "gore," whose Indo-European root means "spear," and Stephen's image of the general leaning on his spear in the next paragraph presenting his thoughts. Joyce and his young character's knowledge of etymology from reading Skeat's *Etymological Dictionary* makes such associations probable.[21] Like the later part of "Telemachus," much of "Nestor" consists of dialogue and the direct and indirect report of Stephen's consciousness.

"Proteus" starts with an entire paragraph of Stephen's thoughts rendered in the first person, followed by the narrator's brief description of Stephen's actions in third person: "Stephen closed his eyes to hear his boots crush crackling wrack and shells" (U 37). The narrator's diction resembles Stephen's thoughts, for he uses "wrack," just as Stephen thinks of "seawrack" in the preceding paragraph. Unlike the two earlier episodes, much of "Proteus" consists of quoted interior monologue reporting Stephen's thoughts directly in first person. But the narrator asserts his presence, and his distance from Stephen, by speaking from time to time in the third person. In "Proteus" that distance and the felt gap between reader and character has diminished greatly from the beginning of "Telemachus." In the style of "Proteus," even the passages presented in the third person often suggest the flow of Stephen's thoughts and the intimate relationship of narrator and reader to character.

Like the narration in *A Portrait*, to which it is closely akin, the narration in the early episodes of *Ulysses* does not sustain completely the sort of broadly generalizing description I have just given. It does not because its variegated texture provides evidence for complicating and modifying the description. When we look closely at the style of "Telemachus," we discover from the outset anticipations of the mixed voices we find in "Proteus" and in later episodes. But that mixture does not occur at length in "Telemachus." It becomes more prominent and emphatic when viewed retrospectively, once the implications for voice have begun to emerge vividly. Joyce's strategy resembles the one he uses in *Dubliners* by starting "The Sisters" in a mode whose potential will not be fully explored until later in the narration.

The teller in "Telemachus" is no commentator openly generalizing about the action's meaning in the manner of many nineteenth-century English novels. He reports the story's setting and action, presenting without explicit comment details of description, movement, and speech, as in the episode's first few sentences:

> Stately, plump Buck Mulligan came from the stairhead, bearing a bowl of lather on which a mirror and a razor lay crossed. A yellow dressinggown, ungirdled, was sustained gently behind him by the mild morning air. He held the bowl aloft and intoned:
> —*Introibo ad altare Dei*. (*U* 2–3)

Especially by comparison with a passage we come to shortly, this introductory paragraph is not highly adjectival. And its adjectives do not raise prominently any question about their source or their referent. It is possible to read every adjective in a description as implying an act of judgment. But here the adjectives, even "stately, plump," evoke primarily a referential physical reality as the scene rather than a state or act of mind in character or teller. The colored, unfastened gown blows gently in a breeze that is neither uncomfortably hot nor cold. Like the language of much of *Dubliners*, the first few pages of *Ulysses* can create the impression of a narrating presence as detached, objective observer of external details. The complicating factor in *Ulysses*, as in *Dubliners*, is the focus on psyche as well as on scene. In "Telemachus," narrator and reader observe Stephen Dedalus in the act of observation. Since the teller shares his apparently detached stance with the character, the style initiates subtly the parallel between narrator and character that recurs frequently. For both, the initial detachment is only one pose among many, though each returns to it regularly. Through stylistic variations, reader and teller fluctuate between observing the character and being engaged by his thoughts.

To introduce Stephen's entrance shortly after Buck speaks the words from the Mass, the narrator describes Stephen as having "looked coldly" at Mulligan's visage. At the same time he reports both Stephen's act of observation and Buck's appearance through apparently scrupulously mean, discrete details:

> Stephen Dedalus, displeased and sleepy, leaned his arms on the top of the staircase and looked coldly at the shaking gurgling face that blessed him, equine in its length, and at the light untonsored hair, grained and hued like pale

oak. (*U* 3)

The language nearly strips Buck of human lineaments. Like one of the grotesques in "Circe," Buck is reduced to the purely physical actions of "shaking" and "gurgling." His face is compared to that of an animal; his hair, to wood. In ways that resemble passages in *Dubliners*, here through metaphor and simile an interpreting presence asserts itself by making comparisons. But the source of the language is not entirely clear. It may be the teller. Or it may be Stephen, who sees Mulligan through his early morning displeasure, which motivates a cold detachment as a symptom of antagonism. In these comparisons, and in this whole sentence, the style becomes more adjectival than in the few sentences that have preceded. Because of the adjectives, psyche begins to merge with scene, and the teller's view, with the character's.

Some of the modifiers are not descriptive in any simple, physical way. By contrast with "ungirdled" in the first paragraph, "untonsored," for instance, tells us what Mulligan's appearance does *not* resemble rather than what it *does* resemble. His morning ritual includes shaving his face, not his head. Even the source of "displeased and sleepy" is ambiguous. We do not know whether Stephen looks out of sorts and disheveled to Buck or to the teller or whether the teller is reporting the way Stephen feels independently of the way he looks. The adverb "coldly" is no easier to gloss univocally. We cannot pass off these ambiguities as either accidental or insignificant. Joyce could have avoided them easily by identifying the source with the kinds of phrases we have encountered in his earlier writing. He could have used "who felt" or "who seemed to Mulligan" to introduce the adjectives "displeased and sleepy" describing Stephen. But he chose not to.

The interplay between scene and psyche in the teller's language comes to a head briefly and abruptly with the insertion of a single word, "Chrysostomos," in the next lengthy description of Mulligan's actions:

> He peered sideways up and gave a long low whistle of call, then paused awhile in rapt attention, his even white teeth glistening here and there with gold points. Chrysostomos. Two strong shrill whistles answered through the calm. (*U* 3)

We can understand this word in at least two ways, both developed in the later narration, neither sustaining the convention of an externally referential style. We hear the word as emanating from Stephen Dedalus's allusive mind when he links Mulligan with the "golden-mouthed" father of the early church, St. John Chrysostomos.[22] In this reading, the interior comment duplicates the narrator's descriptive reference to Mulligan's appearance. Consequently, we might be tempted to distinguish the repetition of teller's view and character's from some later conjunctions of their words in which the character completes or extends what the teller says. But even this early in the narration such an extension takes place. The character goes beyond the teller by passing a judgment, perhaps a largely ironical judgment, on Mulligan's rhetorical abilities. Because the adjective is *allusive* as well as metaphorical, it introduces more explicitly than have the earlier metaphorical comparisons the mimesis of character's mind. The narrator will soon begin to use that mimesis more frequently and at greater length in the initial style.

Within the referential assumptions of that style, the reading of "Chrysostomos" as mimetic of mind seems incontrovertible. But, because that mimesis has not yet been fully established on the first page, we may read the allusion as the narrator's language rather than the character's. It amounts to an epithet, like the epithets, including *polytropos*, that Homer uses extensively in the *Odyssey*. In context, "Chrysostomos" is Joyce's equivalent for the Homeric epithet of the *Odyssey*'s invocation. The context makes it apply to a speaker, and by extension to a writer, who is golden-mouthed because he is full of oratorical, stylistic contrivance. The epithet, then, applies to the teller of this tale. Some of the other epithets mentioned in the initial style, such as "bullockbefriending" (*U* 36) from the end of "Nestor," we attribute unhesitatingly to Stephen's mind. But by then the stylistic conventions have taken hold. While our sense of the initial style undermines the assignment of "Chrysostomos" to the narrator by supporting the attribution to Stephen, other aspects of the narration counter the effect of that style's conventions. The allusive elements within some of the early episodes, together with the self-referential aspects of the later various styles, make the alternate reading plausible. The choice of interpretations depends on our frame of reference. And *Ulysses*, with its odd title and its spectrum of styles, employs both frames of reference, which become available together in a retrospective reading. With the single word "Chrysostomos," we encounter both the first instance of quoted interior monologue in *Ulysses* and the first significant disruption, after the title, of mimetic assumptions. As so often, Joyce throws us off balance near the start by suggesting, before we are prepared to deal with the implications, what the narration will eventually become—what, in fact, it already is.

After this proleptic disruption, the teller proceeds to establish the alternation between external and internal action unobtrusively by introducing Stephen's thoughts gradually into his third-person narration. He does so by employing a third-person report of Stephen's consciousness as psycho-narration before any further direct presentations of it as quoted monologues. The translation of Stephen's thoughts into the normal grammatical units of the narrator's discourse circumvents the kind of jolt in the narration's rhythm caused by "Chrysostomos."

The teller begins to attenuate the sense of distance between himself and his character by presenting Stephen's memory of his dream about his mother. These passages concerning the dream make up the first sustained penetrations of the character's mind in *Ulysses*. Consequently, through repetition and shifts in style, the dream of the mother takes on special significance long before its enactment in "Circe." The first of these passages begins with an echo of the initial description of Stephen: "Stephen, an elbow rested on the jagged granite, leaned his palm against his brow and gazed at the fraying edge of his shiny black coatsleeve" (*U* 5). As in the earlier passage, Stephen is leaning, and the narration focuses on discrete, external details. But the echo results in an incongruity in the description, a kind of dislocation in the presentation of scene. That incongruity prepares for the shift to Stephen's thoughts presented explicitly here rather than implicitly and ambiguously, as in the earlier passage. Now the verb describing Stephen's posture, rather than contributing primarily to a coherent physical portrayal, becomes a signal that he is thinking. Before, he leaned part of his body against something, as we would expect, "his arms on the top of the staircase," and looked at Mulligan. Although Stephen continues to lean and to gaze, the syntax is now, at the least, odd. It suggests that he leans his palm against his brow rather than the other way around. If there were commas after "leaned" and "brow," the description would be more coherent, but those commas are absent. The teller's decision to make the sentence's syntax and its verbs evoke the earlier sentence through repetition affects the description of scene. That scene now matters less than Stephen's mind, which the verbs "lean" and "gaze" work to introduce despite their ostensible meanings.

In *Dubliners* Joyce uses a similar posture together with sense perceptions to introduce thought, though with a different effect—for instance, in the first paragraph of "Eveline": "She sat at the window watching the evening invade the avenue. Her head was leaned against the window curtains and in her nostrils was the odour of dusty cretonne. She was tired." Such a passage clearly differs in its linguistic texture and its impact from either of the passages involving leaning early in "Telemachus." The use of the verb "lean" in a copulative construction rather than as an active verb creates a greater distance from the character's static pose. And the passage lacks adjectives almost completely, while both descriptions of Stephen's pose include adjectives evoking sensuously the details of his surroundings and his stance. Those details anticipate the intimate rendering of his mind to come. The distance between scene and psyche in "Eveline," then, is much more emphatic than in "Telemachus." In that episode, the narrator moves almost directly into psycho-narration to begin establishing quickly the initial style's conventions: "Pain, that was not yet the pain of love, fretted his heart. Silently, in a dream she had come to him after her death" (*U* 5). The word "Chrysostomos" aside, the teller introduces us to the different possibilities of his variable mode of narration gradually. Stephen's posture at first is essentially physical, and adjectives hint ambiguously and indirectly at a consciousness in the scene. Stephen's leaning as part of the physical scene becomes, in the teller's second presentation of it, the explicit context for his thoughts about the dream presented largely as psycho-narration. The later passages in "Telemachus" concerning Stephen's dead mother and the dream (*U* 9–10) introduce both narrated and quoted interior monologue. By the end of "Telemachus" the teller has deployed the basic range of strategies he will use repeatedly in the early episodes.

The dream of the mother may be interpreted in various ways. In light of "Circe" and "Scylla and Charybdis," we can take the dream as a metaphor for aesthetic creation, like the visitation of Hamlet's father to Hamlet, or like Stephen's repeating of his father's tale of the moocow at the start of *A Portrait*. From that perspective, one detail stands out especially vividly, Stephen's recall of his mother's "shapely fingernails reddened by the blood of squashed lice from the children's shirts" (*U* 10). This memory, juxtaposed with Stephen's thoughts about the dream, anticipates the gruesome enactment in "Circe." The involvement of Stephen's mother as creator with her offspring differs substantially from the ostensible withdrawal of the artist carefully paring his nails in Stephen's aesthetic theory in *A Portrait*. That earlier image emphasizes distance; this one, immanence. In *Ulysses* the artist as teller's role involves both.

The shifts in setting and action in "Telemachus" reflect and reinforce the increasing intimacy of the style. Just as the narrator shifts focus from external to internal, from a relatively detached observation to an involved rendering, the setting changes from claustrophobic enclosure to open spaces. Beach replaces tower, and the sea replaces small containers: the bowl of lather, the white china bowl full of bile, the jug and cups of milk. By the episode's end, vigorous movements, including walking, running, and swimming, displace the cramped, passive postures of leaning and sitting. The characters achieve primarily a physical release. The narrator's style, on the other hand, is released from detachment and from the accompanying potential for a cold reduction of characters to immobile, external details. That release creates the possibility for the reader's intimacy with the character's mind unlike anything the characters themselves experience in this part of the narrative. The parallel movements of narrative and narration in "Telemachus" initiate a development that reaches its limit in a merger when teller fuses with character in "Penelope." Just as an exponential curve approaches its limiting value near infinity, in "Penelope" a character achieves a climactic release from physical surroundings when the teller's intimacy with character becomes greatest.[23]

Early in *Ulysses* the narrative deals with psychological rather than stylistic withdrawal and involvement. The initial style's vacillating form bears a direct, sometimes antithetical, relationship to Stephen's and Bloom's psychological states. The teller's ability and tendency to adopt the character's perspective, allowing us to do so as well, run counter to the alienation and withdrawal that occur at times in the narrative. In this regard the antagonism among critics toward Joyce's abandoning the initial style after "Hades" reflects the strong effect the initial style has as intimate narration. For some critics, Joyce's turning away from the mimesis of consciousness amounts to an assault on character that reinforces rather than counters the psychological alienation. This antagonism arises from normative, referential critical assumptions about literature together with the great success of the initial style as referential. I take instead a more positive view concerning the later narration. Joyce's violent shift in style works as part of a large sequence to suggest the relationship between teller, as all in all, and character rather than emphasizing the absolute distance between them. In this interpretation, the referential view is only one among many possible attitudes toward literature. One connotation of *relation* here involves the link between teller and character as parent and child within a familial, generative context of the sort Stephen perceives in *Hamlet*. And relations have to do with sexual intimacy, as Henry James's comments on narrator, character, and reader make clear.

In "Telemachus," Stephen reacts defensively both to his memory of his mother and to Mulligan. Anticipating the *"Non serviam"* (*U* 582) of "Circe," he denies in thought the obligation his mother represents: "No, mother. Let me be and let me live" (*U* 10). Thinking of himself, with respect to Mulligan, as an isolated, embattled figure, Stephen conceives of his art in terms of parry and thrust: "Parried again. He fears the lancet of my art as I fear that of his. The cold steelpen" (*U* 7). While Stephen associates Mulligan, a medical student, with the scalpel, Mulligan has dubbed him "Kinch the knifeblade." In their verbal fencing Stephen uses language as a shield for coldly keeping others at a distance while the teller uses language to represent thoughts:

> He had spoken himself into boldness. Stephen, shielding the gaping wounds which the words had left in his heart, said very coldly:
> —I am not thinking of the offence to my mother.
> —Of what, then? Buck Mulligan asked.
> —Of the offense to me, Stephen answered. (*U* 8–9).

Stephen constantly speaks coldly or bitterly:

> Drawing back and pointing, Stephen said with bitterness:
> —It is a symbol of Irish art. The cracked looking-glass of a servant. (*U* 6)

His physical act of drawing back indicates his habit of psychological withdrawal. Like Shem the Penman, he screens himself from the world by projecting squidlike an image of himself as a defense (*FW* 185–86). But the screen is also a mirror reflecting Stephen's face, as does the mirror Buck actually holds up to him:

> —Look at yourself, he [Mulligan] said, you dreadful bard.
> Stephen bent forward and peered at the mirror held out to him, cleft by a crooked crack on end. As he and others see me. Who chose this face for me?

This dogsbody to rid of vermin. It asks me too. (*U* 6)

Joyce uses the mirror in "Telemachus" to indicate the style's developing direction. Before holding it up to Stephen's face, Mulligan has literally held the mirror up to nature (Lynch, Mulligan's substitute in "Circe," actually uses that phrase, as we have seen [*U* 567]): "He swept the mirror a half circle in the air to flash the tidings abroad in sunlight now radiant on the sea" (*U* 6). Like some of the teller's language, the mirror reflects an external world. But when Stephen looks in the mirror the second time Buck holds it out, the mirror introduces an instance of the other kind of reflection the teller's style has begun to include. "Circe" marks a further stage in Joyce's use of the mirror, one pointing toward the goal of the styles: to link artist and citizen, writer and reader, in the literary text as looking glass. That linkage occurs because the styles, like the image Bloom sees of himself in a mirror in "Ithaca," are "aliorelative" as well as "ipsorelative" (*U* 708). However discrete each style may seem, together they enable a dynamic process that involves teller and reader.

At this point in his development, Stephen illustrates but does not yet comprehend the paradox of his squidlike, defensive use of language. He embodies truth, but does not know it. The description of Shem the Penman's creations in the *Wake* captures that paradox, for he not only shields himself from the world but the screen he makes from the material of his world constitutes his identity. Stephen's unenviable position, like Quentin Compson's in Faulkner's *The Sound and the Fury*, involves rejecting the past that has made him. Although he would reject the material his imagination works on so intensely in his thoughts, his language as shield is also the highly polished self-reflecting surface the creating consciousness cannot avoid. Like the narrator and like Shakespeare as Stephen characterizes him, when Stephen walks out, his steps tend toward himself. He even admits in thought in "Telemachus" that he is "another now and yet the same" (*U* 11), that he cannot escape what he has been. Unlike Buck, who claims to remember "only ideas and sensations" (*U* 8), Stephen's vivid memories constantly "beset his brooding brain" (*U* 10). Try as he will to become detached from his past, he cannot disengage himself completely.

In "Nestor," as the teller moves more frequently into his mind, Stephen becomes more engaged by those around him in spite of his aloof attitudes. The episode is composed of two parts, each concerned with Stephen's relationship to his auditors. In "Telemachus" we see Stephen vis-à-vis both his peers and, implicitly, the teller. In "Nestor" the reader sees him in his public role as teacher, in relation first to his students, then to the headmaster. As in the late sections of *A Portrait*, Stephen's public and private voices become prominent. Consequently, they are our basis for judging him, especially later after his public performances in "Aeolus" and "Scylla and Charybdis."

The ambiguity of voice in "Nestor" can be quite pronounced, as in the following passage:

> A bag of figrolls lay snugly in Armstrong's satchel. He curled them between his palms at whiles and swallowed them softly. Crumbs adhered to the tissues of his lips. A sweetened boy's breath. Welloff people, proud that their eldest son was in the navy. Vico Road, Dalkey. (*U* 24)

At first the paragraph might seem nearly evenly divided between the teller's perspective and the character's: the first three constructions, grammatically complete, employing verbs in past tense and pronouns of the third person emanating from the teller and the three grammatical fragments that follow coming from the character. But the teller's epic preterite does not entirely disappear in the second half of the passage. We can read "was" as Stephen's present tense transformed by the teller *or* as Stephen's reference to a past situation. The former reading seems more likely; the parents would be proud of present service rather than past. Consequently, the predicate is the teller's. The continued use of third-person pronouns without any switch to first person also complicates our attributions. The references in third person throughout the paragraph could even be Stephen's, for not one of them refers to him. Even the adverbs "snugly" and "softly" in the grammatically complete sentences suggest the judgments of a consciousness in the scene, especially when we do hear such a consciousness almost immediately.

Often in *Ulysses*, context influences our attributions. But here the snatches of dialogue reported by the narrator preceding and following the paragraph provide no determinative clue about the voice speaking in the passage they frame. Unlike the passages in "Circe" and in other late episodes that insist on the narrator's primacy, in this paragraph, two currents of thought continually merge and diverge ambiguously. They do so because the narrator combines observations of scene not obviously mediated by the character's mind with language that resembles a fragmented quoted monologue. In fact, the presentation of scene reflects the character's possible perspective as well as the teller's, and it includes some language that could be the character's diction. The constructions that look like quoted monologue are actually closer to narrated monologue because of tense and pronoun.

A similar complication arises in passages like the following, in which present tense does not indicate a quoted monologue, at least not the character's:

> That phrase the world had remembered. A dull ease of the mind. From a hill above a corpsestrewn plain a general speaking to his officers, leaned upon his spear. Any general to any officers. They lend ear. (*U* 24)

While the apparent grammatical completeness of the first sentence may encourage us to hear it as the teller's, the sort of general comment it contains sounds like Stephen's mind. Reading it as narrated monologue, we understand the teller's "had" as Stephen's "has." We can even read it as a relative clause rather than a complete sentence. The rest of the paragraph is odder still. Stephen seems to contemplate how the general who spoke the phrase might be thinking easefully. We may well want to read the third construction as part of Stephen's grammatically fragmented quoted monologue, but it only looks syntactically anomalous because of the single comma intervening between subject and verb. If we add another comma after "general," the sentence echoes closely the earlier ones describing Stephen in a posture of thought. The incongruity has been shifted from the physical description of brow in relation to hand to our experience of the syntax. From this perspective, the verb "lean" forms part of Stephen's physical description of the general *and* introduces the general's thoughts to come. We can now read the next two constructions as both part of Stephen's comparison of himself to the general and his representation of the general's thoughts. We can even read the last sentence's statement in the present tense in several ways. That present tense is gnomic, or iterative, because it refers to all soldiers and all students listening to superiors. And it is definite because it refers to the general's sense of the officers' attention, or to Stephen's sense of the students', or to both. In that last case, the definite reference would also be dual.

Not only is there no simple alternation of voices here, but the mixture of voices involves Stephen's and the general's, not just Stephen's and the teller's. I pay such close attention to this passage because it complicates considerably our sense of the form quoted monologue can take in these early episodes. Instead of announcing its difference from the narrator's discourse in third person and past tense, this quoted monologue uses both. It contains no first-person pronouns. And its single present-tense verb is gnomic rather than only definite. In addition, Stephen's presentation of the general's posture echoes the teller's earlier descriptions of Stephen. There is no simple alternation in the initial style between teller's and character's passages. Each can evoke the other's language and in so doing undermine any suggestion of absolute distinctions between them.

In the first pages of "Nestor," Joyce compresses the kind of shift in attitude Gabriel Conroy experiences in "The Dead" when, after performing for an audience from whom he distinguishes himself, he discovers a common bond with that audience. Because Stephen barely controls his students and belongs to a social class different from theirs, he feels his separation from them: "In a moment they will laugh more loudly, aware of my lack of rule and of the fees their papas pay" (*U* 24). Like both the aesthetic theory of *A Portrait* and the story Stephen recites in "Aeolus," the riddle he inflicts on his students about the fox burying his grandmother emphasizes his defensive sense of separation. But Stephen's nervously maintained distance dissolves when he confronts Cyril Sargent:

> Like him was I, these sloping shoulders, this gracelessness. My childhood bends beside me. Too far for me to lay a hand there once or lightly. Mine is far and his secret as our eyes. Secrets, silent, stony sit in the dark palaces of both our hearts: secrets weary of their tyranny: tyrants willing to be dethroned. (*U* 28)

Part of this paragraph's force comes from the unambiguous assignment of it to Stephen's consciousness through the repeated use of first person and present tense. As in *Dubliners*, Joyce employs his techniques for presenting mind to emphasize special moments in the character's thoughts.

This single moment of sympathy for the young boy, however strong in itself, does not counter wholly Stephen's continuing defensive attitude toward others, especially Haines and Mulligan. Perhaps it even explains partially that attitude. He still thinks of himself as embattled, as needing to parry and thrust. But his goal is to *sustain* the verbal combat rather than to defeat absolutely the audience he must have. He even plans his remarks in advance: "For Haines's chapbook. No-one here to hear. Tonight deftly amid wild drink and talk, to pierce the polished mail of his mind" (*U* 25). And he admits that Haines means him no harm: "The seas' ruler. His seacold eyes looked on the empty bay: history is to blame: on me and on my words, unhating" (*U* 30). Still, Haines's detachment, like a scrupulously mean narration, can evacuate its object of positive meaning. "Unhating" here indicates not the opposite of hatred, which, according to Bloom in "Cyclops" is love (*U* 333), but an attitude closer to indifference. The attitude Stephen discerns lacks the passionate intensity of the croppy boy's decision to bear no hate in the song Bloom hears during "Sirens." Stephen appraises his own antagonisms justly when he compares his verbal jousting to the sports his students engage in on the playing field: "Again: a goal. I am among them, among their battling bodies in a medley, the joust of life. You mean that knockneed mother's darling who seems to be slightly crawsick? Jousts" (*U* 32). Stephen's pose of solitary heroism actually gives him the means for continuing his engagement with his antagonists as a kind of game.

Like some of Stephen's entries in his journal at the end of *A Portrait*, his encounter with the headmaster in "Nestor" reveals Stephen's ability to laugh at himself rather than taking himself seriously all the time. The situation tests Stephen's ability to react sympathetically, or at least good-naturedly, for he is faced not with a child but with a crotchety, argumentative old man who trivializes Stephen's own jousting metaphor when he says: "I like to break a lance with you, old as I am" (*U* 35). Stephen does not hesitate to disagree with Mr. Deasy; for instance, when he surprises the schoolmaster by implying that everyone, not only the Jew, has "sinned against the light." But despite his antagonism to Mr. Deasy, Stephen finally laughingly aligns himself with his would-be adversary by promising to carry out his request:

> The lions couchant on the pillars as he passed out through the gate; toothless terrors. Still I will help him in his fight. Mulligan will dub me a new name; the bullockbefriending bard. (*U* 35–36)

This passage provides a stylistic culmination for the episode in one way by moving close to the kind of fused narration that occurs more vividly in some later episodes narrated in the initial style. The language of teller and character overlaps when Stephen decides to help Deasy by adopting his perspective however briefly and tentatively. And he adopts a perspective he thinks Mulligan might have taken.

Although short, the passage bears comparison with the conclusion of "The Dead," in which Gabriel Conroy has become the spokesman for others. While Stephen's identification in this passage is not so intense as his sympathy for Cyril Sargent, it has some of the same qualities. The teller marks the difference stylistically by rendering Stephen's thoughts here not as unalloyed quoted monologue, as in his reaction to the boy. Instead, the teller indicates his own presence. That indication creates some sense of distance in the narration, however gently, by mixing past tense and references to Stephen in the third person with the grammatical fragmentation and first person typical of quoted monologue. The style reflects as well the character's ambivalence, his mixed feelings of amused involvement and detached judgment. Stephen understands that Deasy is only a toothless terror, as helpless nearly as Cyril Sargent, but he will fulfill the request nevertheless.

After this passage the episode's style moves quickly to a sort of closure different from this mixture. When Mr. Deasy comes running after Stephen for a final repartee, the episode's last scene balances its opening one with another exchange of questions and answers. In that opening, the dialogue between Stephen and the students was a prelude for Stephen's eventual identification with one of them rendered as quoted monologue. By contrast, the dialogue at the end removes us from Stephen's thoughts and marks his, and our, withdrawal from alignment with the schoolmaster. Consequently, the episode ends not with quoted monologue but with direct discourse and with the teller's detached, ironic description of Mr. Deasy in third person and past tense: "On his wide shoulders through the checkerwork of leaves the sun flung spangles, dancing coins" (*U* 36). We can read the teller's withdrawal and irony as equivalents for Stephen's, whose thoughts are not rendered directly. The careful alignment and counterpoint of teller's language with character's interior view is in the same developmental line as the endings of some of Joyce's stories, especially "Eveline" and "Counterparts."

At the beginning of "Proteus" the teller reverses his withdrawal by injecting us into Stephen's interior language. He does so by setting the complexity, vivid language, and vitality of Stephen's mind apparently free to play at will on the world around him, unhindered by the distracting conversation of others. In this regard, "Proteus" resembles V.2 in *A Portrait*, for there too the reader is privy to the creative energies of Stephen's mind during a sustained portion of the narration. In its apparent liberation from constraints, "Proteus" anticipates both "Circe" and "Penelope," the book's two other end points. The relatively free play of the character's mind in "Proteus" is matched in "Circe" by the narrator's liberties with style and narrative. And it is extended in "Penelope," for there the reader is within the consciousness of a character not only briefly and intermittently but for an entire episode without interruption.

"Proteus" is climactic in part because it completes the movement initiated in "Telemachus" from enclosed spaces to open ones. Released from the confines of the school, which reiterate the earlier enclosed spaces, Stephen finds himself again by the sea, not for just a few moments but for the whole episode. The release from physical constraints includes a turning away from the external world itself. In one passage, Stephen contrasts the silent tower's stifling enclosure with the freedom of movement possible on the strand, where he can be alone and turn inward:

> The cold domed room of the tower waits. . . . In the darkness of the dome they wait, their pushedback chairs, my obelisk valise, around a board of abandoned platters. . . . A shut door of a silent tower entombing their blind bodies, the panthersahib and his pointer. . . .My soul walks with me, form of forms. So in the moon's midwatches I pace the path above the rocks, in sable silvered, hearing Elsinore's tempting flood. (*U* 44)

When he shifts his attention from the interior of a domed space to the interior of his own head, Stephen begins to will the literary parallels that inform his life. He places himself self-consciously in the romantic atmosphere of the sea coast and casts himself in Hamlet's role. Stephen's choosing of roles presents within the narrative the kind of choice the book's teller makes by associating himself with mythic and literary precursors. And the fluctuations of Stephen's thoughts in this episode suggest that his identity is as allotropic as the teller's.

Stylistically Joyce moves beyond both "The Dead" and part V of *A Portrait* by allowing the character more apparent autonomy as teller than previously in the context of narration in third person. The character's thoughts carry the burden of narration in ways only hinted at in the earlier episodes and works in the longer passages focusing on a character's mind. Stephen's approach to parity with the teller emphasizes the blending of inner and outer perspectives and of teller's and character's views and voices already initiated in the preceding episodes. The effect of the style resembles that of V.2 in *A Portrait*. As with Stephen's villanelle, we perceive the mind represented in the narrative functioning like the teller's mind implied by the narration. In what amounts to an allusion to Stephen's earlier act of writing in another work, the teller presents him again composing verses about a woman: "She trusts me, her hand gentle, the longlashed eyes. Now where the blue hell am I bringing her beyond the veil? Into the ineluctable modality of the ineluctable visuality. She, she, she. What she?" (*U* 48). The effect differs from *A Portrait* since Stephen calls the reality of his own imaginative creation into question. By doing so he captures in an odd way the double effect of Joyce's narration in *Ulysses*. To describe Stephen's thoughts together with the immediate and general stylistic contexts for them we have to resort again to constructions recalling "The House That Jack Built." Joyce writes a book whose teller evokes at the beginning the mind of a character as if it were a real presence. But in the act of composing verses the character creates within the narrative another fictional figure whom he speaks of as if she were a real presence, only to undermine her reality, just as aspects of the teller's later narration will undermine our sense of Stephen's reality. The parallel between teller and character goes beyond the similarity that any representation of consciousness in fiction will almost inevitably suggest. Here, the movement of the character's thoughts anticipates one of the narrator's large strategies of narration.

The style in "Proteus" reveals the ambiguous relationship between teller and character in various ways, as for instance in the following sentence, which introduces a series of images juxtaposed as grammatical fragments:

> A porterbottle stood up, stogged to its waist, in the cakey sand dough. A sentinel; isle of dreadful thirst. Broken hoops on the shore; at the land a maze of dark cunning nets; farther away chalkscrawled backdoors and on the higher beach a dryingline with two crucified shirts. Ringsend: wigwams of brown steersmen and master mariners. Human shells. (*U* 41)

The adjectives "stogged" and "cakey" suggest Stephen's ideolect. But the sentence begins with a complete grammatical construction in the past rather than the present tense, suggesting the narrator's view rather than the character's. Only when we reach "stogged," a past participle as adjective rather than a verb in past tense, do we begin to read the perception as Stephen's. That reading is confirmed once we reach the string of images devoid of third person and past tense. Retrospectively, we can read "stood up" as either a past participial phrase used adjectivally or as a predicate in past tense. Porter bottles, of course, do not normally stand up, but this one, a "sentinel" with a "waist," may do so, for Stephen and the reader, in imagination.

This sort of passage occurs frequently in "Proteus." And the teller interrupts the flow of Stephen's thoughts less often than earlier, allowing him to become a narrator-within-the-narration, duplicating the teller's constant shifting between internal and external views. In one section, for instance, though much of the language of narration occurs in third person and past tense, we read it as Stephen's perceptions (*U* 46–47). By not making his presence obviously felt in these pages, the teller encourages us to treat the passages as direct presentations of Stephen's mind rather than mediated ones. In this particular case, after noting a man and woman on the strand, Stephen adopts a mode of discourse resembling the narrator's, for he becomes an observer and describer of events in an external world: "Their dog ambled about a bank of dwindling sand, trotting, sniffing on all sides. Looking for something lost in a past life" (*U* 46). While we could read the past tense as the teller's language, we tend not to once we reach the string of present participles, which encourages us to take the sentence as a rendering of a scene Stephen perceives in the present. Through grammatical fragmentation, by separating the final participial phrase and continuing it in the character's ideolect, the teller creates the impression of our being in Stephen's mind. It is as if Stephen were turning the scene immediately into a vignette at the moment of perception. Perception and storytelling, both Stephen's telling and the narrator's, become nearly fused.

The narrator continues in this vein for almost a page, quoting speech that Stephen hears without using an *inquit* phrase and allowing Stephen to narrate in third person and past tense: "Something he buried there, his grandmother." Just as the teller shifted in "Telemachus" from the reporting of external action and speech to presenting Stephen's consciousness through the dream of his mother, Stephen shifts abruptly from his internal description of what happens before him to his memory of the dream he has had the night before: "After he woke me up last night same dream or was it?" (*U* 47). Once he has recounted the dream to himself, Stephen returns to his perceptions of the cocklepickers, which we hear as description. Like the teller, Stephen switches back and forth between an internal and an external world and even shifts from sense perception to memory and imaginative revery. But, however vivid and sustained Stephen's thoughts may be in "Proteus," the narrator always eventually reasserts his presence by using third-person pronouns and the past tense in ways that mark them as primarily his own language.

In his fluctuation between first- and third-person pronouns, the teller exercises, and allows us to exercise, and to recognize, the mind's protean power. In the narrative Stephen sometimes exhibits that power as an imaginative ability to take on different identities; for example, when he identifies with a changeling who lived in Dublin during 1338, the year the Liffey froze: "Their blood is in me, their lusts my waves. I moved among them on the frozen Liffey, that I, a changeling, among the spluttering resin fires. I spoke to no-one: none to me" (*U* 45). Stephen's notion of his own identity and our sense of it based on the style involve not a static ego but instead a series of related personae always in flux, changing through time yet still the same. During the day, both Stephen and Bloom think of themselves as changing or having changed, Stephen most memorably in "Scylla and Charybdis." Stephen's thinking of himself as a shape-changer and the narrator's presenting him as a mental flux fulfill the Homeric correspondence suggested by the third episode's deleted title. But, as in "Circe," the correspondences themselves tend to be protean. We are dealing with a prismatic text refracting its would-be original into a rainbow as the teller weaves his rainbow coat. Consequently, when we ask who is Proteus in *Ulysses* and what is protean about this episode, no one answer will suffice. The book constantly overturns any categorical formulations, some encouraged by Joyce himself, who distributed his well-known schema, parts of which Stuart Gilbert was the first to publish in *James Joyce's "Ulysses."*[24]

By reaching this conclusion, the reader answers the questions by reformulating them in an affective context, for our response to *Ulysses* in its relations to the *Odyssey* and in other ways is protean. From one point of view Stephen is Proteus because of the flux of his thoughts. But Stephen also resembles Menelaus, for he would try to capture Proteus, try to stop the flux that is himself, or at least attempt to order it by finding the "word known to all men" (*U* 49, 581). The narrator resembles Menelaus as well, for he has succeeded in capturing the flux of Stephen's thoughts within the matrix of his third-person narration. Likewise the reader becomes Menelean by striving to make sense of what seems at first, and even subsequent, consideration a chaotic episode whose narrator and character, outer and inner views, can be difficult to distinguish and to interpret. All these parallels potentially generated in our response compose the reader's protean role. One final parallel will be the periodic focus in our discussion of the remaining episodes: the narrator is Protean, and he is Odyssean. Stephen as shape-changer never surpasses the narrator's chameleonic abilities. More than any of his mutable characters, the narrator deserves the epithets *polymetis* and *polytropos*, the primary epithets of Odysseus, which are often translated as "wily" but mean more precisely "of many contrivances," "of many turns," or, perhaps most felicitously, "skilled in all ways of contending."[25]

"Odyssey": "Calypso"—"Hades"

By devoting the first three episodes of the second part to Bloom's morning, and by employing the same range of stylistic techniques as earlier, Joyce creates a similitude between Stephen Dedalus and Leopold Bloom like that between bard and wanderer in the *Odyssey*. While the range of techniques is the same, in Bloom's episodes they create different effects than earlier. The difference has to do with the book's chronology and its Homeric descent. By taking us through the morning to noon and then returning to a scene of breakfast in preparation, the teller violates the referential conventions concerning chronology that the narration has followed up until now. We can think of the longer representations of

Stephen's thoughts interspersed between direct discourse and description as digressive, but they are not digressive in any especially distracting way. We learn quickly to incorporate the possibility of longish meditations occurring briefly to the character into our referential view of the narrative. But with "Calypso" a much lengthier digression begins, a digression three episodes long, which, when complete, takes us just past the ending time of "Proteus." Shortly following that juncture in the plot, the first extreme variation on the initial style begins. Consequently, the digression yields to an episode that undermines the narrative's referential aspects in a new way. But the digression itself has already begun the undermining. The initial style, then, as primarily mimetic ceases with the beginning of "Calypso," insofar as that style's conventions include a relatively consistent temporal presentation with only slight breaks between episodes, always as part of the forward movement of the story's chronology.

The large structure of narration in the first six episodes anticipates the coordination of simultaneous actions in "Wandering Rocks." In both that episode and the first six, the narration serves the metaphorical and comparative linkage of bard to wanderer. I stress the similarity of the first two triads to the much later, seemingly more eccentric "Wandering Rocks," though that similarity is by no means exact, to avoid overemphasizing the local effects of the initial style's techniques on our description of the book's literary realism. To remind the reader of the disparity between our expectations for an orderly chronological development and the shift that has just occurred, the teller reports Bloom's intention to write a story based on his actual observation of Molly's actions and speech. His work toward writing that story takes the form of a chronicle: "Might manage a sketch. By Mr and Mrs L. M. Bloom. Invent a story for some proverb which? Time I used to try jotting down on my cuff what she said dressing. Dislike dressing together. Nicked myself shaving. Biting her nether lip, hooking the placket of her skirt. Timing her. 9.15. Did Roberts pay you yet? 9.20. What had Gretta Conroy on? 9.23. What possessed me to buy this comb? 9.24. I'm swelled after that cabbage. A speck of dust on the patent leather of her boot" (*U* 69). The teller of *Ulysses*, too, structures his narration around a chronicle of the hours of the day, as Joyce's schemata and John Henry Raleigh's *The Chronicle of Leopold and Molly Bloom* abundantly demonstrate.[26] But the chronicle contains disconcerting shifts, gaps, and discontinuities, not only in the later episodes, as between "Cyclops" and "Nausicaa," but just as oddly in the midst of the initial style.

Even before "Aeolus," the teller's style is no transparent vehicle for the narrative. In "Calypso," it includes its own countermovement in a way that is not the case in the "Telemachiad." This is so in part because Bloom thinks of several stories whose styles differ from the episode's narration. The insertion of these other stylistic possibilities within the initial style makes us sense, more fully than we would otherwise, that a choice of techniques stands behind the telling. Bloom's brief chronicle, itself an example of the teller's quotation of interior monologue, reports only details of action and scene along with speech as direct discourse. It does not include the mimesis of mind so central to the book's narration. Just before Bloom considers writing his own sketch, he has been reading Philip Beaufoy's *"Matcham's Masterstroke"*:

> It did not move or touch him but it was something quick and neat. Print anything now. Silly season. He read on, seated calm above his own rising smell. Neat certainly. *Matcham often thinks of the masterstroke by which he won the laughing witch who now.* Begins and ends morally. *Hand in hand.* Smart. (*U* 69)

Beaufoy's rendering of his character's thinking in third person and present tense differs from the initial style. And apparently, the narrator of *"Matcham's Masterstroke"* provides a moral, perhaps a commentary in the third person, as the story's conclusion. Luckily we never hear the conclusion. Bloom's reaction to Beaufoy's story contrasts with the effect the style of "Calypso" often has on us. The initial style's intimacy insures that we feel moved and touched, that we do not read on calmly and unperturbed. We are moved by the narration of "Calypso" and the other early episodes, because the teller seems to present the character's thoughts directly. We sense an immediacy of mind not just in the quoted and narrated monologues and in the psycho-narration but in many of the passages narrated in third person that do not announce themselves explicitly as renderings of thought.

As in the "Telemachiad," the impression of a consciousness in the scene arises from the adjectives. We are even more aware of adjectives in "Calypso" than earlier because the teller provides bases for judging their density and specificity through contrasts. One of those bases is the line Bloom reads from Molly's book, *"Ruby: the Pride of the Ring"*: *"The monster Maffei desisted and flung his victim from him with an oath"* (*U* 64). The line stands out in context as devoid of adjectives except for the single noun *"monster"* used attributively. We have only to look at the opening paragraph of "Calypso" to sense the large difference between the styles, both relying on a narrator's third person and past tense:

> MR Leopold Bloom ate with relish the inner organs of beasts and fowls. He liked thick giblet soup, nutty gizzards, a stuffed roast heart, liver slices fried with crustcrumbs, fried hencod's roes. Most of all he liked grilled mutton kidneys which gave to his palate a fine tang of faintly scented urine. (*U* 54–55)

Unlike the line from *"Ruby,"* this paragraph is densely crusted with modifiers. The style is so highly adjectival that several nouns (giblet, roast, crust, hencod, and mutton) are used attributively rather than nominatively. The adjectives all contribute to an impression of the dense specificity of Bloom's thoughts and perceptions.

Another basis for measuring that effect, as well as for creating it, involves the style of the earlier episodes. The development of the initial style up to this point in the narration encourages us to read modifiers as evocative of the character's mind. We read them that way almost automatically after our experience with the "Telemachiad." But the teller's return to the narrative's chronological beginning sends us back stylistically as well as temporally to the opening paragraph of "Telemachus." By comparison, the modifiers in "Calypso" are more prominent, and our sense of a mind in the scene is stronger. Even once the conventions of the initial style become established, we do not encounter a passage in the "Telemachiad" like the opening of "Calypso." We do not because the sensual, perceptual quality of Bloom's thoughts differs so substantially from Stephen's allusive, self-regarding consciousness. There is, however, an allusion in the narration of this opening scene, one that the character does not perceive. That allusion initiates a counterpoint between the first three episodes and the next three. By invoking the Homeric perspective suggested by the book's title, it puts a twist in the teller's tale that cannot be accounted for within the context of a referential style, even one representing consciousness.

I am referring to the contrast and parallel between Mulligan's parody of the Mass and Bloom's thoughts about breakfast. Although *Mulligan* chooses to speak the words of the Mass, *we* read them as indicating as well the teller's allusion to the Homeric invocation to the Muse, especially once the teller reports Mulligan has "called up," or invoked, Stephen to "come up" (*U* 3). Buck Mulligan cannot possibly intend this allusion, because he does not realize he is a character in a scene at the beginning of a book with an epic title. Now, in "Calypso," Bloom's thoughts about inner organs provide a transmogrified, because pagan, counterpart to Mulligan's Christian reference. The transmogrifying shift moves us even closer to the *Odyssey* than do Buck's words. Bloom's gustatory preferences suggest a ritual and a sacrifice, though neither is Christian. The relevant action from the *Odyssey* is the sort of ritual mentioned in *Odyssey* XII during Odysseus's narration of the episode in which the crew slay and consume the sun's cattle. As part of the ceremony Odysseus's men perform before eating, they broil the animal's entrails:

> Straightway they drove off the best of the kine of Helios from near at hand, ... the fair, sleek kine, broad of brow. Around these, then, they stood and made prayer to the gods, plucking the tender leaves from off a high-crested oak; for they had no white barley on board the well-benched ship. Now when they had prayed and had cut the throats of the kine and flayed them, they cut out the thigh-pieces and covered them with a double layer of fat and laid raw flesh upon them. They had no wine to pour over the blazing sacrifice, but they made libations with water, and roasted all the entrails over the fire. Now when the thighs were wholly burned and they had tasted the inner parts, they cut up

the rest and spitted it. (Book XII, ll. 355–66)

Joyce continues the parallel jokingly later in "Calypso." In *Odyssey* XII Odysseus says he learned of the crew's violation when he encountered the smell of the cooking (ll. 366–69). After Bloom has explained "Metempsychosis," "what the ancient Greeks called" reincarnation (*U* 65), to Molly, she alerts him to "a smell of burn," which he "hurried out towards": "Pungent smoke shot up in an angry jet from a side of the pan. By prodding a prong of the fork under the kidney he detached it and turned it turtle on its back. Only a little burned." In *Ulysses*, the burned part goes not to the gods but to the cat. (In the corresponding scene in "Telemachus," Mulligan uses priestly language again as he serves breakfast [*U* 12].)

My assertion that there is a reference to *Odyssey* XII as the counterpart for Mulligan's invocation might seem far-fetched, if it did not receive confirmation in the *Odyssey*'s beginning. In the midst of his invocation, Homer mentions Odysseus's adventures in general but cites only one as the cause of his shipmates' downfall: "Yet even so he saved not his comrades, though he desired it sore, for through their own blind folly they perished— fools, who devoured the kine of Helios Hyperion" (Book I, ll.6–9). Because Homer, after requesting that the Muse begin the story where she wishes, starts narrating Odysseus's sojourn with Calypso, Joyce has ample warrant to allude to the ritual sacrifice as part of his "Calypso." Both initial scenes in *Ulysses* involve breakfast because Poseidon feasts in *Odyssey* I in the land of the Ethiopians: "There he was taking his joy, sitting at the feast" (Book I, l.25). This sort of allusive reading casts a different light on the narration than does the referential impression created by the style's circumstantial details. It would be hard to maintain that this other sort of mimesis, the teller's imitation of an earlier author's text, is less important in our response to *Ulysses* than the details of the initial style. Our perspective oscillates between two positions. We are moved and touched, as Bloom is not when he reads Beaufoy, but we also recognize what Bloom responds to in "*Matcham's Masterstroke*," the teller's ploys as "something quick and neat. . . . Neat certainly."

In this second triad, the teller need not move so gradually into the direct mimesis of mind using quoted monologue as in earlier episodes, because he can depend on the reader's having learned the conventions already. Consequently, we do not receive as emphatically as in the "Telemachiad" the impression of moving more deeply and frequently into the character's mind as Bloom's episodes proceed. As with Stephen, though, we come to know Bloom better. But we see him in more public contexts, in the contexts of social rituals, such as the funeral, and in relation to the direct discourse so prevalent in "Hades" rather than through the isolated self-communion of "Proteus." We can guage the relative stability of the teller's perspective in the second triad in comparison with the first by looking again at the beginnings of episodes. When we do that, we do not discover the teller's increasing proximity to the character's mind in each successive beginning. Instead each episode starts essentially the same way, with at least one substantial sentence in third person, which we understand as the teller's, preceding the quoted monologues. There are differences among these paragraphs, of course. Perhaps the beginning of "Calypso" is the most unusual, because the teller's choice of the verb "like" makes it psycho-narration. It is a sort of pscyho-narration we do not encounter often in *Ulysses*, for it focuses not so much on immediate sensation or thought as on the character's habits. Stephen is displeased and sleepy on this specific morning, but it is not just today that Bloom enjoys his kidneys. After "Proteus" only two episodes, "Lestrygonians" and "Penelope," begin with direct evocations of the character's thoughts. In both those episodes, the mimesis of mind includes language differentiating it from the first two triads. And we read that language against the background of intervening styles different from the initial one. In this second triad the style is almost always somewhere *between* the extremes of proximity to the character's mind of "Proteus" and the more distant first paragraph of "Telemachus," hardly ever near those extremes. Consequently, teller's and character's views are often thoroughly mixed.

Although he keeps within these limits, the teller uses his techniques to create new effects. Besides the reiterated presentation of Bloom's thoughts, he gives us ways of becoming aware of the style and how we read it by including stylistic jokes. I call them jokes because they rely on incongruities in the narration to jostle us out of our habitual pattern of referential reading. Like Stephen thinking of his own carefully elaborated theory in "Scylla and Charybdis," we can laugh to free our minds from our minds' bondage (*U* 212). If we decide in advance that it would be indecorous to laugh either about or with the narration, we may fail to perceive the incongruities in its apparatus.

In the second paragraph of "Calypso," the teller moves toward quoted monologue quickly by employing the other techniques first in a perambulatory fashion. The joke begins already, in a way that anticipates the bumbling style of "Eumaeus," another of the book's episodes that is a beginning. The first sentence of the second paragraph, an instance of psycho-narration, takes us away from the character's habitual thoughts by stating forthrightly what is "in his mind" on this day:

> Kidneys were in his mind as he moved about the kitchen softly, righting her breakfast things on the humpy tray. Gelid light and air were in the kitchen but out of doors gentle summer morning everywhere. Made him feel a bit peckish. (*U* 55)

The teller's language incongruously places physical organs *in* (rather than simply *on*) his character's mind. The sentence works as do many in the initial style by presenting physical activities together with mental ones. But by playing on the ambiguity between physical and mental in the word *mind*, Joyce uses the assertion of thought to place the kidneys in Bloom's head. We can, of course, choose to suppress the incongruity, especially because the rest of the sentence and the remainder of the paragraph are relatively innocent of such twists. We find out shortly that "her" refers to Molly. "Humpy" and the other adjectives evoke Bloom's consciousness, as does the suppression of the verb in the second sentence's second clause. If we delete the period and combine the second and third sentences, we have another instance of psycho-narration, one that tells us in the third person and past tense how Bloom feels. Joyce easily transforms one technique into another by simply adding a mark of punctuation to create grammatical fragments. The last sentence as it stands is narrated monologue rather than psycho-narration. We understand it to mean "makes *me* feel a bit peckish." In this paragraph, then, we find external and internal, physical and mental, combined in the teller's language, and we hear what we often do in the initial style: two streams of thought, that of the character and that of the narrator, who translates the contents of the character's mind into the relatively conventional syntax of a third-person narration. The teller shifts almost immediately after this paragraph into the quoted monologues by simply omitting verbs and pronouns or by using present tense and first person.

Bloom's initial thoughts and perceptions presented this way dwell largely on the cat. As with the hilarious allusions to the Homeric sacrifice to the gods, the cat plays an important role in setting the humorous perspective by which the teller allows us to share and to enjoy his manipulations of style:

> The cat mewed in answer and stalked again stiffly round a leg of the table, mewing. Just how she stalks over my writingtable. Prr. Scratch my head. Prr.
>
> Mr Bloom watched curiously, kindly, the lithe black form. Clean to see: the gloss of her sleek hide, the white button under the butt of her tail, the green flashing eyes. He bent down to her, his hands on his knees.
>
> —Milk for the pussens, he said.
>
> —Mrkgnao! the cat cried.
>
> They call them stupid. They understand what we say better than we understand them. She understands all she wants to. Vindictive too. Wonder what I look like to her. (*U* 55)

I quote this section at length because it seems to me extraordinary and extraordinarily funny when read with an ear for the teller's self-consciousness about his own style, a self-consciousness revealed already by "kidneys were in his mind." In *Anna Karenina* (Book VI, chapter 12), Levin speaks to his hunting dog, Laska, and Tolstoy's narrator renders the dog's thoughts at length, but in "Calypso" Bloom has a dialogue of sorts with the cat.[27] He even goes beyond dialogue by translating the cat's purr, which is reported as part of his own quoted monologue, into the cat's quoted interior monologue,

"Scratch my head." There is nothing especially unusual about human beings treating pets as if they too were human. But that kind of treatment presented as the character's attributing thoughts, however playfully, to a cat in a narration filled with thoughts ascribed to the character adds up to a laugh. And it recalls Stephen's attitude toward the woman in his poem, whom he realizes he is thinking of as a presence. In "Calypso," the ludicrous tableau with the cat yields to Bloom's related encounter with Molly:

> —You don't want anything for breakfast?
> A sleepy soft grunt answered:
> —Mn.
> No. She did not want anything. (*U* 56)

He translates her first utterance in the narrative, her sleepy grunt, like the cat's purr, into a response and a verbalized desire. We shall consider this passage again when we examine the final episodes and Molly's last utterances.

One other aspect of the narration in the second triad deserves mention because of Joyce's supreme skill in employing it, at times for comic effect. I refer to the subtle modulations between statements in the third person and past tense and the character's interior language. Often, the transition involves adjectives that might be Bloom's. And it can also involve a combination of narrated with quoted monologue to create a shift from narrator's to character's voice. At times the adjectives and the shifts in perspective give us material for doing a double take, for realizing the incongruity we have just encountered and generated in our reading.

Often the teller shifts from a third-person perspective to the first person by employing language we can take in two ways, as in the following passage presenting Bloom's leaving the house for the butcher's: "On the doorstep he felt in his hip pocket for the latchkey. Not there. In the trousers I left off. Must get it" (*U* 57). There is no clear distinction here between scene and psyche, though the shift from grammatically complete to grammatically incomplete statements may encourage us to make such a distinction. Even in the first sentence, we are in the character's mind, since only Bloom can know what he feels for, though "pocket" and "latchkey" have physical referents. The effect is like that of the adjective "untonsored" at the beginning of "Telemachus." We find out what one of the character's fails to discover in the scene. The teller also evokes Bloom's mind by a linguistic slippage, through the use of a verb that could introduce a presentation of thought in psycho-narration but that does not in context. Here "felt" negotiates an elision between a physical act, sense perception, and thought. The teller observes a physical act, Bloom's *feeling* for something that, when his sense of touch does not find it, Bloom *feels* he "must get." Teller and character share the burden of narration through the shift from feeling to feelings that evokes sense perception triggering thought. And we share that burden as well insofar as we expect "felt" to introduce thought.

Such a shift from description to thought becomes comic when the elision is less gradually modulated than in the passage about the key. For instance, as Bloom leaves we learn that he takes his hat down from its peg:

> His hand took his hat from the peg over his initialled heavy overcoat, and his lost property office secondhand waterproof. Stamps: stickyback pictures. Daresay lots of officers are in the swim too. Course they do. The sweated legend in the crown of his hat told him mutely: Plasto's high grade ha. He peeped quickly inside the leather headband. White slip of paper. Quite safe. (*U* 56)

The first sentence seems straightforward enough, but its two parts are virtually antithetical in focus. The first one deals with the discrete details of physical scene: Bloom's hand, his hat, the peg, the coat that is initialled and heavy. The only detail that we cannot account for visually is the word "initialled," suggesting perhaps that Bloom's initials are inside the coat somewhere. Only Bloom could know that, not any teller simply reporting scene. We probably would pass over "initialled," except that the remainder works the same way, revealing what only Bloom could know while creating the effect of a physical description. We hear as if it were descriptive what no observer except Bloom could realize about his waterproof: not that it is brown, dirty, torn, or wrinkled, but that he obtained it secondhand at a lost property office. The second sentence using the third person and past tense, the one that reports what Bloom sees inside the hat, also engages the reader's attention in a special way, because it fails to do what the earlier sentence does: supplement the perception of scene with thought. Bloom knows already what the reader is asked to figure out: that the "t" of the word "hat" has been worn away. We learn what Bloom knows when we add what the hat mutely tells Bloom to what the narrator tells us; Bloom is looking into a hat, not into a "ha." Our response includes another sort of "ha" as well as an "aha."

Once we begin to catch on to these quick switches in perspective among scene, sense perception, and thought, some of the teller's effects become very funny, because they fool us *and* give us a perspective for sensing what the style is doing to us. There is, for instance, the wonderful final paragraph of "Lotus-Eaters" with its description of Bloom in the bath:

> He foresaw his pale body reclined in it at full, naked, in a womb of warmth, oiled by scented melting soap, softly laved. He saw his trunk and limbs rippled over and sustained, buoyed lightly upward, lemonyellow: his navel, bud of flesh: and saw the dark tangled curls of his bush floating, floating hair of the stream around the limp father of thousands, a languid floating flower. (*U* 86)

We can easily take this passage to be the narrator's physical description, his realistic representation, of Bloom actually in the bath, albeit a description whose diction suggests the infiltration of the character's thoughts into the narration. But the passage is not such a description by the narrator. We tend to read it that way because of its length and because the narrator replaces the initial verb "foresaw," a verb of thought, twice with the verb "saw," indicating sense perception. The physical details of a scene Bloom only imagines—based, of course, on past experience—create the impression of a physical reality. The effect is like the reversal between figure and ground in certain optical illusions. And it is related to the sort of narration we have encountered in "Proteus" when Stephen's mind largely takes over the job of the telling. By moving into Bloom's mind, the teller creates the impression not only of being in his character's consciousness but of his character's actually being where he is *not* in the narrative. If we can manage not to forget the introductory, controlling verb "foresaw" and its prospective implication, when the teller says Bloom saw (past tense) something, we understand that Bloom imagines (present tense) himself at some future time seeing something. Because this is Bloom's vision of himself, we understand "his navel, bud of flesh," as "*my* navel." What "he saw" is actually what he will see as "I" in the future if his act of foreseeing in the present, which is reported in the past tense, actually comes true. Joyce manages to keep us engaged and amused through such modulations of style and their eddying implications.

Because of the book's stylistic fluctuations, we sense its double vision even in the first six episodes. We perceive Bloom both as a presence and as the effect of the teller's stylistic manipulations. The language that creates an impression of reality also announces its own stylistic, and sometimes mythic, convolutions. In the persistent flower motif of "Lotus-Eaters" and in the other Homeric allusions (e.g., to the invocation), we discern the teller's role in generating those complexities. That role is also inscribed in the self-conscious aspects of the initial style, especially in the contrasts and twists the teller gives to referential conventions. Toward the end of "Hades," Bloom's thoughts focus on different gradations of illusion that are possible in art. His thoughts reflect the narration's double focus, the manner in which it invites the reader both to become intimate with Bloom as a presence and to view him as the effect of the teller's language, even in the initial style. He sees a bird perched on a tree branch and thinks the live bird looks stuffed, like the embalmed owl alderman Hooper presented him as a wedding gift. Then he sees an image of the "Sacred Heart," apparently a stylized carving on one of the monuments in the cemetery, thinking that it should be turned sideways and painted red for the sake of greater realism. Finally, he remembers the story of a painting by the Greek artist Zeuxis, whom he confuses with another painter, Apelles, whose name he thinks is Apollo: "Would birds come then and peck like the boy with the basket of fruit but he said no because they ought to have been afraid of the boy. Apollo that was" (*U* 113). The story Bloom alludes to concerns a painting by Zeuxis of a boy with a basket of grapes. The fruit looked so natural that birds tried to eat it.[28] Bloom has now gone the beginning of "Calypso" one better. There he treats the cat as if she were a thinking presence. Here he ponders animals that treat art as real presences. The narration in these episodes, the trompe l'oeil painting, and the thoughts of the cat are all "genuine forgeries," at once seemingly real and obviously created.

VARIOUS STYLES: "AEOLUS"—"CIRCE"—WANDERINGS

Style and the Memory of Things Past

In *Ulysses*, Joyce gives us the material for constructing several analogies to explain the sharp shift in style announced typographically by the headlines of "Aeolus." The primary analogy involves the wanderings of Odysseus. The book's title and the pattern of shifts in style from initial to various and finally to the ultimate ones provide the most convincing support for interpreting the narration as symbolic action. In that symbolic action, the author as teller strives to actualize his relationship to epic precursors through adventurous wanderings of style. In those wanderings, the teller's identity, like his character's, is allotropic. We encounter not a series of absolutely distinct personae but a sequence of overlapping and mutually defining styles creating perspectives by incongruity. The narration projects attitudes toward identity and toward the authority of style in fiction that undermine some readers' expectations. Those attitudes become intertwined because the book's styles as allotropic forms reinforce the notion of identity as chameleonic. The teller has no centered self and no proper style suggesting a unified ego. Rather, he constructs an image for himself as variable, as shifting, out of the multitude of styles he could choose for his narration. That self-image and the book embodying it resemble Wallace Stevens's "Thirteen Ways of Looking at a Blackbird" in the conceptions of style and perspective they project. If there are various ways of looking, each only one among many modes of consciousness, then a unitary approach falsifies experience. The alternative to employing such a falsifying style is to write in a multitude of styles, enough to suggest that the number of ways to look and to write is, at the least, very large and, potentially, inexhaustible. There is no unreliable narration here, simply the determined unfolding of some complex notions about identity and language.

Joyce contains the chaotic tendency of the proliferating styles by giving them a Homeric shape and meaning. We come to understand the style's meaning through the guidance provided by the book's narration and its narrative. With regard to the narration, we understand the episodes of the "Odyssey" after "Hades" by contrast with the initial style. Later in the process of reading, we understand them by contrast with "Penelope" as a final episode that returns to ostensibly referential principles. In the narrative, we have Stephen Dedalus's commentary on Shakespeare as a source of analogies for the shift in styles, analogies that are occasionally openly Homeric. In addition, and relevant to both the referential style and Stephen's theory, the narrative emphasizes, largely by failing to represent it directly except in "Penelope," Molly Bloom's sexuality, in particular her adultery. The sexual implications of technique in the initial style combine with the adultery of the narrative and with aspects of Stephen's commentary to illuminate the epical wanderings in style as the artist's image. Like Shakespeare's twenty years in London and Odysseus's twenty years away from Ithaca, the narrator's wanderings in the various styles include his exile from the spouse.

In his metaphoric exile the teller either transforms or largely neglects the intimate referential narration that for Henry James includes the possession of one being by another through the mutual assisting among teller, character, and reader. This stylistic exile is not absolute, for the initial style does not disappear entirely. Its presence in the later episodes of the various styles amounts to a memory of what has been lost. Joyce returns to it in "Nausicaa" to present Bloom contemplating his loss of intimacy with Molly. When that recollected intimacy reasserts itself in the narrative, as in both "Nausicaa" and "Penelope," a referential style returns. It returns with a difference that involves a heightened intensity generated by its temporary absence and a sense of stylistic relativity less fully available in the early episodes of *Ulysses*. In his letter to Harriet Shaw Weaver about the styles, Joyce hints at the rationale for his returns to the initial style: that style comes to represent the wandering character's and the reader's longing for the rock of Ithaca and all it suggests.

There is, then, a kind of polygamy as "spouse-breach" (*U* 47) at work in the narration of *Ulysses* in the teller's relationship to his characters and to his Muses. That polygamy resembles Shakespeare's life in London as Stephen describes it: "Twenty years he dallied there between conjugal love and its chaste delights and scortatory love and its foul pleasures" (*U* 201). Shakespeare never abandons the one love wholly for the other but dallies *between* them. He carries with him "a memory in his wallet" of "*the girl I left behind me.*" According to Stephen, "that memory . . . lay in the bedchamber of every light-of-love in London" (*U* 190–91). In the wanderings of style and story, "Circe" and its nighttown represent the "scortatory love and its foul pleasures." Bloom wanders between Molly's bedchamber and nighttown, always carrying with him memories of his wife, to whose bed he finally retires. In his stylistic "Odyssey," the teller dallies between the referential, initial style and the self-referential style of "Circe" before returning to the representation of mind. During his dallying the teller's language sometimes reverts or alludes to the initial style, but, even when it does not, *we* carry the memory of that style with us in our reading as wandering.

The teller's hankering after strange stylistic gods in the book's middle is no mistake, as some critics, most prominently S. L. Goldberg, would have us believe, though it is errant in the etymological sense (L., *errare*, to wander):[29]

> —The world believes that Shakespeare made a mistake, he [John Eglinton] said, and got out of it as quickly and as best he could.
> —Bosh! Stephen said rudely. A man of genius makes no mistakes. His errors are volitional and are the portals of discovery. (*U* 190)

Just as Shakespeare's original error, his bond to his spouse, yields to his other errors as wanderings and as portals of discovery, Joyce's initial style becomes but the first in his errant sequence of styles. The volitional errors of a wandering telling become portals of discovery because they contribute to the artist's tracing of his ancestry and his image. As Stephen says of Shakespeare, "his own image to a man with that queer thing genius is the standard of all experience, material and moral" (*U* 195). The shape of that image includes stylistic "spouse-breach" as a sundering in anticipation of reconciliation, which Stephen asserts twice to be descriptive of Shakespeare's life (*U* 193, 195) and which we understand as descriptive of Odysseus's story as well. Finally, it describes *Ulysses*, too.

Stephen mentions both the sundering and an ultimate reconciliation using sexual metaphors. Before commenting on Shakespeare's twenty years in London, he alludes to the Trojan War: "—Antisthenes, pupil of Gorgias, Stephen said, took the palm of beauty from Kyrios Menelaus' brooddam, Argive Helen, the wooden mare of Troy in whom a score of heroes slept, and handed it to poor Penelope" (*U* 201). If we take "the wooden mare of Troy" as a metaphor of narration, it reinforces our sense of the teller as Odyssean but also as Daedalian and Protean. His stylistic strategy in the book's middle amounts to creating a wooden horse, as Odysseus did, that resembles Daedalus's famous artifice to enable copulation. The wooden horse turns out to contain an apparent multitude of presences. The maker's ultimate strategy in creating the artifice is to end his exile from home, to gain an entry that allows him to return to his spouse stylistically in "Penelope." Eventually, like Shakespeare and Odysseus, the teller will return to his origin: "He returns after a life of absence to that spot of earth where he was born, where he has always been, man and boy, a silent witness and there, his journey of life ended, he plants his mulberry tree in the earth. Then dies. The motion is ended" (*U* 213). In that ending Penelope replaces the wooden mare of Troy. The mulberry tree then turns out to be both the plum tree as "the heaventree of stars hung with humid nightblue fruit" (*U* 698) and the olive tree, the secret of the bed only Odysseus and Penelope know. Through style, mulberry tree becomes muliebrity, and the labor of great-rooted blossoming becomes singing.

The ending of the motion involves the artist's finding "in the world without as actual what was in his world within as possible" (*U* 213). In *Ulysses* that discovery for teller and reader is the stylistic revivifying of our temporarily moribund relationship to character as spouse when character becomes interior paramour. Once the teller in *Ulysses* can represent a character as internal voice—that is, as consciousness and as Muse—and simultaneously as a separate persona for telling, he achieves that final motion by experiencing "the economy of heaven, foretold by Hamlet," in which "there are no more marriages, glorified man, an androgynous angel, being a wife unto himself" (*U* 213). In this economy the architect of the horse, who also rides within the horse, becomes indistinguishable from Penelope the weaver. The movement in "Aeolus" away from the intimate rendering of consciousness turns out to be part of the motion that includes a sundering anticipating reconciliation. It begins anew the eddying motion, already under way in the initial style, toward an ending that takes us back to our origin. But first we must wander before we find that ultimate portal of discovery.

"Aeolus"—"Wandering Rocks": From the Rock to the Wanderings of Rocks

Every power in nature must evolve an opposite in order to realize itself and opposition brings reunion.
—Joyce, *Letters* II, 226

Without Contraries is no progression.
—William Blake, "The Marriage of Heaven and Hell"

Although stylistically and typographically "Aeolus" marks clearly the break from the initial style, many of the episodes written in the various styles, especially the first four, rely heavily on the earlier referential techniques. In these episodes, the techniques are either directly employed or transformed in ways that remind us of the style that has been left behind. After "Wandering Rocks," the transformation of the initial style, as in "Sirens," reaches a more extreme stage. "Sirens" as stylistic turning point reflects the crisis of the narrative, for during "Sirens" Boylan goes to keep his appointment with Molly. The turn in the narration corresponds to the strongly suggested possibility of Bloom's loss of his spouse in the narrative. From then on, the narrator returns to the earlier style at length only in "Nausicaa." There, that style and the narrative evoke Bloom's intense longing for home in the midst of his wanderings. By returning to the mimesis of consciousness in "Nausicaa," the narrator realizes stylistically a correspondence with the *Odyssey* by allowing the character again to take over the telling, as Odysseus does after his encounter with the Phaeacian princess.

Before "Sirens" Joyce moves toward the more extreme wanderings of style in a manner consonant with the strategies we have seen him use in earlier works and at the beginning of *Ulysses*. Just as he introduces the quoted monologue in "Telemachus" virtually without preamble by inject-ing the word "Chrysostomos" into his narration in third person, with "Aeolus" he injects without explanation seemingly foreign elements into the narrating mode he has firmly established. With both "Chrysostomos" and the headlines of "Aeolus," he knocks us off balance and then reverts to a more gradual movement toward the new aspects of style. The crucial difference in "Aeolus" is the reiterated employment of the new techniques for an entire episode before the reversion to the earlier style. After "Aeolus," we do not encounter substantial typographical irregularities until "Scylla and Charybdis," and there they occur only briefly and intermit-tently. Eventually, we encounter something like a headline again when we reach the odd headnote of "Sirens."

From the perspective of style, then, "Aeolus" is a temporary stage heralding the sort of narration that will be sustained more consistently after "Wandering Rocks." We can think of the style in "Aeolus" and in the episodes immediately following it on analogy with the initial style as the interaction of two views of the narrative. While in the initial style both views are referential, in these early episodes of the various styles, only one is referential. The narrating situation is complicated, because now the initial style, itself a compound, constitutes the referential pole of the interaction. Earlier we have heard two voices and two sets of grammatical markers in the alternation between narration in third and first person, a narration that has tended often toward a mingling of narrator's and character's voices. In "Aeolus" we discover another alternation: between the new elements of style, especially the headlines, on the one hand, and passages narrated in the earlier manner, on the other. But we also perceive a mingling of the seemingly antithetical aspects of style, a mingling as strange as, but also no stranger than, the interplay of third and first person in the referential style. The narration of *Ulysses* proceeds by doublings and fusions. The third-person narration with which "Telemachus" begins soon becomes a narration involving the dialectical interplay of third and first person. Then, in "Aeolus," that kind of narration is replaced by the interplay of self-referential and referential strategies of telling, the latter retaining and extending the earlier mixture of linguistic forms.

It would seem at first that we would want to distinguish sharply the two large strategies of the telling, the referential and the self-referential, in "Aeolus" and the later episodes. While we can distinguish them to a certain extent, finally they are no more absolutely distinct than the third- and first-person elements of the initial style. They, too, merge and diverge. In suggesting that the Aeolian style is fused and mixed, I reject the notion that, as one critic of *Ulysses* has recently asserted with particular clarity, the "narrative norm of the first six chapters continues in 'Aeolus,' providing stability and continuity": "For as bizarre as the headings may be, the texture of the narration beneath them is largely that of the first six chapters: a combination of dialogue, interior monologue and third-person narration."[30] The mimesis of mind early in *Ulysses* as protean process, both a protean process of mimesis and a protean process of mind, belies this assertion. As we have already seen, the fluctuating combination of techniques in the initial style provides no simple "stability and continuity." Instead, it yields a complex, variable narration in which narrator's and character's voices mingle and separate in subtle ways.

Like the initial style's third and first persons, the seemingly disparate elements in "Aeolus" tend to merge; they are not segregated in the headlines, on the one hand, and in the passages following the headlines, on the other. Although the headlines were added to "Aeolus" after its publication in *The Little Review*, the narrator has not merely taken a narrative that is essentially the same stylistically as the preceding episodes and added the captions. Instead, the initial style has been modified even in the passages that follow the headlines. The change draws greater attention to the act of narration. The modification is basically the addition of more Homeric allusions and ones that are more obvious than in earlier episodes. As many critics have pointed out, these allusions include references to the wind and examples of linguistic analogues for wind, rhetorical devices as windy language. From the episode's first page, these devices appear so blatantly that we could not ignore the manipulations of language even if the headlines were absent. In the page-long segment following the caption "SAD," at least six allusions to wind occur (*U* 125). And there is the well-known example of chiasmus early in the episode: "Grossbooted draymen rolled barrels dullthudding out of Prince's stores and bumped them up on the brewery float. On the brewery float bumped dullthudding barrels rolled by grossbooted draymen out of Prince's stores" (*U* 116). Whether or not we know the technical names of the devices, we cannot fail to note the contrast with the initial style.

Arnold Goldman has remarked that "Aeolus" "forms a kind of half-way stage between what has preceded and what is to come": "In it we may read the continuing human action, in which the events in Dublin are a *mimesis*, behind the narrative presentation."[31] While the episode *is* an intermediate stage, including both the initial style and new elements, it seems at least curious to describe a mimesis going on "behind the narrative presentation," as if a mimesis could be distinct from the narration. Mimesis involves a mode of presentation, a certain kind of literary style, one that does not call vivid attention to itself as composed of self-conscious, literary conventions. Just as a mimetic style always has self-referential aspects (as we have seen already for the initial style), a self-referential style necessarily has some mimetic aspects, as in "Circe." In "Aeolus," the narrator plays with this mutuality by openly mingling self-referential and mimetic. Although the new style does not destroy wholly our sense of a continuing action in the narrative, it modifies the illusion that the action is anything but fictive. And it breaks the continuity in the style of telling. The narrator's wanderings have begun.

Like S. L. Goldberg and many other critics of *Ulysses*, Goldman assumes the initial, mimetic style of the first six episodes to be a kind of ideal narration because it is referential. That bias is clear in his attitude toward Homeric correspondences in "Aeolus": "While figures of speech and 'wind' allusions are generally worked into the dialogue, and ideally, one might suppose would not stand out, functioning equally as part of the human action, I doubt if this is the experience of most readers."[32] The change in style undermines the assumption that the initial style is more than a convention, like that at work in many novels written before and after *Ulysses*. Consequently, Goldman wishes the allusions to wind and the rhetorical devices had been included less obviously within the initial style. If Joyce had so attenuated them, then the style of the passages following the headlines would be indistinguishable from the initial style, for the reader would be unable to perceive the change. As Goldman admits, "the experience of most readers" includes their perception of the new elements in the style besides the headlines, for there are passages such as the one employing chiasmus. In fact, the allusions to wind and the figures of speech act as bridges between the headlines and the initial style.

Goldman explicitly rejects the possibility of fusion both in "Aeolus" and generally in *Ulysses* as any "part of the book's meaning": "We experience both reactions, and keep them distinct. It [the Aeolian style] is one of a large number of instances in which the book forces us to keep separate the way it talks about things and the things it is talking about."[33] On the contrary, the first two pages of "Aeolus" suggest a fusion in the new style rather than a complete sundering. The passages following the first three headlines resemble stylistically the beginning of "Telemachus," for they report in third person the external details of scene and, in the third passage, a dialogue between two characters, Bloom and Red Murray. Bloom's thoughts are rendered briefly in that passage and more fully in the fourth. Although the juxtaposing of the first two headlines with the prose following them may create at the outset a feeling of disjunction, in the case of the first passage, the contrast is due largely to typography. We can read the first headline, "IN THE HEART OF THE HIBERNIAN METROPOLIS," as an introductory prepositional phrase forming part of the first sentence. Changed to conventional typography, the first sentence of "Aeolus" would read this way: "In the heart of the Hibernian metropolis before Nelson's pillar trams slowed, shunted, changed trolley. . . ." While the phrase printed as a headline is obviously stylized, it is no more so than the final sentence of "Nestor," or many others in the first six episodes.

The passage following the third headline, "GENTLEMEN OF THE PRESS," begins with the example of chiasmus. Again there is a contrast between headline and passage, even a contrast within the passage between the first paragraph and the remainder, which includes mimesis of mind in the initial style. This contrast internal to the passage indicates the slippage between the seemingly antithetical stylistic elements. The juxtaposing of headline, chiastic passage, and report of dialogue tends to blur any absolute distinction between the caption and the accompanying passage. While the word order of the first sentence of the chiasmus jars slightly, that sentence could conceivably be the beginning of a passage in the initial style. Only when we reach the second sentence is our expectation that the paragraph will be in the earlier mode undercut.[34] With this clear deviation from the initial style, the paragraph modulates between the headline and what follows, for it resembles typographically narration in the initial style and begins as a passage in that style might. As in the opening paragraph of "The Sisters," the oddities of the language invite us to reconsider what we have just read and to revise our expectations for reading further.

In the passage after the fourth headline, a paragraph beginning in the initial style includes an allusion to the chiastic paragraph in the phrase "Dullthudding Guinness's barrels" (U 117). Because of the earlier passage, we cannot read the phrase simply as a representation of Bloom's thoughts, as we might without the chiasmus. While technically the words do not deviate from the initial style, we read them differently. This is often the case in "Aeolus": the passages may resemble the earlier referential style formally, yet their affective impact can differ considerably. At the end of the same paragraph, the rendering of Bloom's thoughts includes unexpectedly an example of *anaphora*: "The broadcloth back ascended each step: back. All his brains are in the nape of his neck. Simon Dedalus says. Welts of flesh behind on him. Fat folds of neck, fat, neck, fat, neck" (U 117). The mimesis of mind now appears simply to be one part of the narrator's continuing exercise in rhetorical virtuosity. But the shift is not as radical as it might at first seem, for that mimesis has been only part of the teller's stylistic project all along.

In the new context passages that we would take in an earlier episode as purely in the initial style have pushed past its limits. There is, for example, the matter of the teller's metaphors. In "Hades," when we hear of Father Coffey's "fluent croak" and "toad's belly" (U 103), we take the metaphors as originating in Bloom's thoughts, even though they do not occur as part of quoted monologues. But in "Aeolus" only a few pages later we are less likely to attribute the treatment of Myles Crawford as a rooster (U 126, 136) to either Bloom's or Stephen's thoughts. As in *Dubliners*, metaphors can emphasize the act of telling as independent of the character's actions and thoughts. We read "Aeolus" with a kind of oscillating perspective that goes beyond the interplay of first and third person. This perspective recognizes the initial style but also perceives, fused with it, new elements indicative of a different attitude, including allusions to wind, rhetorical tropes, and headlines, not all of which can be easily separated from the referential style. Unless we are willing to assume prescriptively that the initial style is normative as narration, we cannot treat the new elements as intrusive. And we cannot separate the way the book "talks about things" from "the things it is talking about." Instead, the structural relations between narration and narrative in *Ulysses* are among its most arresting features, ones that make it Joyce's great achievement, worthy of its Homeric predecessor.

At the same time as he characterizes the new elements as intrusions, Goldman assigns them to a "non-human" narrating voice that mimics examples of language, such as headlines, public notices, and legal writ, whose "*origin* is not vocal."[35] There is obviously a negative judgment being passed here on the ostensibly "non-human" voice. Presumably, Goldman attributes the parts of the episode narrated in the initial style to a narrating voice that is human and, therefore, good. This kind of harsh contrast and evaluation is untenable, primarily because it does not account for the melding of the seemingly antithetical elements in the new style, a melding that makes us read the initial style in new ways. When we try to limit arbitrarily the possibilities of the protean narration by imposing critical standards of decorum, the narration, like Odysseus, eludes the attempt to imprison it. As D. H. Lawrence asserts in another context, when we "try to nail anything down, . . . the novel gets up and walks away with the nail."[36] Instead of objecting to the newly introduced elements of style as obtruding into the realism, after "Aeolus" we can read the initial style retrospectively. When we do, we understand that it is both nonhuman and human, impersonal and personal, arbitrary and natural, as is the new style.

We cannot distinguish between the Aeolian style and the initial one as more or less human, more or less normative, on the basis of their relationships to human speech as somehow primary and authenticating. The test of vocal origin opens even the initial style to the charge of being arbitrary in its linguistic form. Quoted and narrated monologues are emphatically *not* human speech in some pure form but stylized literary forms presenting thought through the mediation of linguistic conventions. The ideal of pure speech independent of arbitrary conventions is a mystification. The conventions of the monologues early in *Ulysses* include such oddities as the substituting of third person and past tense for the character's thoughts in first person and present tense, the translating of thought by the narrator into conventional syntactical units, and the presenting of thought, through grammatical fragmentation and ellipsis, not as spoken but as presyntactical or elliptically syntactical. If the fragments composing many of the quoted monologues in *Ulysses* were actually spoken, a listener might well take them to be mad gibberish, like Othello's ravings about goats and monkeys. Furthermore, the narrative of "Aeolus" provides examples of human speech itself as conventional and arbitrary by including three examples of highly stylized speech within the action. Ned Lambert's reading of Doughy Dan Dawson's speech, J. J. O'Molloy's recitation from Seymour Bushe's remarks at the Childs murder case, and Professor MacHugh's rendition of John F. Taylor's speech on the Irish language are all examples of human speech. But they are no less and no more stylized than Stephen Dedalus's scrupulously mean story or the narration in *Ulysses*, whether in the initial style or in one of the later styles. The various styles make clear from their start in "Aeolus" that the narration of *Ulysses* in all its episodes—unlike the language of certain characters within the narrative, such as Lambert, O'Molloy, and MacHugh—is *not* primarily an imitation of real action and speech that exists prior to the teller's language. Although it may be that sort of imitation from time to time, its imitative aspects are often more subtly allusive.

The narration of "Aeolus," as well as the narrative, alludes to the opening of the Aeolian bag of winds, which occurs early in Odysseus's wanderings and prolongs them. Once the narrator has begun modifying the initial style by supplementing it with new elements, he has opened a bag of narrating techniques that makes difficult any direct return to the stylistic rock of Ithaca. Instead of a single style as an ostensibly stable rock, we have many styles as wandering rocks. As Eliot's Gerontion asks, "After such knowledge, what forgiveness?" After Pandora's box has once been opened, how can it be closed again? As Stephen suggests in "Scylla and Charybdis," the artist's wanderings can have a positive result when the errors are actually portals enabling the discovery and expression of the artist's image. Here, the introduction of new stylistic elements continues the motion that ends only in "Penelope," the motion of stylistic divagations by which the teller traces his own image back to Homer as he voyages forward *and* backward toward the mimesis of mind again.

In the earlier episodes narrated in the initial style, the teller includes numerous jokes in his narration, some of which encourage our self-consciousness about the style. "Aeolus" also includes such jokes about style in both narration and narrative. In the narration, though they may occur in the seemingly purely referential passages, they often concern the elements that have been added. The crossing of reference enhances the incongruity. The teller's insertion of headlines is like Bloom's early conversation with Mr. Nannetti, the foreman, in which he converses by "slipping his words deftly into the pauses of the clanking" (*U* 120). Or, as Simon Dedalus suggests in response to Ned Lambert's recital of Doughy Dan's speech about reforestation, the purveyor of this idiosyncratic, elaborate style has been "changing his drink" (*U* 123), presumably with ill effect on his rational faculties. The headlines resemble the disruptive sound that interrupts MacHugh's version of Taylor's speech on language: "A dumb belch of hunger cleft his speech" (*U* 143). The cumulative effect of these references in their context amounts to a joke itself about the initial style, for the references are themselves examples of the insertions they indicate. Embedded in passages that look like the initial style, the insertions can divert our attention from that style toward its ostensible opposite. They have at least two meanings and two referents, one of which involves a style of narration.

Stephen's story provides the best joke of all. For the reader its implications include both the style of narration and styles in the narrative. We encounter here one of the ways Joyce has extended the self-consciousness about narration suggested in earlier episodes through quotation, especially in the quoting of *"Ruby: the Pride of the Ring"* and *"Matcham's Masterstroke"* during "Calypso." We see stylistic contrasts typographically in both "Calypso" and "Aeolus" because of the difference between the italic type and the roman. In "Aeolus" the contrast is more emphatic because more sustained; the passages in italics occur more frequently and at greater length than in "Calypso." And the contrast is more complicated because so many more styles are involved. In the narrative, Stephen's story begins to create the effect he wants on his auditors only once he has given it a title, *"A Pisgah Sight of Palestine or the Parable of the Plums."* As in Joyce's revising of the episode, the caption appears after the narrative has been completed; it is an afterthought that makes the point of the story clear. Once it does, Professor MacHugh sees with good-humored admiration that Stephen is alluding to the earlier speeches and making fun of them. He has tried to puncture their high-blown eloquence with the spare language of a referential style. After several examples of the high style in the narrative of "Aeolus," Stephen has indicated an entirely different way to proceed by producing a vignette in a contrasting style with an incongruous caption. And that is largely what the teller has done as well by taking Stephen's telling *in* the narrative and translating it into a principle *for* the narration containing it. After several episodes in the initial style, the teller indicates an entirely different way to proceed by producing an episode divided into vignettes written in a modified initial style with incongruous captions. For Stephen, the high style amounts to what Bloom in "Lestrygonians" calls "flapdoodle to feed fools on" (*U* 161). Like the narrator, Stephen juxtaposes one style with another, allows one style to respond to another's limitations, without making any explicit comment.

In "Aeolus" Joyce creates a relationship between narration and narrative that, like aspects of the *Wake*, requires language resembling "The House That Jack Built" for adequate description. In anticipation of the *Wake*, the episode involves printing in both style and story; typesetting has become part of the setting and an aspect of style. The isomorphism between telling and action in "Aeolus" even takes on a developmental implication like that of V.2 in *A Portrait*. Stephen is again in the process of generating a literary work, albeit a minor one, in the narrative, a vignette that perhaps contributes in some way to the collection of stories not yet written whose title he thinks of just before beginning his narration: "Dubliners" (*U* 145). Unlike V.2, the teller does not give us at length language suggesting the mental process of gestation by which Stephen goes "on now," decides to "dare it" and to "let there be life" (*U* 145). But the implication of the writing of the villanelle asserts itself here as well; the process of creation occurring in *Ulysses* gives us a version of the book's origin. The same kind of allusive mind capable of assigning a mythic title to a realistic narrative might eventually entitle mythically the story of a day's wanderings in Dublin. That would be the story Myles Crawford urges Stephen to produce in order to "put us all into it" (*U* 135).

Even the headlines suggest in their sequence the contrast and the link between a high, conventional style and a more irreverent modern idiom. Stuart Gilbert seems to have been the first to point out the changing style of the headlines: "The style of the captions is gradually modified in the course of the episode; the first are comparatively dignified, or classically allusive, in the Victorian tradition; later captions reproduce, in all its vulgarity, the slickness of the modern press."[37] The break between the headlines in a traditional style and the ones in a more modern style takes place when Stephen Dedalus enters the newspaper office. The first headline after his entrance, the quizzical "? ? ?" (*U* 132), initiates a series that produces eventually such lengthy, and comic, Homeric ones as: "SOPHIST WAL-LOPS HAUGHTY HELEN/SQUARE ON PROBOSCIS. SPAR-TANS/GNASH MOLARS. ITHACANS VOW/PEN IS CHAMP" (*U* 148). While "classically allusive," the headline is no longer "in the Victorian tradition." The contrast between the earlier headlines and the later ones reiterates the contrasts among styles in episode and book. The contrasts involve the differences between the recitations and Stephen's narration, but they also suggest the difference between the initial style and the Aeolian one and between the great tradition of English fiction and Joyce's book. The quizzical headline, like "Aeolus" itself, announces a new element in the situation that changes it beyond rectification. Even so, after Stephen enters and the headlines become more flamboyant, there are several returns to captions resembling the early ones, such as "A POLISHED PERIOD" (*U* 140) and "INTERVIEW WITH THE EDITOR" (*U* 146), just as there will be recalls of the initial style in the episodes to come.

The return to the initial style with a difference occurs immediately, in the narration of "Lestrygonians." The styles of "Lestrygonians," "Scylla and Charybdis," and "Wandering Rocks" include technical modifications that make them all post-Aeolian versions of the initial style. In addition, our attitude toward the earlier style has changed in response to the substantial modifications of "Aeolus." In "Lestrygonians," it is as if returning in the narrative to Bloom, for the most part alone and in thought, makes the partial stylistic reversion possible, while Stephen Dedalus's prominence in "Scylla and Charybdis" reinforces the movement beyond the initial style or channels it in new directions. As in "Circe," the teller establishes the appearance of a workable convention in the narration only to abandon it. The later episodes, in all of which Bloom appears at length, are not narrated primarily in a modified initial style, and their flamboyance is not always clearly linked to Stephen's presence. The change in styles has a basis other than the thoughts and actions of the characters in the narrative, though their appearance plays its part as an important factor.

In the three episodes between "Aeolus" and "Sirens," the teller takes the referential style and turns it, like a glove, inside out to create its own opposite from itself. He does so by pushing to extremes the implications of the language and referential assumptions making up the initial style. The styles that emerge no longer create essentially a mimetic effect. The rock of Ithaca has been fragmented into various rocks: the "PINEAPPLE ROCK" (*U* 151) of "Lestrygonians," the rock of the monster Scylla, and the wandering rocks that roam the streets of Dublin. Several strategies of narration effect the transformations leading up to "Sirens" and the later episodes. The teller exaggerates selected aspects of the initial style, especially the fusion of first- and third-person perspectives, to create stylistic incongruities. In doing so, he indicates the limits for presenting certain states of mind realistically in referential language. And, in "Wandering Rocks," he evokes the multiplicity of physical and mental actions that would make up a real world like the fictional one the initial style suggests. By presenting views of a multitude of actions and minds, the narration taxes and finally overcomes our tendency to read only referentially, to read without a clear awareness of the various choices that stand behind the telling.

In both "Lestrygonians" and "Scylla and Charybdis," the incongruities arise as some apparent disequilibrium in the relationship of teller's voice to character's voice that has been established earlier in the narration. The fusion of perspectives is no longer decorously underplayed and well-modulated. Instead, grammatical oddities, usually involving modifiers, pronouns, and tense, prevent us from reading the styles as transparent vehicles for plot. In "Lestrygonians," for instance, we find the following description (if it can be called exactly that) of Bloom walking: "Mr Bloom, quick breathing, slowlier walking, passed Adam court" (*U* 167). With its interpolated modifiers, the sentence is as much evocative of Bloom's state of mind as it is descriptive of his actions. We have, of course, seen combinations of physical sensations, emotions, and actions in earlier episodes. And there are passages of description, like this one from "Calypso," that include modifiers apparently emanating from the character's thoughts: "A cloud began to cover the sun wholly slowly wholly" (*U* 61). The oddity in "Lestrygonians" has been increased through the coinage of "slowlier."

Ordinary words in ordinary combinations are no longer sufficient. Taken referentially, the later passage suggests Bloom's emotional and physical agitation as he thinks of Boylan and Molly together. When that agitation increases, the narrator transforms his language even more, until finally the representations of mind placed within statements spoken in third person no longer function only referentially.

The teller shortly reaches one limit of the initial style's capacity for expressing feelings, as in the following passage: "A warm human plumpness settled down on his brain. His brain yielded. Perfume of embraces all him assailed. With hungered flesh obscurely, he mutely craved to adore" (*U* 168). There are other examples in the episode of this sort of narration, in which the narrator's language points implicitly to the process by which mute cravings become readable style: "A warm shock of air heat of mustard haunched on Mr Bloom's heart" (*U* 172–73).[38] In the midst of representations of mind in third person, the mimesis announces itself as diegesis, as mediated by the teller's craft. The language begins to be as mixed as what it sometimes describes, the combining of different kinds of food in Bloom's digestion: "Wine soaked and softend rolled pith of bread mustard a moment mawkish cheese" (*U* 174). In this style, predicates and past participles used as adjectives can become indistinguishable, as do teller and character, once the fragmented and ambiguous syntax of quoted monologue becomes a pattern for third-person statements, such as: "Touched his sense moistened remembered" (*U* 175–76).

Joyce faces the problem of the referential style's limits by evoking them and then going beyond them. He turns those limits to his advantage by giving them a new function, to indicate the act of telling within the mimetic narration. We have seen him reaching those limits before. For instance, at the ends of "Eveline" and "A Painful Case," the teller's language and the character's interior voice diverge when the emotion can no longer be presented directly as referential language. In both those stories, instead of continuing the representation of mind, the teller uses metaphorical language briefly, then stops the narration. In *Dubliners*, reaching the limits of the mimetic style means reaching the end of the telling. In *Ulysses*, the teller goes further by combining syntactical forms, first- and third-person pronouns, present and past tenses. While the combination does represent the character's agitation through grammatical irregularities, it also draws attention to the style. The teller gradually approaches the limit he reaches and then breaches in the final sentences of "Lestrygonians."

He modifies the initial style, first in "Aeolus," then in "Lestrygonians," in one way by exaggerating the combinations of style and of voice. In "Aeolus," or example, the teller inserts into his own statement in third person and past tense Bloom's thought in the present tense and implied first person: "Mr Bloom, glancing sideways up from the cross he had made, saw the foreman's sallow face, think he has a touch of jaundice, and beyond the obedient reels feeding in huge webs of paper" (*U* 120). The sentence that follows in the next paragraph about Bloom's "slipping his words deftly into the pauses of the clanking" emphasizes the *teller's* interpolations of thoughts as well as headlines. In the initial style, similar interpolations occur realistically within the quoted monologues, as in "Lestrygonians," when Bloom remembers Molly's "O rocks" (*U* 64, 154) from "Calypso." But when lengthy interpolations begin to appear in the teller's third-person narration, the memory and imagination formerly limited to the character's mind emerge as highly visible aspects of the teller's style. They are *his* memory and imagination.

The most arresting combinations and interpolations in "Lestrygonians" occur at the episode's end, in the sentences representing Bloom's response to seeing Boylan on the street, and especially in the culminating one: "His hand looking for the where did I put found in his hip pocket soap lotion have to call tepid paper stuck" (*U* 183). The compound forms that characterize the style of "Lestrygonians" at its most extreme, focusing as they do on loss and agitation in the narrative, represent Bloom's state of mind. But they allude as well to Odysseus's longing for home and, in this example, to his grief at the loss of his ships and men, and to his furious, successful attempt to escape the Lestrygonians in *Odyssey* X. In addition, they mark the teller's progress beyond his own earlier style at the same time as they provide a countermovement to the loss in the narrative. As with Bloom's deep sense of bereavement, the change in style takes hold because it is "useless to go back": "Had to be" (*U* 168). The errant style compensates for loss of what cannot be retrieved by transforming, as in Stephen's theory about Shakespeare, loss into gain when the style moves away from mimesis in order to move back to it again.

In "Scylla and Charybdis," the teller modifies his style by extending the initial style. He does so by developing an extreme form of the stylistic contagion we have seen before, the apparent infiltration of the character's language into the third-person language of the telling. Now there is no emotional agitation as the locus for a representation of mind. Instead the teller modifies his diction, not just as context for presenting thoughts, but also in the *inquit* phrases, as the context for presenting speech. Like the shift in the headlines that occurs in the middle of "Aeolus," a shift takes place in the middle of "Scylla and Charybdis." Like the book itself, the second half is considerably stranger than the first. As in the comparison of Myles Crawford to a rooster in "Aeolus," in "Scylla and Charybdis," there is no absolutely clear relationship between teller's language and character's mind in the unusual *inquit* phrases, in the musical score for the "Gloria," in the parody of the Apostles' Creed, or in the typography of verse and drama.

Even more fully than in "Aeolus," the initial style has been transformed in ways that make it impossible for us to divide the language of "Scylla and Charybdis" neatly into passages in the initial style and into the other elements that, like headlines, have been interpolated. This is especially true of the *inquit* phrases. Metaphors have now replaced the formerly unobtrusive identifications of speakers in the direct discourse. The characters do not merely "say," they purr, sneer, ask with elder's gall, censure, oracle, say superpolitely, wax wroth, warn occultly, say with tingling energy, ask with their eyebrows, quoth, groan, or philosophize, among their other modes of speaking. Eventually, even the speakers' names are transmogrified along with the verbs of speaking: Secondbest Best, Second Eglinton, Monk Mulligan, Sonmulligan, John Eclecticon, Eglinton Johannes. This change is extreme because it involves for the first time the language providing the frame for quoted speech calling attention to itself. We have seen stylistic infection of the teller's third-person statements before, but not in the *inquit* phrases. Not only is the change not clearly linked to a character's thoughts, but unlike the metaphors in "Aeolus," which occur only sporadically, now they occur too often to be easily overlooked.

Direct discourse, the bastion of the referential style in its appearance of unmediated presentation, begins to be treated oddly in another way when words from quoted speech appear in the teller's statements in disconcerting repetitions. This is also something new in the book's styles. When the repetition occurs in Stephen's mind, as when he combines "Fred Ryan" into either the sound image or the written image, or both, that the teller renders orthographically as "Fraidrine" (*U* 214), we take it as part of the mimetic style. But when it occurs in the third person, we may conjecture that the narration has begun to imitate the process of Stephen's consciousness not through direct presentation of verbalized thoughts but by translating his mental activity into other strategies for narration. Such a structural imitation differs considerably in its effect from the initial style's mimesis of consciousness. We are not reading *what* Stephen thought but a style that presents the teller's translation into third-person narration of the *way* he conceives Stephen's thinking to be structured: as repetition, often with a difference. For instance, the librarian's statement that "the mocker is never taken seriously when he is most serious" (*U* 199) is taken up mockingly by the teller in his assertion that "they talked seriously of mocker's seriousness" (*U* 199). Besides repeating the character's language, this assertion is also a kind of extended *inquit* phrase replacing the dialogue, which the teller does not report.

Stephen's mind would seem the locus of many of these oddities in the narration, because their object is always the language and speech of the other characters. But, as in the narrated monologue, if these are Stephen's thoughts, they have been transformed into the narrator's third-person remarks, which, as in this case, can include Stephen as their object. *He* is one of the characters identified as "they." The narrator goes even further when he includes the musical score, verse, and dramatic form, allowing them to appear without ascription and sometimes at length. We can read these anomalies as things Stephen thinks of fleetingly in the narrative, though their length in the narration makes the teller's acts of mediation clear. Inevitably, in the wake of the initial style we try to naturalize the language by taking what appears without attribution to be somehow a mimesis of mind. That naturalizing process becomes increasingly difficult as *Ulysses* proceeds.

"Wandering Rocks" provides an interlude or *"Entr'acte"* (*U* 197), to adopt the word Stephen thinks of when Buck Mulligan enters the library. The episode divides the book, just as Buck's entrance divides "Scylla and Charybdis," into two parts, the second stranger in style than the first. As the tenth episode, it shares the middle of the way with "Scylla and Charybdis." These two episodes are central in their use of some defining metaphors for the narration and the narrative: voyaging between opposites, wandering, and the rocks. "Wandering Rocks" is as representative of the book's whole project as Bloom and Stephen are representative of humanity within its narrative. The characters' roles in that regard depend in part on the eccentric narration. Joyce jokingly invokes the episode's representative quality by having it repeat what has gone before, though not in such detail as in "Circe." Father John Conmee's appearance in the first section matches Buck Mulligan's mocking adoption of the priestly role at the narrative's beginning. At the end of the nineteenth section we hear that Almidano Artifoni disappears through a door, just as Bloom has passed through the gateway at the end of the previous episode.

The narration also reminds us of what has gone before. It pushes again beyond the initial style's limits while relying on that style in a way related to the attempt in "Lestrygonians" to represent emotional agitation. Another kind of activity turns out to exceed a referential style's grasp: the realistic representation of the multitude of physical and mental acts populating the world suggested by the initial style. In order to represent the simultaneity, or near simultaneity, of many actions and thoughts occurring in different locations, the teller breaks bits of the narrative presented in the initial style free from their moorings in separate vignettes and lets them drift into the narration of other sections. Through this infiltration, he makes explicit what was implicit in the counterpoint among the first six episodes: the acts of selecting and arranging that stand behind the narration, no matter how realistic it may seem in its local effects. This is the sort of arranging we have seen Stephen Dedalus actually practising in the preceding episode. The strategy thoroughly undermines the realistic impression by violating any would-be unity of scene and action. As in "Lestrygonians," though with a different result here, the initial style's assumptions when carried to extremes produce techniques that announce realism's boundaries.

The metaphor of wandering describes the style in "Wandering Rocks" as well as the narrative, for the teller lets the narration's focus as well as the characters wander. That double wandering applies to the whole book, with its wandering characters and styles. Bloom, the "wandering Jew" (*U* 217), and Stephen, "wandering Aengus" (*U* 214, 249), are joined here by all the other peripatetic figures and by the teller as wanderer. Although there is much irony directed at the wanderers, the teller's having set all these characters in motion creates an effect more positive than ironic. We see Bloom and Stephen now as representative of all the voyagers. In this role, they resemble Gabriel Conroy, who would distinguish himself from the group he finally identifies with as spokesman. We too are among the travelers, for within the narrative several of the prominent ones, Father Conmee, Stephen Dedalus, and Leopold Bloom, engage in our activity. They are all readers. Like Conmee, we read the hours of the day, though in a book much different from his. The metaphor of wandering, here *as reading* and in other forms elsewhere in *Ulysses*, emphasizes the mingling of activities—telling, reading, thinking, eating—that reveal the humanity shared by teller, characters, and readers.

In section thirteen, Stephen has a moving insight about the common plight joining him to his sister, who has just bought a tattered French grammar. As defensive as he is ("Shatter me you who can"), Stephen now sees himself in another person, as he has seen himself in the young student Cyril Sargent in the schoolroom of "Nestor." His sister Dilly, like the other shade Stephen associates her with, his dead mother, is the shadow of his own mind (*U* 243). Although he feels unable to keep Dilly from drowning in the morass of the Dedalus family's poverty, Stephen can sympathize with her. He indicates his involvement briefly by his monosyllabic "We," a word that, like Molly's "yes," marks a strong emotional bond based on memory and common experience. As we read, we earn both of these bases *aesthetically* in our relations with teller and characters: a memory of the initial style and the common experience of wandering. Together they point to the shared experience and heritage of being human.

Like Stephen's acts and thoughts as both artist and reader, the activities of teller and readers involve rocks in the metaphorical way Stephen thinks about them in relation to old books. At the beginning of the thirteenth section, before Stephen reaches the book cart, he watches a lapidary at work and thinks of the gems the craftsman handles. When Stephen addresses himself as "you who wrest old images from the burial earth" (*U* 242), he links his art to the lapidary's craft and to the ghostly voices of his commentary on Shakespeare. The gems Stephen would resurrect as images are the old books as old stones of a cultural past to which he would give a living setting. His desire recalls his delight in *A Portrait* at having the pages of his well-used Horace worn, touched by hands that revivified dead languages and dead authors (*P* 179–80). As in the narratives of the *Wake* and the metaphor of its title, the resurrection of stones and books from the cultural midden resembles Stephen's remembering his dead mother and seeing her image before him in his sister's visage. Progeny, either literal or literary, have the power to wake the dead by wresting the past from burial.

By revivifying the *Odyssey* and other texts through style and story the episodes of *Ulysses* achieve Stephen's goal. The composite styles of the four episodes preceding "Sirens" do so by mixing the initial style with elements ostensibly antithetical to it. The fusion of opposites creates a vivid parallel between teller and characters as avatars of Odysseus. While they provide stylistic analogues for Stephen and Bloom as mediators between extremes in the narrative, the mixtures also enact Odysseus's sailing between two dangers, most obviously Scylla and Charybdis. In each episode characters and teller voyage in their different ways between opposed attitudes and styles. Structurally, the connection between the two characters is especially clear in "Lestrygonians" and "Scylla and Charybdis," because Stephen and Bloom occupy similar positions regarding the opposing attitudes. By choosing a different order from Homer's and placing these two episodes together early in the various styles, Joyce emphasizes the link between Stephen and Bloom. Then, in "Wandering Rocks," they both miss, though only physically and by chance, the priest and the politician representing the ostensible opposites. The reiterated oppositions create an interpretative frame for our reading in which teller and characters will continue to wander in tandem, encountering, experiencing, and overcoming siren temptations and cyclopean viewpoints in the story and the styles. The parallel includes the teller as well as the characters, for all three, like Odysseus, survive extremes not by avoiding them but by experiencing them. In the full course of his wanderings Odysseus does not actually avoid either Scylla or Charybdis completely; instead, he survives both.

Richard Ellmann has pointed out that "Lestrygonians" "is generated mostly out of two different attitudes toward food and sexuality."[39] George Russell and Blazes Boylan, who appear briefly, represent the contrasting attitudes toward both. When Bloom sees the poet and thinks that he and his companion, who may be Lizzie Twigg, are emerging from a vegetarian restaurant, he calls them "literary ethereal people," "dreamy, cloudy, symbolistic Esthetes" (*U* 166), innocent of sexuality.[40] By contrast, Blazes resembles the carnivores that Bloom finds so disgusting in the Burton Restaurant. Blazes' sexual relationship with Molly, associated with the Plumtree's Potted Meat he brings her, is the antithesis of Russell's chaste literary friendship with Lizzie Twigg as Bloom conceives it.

Ellmann's description of Bloom's lunch in Davy Byrne's pub after he leaves the Burton Restaurant captures Bloom's combining of carnivorous and vegetarian extremes:

> The two poles of this chapter, one white and one red, one fleshless and the other flesh-and-bloody, are now energized, and Bloom is forced to make an existential choice or go without his lunch.
> In this jesuitical crisis he enters Davy Byrne's pub. First he orders a glass of

burgundy, vegetable in origin but quite altered from its original. But the main decision is still to come. He is tempted a little by sardines, and remembers his childhood nickname of "Mackerel"; fish can survive in water as neither meat-eating nor vegetable-eating landlubbers can. But he hits on a better choice, a cheese sandwich, because cheese is neither vegetable nor meat: it is formed from mammal's milk without slaughter, and enclosed in bread which is vegetable in origin but reconstructed by man.[41]

Bloom's thoughts about sexuality in "Lestrygonians" also mediate between the ethereal and the grossly physical. As he passes the office of the *Irish Times*, he thinks about the answers he received to his ad for a "smart lady typist to aid gentleman in literary work" (*U* 160). From among the responses, he chose Martha Clifford rather than Lizzie Twigg for his *correspondance*. While Bloom's relationship with Martha involves letters, it is not exactly literary, and it has an overt sexual aspect lacking between Russell and Miss Twigg. But Bloom is careful not to let the sexual overtones of his epistolary flirtation become a physical relationship like Molly and Blazes's. Bloom dallies between the chaste and the scortatory in his attitudes toward love.

In contrast to his *correspondance*, Bloom's memories of his lovemaking with Molly on Howth provide a more poignant alternative to both lust and spirituality. While two flies apparently copulate on a windowpane, Bloom ruminates, thinking at length about how "she gave me in my mouth the seed-cake warm and chewed" the day they first made love:

> Mawkish pulp her mouth had mumbled sweet and sour with spittle. Joy: I ate it: joy.... Flowers her eyes were, take me, willing eyes.... Hot I tongued her. She kissed me. I was kissed. All yielding she tossed my hair. Kissed, she kissed me.
> Me. And me now.
> Stuck the flies buzzed. (*U* 176)

As Ellmann remarks, Bloom's memory is his weapon against the extremists.[42] Bloom's recollections combine the intensely physical and potentially revolting with an idealizing, sentimental attitude. Molly is flower and woman, plant and animal. His thoughts reveal passion, but, mediated by time and sentiment, this passion is unlike Boylan's lust. Even so, the kisses were real, physical kisses, not the fleshless, literary ones of Stephen's verse in "Proteus" (*U* 48–49).

Bloom's memory connects past and present as well as food and sexuality: "Me. And me now." He answers his own earlier question, "Am I now I?" (*U* 168), and modifies his previous assertion: "Can't bring back time" (*U* 168). Because of memory, the past is not wholly dead, nor is "me now" utterly divorced from "me" then. Stephen's thoughts in "Proteus" and in "Scylla and Charybdis" project a similar attitude, one that we see in the styles as well. The teller, like his characters, passes through seemingly discrete but connected stages. By combining two stylistic tendencies, one of which is past, "Lestrygonians" makes the distinctions between those tendencies seem less than absolute. The modified form of the initial style, as an allusion to its earlier form, like Bloom's memory of Howth, re-creates what is past not exactly as in the original, but in a recognizable form.

The episode's final scenes reiterate in images of blindness and sight both Bloom's difference from the extremists and his relationship to them. He sees a blind stripling with a slender cane standing at the curb side and helps him cross the street. As we discover in "Sirens," the stripling is a piano tuner on his way to the Ormond Bar. Stephen resembles the blind man in various ways. Both carry sticks; one a cane, the other an ashplant. Stephen contemplates being blind at the start of "Proteus," when he uses his ashplant to tap his way along the beach with eyes closed (*U* 38). In "Circe" he plays the piano with his eyes shut (*U* 517) and mentions his poor eyesight (*U* 556, 560), which in the context indicates that he is probably blind drunk. Both look priestly (*U* 181, 388). And Bloom leads each past a horsedrawn vehicle. Both are linked with George Russell's idealizing, literary, dreamy mentality, though Stephen's interest in theosophy as protection from the physical is now part of his past.

Bloom's more full-bodied, less aesthetic attitude toward life sets him apart from both Stephen and the stripling as he conceives him to be. Bloom sees physically and figuratively what the stripling fails to see and what Stephen sees only imperfectly. His vision and attitudes also differ from Boylan's. After helping the stripling cross the street, Bloom sees Boylan, who does not see him because of the "light in his eyes" (*U* 183). He perceives what Boylan is blind to: a basis for human action in concern for others rather than primarily in self-interest. As he hurries into the museum grounds, "his eyes beating looked steadfastly at cream curves of stone," when he gazes at the statues he thinks of several times during the day. His meditation on the statues earlier in "Lestrygonians" indicates how he survives the extremes evoked by the concluding scenes:

> His downcast eyes followed the silent veining of the oaken slab. Beauty: it curves, curves are beauty. Shapely goddesses, Venus, Juno: curves the world admires. Can see them library museum standing in the round hall, naked goddesses. Aids to digestion. They don't care what man looks. All to see. . . . Suppose she did Pygmalion and Galatea what would she say first? . . . Lovely forms of woman sculped Junonian. Immortal lovely. And we stuffing food in one hole and out behind: food, chyle, blood, dung, earth, food: have to feed it like stoking an engine. They have no. Never looked. I'll look today. (*U* 176)

As in his long memory of Molly on Ben Howth, which immediately precedes these thoughts, Bloom idealizes the physical, especially the sexual. But the statues are not entirely ethereal for Bloom. Recognizably human in shape, the "lovely forms of woman," are not merely "a form in his mind's eye" (*U* 182) as they would be for the stripling according to Bloom. Although the mention of Pygmalion and Galatea reiterates their resemblance to the human, Bloom realizes that the statues are not alive and do not participate in the gross animality of human digestive processes. Here we encounter another version of the incongruity we saw in Bloom's thoughts about trompe l'oeil in "Hades." A character in a literary work supposedly digesting his lunch thinks about figures in works of art not participating in normal human processes. The statues' place among the sexual contrasts of the episode resembles the cheese's function among the nutritive contrasts. Like cheese, which "digests all but itself" (*U* 172), the statues are "aids to digestion" (*U* 176). The cheese, like the artist in his work, according to Stephen, combines extremes by providing the element that is all in all.

Bloom's voyeurism throughout the day (in "Lotus-Eaters" when the tram blocks his vision; in "Nausicaa" with Gerty MacDowell; in his epistolary flirtation with Martha Clifford) combines the opposed tendencies toward brutal sexuality and toward spirituality into a sensuality that is not brutal. Bloom's glancing at the statues near the episode's end indicates his double vision. He avoids the blindness of Russell and the stripling and of Blazes Boylan. Although Bloom's combining in thought the idealized and the physical, the artistic and the ordinarily human, does not make him an ideal character, in context his attitudes and actions are more attractive than the alternatives. Because of the unsentimentalized presentation, we perceive Bloom as at times ludicrous and ineffectual in his human frailty but as always more appealing than the world he inhabits. Like Bloom, we may choose not to sentimentalize and not to castigate in unalloyed ways. Instead, the details of *Ulysses* encourage us to choose the more complicated and compelling middle way involving a double vision of Bloom's actions, which the teller matches in his double styles.

In "Scylla and Charybdis" Stephen encounters extremes similar to the ones Bloom skirts but chooses from and transforms selectively. In his case, the alternatives clearly have implications for the book's form, because they involve attitudes toward literature. Richard Ellmann identifies some of the extremes the episodes share:

> For Stephen, Mulligan's indifference to the soul is akin to Russell's magnificent aversion to the body, and he joins these two adversaries together by a telegram, sent earlier, but now read aloud by Mulligan: "The sentimentalist is he who would enjoy without incurring the immense debtorship for a thing done." (It is a quotation, acknowledged later, from Meredith's *The Ordeal of Richard Feverel*.) Stephen is adroitly combining the two enemies of men's reason which contended in the previous episode, rarefaction and brutalization. The two seeming contraries share sentimentality, because both are divorced from context, neither being willing to recognize the other. They nonetheless attract each other, as is demonstrated by Russell's invitation to Mulligan, rather than to Stephen, to come to his house.[43]

The telegram is a version of Telemachus's criticism of the suitors' pillaging of his heritage at the beginning of the *Odyssey*. In *Ulysses*, the suitors vie to seduce Stephen's imagination as Muse and spouse. Mulligan replaces Boylan as brutality's representative. With his head wagging and lolling to and fro (*U* 199, 217), he stands as the episode's Scylla. Russell, associated with images of water and engulfment, acts as its Charybdis. He dwells on "formless spiritual essences" and the "deepest poetry" (*U* 185), as deep and formless as the whirlpool.

In their attitudes toward action Stephen and his two adversaries differ considerably, as Ellmann has pointed out:

> For Mulligan things done are inconsequential, for Russell things done are illusory, so in a way neither may be said to do anything. Stephen, however, admonishes himself, "Do and do. Thing done," and later, "Do. But do. Be done to," "Act. Be acted on." And he remarks of Shakespeare, "He acts and is acted on."[44]

As in "Aeolus," Stephen does by talking, by manipulating language to create an effect on his auditors. As in "Nestor" and "Aeolus," he acts and speaks to protect himself. He defends himself, parrying and thrusting with opponents. His words are a poison poured into the ears of his listeners (*U* 196). Like the lapwing he thinks of (*U* 210), Stephen hides his nest from others.[45] Because he fabricates his theory as a fiction that he finally disclaims, we can take his acting as theatrical. Like Shakespeare, Stephen as playwright and actor both writes and speaks his lines. Although he denies his own theory, his act convinces the audience. Stephen's pretense is genuine and effective. It implicates the audience in the fiction but leaves him free to disavow his own position.

However defensive Stephen may be, the attempt to turn listeners into accomplices creates a bond between him and them. The initial gap between himself and at least one of his auditors disappears, if only momentarily, by the time Stephen concludes. Like Socrates in the Platonic dialogues, he has managed to let his interlocutor, John Eglinton, reach the conclusion for himself. Stephen's relation to Plato revealed in the form of his discourse sets him clearly apart from Russell, who is interested only in "eternal wisdom, Plato's world of ideas" (*U* 185). Mulligan's Platonism is the sort that banishes the poet from its republic. Stephen must both "act"—that is, do and dissemble—and "be acted on." He does both by designing a dialectical discourse that involves his listeners actively, just as the narrator's techniques involve us actively in the process of reading. Both here and in "Aeolus" Stephen's storytelling, like the narrator's, resembles Odysseus's verbal heroics. Odysseus's narration to the Phaeacians keeps his auditors involved and encourages them to act on his behalf.

The episode's numerous dichotomies—spirit and flesh, male and female, art and life, past and present—combine into an all-inclusive whole.[46] In

Stephen's theory of *Hamlet*, Shakespeare's art and life interfuse totally, and the ideal artist is androgynous. Stephen resembles Odysseus insofar as his commentary suggests an escape for the artist from the baleful conse- quences of the various oppositions. But the fusion that marks the mature Shakespeare as Stephen presents him is an abstract and future possibility for him, not an attained actuality. Like Bloom in "Lestrygonians," Stephen thinks about himself as both past and present. He combines continuity and discontinuity in a single line: "I, I and I.I." (*U* 190) He and Bloom are each "I by memory because under everchanging forms" (*U* 189). Even his tone mediates between Russell's solemnity and Mulligan's frivolity. Despite his defensive disclaimer, Stephen's discourse is not just a whimsical joke. He wanders knowingly from the facts of Shakespeare's life in order to reach a conclusion he takes seriously. But he recognizes the limits of his own commentary and, implicitly, the limitations of Russell and Mulligan, which he skirts by laughing at himself: "He laughed to free his mind from his mind's bondage" (*U* 212). Like the teller, Stephen understands his narration's incongruities. The narrator of the fiction and the narrator within the fiction are both "jocoserious" (*U* 677). They engage in a paradoxical solemn clowning that includes shifts in tone and strategy worthy of crafty Odysseus.[47]

The mixed tone arises from the grafting of one style onto another in the transforming of the initial style into a self-referential one by addition of incongruous elements. Through dramatic form here and in "Circe," the teller, like Stephen as writer and speaker of his own lines, asserts his resemblance to the Shakespeare of Stephen's theory, who is all in all. Like the teller of *Ulysses*, Stephen begins with a detailed description of an external scene, as in "Telemachus," and ends on a note of androgyny that implies the fusion of artist and character, teller and tale, as in "Penelope." In between, he wanders in various ways. Like some of Shakespeare's themes as Stephen describes them, in this and other episodes, the book "doubles itself in the middle. . . , reflects itself, . . . repeats itself. . . . It repeats itself again" (*U* 212). As ideal artist, Shakespeare presents elements of a contemporary work, Sidney's *Arcadia*, "spatchcocked on to a Celtic legend older than history" (*U* 211), a combination Eglinton compares to mixing "a Norse saga with an excerpt from a novel by George Meredith" (*U* 211). The connection to *Ulysses* is clear, for its author also fuses contemporary events with a myth in order to emphasize the Shakespearean themes of banishment, usurpation, and adultery, ulti- mately resulting in a return.

As for Stephen's wanderings between his beginning and his conclusion, like the teller's wanderings, they are always under control. Because of Stephen's fragmented delivery, his theory at first seems overly complicated and confusing. His discourse is punctuated by the comings, goings, and other interruptions of his auditors, whose attention he is at pains to hold.

Confusions arise from Stephen's dialectical method, his means for evoking and combining contraries. The method is as important as his conclusion, which it reinforces. After employing local color to describe the scene in detail, Stephen baldly identifies Shakespeare with Hamlet's father rather than with Hamlet himself (*U* 188–89). Shortly thereafter, John Eglinton counters him: "—I was prepared for paradoxes from what Malachi Mulligan told us but I may as well warn you that if you want to shake my belief that Shakespeare is Hamlet you have a stern task before you" (*U* 194). Stephen and Eglinton then carry on most of the discussion. Together they appear to compromise on the conclusion Stephen had in mind all the while:

> —The truth is midway, he [John Eglinton] affirmed. He is the ghost and the prince. He is all in all.
> —He is, Stephen said. The boy of act one is the mature man of act five. All in all. In *Cymbeline*, in *Othello* he is bawd and cuckold. He acts and is acted on. Lover of an ideal or a perversion, like José he kills the real Carmen. His unremitting intellect is the hornmad Iago ceaselessly willing that the moor in him shall suffer. (*U* 212)

Although Stephen's theory comes out in bits and pieces, he gives the argument shape without simply imposing it as a lecture. One of his internal dialogues asserts obliquely that his verbal meanderings have a purpose:

> What the hell are you driving at?
> I know. Shut up. Blast you! I have reasons.
> *Amplius. Adhuc. Iterum. Postea.*
> Are you condemned to do this? (*U* 207)

The Latin words for "furthermore," "heretofore," "once again," and "hereafter" are rhetorical phrases marking different states of Scholastic argument.[48] They indicate that Stephen's argument has a structure and purpose not at first apparent to anyone else. His posture toward his audience resembles the one Joyce takes in his letter to Harriet Shaw Weaver. Both teller and character travel a circuitous, tortuous route to the conclusion of their narrations, which they have in mind from the outset. The wandering is necessary in order to reach the goal, which includes the listener's active participation. At times in his long, seemingly discontinuous presentation, Stephen shocks and cajoles his listeners into involving themselves in the argument. Like many detractors of *Ulysses* and *Finnegans Wake*, some members of his audience deride his antics; others simply withdraw.

Stephen's conclusion surpasses in intensity and eloquence any of the oratorical styles of "Aeolus." By doing so, together with other intensely presented, complex parts of his discourse, both internal and spoken, the conclusion indicates Stephen's potential stature as an artist while it defines the kind of artist he would become:

He found in the world without as actual what was in his world within as possible. Maeterlinck says: *If Socrates leave his house today he will find the sage seated on his doorstep. If Judas go forth tonight it is to Judas his steps will tend*. Every life is many days, day after day. We walk through ourselves, meeting robbers, ghosts, giants, old men, young men, wives, widows, brothers-in-love. But always meeting ourselves. The playwright who wrote the folio of this world and wrote it badly (He gave us light first and the sun two days later), the lord of things as they are whom the most Roman of catholics call *dio boia*, hangman god, is doubtless all in all in all of us, ostler and butcher, and would be bawd and cuckold too but that in the economy of heaven, foretold by Hamlet, there are no more marriages, glorified man, an androgynous angel, being a wife unto himself. (*U* 213)

Finally emerging from Stephen's wandering theorizing is a general conception of the artist and of artistic creation rather than a convincing interpretation of Shakespeare, for Stephen knowingly distorts biographical facts to fit the argument: "Don't tell them he was nine years old" (*U* 210). Little by little Stephen has anticipated these final statements, extrapolated from particular points he has made about one artist. The passage, like the writing of the villanelle in a *A Portrait*, gathers bits and pieces of earlier discourse as the speaker forges an autonomous work that can stand by itself and stand for the work containing it. As we have already seen in various ways, *Ulysses* itself validates in some of its details Stephen's general orientation and his specific conclusion. In "Penelope," the most vivid connection between the theory and the book containing it emerges when the concluding style turns out to have been foretold by Stephen in the final lines of his peroration. For Stephen, in every act of artistic creation, the artist reproduces himself. Ultimately, the artist fathers his whole world, because living necessarily involves reading the book of the self, meeting the self at every going forth. And all the goings forth of the artist's life, whether literal or literary, are the "grist to his mill" (*U* 204). When Stephen asserts that the poet of *Hamlet* "was and felt himself the father of all his race" (*U* 208), he grants him the stature of having fulfilled Stephen's own highest expectation, stated at the end of *A Portrait*, "to forge in the smithy of my soul the uncreated conscience of my race" (*P* 253). And that is exactly the stature Joyce aspires to in the telling of *Ulysses*.

Stephen nearly says without ever quite doing so that his remarks are to be taken in their most general sense. Even before the peroration, Shakespeare has become virtually an anonymous poet who could be any artist: "Rutlandbaconsouthamptonshakespeare or another poet of the same name in the comedy of errors" (*U* 208). The conclusion shifts in its final generalizing from the artist (He), whether identified or anonymous, to everyone (We), in a strategic use of the first-person plural pronoun, as in the thirteenth section of "Wandering Rocks." That "We" includes us. Not only the artist but each person always meets himself, finding "in the world without as actual what was in his world within as possible" (*U* 213). As S. L. Goldberg has said, "the basic activity of the citizen is the basic activity of the artist."[49] That activity includes the continuous rewriting of the world's folio according to the imagination's script. In the reading and the writing of *Ulysses*, it involves the structural relationship between style and story that makes our reading as rewriting possible.

"Sirens"—"Circe": Loss, Temptation, Limitation, Resignation, Release

In its focus on a multitude of actions, thoughts, and characters, "Wandering Rocks" anticipates in one way what is to come in the remaining episodes of part II: the book's increasingly assimilative, or encyclopedic, aspect. While the *narrative* in "Wandering Rocks" tends to be assimilative, in the later episodes the style becomes encyclopedic, most obviously in the chronological compendium of English prose styles in "Oxen of the Sun." In that compendium, the narration becomes what it calls itself, a "chaffering allincluding most farraginous chronicle" (*U* 423). By means of parody, Joyce extends and intensifies the debunking of style that has already been taking place.

As always in *Ulysses*, the narration's forms and implications bear some relation to the *Odyssey*. The encyclopedic style provides one version of the epic catalogue. But, more specifically, "Oxen" and the other episodes amount to the teller's slaying of sacred cows, including his own. Once the sacred beasts have been slain, narrative and narration reach a point of partial closure that is also an opening onto something new. In the *Odyssey* and in *Ulysses*, the episodes involving Aeolus and the Sun's cattle mark important developments in the wanderings. The stupidity, greed, and lack of discipline among Odysseus's crew first prolong their voyage home after they leave Aeolia and then insure their destruction after their sojourn on the island of the Sun. In *Ulysses*, the release of the stylistic winds initiates the move toward the vision of stylistic relativity most evident in "Oxen" but also present in the other episodes after "Wandering Rocks" and in all the book's styles considered together. "Oxen" codifies the parodic tendency of "Sirens," with its extreme version of the initial style, "Cyclops," with its Irish pub-crawling storyteller and its contrasting bombastic language, and "Nausicaa," with its parody of magazine love stories. The extensive use of parody and encyclopedic narration sharply differentiates the styles in the latter half of part II from the earlier ones.[50]

In the movement toward the parodies of "Oxen," various Homeric motifs inform the narration, each contributing to the book's stylistic catalogue of Homeric elements. As Bloom moves through the afternoon and evening, struggling internally with his perplexing domestic situation, the teller presents him in various styles, which compose a Homeric rendering of Bloom's interior wrestling. They form the basis for our experience of teller and character's mutual wanderings. In "Sirens" the voyage between opposing attitudes becomes a contrast among siren temptations: the voices Bloom hears and the attitudes he adopts as he speaks to himself. These voices represent one-sided views, like the contrasting single-minded attitudes of the voices in "Cyclops." In isolation, the voices are as unsatisfying to the weary wanderer as Nausicaa is to Odysseus and as the style associated with Gerty MacDowell in "Nausicaa" is to our sense of Bloom's experiences. Like the initial style, each element of the wandering styles provides only a partial, both limited and biased, view requiring other styles and combinations of opposing styles for the narration to proceed dialectically. The dialectical procedure moves us toward something different from the other styles, something more satisfying emerging out of the context of the whole. What emerges is not a narrow-minded style but a "myriadminded," polytropic sequence of styles, including siren, cyclopean, and parodic elements, though not limited by them.

The catalogue of motifs on the first pages of "Sirens" initiates the encyclopedism of the book's second half. Stylistically, like "Aeolus," "Sirens" provides a catalogue of examples, not of rhetorical devices but of nearly all the ways the teller has modified the initial style so far. The only omissions among the earlier changes are the one's involving odd typography: headlines, verse, musical score, and dramatic form. Instead of headlines, we have the headnote at the episode's start. And the teller renders one effect of the musical score of "Scylla and Charybdis" in his presentation of singing. By funneling the modifications into a single episode, the teller emphasizes their cumulative effect, the transforming of the initial style into something wildly different. As in earlier episodes, the narrator provides a metaphor, this time a musical one, characterizing the narration. Like the two barmaids who laugh uncontrollably at the episode's beginning, the teller is "ringing in changes" (*U* 260), ringing his stylistic bells with all possible variations. The variations include the presenting of simultaneously occurring actions, modified *inquit* phrases and names of speakers, examples of rhetorical devices (such as chiasmus: "Like lady, ladylike" [*U* 264]), mixtures of third- and first-person language in single sentences, and the teller's repetition of words and phrases from the characters' thoughts and speech. Although there is a cumulative effect within the episode from the juxtaposing of all these stylistic variations, the effect becomes most immediate and pronounced when several modifications occur together, as in the presentation of Bloom's purchase of stationery: "Two sheets cream vellum paper one reserve two envelopes when I was in Wisdom Hely's wise Bloom in Daly's Henry Flower bought" (*U* 263). Although the sentence appears to begin as Bloom's quoted monologue, we may also read it as a description in third person and past tense of his purchase. But in the description, which includes Bloom's thoughts in first person, the teller reverses the normal word order, refers to Bloom by his alias, and repeats Bloom's thought about "Wisdom" as the epithet "wise."[51]

Besides combining his earlier techniques in new ways, the teller introduces ones we have not seen before, such as his fragmented, dispersed presentation of some of his statements. When Simon Dedalus enters the bar at the Ormond Hotel, we learn that "he was" (*U* 261) on one page, but only what he was, "dry" (*U* 262), on the next, after both conversation and description intervene. The new changes the teller rings are sometimes retrospective, sometimes prospective. The retrospective ones include the allusion to what Bloom enjoys eating, mentioned in the first paragraph of "Calypso" (*U* 55, 269), and a nearly verbatim repetition from one of Stephen's quoted monologues late in "Scylla and Charybdis": "In Gerard's rosery of Fetter lane he walks, greyedauburn. One life is all. One body. Do. But do" (*U* 280, cf. 202).[52] The teller seems to be responding to Bloom's thoughts about Shakespeare and about something being "done anyhow" by inserting between them without explanation this allusion to the earlier episode. The prospective variations anticipate aspects of style in the next three episodes, especially the descriptions of scene and action in language other than a referential style. As in these later episodes, we encounter interpolations. And odder yet, the teller narrates one event in several ways; for example, in the three versions, all reported as indirect speech, of Richie Goulding's comments about Simon Dedalus's singing *'Twas rank and fame* in Ned Lambert's house (*U* 276–77).

With "Sirens" a break occurs in the style of narration as sharp as the break of "Aeolus." The shift involves both the teller's presentation of Bloom's situation and his exploring of styles other than the initial one, some of whose limits we have already encountered. Like Stephen Dedalus formulating publicly his aesthetic theory, he manages to narrate in a way that contains a disclaimer of the reality of the story he tells. As in Stephen's discourse, the narration communicates a story, but it does much more than that: it allows its teller to enact one version of the story's pattern and implications in the action of telling. The teller represents Bloom's thoughts and his attempt to keep busy, to avoid thinking too much about Molly and Blazes, in ways that enable him to translate Bloom's activities into Odyssean principles and patterns of narration. It does not matter that the story, like Stephen's theory, is not literally true; its truth goes beyond the limits of the merely literal.

As always, the narrator works by strategies of indirection, through metaphors in the narrative that are also metaphors of narration, and Bloom's strategy of survival is usually one of indirection and substitution rather than direct confrontation. In one of his most poignant moments, Bloom expresses a deep sense of loss in his comment on the lyric Simon Dedalus will sing, *All is lost now*: "—A beautiful air . . . I know it well" (*U* 273). Like the narration, Bloom's statement tells us at least two things at once. His attitudes in this episode, and in general, mix skepticism with a commitment to strong emotions. The teller reflects that mixture in his fusion of self-conscious artifice and referential narrative. Repeatedly Bloom hears, considers, then expresses judgment skeptically and humanely in his thoughts and actions. The mixture, which we have seen before, resembles the voyage between opposites, Scylla and Charybdis, or carnivores and herbivores, presented here in Bloom's response to the singing and to his meal. The former is potentially intoxicating, the latter not. He feels, and will continue to feel, pain, but he always finds some release, some way to exorcise partially the pain within him and to sing with a different voice, as he does in a comic way when he passes gas at the episode's end.

Rather than succumb wholly to the siren song of sorrow and its intoxicating effect, Bloom hears the song, responds, but then continues on his way, deciding not to linger there. He chooses cider rather than the stronger, debilitating drinks of the barroom singers. In the acts of singing, the teller develops a metaphor that points toward the book's conclusion. For Bloom, the most important singing occurs not in the Ormond Bar but in his mind, in the memory of his first meeting with Molly (*U* 275), when he assisted her by turning the pages of her music, and in his largely suppressed anticipation of Molly's appointment with Boylan. For Bloom, as for Odysseus, the absent spouse from the past takes precedence over any siren calls in the present, however seductive they may be.

The teller handles the singing in "Sirens" in two opposing ways. On the one hand, he shows its powerful effect on Bloom, who identifies momentarily with the performer, Simon Dedalus, and with the song, Lionel's air *M'appari* from Flowtow's *Martha*:

> Alone. One love. One hope. One comfort me. Martha, chestnote, return.
> —Come!
> It soared, a bird, it held its flight, a swift pure cry, soar silver orb it leaped serene, speeding, sustained, to come, don't spin it out too long long breath he breath long life, soaring high, high resplendent, aflame, crowned, high in the effulgence symbolistic, high, of the ethereal bosom, high, of the high vast irradiation everywhere all soaring all around about the all, the endlessnessnessness . . .
> —*To me*!
> Siopold!
> Consumed.
> Come. Well Sung. All clapped. She ought to. Come. To me, to him, to her, you too me, us.
> —Bravo! Clapclap. Goodman, Simon. Clappyclapclap. Encore! Clapclipclap. Sound as a bell. Bravo, Simon! Clapclopclap. Encore, enclap, said, cried, clapped all. (*U* 275–76)

The variety of compound names appearing later in the episode reiterates the fusion of singer and listener, singer and operatic character: "Lionel Simon"

(*U* 276), "Lionelleopold" (*U* 288), "Simonlionel" (*U* 289), "Henry Lionel Leopold" (*U* 290). As it stresses this fusion, the narration presents Bloom's experience as another one of those scenes encouraging our self-conscious reflection about the reality of a character in a literary work and about our relationship to him. We, too, listen to the rendering of a fictional character's singing, the teller's narration of Bloom's interior voice, with which we can identify.

As in earlier episodes, especially "Lestrygonians," the teller indicates the style's limitations, its inability to present intense emotion without calling attention to the language of presentation. While the style is evocative, it points to that lack of full presence that Bloom himself considers just before the song's conclusion, when he thinks about not being able to see Simon Dedalus as he sings: "Wish I could see his face, though. Explain better" (*U* 275). Both the sublime and the ridiculous indicate the limits of the style. Both the mannered, highly adjectival language of Bloom's response and the comic language presenting the applause deflate the effect of the fusion. "Clappyclapclap" and the other words indicating applause, some reported as if they were speech, work together with the climax's overblown language to provide an antidote as anticlimax, just as Bloom's flatulence later provides a corrective comment on the self-indulgence of the singing and drinking in the bar. As the musical score in "Scylla and Charybdis" suggests, the language of referential narration cannot present fully the impact of the human voice in song, because that voice is always lost in a mediation. In part because of its inaccessibility to teller and character, the experience of singing as both aesthetic and sexual becomes the object of desire that each in different ways voyages toward as goal. Molly Bloom the singer represents that goal.

In both "Cyclops" and "Nausicaa," Bloom continues to reject the intoxicating effect of siren calls and cyclopean views by responding in his more complicated, mixed ways. Consequently, the criticisms of him as "neither fish nor flesh" (*U* 321) and as "one of those mixed middlings" (*U* 338) turn out to be unintended compliments. Bloom's mixtures and shifts of attitude are not self-defeating. In "Cyclops," for instance, he presents the antithesis to Bob Doran's drunken swerving between sentimentality and belligerence. Bloom is capable of "twisting around all the opposite" (*U* 333), depending on the circumstance. We see such a shift in his assertion that "love" is "the opposite of hatred" and that "force, hatred, history" are not "really life" (*U* 333), immediately following his strong statement about persecution. As his final remarks provoking the Citizen's violence show, Bloom can be aggressive too, when he decides the issue is worth the effort. Together, his moods of sentiment and anger, which never become mere self-indulgence, reflect the ambivalence Bloom feels about his situation at home, especially his sense of loss coupled with a belief that he is at least partially to blame.

The narration raises the shifting motion of that ambivalence to its principle of expression by yoking the episode's two cyclopean voices, the thersitical voice of the pub-crawling speaker and the bombastic style that Joyce referred to as the voice of the epic.[53] The teller presents the struggle in Bloom's consciousness not referentially as a mimesis of verbalized thoughts, but indirectly as the conflict between opposed tendencies of style and interpretation. At times the voices narrate apparently unrelated or tenuously related events. At times one picks up the narrative where the other has left off. Finally, in the episode's concluding paragraph, the narrator combines them in a single sentence, recalling the ending of "Lestrygonians," by completing the epic voice's statement with a simile appropriate to the thersitical voice: "And they beheld Him even Him, ben Bloom Elijah, amid clouds of angels ascend to the glory of the brightness at an angle of fortyfive degrees over Donohoe's in Little Green Street like a shot off a shovel" (*U* 345). This merger and the similar ones earlier in the episode belie the propensity of some critics to speak as if there were a separable "pair of narrators"[54] or a "new narrator of Chapter Twelve," meaning the thersitical one, being interrupted by Joyce.[55] As in earlier episodes, the teller pokes fun at the tendency of his own style, here by drawing attention to the conflict and merger through a joke. He imposes a particularly incongruous stylistic merger by combining the positions of the antagonists in the telling. The merger is like Constable MacFadden's resolving the conflict "among F. O. T. E. I. [the Friends of the Emerald Isle] as to whether the eighth or the ninth of March was the correct date of the birth of Ireland's patron saint": "The baby policeman . . . quickly restored order and with lightning promptitude proposed the seventeenth of the month as a solution equally honourable for both contending parties" (*U* 307–8).

A similar combining of stylistic tendencies takes place at the end of "Nausicaa." As in "Cyclops," we encounter two substantially different styles, not alternating frequently as in that episode but each sustained instead for half the narration. Within the focus on Gerty MacDowell and her friends in the style of the first half and on Bloom in the modified initial style of the second, the narrator includes references to the religious service whose music the characters hear on the strand. Although the reporting of Bloom's thoughts resembles the initial style of his previous episodes, at least two modifications distinguish it. In one, the narrator employs the third person far less frequently than in his early use of the initial style. Besides the single lengthy paragraph narrated wholly in third person and past tense (*U* 379) in Bloom's part of the episode, the teller uses quoted monologue virtually without interruption from the time he switches to Bloom's perspective until the episode's last three paragraphs. The quoted monologue of the paragraph before the narrator's concluding ones ("O sweety all your little girl white" [*U* 382]) departs from the initial style by giving us briefly an unpunctuated, seemingly autonomous, first-person monologue, like that of "Penelope." In this paragraph, the episode's narration points beyond the initial and various styles to the book's conclusion.

We encounter Bloom in a period of fatigue. He is alone thinking, unsupported by the comforting distractions of daytime experience that he has given his attention to earlier. As I have mentioned, the return here to Bloom's mind works in several ways to forge a link with the *Odyssey*. Like Odysseus on Scheria, Bloom longs for what he has lost, and he tells his own story. Furthermore, like Odysseus, he finds the young girl he meets inadequate to the memory of his spouse, just as we find the cliché style associated with her to be limited and immature. The initial style reasserts itself as a return to memories of the spouse, though Bloom, like the reader, realizes "returning not the same" (*U* 377). Still, we and Bloom do return, return to his thoughts about Molly, which have ceased for us and which presumably Bloom has avoided since his watch stopped at the crucial hour: half past four. Bloom needs to occupy himself during the afternoon and evening in order to keep from going home before he can find some release for his feelings. He vents himself in various ways, comically by his flatulent response to the events in the Ormond Bar, angrily in his outburst at the Citizen, and sexually by masturbating on the beach. Even though Bloom admits that "aftereffect not pleasant" (*U* 370), he is grateful for the release of masturbating: "Did me good all the same. Off colour after Kiernan's, Dignam's. For this relief much thanks" (*U* 372). The more limited style of the episode's first half marks a failure to find release. That style is what Gerty claims Cissy Caffrey is not: "One of your two-faced things, too sweet to be wholesome" (*U* 353). Its duplicity emerges most clearly when we learn that the style is a mask of clichés hiding Gerty's bitterness about her deformity and her incipient old maidenhood. Bloom himself thinks about the effects of frustration, abstinence, repression, and duplicity when he refers to the nuns' supposed inventing of barbed wire and to the girlfriends, like Hermia and Helena in *A Midsummer Night's Dream*, whose antagonism toward one another eventually surfaces *(U* 369).

Through their multiple perspectives ("Colours depend on the light you see" [*U* 371]), Bloom and the teller avoid the hypocrisy and self-deception by which one style becomes the unselfconscious mask for its opposite. Bloom does so by finding releases and by trying to take a second point of view that modifies one limited to loss and hurt. When he recalls his encounter with the Citizen, one of the substitutes for Boylan in his thoughts, Bloom finds a way to forgive him by adopting that other view: "Suppose he hit me. Look at it other way round. Not so bad then. Perhaps not to hurt he meant" (*U* 380). And he recommends laughter as part of self-knowledge, though he by no means laughs at this juncture in the day's events: "Ought to go home and laugh at themselves" (*U* 380). The narrator employs both strategies to alleviate our sense of Bloom's pain. He does so by providing perspectives by incongruity in the final paragraphs, which dovetail the sentimental and the gross in a jocoserious way. When the "Cuckoo," signifying cuckoldry and madness as well as the time, punctuates both the episode's styles, this anticlimactic antidote for maudlin attitudes toward Bloom evokes our laughter. The narrator avoids duplicity by having his style announce its double nature and shifting implications. The stylistic wandering here allows us a release, not of the sexual sort that Bloom finds, but of the kind Stephen Dedalus achieves in "Scylla and Charybdis" when he laughs (*U* 212).

The laughter of release echoes throughout "Oxen of the Sun," with its parodies as the teller's slaying of sacred literary beasts. It continues countering the situation Bloom faces, one potentially close to that of "Nausicaa." Bloom's various losses, especially the death of his infant son, may well disturb him. By assuming a parental attitude toward Stephen, Bloom finds a gain rather than only more reminders of loss. When he takes that attitude, Bloom negotiates a crucial turn in the day's events, one that gives him the chance to channel his attention and energies in a way he finds satisfying. The narrator, too, accomplishes a reversal, one extending and culminating his stylistic wanderings, though it leads to another adventure that is its metaphorical opposite. For Bloom, the losses provide a liberation for experiences of a new sort.

Loss is the teller's gain, too, for he can make death a birth. That reversal as gain occurs when the slaying of sacred literary cows becomes the vehicle for creative extravagance. The tour de force that provides one of the book's longest laughs in "Oxen" demonstrates that, like Odysseus, this teller is "skilled in all ways of contending." The teller puts all these styles behind him, each with its different interpretative limitations, just as he has put the other styles of the day behind him on his chameleonic progress toward the new styles of "Circe" and "Penelope." "Oxen" clears the way for "Circe," the episode whose primary metaphor is not slaying but its opposite, the resurrection of the dead. That resurrection includes the rising up of the unconscious mentioned in "Oxen" but evoked more fully in "Circe" and in "Penelope":

> There are sins or (let us call them as the world calls them) evil memories which are hidden away by man in the darkest places of the heart but they abide there and wait. He may suffer their memory to grow dim, let them be as though they had not been and all but persuade himself that they were not or at least were otherwise. Yet a chance word will call them forth suddenly and they will rise up to confront him in the most various circumstances, a vision or a dream, or while timbrel and harp soothe his senses or amid the cool silver tranquillity of the evening or at the feast at midnight when he is now filled with wine. Not to insult over him will the vision come as over one that lies under her wrath, not for vengeance to cut off from the living but shrouded in the piteous vesture of the past, silent, remote, reproachful. (*U* 421)

In "Penelope" what waits for us and for Bloom is not an *evil* memory but it *is* "hidden away" in "the heart," like Bloom's first encounter with Molly: "Singing. *Waiting* she sang" (*U* 275). And in "Circe," we encounter a vision or dream that is as much ours and the teller's as the characters'. When the narration points beyond referential and self-referential styles, beyond style itself, by presenting mental activity, including writing, as a descent into an underworld and a resurrection of the dead, we reach a telling that attempts to carry us back to origins, back home.

The voyage back involves a kind of *Nachträglichkeit*, or belated recognition, for teller, character, and reader.[56] For all of us, as for Odysseus, the encounter with Circe becomes a means for reaching the underworld and for continuing the journey home. At the end of "Circe," Bloom's unexpected vision of Rudy underscores his paternal attitude toward Stephen, an attitude reaffirming his tie to spouse and to home. For the teller, the underworld of the mind, with its memories of literary, cultural, and personal pasts, propels us toward a future in which we experience and recognize that underworld as our own place of habitation. Through the story and style's *Nachträglichkeit*, the reader of "Circe" and of the "Nostos" perceives the book's past and past parts of the book coming back in new guises, asking for recognition. "Circe" turns out to be "Hades" with a difference. And the "Nostos," by sending us back to the "Telemachiad," allows us to know the beginning and the end of the telling in the wake of our wanderings.

ULTIMATE STYLES: "EUMAEUS"—"PENELOPE" —ENDS AND BEGINNINGS

Every limit is a beginning as well as an ending.
—George Eliot, *Middlemarch*

. . .the ends and ultimates of all things accord in some mean and measure with their inceptions and originals. . . .
—"Oxen of the Sun" (*U* 394)

Various kinds of homecoming, return, and recovery occur in the "Nostos" of *Ulysses*. Besides physically returning to his house at 7 Eccles Street after a day of wandering, Bloom returns to Molly by reaffirming his commitment to her as a spouse despite her liaison with Boylan. The tension about his marital situation evident in Bloom's thoughts and actions and in the teller's styles in earlier parts of *Ulysses* dissipates in these episodes, especially in "Ithaca," when Bloom consciously reconciles himself to Molly's adultery. In her monologue Molly returns through memory by turning back to special incidents of the past. For Stephen, the action involves his recovery after his debauch, then his leave-taking. The teller also turns back and takes his leave. Stylistically, he returns to presenting characters' thoughts and actions referentially, though not in the initial style, and he withdraws, as at the end of *A Portrait*, by ostensibly relinquishing the teller's role to a character.

In numerous ways, the narration alludes to earlier episodes through recalls of both initial and various styles, but especially in the connections between the "Nostos" and the "Telemachiad." Because "returning [is] not the same" (*U* 377), the recalls involve significant differences. Often the modifications dominate our sense of a stylistic return. In certain ways, these final episodes are closer in kind to the earliest episodes in the various styles than they are to the other parts of *Ulysses*, to either the late episodes of the "Odyssey" or the book's first two triads. Like "Aeolus," they form a half-way stage that mediates between the initial style and the more extreme various styles. The representation of mind and action now occurs in a narration that, unlike the initial style, insistently calls attention to its own language. Obtrusive aspects of style blend with presentations of mind into a selective, but thorough, mixture of earlier stylistic tendencies.

Despite the mixtures, we encounter a sustained style in each final episode from the beginning. In "Eumaeus" we find from the outset a verbose, pompous narration, which continues throughout. The teller frequently editorializes, as when he says that Bloom bucked Stephen up "in orthodox Samaritan fashion" (*U* 613). And he translates characters' speech and thoughts into a homogeneous, bumbling style. Like Stephen's mind as the first paragraph of "Eumaeus" describes it, the episode's style is "not exactly what you would call wandering but a bit unsteady." This is not a wandering style but one of homecoming that seems homely, or even homemade. The style is both culminating and "preparatory to anything else" (*U* 612–13). In "Ithaca" no matter what aspect of the characters' actions, thoughts, and situation the teller considers, he maintains a uniform stance and style. He is always scrupulous about details, seemingly objective, encyclopedic, and fond of the language of mathematics and science. Only at the end of the episode does the narration evoke the character's interior voice, and even there it does so within the form of "catechetical interrogation" (*U* 735). The shift acts as a transition to "Penelope." Unlike the other episodes, in the final one the teller limits the language to Molly's thoughts in first person. Her thought as language is associative and grammatically fragmented, often focused on the past, and sometimes onomatopoeic. There are neither sharply contrasting styles within Molly's thoughts nor interruptions in the third person to disturb the style's homogeneity and flow. But there are some well-modulated changes in register, particularly at the end. As I suggested briefly at this chapter's beginning, we perceive the narrator's presence despite the lack of third-person statements. We sense that presence in the change of register that the shift to this new style effects and in the modulations within the style.

"Nostos" and "Telemachiad": The Schemata

Although the narration moves from the dual and multiple voices earlier in *Ulysses* to the singular ones of the "Nostos," the final episodes provide a return by recalling the "Telemachiad." Each of the final episodes is linked by a variety of echoes and transformations to its counterpart among the first three. In the "Nostos," Joyce provides counterpointing with the early triad in parallels and contrasts that match, complete, or redirect the book's initial tendencies. Using the Linati and the Gorman-Gilbert schemata, we can trace the parallels and contrasts along with spatial and temporal connections between the book's early and late parts.[57]

In the Linati schema the general headings specify the time of day. The first six episodes move from "I. *DAWN*" (first triad) through "II. *MORNING*" (second triad) to "*NOON*," at which point "Aeolus" begins. The beginning of "*DAY*" is not indicated until "Wandering Rocks." This seemingly belated entry is withheld from the triad that "Aeolus" initiates, presumably because the first three episodes in the various styles are, like the "Nostos," different from the later episodes of wandering. "III. *MID-NIGHT*" marks the end of the "Odyssey" and the various styles and points to the commencement of the "Nostos." Directly beneath that heading two parenthetical notations suggest fusion: "(Fusion of Bloom and Stephen) (Ulysses and Telemachus)." The "Nostos" proceeds from midnight to a final, indeterminate time indicated by the hyphenated entry after "Penelope" reiterating the fusion of characters with one another and with mythic counterparts.

At the end of the Linati schema, the following alignments indicate the connections between characters, their counterparts, and times of day:

DEEP NIGHT   –   DAWN

Ulysses (Bloom)   Telemachus (Stephen).

Definite and iterative become one when dawn and deep night merge. And so do prospective and retrospective, because *Ulysses* has returned temporally to a beginning by reaching the point in the diurnal cycle just prior to "Telemachus." The new "*DAWN*" differs from the previous one not simply as the start of a different day, but because of its connection to "*DEEP NIGHT*." The narration's spiral, rather than linear or circular, movement anticipates the cyclical vision of the *Wake* as "vicociclometer" (614.27). The twelve hours and nine episodes from noon to midnight are narrated in the various styles of wandering. The twelve hours and nine episodes from dawn to noon and from midnight to the new dawn, making up the frame for the other nine episodes, are narrated either in the initial style or in the related ultimate styles. The framing gives the narration a chiastic structure.

Spatially as well as temporally *Ulysses* moves back towards its beginning. In the "Telemachiad" we move outward from images of claustrophobic enclosure to images of increasingly open space. The "Nostos" ostensibly reverses that motion by presenting ever more confined spaces. According to the Gorman-Gilbert plan, the "Scene" of the "Telemachiad" changes from "Tower" to "School" to "Strand," while the "Scene" of the "Nostos" moves from "Shelter" to "House" (actually kitchen) to "Bed." Because of the prolonged presentation of the character's mind, the narrating situation at the book's end resembles the end of "Proteus." In both episodes the all-embracing nature of the character's mind involves simultaneously inward and outward movements, ones not limited by physical scene. Molly in her bed is no more enclosed mentally than Stephen on the strand, though her "Scene" is more narrowly circumscribed physically. With its present participles, Stephen's perception of the Rosevean at the end of "Proteus" leaves us with an expansive view, heralding an arrival: "Moving through the air high spars . . . her sails brailed up on the crosstrees, homing, upstream, silently moving, a silent ship" (*U* 51). That expansive vision recurs in Molly's narration, filled as it is with present participles, and in such images from "Ithaca" as the "heaventree of stars hung with humid nightblue fruit" (*U* 698). But in "Ithaca" the image combines expansion with limitation. The tree with its dark fruit is both mulberry tree and plum tree. It signifies both the fulfillment of Shakespeare's journey home to plant his tree and Molly's adultery, her having eaten the tree's forbidden fruit. The freely moving Rosevean, a ship full of bricks bringing the old salt of "Eumaeus" back to Ireland, has become the comic analogue for the Phaeacian ship turned to stone after returning Odysseus to Ithaca. The end of the "Telemachiad" conjoins momentarily Stephen's physical and mental wandering. The end of the book meshes confinement with its opposite, the wandering mind unlimited by time or place as dawn merges with indeterminate deep night.

Some of the entries in the schemata, particularly those concerning "Technic," indicate the relationships of similarity and difference between the early and the final episodes. While the parallels among techniques are evident in both schemata, they are clearer in the Gorman-Gilbert plan. There, "Telemachus" is "Narrative (young)"; "Eumaeus" is "Narrative (old)." "Nestor" is "Catechism (personal)"; "Ithaca" is "Catechism (impersonal)." "Proteus" is "Monologue (male)"; "Penelope" is "Monologue (female)." The entries in the Linati Schema focus more precisely on the transforming of the initial techniques at the end. Three techniques are listed for "Telemachus": "3- and 4-person dialogue," "Narration," and "Soliloquy." The comment for "Eumaeus" is the more general "Relaxed prose." In this later episode the narrator employs all the techniques indicated for "Telemachus," including multiperson dialogue, third-person narration, and representation of mind, especially psycho-narration. But the context is a more informal prose than in "Telemachus," one lacking the seeming precision of the earlier third-person narration. By employing a relaxed style, the narrator disguises the initial style, both the third-person passages and the characters' thoughts. Like Odysseus returning home and like Bloom, who is *"Incog Haroun al Raschid"* (*U* 586) in "Circe," the teller returns in disguise to his rock of Ithaca as mode of telling. When we see through the disguise, we also see by means of it that all the book's styles, including the initial one, are disguises, personae, masks.

In "Eumaeus," by using clichés to present action, scene, *and* thought, the teller makes the mediating function of style more explicit than in the earlier referential style. Even the reports of speech are often not direct but summarized and transformed; they are translations into the style's "words to that effect" (*U* 638). Because the return with a difference occurs in both narration and narrative, the teller's language often applies to itself as style. We learn of "history repeating itself with a difference" (*U* 655) and of situations being "radically altered since" the "last visit" (*U* 638). Like the man in the shelter who looks like, but not exactly like, "Henry Campbell, the townclerk," the teller adopts "a seedy getup and a strong suspicion of nosepaint about the nasal appendage" and bears "a distant resemblance" (*U* 631) to his earlier stylistic incarnation.

The Linati schema contains three entries under "Technic" for "Nestor," "2-person dialogue," "Narration," and "Soliloquy," corresponding to the three for "Ithaca": "Dialogue," "Pacified Style," and "Fusion." Both episodes present dialogue in the framework of third-person narration; one between Stephen and Mr. Deasy, the other between Stephen and Leopold Bloom. In "Ithaca" style pacifies dialogue by homogenizing it rather than rendering differences through contrasts in linguistic modes, either spoken or thought. The teller has translated what was only an aspect of plot in "Nestor," the questioning and answering occurring among the characters and in their minds, into the principle of the telling.[58] The episode's catechismal form is a dialogue of one. As the narration's "all in all," the teller responds to his own questions. By doing so he achieves one kind of "Fusion" stylistically. In this fusion the teller presents the character's voices, both audible and internal, not as distinct rhythms and dictions but as virtually indistinguishable language. Only at the end of "Ithaca" do teller and character's voices and functions fuse in a different way. When Bloom becomes a "Narrator" (*U* 736) as he tells Molly about his day, the teller's answers to his own questions begin to sound briefly like the character's distinctive mind on the verge of sleep. The large dot after the final question indicates the cessation of the narrating voice as the protagonist falls asleep. The teller no longer answers, because his voice combines with Bloom's conscious thoughts, which now presumably cease.

The single entry in the Linati schema for "Technic" in "Proteus" is "Soliloquy," not monologue. Because there is a third-person context for

Stephen's interior soliloquizing, the "Narration" mentioned for the two previous episodes is still at work, though it is not listed. The two entries for "Penelope"—"Monologue" and "Resigned style"—both indicate a major change from "Proteus": the abandoning of the third person. Autonomous, first-person monologue replaces interior soliloquy, for the teller has resigned his position as the explicit third-person context of the character's thought even more thoroughly than he does at the end of "Ithaca."[59] The narration of "Penelope" resembles not only "Proteus" but that other terminal episode, "Circe." As in "Proteus," the primary focus of the telling is a single character's mind. But as in "Circe," the teller appears to have withdrawn in certain respects. Only the episode's form, not passages explicitly assigned to the narrator through grammatical markers of person, reveals his presence.

"Eumaeus" and "Ithaca": Disguise and the Relativity of Styles

In both narrative and narration, "Eumaeus" concerns lies and disguises. Like the other episodes of the "Nostos," it contributes to the sense of release that marks the book's conclusion. Here and in "Ithaca" the release occurs through laughter as the teller transforms realism into a comic mode aware of its own limitations.[60] Filled as it is with suggestions of mistakes, false information, lies, and disguises, "Eumaeus" encourages us to see all styles as disguises, as "genuine forgeries" (*U* 634).

We have, for instance, the apparent discrepancies in the newspaper's report of Dignam's funeral and in Bloom's narration about his encounter with the Citizen in Barney Kiernan's. When Bloom reads the late edition of the *Telegraph*, he thinks about how its inaccuracies "tell a graphic lie" (*U* 647). Besides the chance typographical errors, such as the omission of the "l" from Bloom's name, which parallels the "t" absent from "Plasto's high grade ha" in "Calypso," the article falsifies the attendance of McCoy and Stephen Dedalus. Through the printing of texts, characters, both typographical and fictional, are made to appear or disappear. Because of Bloom's remark to the reporter after the funeral, the article naively assigns the name "M'Intosh," spelled variously throughout *Ulysses*, to the unknown character in the macintosh. The joke of the episode is on us, because like Bloom we respond to the mistakes and to Bloom's narration about "Cyclops" (*U* 642–43) with referential assumptions about the possible correspondence between language and event. Along with Bloom, we want to correct the article's errors based on our experience, not the experience of being a witness but of having read another account. But the episode's style, along with the recurring implications about style throughout *Ulysses*, keeps reminding us that all supposedly referential narrations are limited and fictional. Consequently, we keep catching ourselves responding referentially.

"Eumaeus" invites us to realize the difficulty, even the impossibility, of choosing absolutely between differing narrations of the same event. When Bloom reads the article about the Gold Cup race at Ascot, he faces a problem like ours, though his reaction is as straightforward as his response to the article about the funeral. The version of the race printed in the paper differs from Lenehan's version in "Cyclops." Lenehan claimed hyperbolically that Sceptre, "Bass's mare," was "still running" (*U* 325), implying that the horse finished last or at least far behind the winner. But the article reports that Sceptre came in third. While Bloom decides that "Lenehan's version of the business was all pure buncombe" (*U* 648), we may well wonder if the newspaper's account isn't simply muddled again. No absolute determination is possible among competing referential accounts, at least not in a fictional text. This point would hardly be worth noting based only on Lenehan's exaggeration and Bloom's belated response, except that Joyce has complicated the situation. We are, in fact, not even sure what Bloom has heard. During Lenehan's report in "Cyclops," because Bloom is engaged in "arguing about law and history" with J. J. O'Molloy and the citizen (*U*, 326), he may not hear the account of the race until Lenehan provides it again later in "Oxen" (*U* 415).[61] We have three versions, while Bloom *may* have only two. The narrations of the episodes, as well as the narrations in them, invite our conjectures as response. Bloom's Shandean response to Stephen's comment about the multiple names of God suggests the difficulty of making a categorical decision: "—Of course, Mr Bloom proceeded to stipulate, you must look at both sides of the question. It is hard to lay down hard and fast rules as to right and wrong" (*U* 643). Or, as we learn in the *Wake*, there is always "another cant to the questy" (*FW* 109.01), another angle to the question and an obstruction to completing the quest. In "Ithaca" Bloom holds to the principle of his statement, and to the principle of the book's styles, when he thinks about Molly's adultery.

Although Stephen can correct Bloom's misinterpretations of the discussion among the Italians outside the shelter (*U* 621–22), some of Bloom's notions about what he sees and hears are not open to easy correction. These aspects of the narrative resemble the old sailor's tattoo, which appears to be frowning one moment and smiling the next (*U* 671). When Bloom asks the sailor if he knows the Rock of Gibraltar, the old salt "grimaced, chewing, in a way that might be read as yes, ay, or no" (*U* 629). Because the sailor refuses to talk about Gibraltar or answer any questions directly, neither the reader nor Bloom can decide with certainty if indeed the sailor means yes. Even so, Bloom acts as if he could interpret the gesture unambiguously as affirmative. The references to Gibraltar and to an ambiguous gesture send us back to Bloom's response to Molly's "sleepy soft grunt," "—Mn," in "Calypso": "No. She did not want anything" (*U* 56). The contrast between our response to the two scenes of interpretation indicates the way *Ulysses* develops from "Telemachiad" to "Nostos," from initial to ultimate styles. The context for interpretation within the narrative and the context for our interpreting the narration have both changed. The change involves our increased sensitivity to the ambiguities of listening and telling because of stylistic relativity and the limitations of language.

In "Ithaca" the teller adopts a principle of style highlighting the change in our reading. In the scene from "Calypso," question and answer raise no particular problems of interpretation. But in "Ithaca," as in Bloom's questioning of the old salt, the answers are no longer satisfying, despite the encyclopedic elaborations. They turn out to raise more questions, which could proliferate indefinitely, reaching no one end. They stop only when Bloom sleeps. Donald Barthelme captures the implications of the catechismal form in his story "The Explanation":

> Q: Are you bored with the question-and-answer form?
> A: I am bored with it but I realize that it permits many valuable omissions: what kind of day it is, what I'm wearing, what I'm thinking. That's a very considerable advantage, I would say.
> Q: I believe in it.[62]

As the "Q" preceding the final declaration in this excerpt suggests, what from one perspective might be an answer is from a different perspective only another question. Not only is every style a disguise, but every style raises questions that cannot be answered within the style's boundaries. Instead, the questions must always be deferred to other frames of reference, which generate answers *and* more questions. In "Ithaca," by allowing a variety of inclusions and omissions, the form causes us to question both style and story. Most prominently omitted is the representation of characters' thoughts in a realistic style like the initial one. Rather than asserting the validity of any single character's perspective or any single style, the narration of "Ithaca," like the narration of the entire book, is ecumenical. In an absurd extension of the metonymic perspective that informs realism, the teller in "Ithaca" treats everything as equally relevant and equally problematic. The characters, like the book's styles, are separate but equal. Each takes on the literal role of a narrator during the episode, not just in thought as so often in the initial style. As narrators, they diverge and converge, disagree and agree, by turns, always seeing things from "different points of observation" (*U* 667).

In both style and story, "Ithaca" encourages laughter at the seemingly inexhaustible proliferations that link stylistic and moral relativism as counterparts. Bloom's culminating attitude toward Molly matches the narrator's implied attitude toward style and toward the imagination. Although Bloom's feelings about Molly include "antagonistic sentiments and reflections" (*U* 734), he can finally reconcile his emotions and reaffirm his commitment to her. He feels "more abnegation than jealousy, less envy than equanimity" (*U* 733). The teller couches Bloom's unspoken judgment in terms reminiscent of the earlier passage in "Ithaca" about squaring the circle (*U* 699):

> If he had smiled why would he have smiled?
> To reflect that each one who enters imagines himself to be the first to enter whereas he is always the last term of a preceding series even if the first term of a succeeding one, each imagining himself to be first, last, only and alone, whereas he is neither first nor last nor only nor alone in a series originating in and repeated to infinity. (*U* 731)

The passage describes the character's situation and the writer's. First and last, like "A" and "O" in the *Wake*'s elliptical letter, turn out to be parts of a continuum in process of repeating itself. As with "the quadrature of the circle," only "a relative degree of accuracy" is possible. Print is unable "to contain the complete tale" (*U* 699), which would include the story of the book's engendering. Despite the difficulties and limitations, teller and character can still choose spouse, Muse, and style on bases other than chastity, accuracy, or completeness.

The laugh or smile provides release from the frustrating limitations of mind and matter without ignoring those limitations. Realizing the difficulties of human experience, the ambiguities of moral judgments, the "irreparability of the past," and the "imprevidibility of the future" (*U* 696), Bloom finds release first in the potential smile and then, his decision made, in the concrete, immediate "satisfaction" (*U* 734) of touching Molly's flesh. As he does so, the teller is about to choose his own final "sotisfiction" (*FW* 161.02, 452.06). For the last time in *Ulysses*, the teller faces and defies the limits of referential language. Through incongruities of narration, he has given us the experience of the almost smile or of the laugh as release. At the same time, he has freed himself from bondage to the limitations of any one style.[63] But to give us something like the experience of touching Molly's flesh, he needs a new style for his ultimate episode.

"Penelope": The Grain of the Voice as Joy

> Well, you know or don't you kennet or haven't I told you every telling has a taling and that's the he and the she of it.
> —*Finnegans Wake* I.8 (213.11–12)

> We shall not cease from exploration
> And the end of all our exploring
> Will be to arrive where we started
> And know the place for the first time.
> Through the unknown, remembered gate
> When the last of earth left to discover
> Is that which was the beginning;
> At the source of the longest river
> The voice of the hidden waterfall
> And the children in the apple-tree
> Not known, because not looked for

But heard, half-heard, in the stillness
Between two waves of the sea.
                                                —T. S. Eliot, "Little Gidding"

Molly's thought that opens "Penelope," "HE NEVER DID A THING
LIKE THAT BEFORE" (*U* 738), applies to the teller as well as to Bloom
the "Narrator" (*U* 736). Like the other episodes of the "Nostos,"
"Penelope" involves repetition with a difference. The teller returns to
earlier aspects of the narration but changes them significantly. When he
reports as apparently unmediated, first-person language Molly's misinter-
pretation of Bloom's words as his ordering breakfast, the teller breaks his
own fast by returning to the mimesis of mind in a style that underplays its
mediating role. But the mediation is not wholly effaced; it still occurs, still
reveals itself as style. "Penelope" completes the oscillation between third
and first person in the initial style by allowing the teller to seem both
immanent and withdrawn. The homecoming to mimesis of mind is a return
to the style of the morning pressed to the limits of its referential implications.
And it is a return to the seemingly autonomous monologue that closes
Bloom's section of "Nausicaa" (*U* 382). The ultimate style, then, brings us
to a home that we have known before and have already seen renovated into
something like its final form in one of the episodes of wandering.

The style of "Penelope" does not just recapitulate some of the book's
earlier language and attitudes. It allows the teller to go beyond the
implications of earlier styles. The teller turns his back on them while also
turning back to them. Finally, he seems to have become wholly invisible, to
have effaced himself by transferring the work of narrating, as at the end of *A
Portrait*, to one of the characters. Style seems to have become the
transparent medium for presenting plot and character. But that transparency is only a special kind of illusion, one that we experience as illusory by
recognizing the seeming transparency to be also a mirror. The connections
between "Penelope" and Stephen's journal and villanelle in *A Portrait*
reveal the episode's odd, compelling conjunctions. The ending of *Ulysses*
resembles both villanelle and journal, for it is both climax and conclusion as
post scriptum and as origin of writing. The initial style's combination of first
and third person comes to climactic conclusion when the style blurs the
distinction between teller and character in a fusion. Narrative and narration
mesh fully when the action in the tale is also the act of telling. Parallel lines
have met and merged. They have because the teller's act of masking as a
female character is also an unmasking that reveals the origin of narration in
mental processes. The new stylistic disguise hides the teller and reveals the
act of hiding.

In the journal and in the writing of the villanelle, we encounter a representation of textual origins in which the narrator appears to fall silent. The
related representation in "Penelope" combines sexuality and writing in a

style representing the origin of writing as an experience like sexual gratification. Molly's thoughts explicitly link writing and love-making. She thinks of men generally that "theyre all mad to get in there where they come out of" (*U* 760). And thinking of poets, Stephen in particular, she asserts that "they all write about some woman in their poetry . . . hell write about me lover and mistress" (*U* 775–76), as Stephen in *A Portrait* has already written about the temptress of his villanelle. In "Penelope," another author has written about her, too, in an attempt to present mental process as our origin, the place we all come from, in a writing that shows "what we have inside us" (*U* 743) as it comes "pouring out . . . like the sea" (*U* 769): "O how the waters come down at Lahore" (*U* 770). Molly's voice, like Anna Livia's at the end of the *Wake*, echoes the sound of distant waters, the headwaters of the Nile, the wellsprings of imagination. The teller has brought us to that source as home to conclude the Homeric pattern of his stylistic wanderings and thereby to forge a final link connecting him to his literary source. The wanderings in Joyce and in Homer end with a return to the place of beginning that we come to know in a new way. The end, or goal, of writing as wandering quest is not to cease from exploring but to continue. "Continuarration" (*FW* 205.14) is "the he and the she of it" as the "taling" of the telling, the tale of the telling and the tail, or finish, of the telling as sexual.

The story of writing that Joyce has inscribed implicitly throughout *Ulysses* reaches its end when "Penelope" fulfills stylistically and conceptually the conclusion of Stephen's comments on aesthetic creation in "Scylla and Charybdis." When the male writer adopts the voice of the book's central female character, the narration achieves "the economy of heaven, foretold by Hamlet . . . , glorified man, an androgynous angel, being a wife unto himself" (*U* 210). As the *Wake* tells us, "the penelopean patience of its last paraphe" is "tailed by a leaping lasso . . . the vaulting feminine libido of those interbranching ogham sex upandinsweeps sternly controlled and easily repersuaded by the uniform matteroffactness of a meandering male fist" (*FW* 123.5–10). By fusing male and female, teller and character, in a narrating situation evoking androgyny and coupling, Joyce brings to culmination the mythic, literary repeating with a difference that informs the entire narration of *Ulysses*. Like Odysseus returning to wife and home, the teller cohabits stylistically with his character as spouse and as interior paramour. In doing so, he matches Homer's act of suggesting but not explicitly presenting the lovemaking of Odysseus and Penelope, heroic voyager and waiting spouse. The episode's singular style fulfills at least two functions simultaneously, as a mimesis of mind and as the imitation of an earlier work. It gives us the capstone of the artifice and the last bodily "Organ" listed on the schemata: "Flesh." Narration and narrative together conjoin flesh and mind as figures for one another. Through that conjunction and the completion of the organs, the author inscribes his work with a "last paraphe." That final signature finishes the literary construction of the book as composite image, not the image of a single person only but of Ulysses as humankind.

When Joyce, like Antisthenes, gives the palm to Penelope rather than Helen, he seems to turn to the chaste and singular and away from the scortatory and multiple, back to the initial style and mimesis, away from the heterogeneous variety of the book's middle. However, the singular has become multiple, for the one now contains the many within itself. The inanimate statue has come alive. Like the photo that Bloom faults in "Eumaeus" because it "could not at all do justice to" "her stage presence," the narration turns into "a speaking likeness," a figure that seems able "to speak for itself" (U 653). When it does we hear within and behind the singular voice other voices, attitudes, and perspectives that make the language live, move, oscillate, vibrate, blossom, dance. The style will not stay in place, will not stay still. It will not in part because of the grammatical ambiguities of Molly's language. It will not as well because we read the final episode not in isolation but in the context of all the other styles and attitudes of the seventeen preceding episodes. We have learned how to read this last episode in a special way, because the sequence of styles has moved us to a final position enabling our active response. Like Bloom in his first encounter with Molly, we turn the pages for her performance (U 275), which we ourselves render. As Henry James says in his preface to The American, at the window of the character's "wide, quite sufficiently wide, consciousness we are seated, from that admirable position we 'assist.' " Our reaction actualizes a Joycean labor theory of aesthetic value in which the process of striving as questing defines our role, the teller's, and the characters'. Like John Eglinton, Stephen's interlocutor and listener in "Scylla and Charybdis," we become the teller's counterparts, for he gives us the material for completing the motion ourselves. When we draw our own, and the teller's, conclusion, like Professor MacHugh after Stephen's narration of his "Pisgah Sight" in "Aeolus," we realize where the elements of the story originate. We are the tale's subject. Molly's "yes" is also "We," the pronoun Stephen uses to respond silently to his sister in "Wandering Rocks," and it is "us," as in Bloom's reaction to Simon Dedalus's song in "Sirens."[64] We discover the teller to be "all in all," and we discern our own and other voices in his story, his story in us.

Our discovery of the link between reader and teller occurs through the character's mediation when the style asks us to undertake a double task of interior singing as writing. We take over the interior voice of Molly Bloom the singer as it takes us over, yet we understand the style as the author's writing, not as any actual voice. We can read the style in this double way only because the book has given us a series of lessons in writing as spiritual, aesthetic exercises. We have learned the nature of the writer's techniques, the medium's qualities and the apparatus of narration that make the book possible, and also the conceptual implications of those techniques. We recognize what the writer knows: the technical aspect of the strategies of narration, which we use to disassemble and reassemble the book's elements. And with that knowledge we put on his power, if only partially. We experience what Roland Barthes calls "the grain of the voice," a kind of singing that is also *"writing aloud."*[65] In that special singing, we hear the physical, fleshly apparatus at work as part of the performance and not covered over. Although Barthes does not mention reading explicitly in regard to the grain of the voice, what he says gives us a way to understand the act of reading *Ulysses*, especially "Penelope": our reading is listening in which we hear our own interior speech as writing. We apprehend the implications and the workings of the stylistic techniques and structures enabling us to hear, as we speak to ourselves, the grain of the voice in the text. As we do, we discover through the mediation of the style presenting Molly Bloom's interior singing the link between reader and writer. In "Penelope" Joyce achieves the subtlest, most compelling expression of his great theme: the relation of the artist and the citizen. When reader becomes writer, or nearly so, the roles of citizen and artist merge by means of style, through narration rather than in the narrative.

"Penelope" provides a consummate, substantiating perspective at the book's end, one underlying the whole self-consuming sequence of styles in *Ulysses*.[66] I call the sequence self-consuming because it keeps us in motion, asking us to use up the styles, to replace one style with another. Joyce once compared "the progress of the book" to "the progress of some sandblast," claiming that "each successive episode . . . leaves behind it a burnt up field" (*Letters* I, 129). Having found that all styles are relative, limited, and expendable, we encounter the final one, which provides a self-consummating understanding of the entire process of self-consumption. The new understanding comes about because the final one represents what stands under all the styles: mental processes, including ones that are outside the province of referential language. By adopting this last style, which presses the mimesis of consciousness toward the nonlinguistic, both as physical sensation and as the unconscious or the imagination, the teller enables the reader to participate in the book's consummation. That joyfully wise satisfaction occurs in the choice of a style that, unlike any of the earlier ones, is not just another style but one that pretends to be the opposite of what we know it is: *unwritten*. The style goes further than the presentation of Stephen's writing the villanelle in *A Portrait*, because "Penelope" does *not* present the as yet unwritten in the process of becoming written. Instead, it employs writing to present what, in the fiction of the narrative, has not been and will not ever be written. The substance of the episode is and will remain beyond the horizon of writing and of reading, always in the realm of the yet-to-be-written, the yet-to-be-formulated, because it is inaccessible to writing.[67] The final style, the end of wandering, in *Ulysses* is also the end of writing as its teleology: to present as style what no style can actually present. We abandon ourselves to a narration that finishes with the abandoning of language at the margin of narrative.

Molly's "yes" marks two boundaries as if they were one; the boundary between the unwritten and the written and between what can and cannot be written. Joyce shows us simultaneously where language stops and where it starts. In his letters Joyce speaks of the stylistic "ports of call" in his aesthetic wanderings of narration (*Letters* I, 204). In the ultimate style, we reach the final port of call and bring the ship of our literary voyaging at last to berth and to birth in its home port. The style stays within the bounds of the written, as it must, but it propels us beyond language in general and specifically beyond the language of *Ulysses* by moving us toward an experience of style like the act of writing as the book's already written words cease. In "Penelope," Joyce employs his teller as gravitational field in two ways at once: to bring us back to earth and to let us reach escape velocity. The book's finish, like the phoenix and like the language and structure of *Finnegans Wake*, consumes itself in its process of generation.

Superhuman, Mirror-resembling Dreams

It would seem that mythological worlds have been built up only to be
shattered again, and that new worlds were built from the fragments.

—Franz Boas

By creating structural relationships between style and story, Joyce aligns
the framework and the details of narration in his post-Romantic epics,
Ulysses and *Finnegans Wake*. In those works, Joyce develops and then
elaborates his styles and narrative structures for embodying in narration a
cultural consciousness, the conscience of his race that Stephen Dedalus
knows in his journal he has yet to create. By the time he published *A
Portrait*, Joyce had already begun transforming representation of mind into
communal speaking in "The Dead." In *Ulysses* he goes further by
developing mimesis of mind in ways that reveal the contradictions
accompanying the attempt to represent processes of mind in referential
language. Using those contradictions, he directs our attention beyond the
objects of mimesis, toward the act of mimicry and its sources. Beginning
with "Penelope," the stream of consciousness becomes a tributary of the
sort that merges in the *Wake* into the context of the whole, the book as
stream and as consciousness. Styles of narration and the characters'
speaking become in Joyce's fiction communal singing, like the singing after
dinner in "The Dead" or like Stephen's act of singing with his ragamuffin
brothers and sisters in part IV of *A Portrait*.

Like Molly Bloom, Anna Livia, the character as river that is the author's
Wake, can "sing us a sula" (*FW* 209.35). Her solo involves us all as her
children and her songs; song of ourselves she sings:

> . . . every dive she'd neb in her culdee sacco of wabbash she raabed and reach
> out her maundy meerschaundize, poor souvenir as per ricorder and all for sore
> aringarung, . . . her furzeborn sons and dribblederry daughters, a thousand
> and one of them. (*FW* 210.1–5)

Her actions are those of the artist collecting and writing tales, the mother
having children, and the imagination resurrecting the past, all as singing,
telling, remembering, and as the river's flowing. From the sack of rubbish
she has robbed, Anna Livia distributes her largesse of merchandise that is
both sea foam (G., *Meerschaum*) and her children, her first-born sons and
tributary daughters as her litter. She creates her thousand and one offspring

as her tales through acts of remembering (Fr., *souvenir*; It., *ricordare*; G., *Erinnerung*) what she has salvaged from the midden of the past. Joyce has moved from representing minds of characters in a referential style to treating consciousness as representative, as synecdochic, of human acts. Mind has become the river, the book, the act of writing and the act of reading, which disseminate and conserve, collect and distribute, carry and deposit litter and letters. Mental processes have become the most ordinary and the most extraordinary of human experiences, ones that link us all to one another and to a past that is within us at the origin of what may sometimes become writing. In his late works, Joyce assimilates remembering and imagining to other acts revealing our common humanity—sexual pleasure, eating, reading, and writing—as climactic processes of consuming, digesting, or producing. Memory and imagination allow us all to sing within ourselves.

That singing is not solipsistic and personal but communal and mythic. It remembers the past, be it personal, cultural, or stylistic. Guided by shared memories traced in the styles of *Ulysses*, reader, writer, and character participate together in mental traveling as wandering of styles and minds. That journey takes us, if not all the way home, at least to a Pisgah sight of the source of consciousness, culture, and language in experiences that may be written about but are never themselves only written. Like Yeats in "The Tower," Joyce strives to produce from past art, including "the proud stones of Greece," a "superhuman/Mirror-resembling dream."[68] That dream is not supernatural but "superhuman" because it gives us a mirror in which we know our own visages and the artist's as the type of wandering humanity searching for home. Joyce wills that dream as legacy to his readers by initiating a never-ending motion of writing and reading, reading as writing, in which his work and ours keeps being thrust "back in the human mind again." The motion has not ended.

APPENDIX 1

The Parts and the Structural Rhythm of *A Portrait*

THE PARTS

Like both *Ulysses* and *Finnegans Wake*, *A Portrait* consists of untitled, unnumbered segments grouped into several parts designated by roman numerals. While the conventions of referring to the episodes of *Ulysses* by Homeric titles and to the chapters of the *Wake* by part and chapter numbers were adopted long ago, no similar convention has developed for *A Portrait*. To facilitate reference to specific sections and to indicate their particular placement within the sectional arrangement of the part, I provide the following scheme. Adopting a convention like that for citing chapters of the *Wake*, in my discussion of *A Portrait* I refer to sections by part and section numbers.

Part and Section	Designation	Pages
Part I		
I.1	Prelude	7–8
I.2	Clongowes (playing field; classroom; infirmary)	8–27
I.3	Christmas Dinner	27–39
I.4	Broken Glasses (smugging; writing lesson, pandybat; rector)	40–59
Part II		
II.1	Blackrock (Uncle Charles; *The Count of Monte Cristo*; Cowyard)	60–65
II.2	Dublin (moving; chronicles; tram; poem to "E— C—"; Fr. Conmee)	65–72
II.3	Belvedere (Whitsuntide Play; Heron and the heretical essay; "horse piss and rotted straw")	73–86
II.4	Cork (father and son; "foetus")	86–96
II.5	Essay Prize and Nighttown	96–101
Part III		
III.1	Lust and the Sodality of the B.V.M.	102–8
III.2	Retreat (sermons)	108–35
III.3	Confession (chapel; kitchen)	136–46
Part IV		
IV.1	Spiritual Discipline	147–53
IV.2	The Director, Priesthood, The Kitchen	153–64
IV.3	The Strand	164–73
Part V		
V.1	The University (breakfast; to school; memory of Davin's	174–216

THE STRUCTURAL RHYTHM

Besides giving brief numerical designations to the sections of *A Portrait*, this schema provides some evidence for a conjecture about the structural rhythm of Joyce's arrangement. A peculiar sort of unity of effect arises from the juxtaposing of fragmented narrative segments. Part of that unity can be traced to expansions and contractions of narrative focus that become a defining configuration for our experience of the text. My conjecture can be translated into structural terms simply by examining the lengths of the various parts and sections. From such an examination we can describe the narrative structure as made up of three units. The first consists of the first three parts, each of about the same length. The second unit is the climactic fourth part, by far the shortest one, about half the length of any of the three preceding parts. The final unit is the fifth part, by far the longest one, nearly twice as long as part II, the briefest of the first three.

I emphasize these proportions because they are also the proportions of the narrative configuration of part V. The unusually long V.1 (longer even than part II), with its heterogeneous mix of scenes, memories, and dialogues, is the equivalent for the first unit of the larger narrative. The writing of the villanelle, V.2, corresponds to the climactic second unit, part IV. The talk with Cranly and the journal, V.3 and V.4, provide a denouement, as does all of part V in the larger scheme. The narrative structure of V, then, duplicates the structure of the entire book. The exact proportions of the narrative segments in my tripartite divisions of the text would be: I–III (140 pp.): IV (27): V (80):: V.1 (43 pp.): V.2 (8): V.3–V.4 (30). If we remove I.1 and V.4 from consideration as prelude and postlude, the ratios become 138:27:73::43:8:23, for a consistent comparative proportion of about 3.3:1. Although the point I am making about the proportions of the narrative units does not depend on such an exact ratio of correspondence between whole and part, the close parallel does support my conjecture.

Joyce stresses this duplicated configuration, one structure nesting within the conclusion of the other, by the way he frames the climaxes of the book and of part V. In both cases, the sections preceding and following the climactic segments are clearly linked. III.3 presents Stephen in the kitchen of his home idealizing and contemplating with anticipation the food that will be his breakfast after Communion the next morning. In V.1 he is again presented in the kitchen eating a greasy breakfast before leaving belatedly for his classes at the university. As I discuss in greater detail in the chapter on *A Portrait*, V.1 ends and V.3 begins with Stephen on the steps in front of the library. In between the two similar scenes of V, he has decided to break with his past and to leave Ireland. Both climaxes act as intervening segments explaining the transformation that has occurred. The two unexpected transformations are connected. The communion Stephen finds in IV is clearly not the one he anticipates at the end of III. It prepares for the inspired union with the temptress of the villanelle, who resembles both Emma, that birdlike woman Stephen gazes at in the final scene of V.1, and the girl he sees on the strand.

Both the large arrangement of sections and the details framing the climactic portions of the narrative contribute to the structural rhythm and duplication. In that replication of structure initiated at the start of V, the book's beginning and its ending merge. Repetition has become a new beginning for Stephen. The ending is only partially distinguishable from the climax, for each marks the beginning of writing. The scene on the strand and the writing of the villanelle merge with one another and with the endings they cause, endings that are also fresh starts. As I argue in my comments on the journal, *that* ending is the book's beginning and a merging of writer with character resembling the conclusion of V.2. The narrative starts again in and by means of its climaxes and its ostensible endings.

The Structure of Allusion in "Circe"

I provide the following chart to suggest how Joyce arranges details of "Circe" in ways that do not depend on a sequence of events as we think of events in realistic narratives. In the left column, I have divided the episode into four parts, which suggest a framework of realistic action. But within that broad framework I have identified details primarily through a rationale that conforms not at all to the canons of realism. The details become important for the reader not because they contribute to actions in a referential world but because they function in one or more of the three patterns of allusion providing structures for the episode. Rather than using narrative action to determine the structures, I employ the structures to identify what some readers may still want to call narrative. If we continue to use that term with reference to "Circe," we do so with a meaning virtually independent of realism, for the events of the narrative have become functions of allusive structures. In literary realism, *mimesis* suppresses *diegesis*; that is, the conventions tend to mask the acts of writing and, at times, of narrating. In "Circe," Joyce subverts those conventions by fragmenting them and using them to evoke irrational thoughts and the act of narration as writing. As they are presented, those thoughts and that act are far removed from literary realism. The list of allusions in the right-hand column, "Events of the Day," is, of course, by no means exhaustive. I have tailored the selection primarily to indicate the orderly recapitulation of earlier and later parts of *Ulysses*, the close connection between "Hades" and "Circe," and relationships to the Homeric and Christian correspondences or to the characters' dreams.

Like an orchestral score, the chart needs to be read along two axes at once, both down the columns and laterally from column to column. In this regard, it resembles the arrangements Claude Lévi-Strauss constructs in his structural studies of myth. His description of the contradictory nature of mythology could be a description of "Circe": "Mythology confronts the student with a situation which at first sight could be looked upon as contradictory. On the one hand, it would seem that in the course of a myth anything is likely to happen. There is no logic, no continuity. Any characteristic can be attributed to any subject; every conceivable relation can be met. With myth, everything becomes possible."[1] The other pole of the contradiction, which counters the "apparent arbitrariness," involves "the astounding similarity between myths collected in widely different regions." In the chart, the left-hand column presents the arbitrary, illogical, discontinuous surface of "Circe." The other columns present structures of meaning undergirding that surface. Although the isolated details of the narrative are arbitrary, their combination is not. As in the structural interpretation of myths, because the bundles of relations creating meaning are likely to be widely scattered, they need to be grouped and reorganized for analysis. Many groupings are possible.

When we read both down and across the columns, we discover that certain parts of "Circe" are especially densely encrusted with allusions. The thick clustering, particularly in the final forty pages, suggests that a climax is underway. This climax is not contained in a narrative as plot but is instead generated in our acts of reading. The intensity of the late pages of "Circe" arises from Joyce's having achieved a synecdochic, or mythic, mode of narration. The details of language and narrative as *parts*, or fragments, point to several wide, interlocking contexts of meaning. Consequently, in this portion of *Ulysses*, Joyce approaches closely the techniques of the *Wake*, in which "a part so ptee does duty for the holos" (18.36–19.01). The synecdochic techniques become mythic when one narrative suggests and merges with many others.

While the dense clustering of references can indicate the importance of parts of "Circe," so can the relative absence of allusions. Here I would invoke one of Freud's principles from *The Interpretation of Dreams*. According to Freud, in dreams the unconscious takes on disguises for expressing itself through attachment to details embedded in a mass of more prominent dream events. Taking that perspective, I would suggest that however important the structures of allusion may be in making sense of "Circe," we should not let them distract us from what they do not explain. We can use the chart, then, to identify those portions of the episode that it seems unable to accommodate.

In two places I have listed parts that do not seem strongly allusive with respect to the principal structures. One is the initial dialogue between Bloom and Zoe (475–78). As Kenner notes in his essay dealing with fantasies in "Circe," this dialogue is exceptional in the episode's narration. It is an exception that proves the rule through contrast, by being largely realistic in a context that is not. The other listing is also exceptional but altogether more important. Part of its significance derives from placement; it immediately precedes, and may be seen as triggering, the thick layering of allusions in the final pages. This part involves Bloom's encouraging the intercourse between Boylan and Molly, who sing together (564–67). The tremendous ambivalence that tries both to hide and to reveal emerges in Bloom's final exclamations: "Show! Hide! Show!" There is good reason for the lack of clear counterparts in the allusive structures. The section presents nearly directly, albeit belatedly, an event that is taboo in the earlier narrative of *Ulysses*. By giving us what Bloom has avoided facing during the day, the section constitutes an instance of *Nachträglichkeit*. It also presents an analogy for the intercourse that the narrator makes available to us finally in the style of "Penelope" and in Molly's thoughts there. In "Circe" the nearly direct presentation of the forbidden moment of lovemaking is linked by juxtaposition to the merging of artist and citizen in the composite image of Shakespeare in the mirror (567). And that reflection, through its connection to "Scylla and Charybdis," suggests the writer's hidden act of aesthetic creation that we experience in reading. Lovemaking and aesthetic making merge to form the unspeakable navel of the dream. The flood of allusions and the close approach to the narration of the *Wake* that follow compose a response to the forbidden event that deflects our attention away from its fleeting representation. Despite the lack of allusions, the apparent exception is not an excursion from the dream but is instead its most crucial moment.

Structure of Allusion in "Circe"

Sections and Events	Homeric Correspondences	Correspondences to Christian History	Events of the Day (Correspondences to Other Parts of Ulysses)
I. Introductory Description; Setting of the Scene (429–33).			I. "Telemachiad" "Telemachus": Realistic presentation of setting, action, and speech.
Whistles call and answer (429).			Mulligan's whistle is answered by the "shrill whistles" of the mailboat (3).
Stephen and Lynch: Words from the Mass for paschal time (430–33).		Creation of light: Stephen's "shattering light over the world" (432).	Stephen and Buck; "—Introibo ad altare Dei."
II. Bloom's Wanderings in nighttown on his way to Bella Cohen's brothel (433–502).	Odyssey XIV: Odysseus visits the hut of the swineherd Eumaeus, who prepares pork for him. Odyssey IX: Odysseus searches for food for his men and sees the smoke rising from Circe's palace.		II. Bloom's "Odyssey" through Dublin on his way back home to Molly.
Bloom at Olhousen's, the pork butcher's; Bloom thinks there is a fire (434).	Odyssey XII: Odysseus sees the smoke indicating the consumption and sacrifice of forbidden meat.		"Calypso": Bloom at Dlugacz's butcher shop; his kidney burns.

Two cyclists and the dragon sandstrewer appear (435).		"Lotus-Eaters": Bloom sees an ad with a cyclist pictured and has his view obstructed by a passing tram.
Bloom's dialogue with his father, Rudolph Bloom (437–38).		"Lotus-Eaters" and "Hades": Bloom thinks of his father several times during the morning, especially during the funeral episode.
Procession of Bloom's women (438–49).	*Odyssey* XI: Odysseus sees his mother and then a procession of famous Greek women in the Underworld.	"Hades": At the beginning of this episode, among other things Bloom thinks in succession of woman's role as mother, of Molly making the bed, and of the soap on which he is sitting.
Marion (Molly) in Turkish costume (439–41).		"Nausicaa" and "Oxen"; Bloom recalls his dream of Molly in Turkish slippers (381, 397); "Penelope": Molly wants a pair of Turkish slippers (780).
Soap-sun rises from the East (440).	Creation of the Sun: "*A cake of new clean lemon soap arises, diffusing light and perfume.*"	"Scylla and Charybdis": Stephen mentions the belated creation of the sun after the creation of light (213).
Bridie Kelly, Gerty McDowell, and Mrs. Breen (Josie Powell) appear (441–49).		
Bloom walks on toward "*hellsgates*" (449).		"Hades": Bloom rides toward the cemetery.

Structure of Allusion in "Circe"

Sections and Events	Homeric Correspondences	Correspondences to Christian History	Events of the Day (Correspondences to Other Parts of Ulysses)
Bloom remarks that "drunks cover distance double quick" (452).	*Odyssey* XI: Odysseus is surprised that Elpenor on foot has beaten him to the Underworld.		"Hades": Bloom says of Dignam: "Got here before us, dead as he is" (101).
Bloom feeds the dog (453).	*Odyssey* XI: Odysseus feeds the shades to enable them to speak.		
Bloom accused and tried (453–73).			
The Dark Mercury appears (456).	*Odyssey* X: Hermes (or Mercury), messenger of the gods, warns Odysseus about Circe.		"Telemachus": Mulligan, whose first name is Malachi, refers to himself as "Mercurial Malachi" (17). "Malachi" means "messenger" (or "angel") in Hebrew.
Dog becomes Dignam, who speaks, confirming Bloom's alibi (472–74).	*Odyssey* XI: Elpenor speaks to Odysseus.		"Hades": Bloom thinks about the dead speaking to us through recordings.
John O'Connell, caretaker of the cemetery, and father Coffey appear (473).			"Hades": Bloom sees both O'Connell and Coffey.
Bloom's dialogue with Zoe starts (475–78).			

240

Bloom's imagined public career (478–99).	The Ministry and Crucifixion of Christ: "He [Bloom] scarcely looks thirty-one" (481). Christ was thirty-one at the beginning of his ministry. Bloom as Christ: "Virag begat Bloom *et vocabitur nomen eius Emmanuel*" (496). Cf. Isa. 7:14. Betrayal of Christ: Reuben J. Dodd appears as Judas, "*Blackbearded Iscariot*" (497). Bloom is clothed in a "seamless garment marked I.H.S." (498). Cf. John 19:23. Bloom exhibits his wounds.	Litany invokes each chapter in turn, beginning with "Calypso."
Bloom burned/Litany of the Daughters of Erin (498–99).		
Bloom's dialogue with Zoe continued: animal imagery (499–502).	*Odyssey* X: Half of Odysseus's crew transformed into beasts.	
III. Bloom and Stephen in the brothel (502–86).	Apocalypse Foreshadowed (505–8). Florry: "They say the last day is coming this summer" (505). "The end of the world!" (506). Reuben J. Anti-Christ appears. Hobgoblin destroys tiny roulette planets. The second coming of Elijah.	"Oxen" and "Circe": Bloom and Stephen in the hospital and in nighttown.

241

Structure of Allusion in "Circe"

Sections and Events	Homeric Correspondences	Correspondences to Christian History	Events of the Day (Correspondences to Other Parts of Ulysses)
Bloom's dialogue with his grand-father, Lipoti Virag, who gives him advice about dealing with the whores (511–23).	Odyssey X and XI: Hermes and Tiresias give Odysseus advice about dealing with Circe and with the shades.	Virag cries "Apocalypse" (520).	
Bloom's confrontation with Bella/Bello Cohen (527–54).	Odyssey X and XI: Odysseus encounters Circe and the bisexual Tiresias.		
Bello: "I can give you a rare old wine that'll send you skipping to hell and back" (534–44).	Odyssey X: Circe tells Odysseus of the libation he must use in order to reach the Underworld.		
Bloom advises Stephen to eat and thinks of his recent feeding of the dog-Dignam (560).	Odyssey X: Odysseus provides food for his crew. Odyssey XI: Odysseus feeds the shades with blood.		
Bloom as flunkey for Marion and Boylan; their singing; composite image of Stephen and Bloom as Shakespeare (564–67).			
Stephen's dreams enacted (571–83): Dream of the watermelon and flying; Simon Dedalus (571–72); dream of	Odyssey XI: Odysseus speaks with his mother in the Underworld.		"Proteus" and "Scylla": Dream of the melon (47, 217). "Telemachus": Stephen recalls his

his mother (579–83).

Stephen strikes the chandelier with his ashplant (583).

Bloom (*Incog Haroun al Raschid*) stops Bella from calling the police (586).

IV. Bloom and Stephen in the Street (586–609).
Private Carr and Stephen (587–602).

Stephen hails Lynch as Sisyphus (587).

Corny Kelleher helps Bloom save Stephen from the Watch (603–8). Arriving with a wreath, he tells the Watch Stephen has won on a horserace, the "Gold Cup."

Odyssey X: Odysseus protects his men from Circe.
Odyssey XIV and after: During much of his homecoming, Odysseus is in disguise.

Odyssey XI: Odysseus sees the shade of Sisyphus.

Odyssey XII: Odysseus returns to Circe's island to bury young Elpenor, who fell drunkenly from the roof of Circe's palace after drinking from her golden cup.

Apocalypse: destruction of light.

Apocalypse: brimstone fires, the resurrection of the dead, the Black Mass (598–600).

dream about his mother (5, 10). Cf. the procession of Bloom's women earlier (438–49).

"Proteus": Haroun al Raschid appears in Stephen's dream of the melon, or "creamfruit" (47).
"Ithaca": Like Haroun in Stephen's dream, Bloom invites him to come in. Then he offers him Molly's cream (677).
Molly has plump "melons" (734).

III. "Nostos": Bloom and Stephen outside nighttown.

"Hades": Kelleher, who works for the funeral home, oversees the burial of Dignam.

243

Structure of Allusion in "Circe"

Sections and Events	Homeric Correspondences	Correspondences to Christian History	Events of the Day (Correspondences to Other Parts of Ulysses)
Stephen in fetal position recites "Who Goes With Fergus?" while Bloom sees his son, Rudy (608–9).	*Odyssey* XI: Elpenor entreats Odysseus to think of his own family (wife, father, and son) when he considers the young man's request for burial. Odysseus then decides to act on his behalf. *Odyssey* XIII: Odysseus undergoes the last portion of his journey back to Ithaca in a deep, deathlike slumber.	Continued Resurrection of the Dead.	"Telemachus": Stephen associates the lyric with his mother. "Penelope": while Bloom reclines in fetal position, "the childman weary, the manchild in the womb" (737), Molly remembers their first walking out together on Howth Hill. "Nostos": Bloom acts paternally toward Stephen.

Notes

1. In the criticism of Joyce's writing, James S. Atherton's *The Books at the Wake: A Study of Literary Allusions in James Joyce's "Finnegans Wake"* (New York: Viking Press, 1959; reprint ed. Carbondale: Southern Illinois University Press, 1974; second, expanded, and corrected edition, Mamaroneck, N.Y.: Paul P. Appel, 1974) is indispensable for anyone interested in allusions in *Finnegans Wake*. Atherton discusses Joyce's allusions under the rubrics "structural," "literary," and "sacred." My commentary differs from Atherton's more extensive treatment in several ways, primarily in scope and emphasis. He identifies and categorizes many of the prominent sources for Joyce's references. I deal instead with the author's attitude toward the literary tradition and with the way he uses that tradition to define his stance as teller of the tale. Inevitably, my discussion overlaps Atherton's commentary in places. I wish to acknowledge my debt to his fine study and to point out that I give much greater importance to Homer and to Joyce's other works in the *Wake* than Atherton does.

As I indicate in the above citation, Atherton's book has appeared in a revised edition. In this new edition, the introductory essay has been recast. It includes a supplementary critical bibliography updating the earlier one, along with an expanded Appendix: "Alphabetical List of Literary Allusions." The new appendix is an extremely useful general guide to the distribution of allusions to particular works and authors in the *Wake*. The revised edition should not be confused with the paperback reprint of the first edition also issued in the United States in 1974.

I wish also at the beginning of my study to draw the reader's attention to Michael H. Begnal's monograph on *Finnegans Wake*, "The Dreamers at the Wake: A View of Narration and Point of View" (in Michael H. Begnal and Grace Eckley, *Narrator and Character in "Finnegans Wake"* [Lewisburg, Pa.: Bucknell University Press, 1975]). Begnal proposes that the voices of numerous dreamers interrupt one another during the course of the narration. He also suggests that a narrator's voice can be distinguished from the other voices. This special voice provides, according to Begnal, a framework for narration as dreaming. While such speculative studies are in order, and while Begnal's conjectures are often worth pursuing, his discussion is not sufficiently detailed to be convincing about where and how we locate the narrator's voice. One of the great, and perhaps insoluble, difficulties of reading the *Wake* concerns distinguishing a narrator's voice from other possible voices projected by the text's language. The problem is an extreme version of differentiating narrator from character in the technique of narrated monologue (also known as *le style indirect libre* and *erlebte Rede*), which I discuss with regard to Joyce's earlier fiction. The difficulty stands behind my choice of the passage from Roland Barthes's *S/Z* as one of my epigraphs. Begnal also insists on calling the *Wake* a novel. That the work is a dream or an interlocking series of dreams, that it is a novel, and that it has a narrator in anything like our usual sense of that term are all questionable assertions in need of lengthy discussion. Given the present state of the interpretation of the *Wake*, any commentary on its telling will be more tentative than treatments of Joyce's narrator, styles, and stories in his earlier works. In this study I try to limit, as well as delimit, the problems inherent in discussing the telling by defining a perspective that focuses on the characters as tellers and on the texts they produce. But there is no gainsaying the problems (see n.7 below).

2. Atherton, *The Books* (1959), p. 45.

3. As Atherton points out in the appendix of *The Books* (1959), "all Joyce's works are mentioned in the *Wake*" (p. 259). He devotes a brief section of his study to them (pp. 106–10).

4. In the appendix of *The Books* (expanded edition, 1974), Atherton provides a long list of

allusions to Wyndham Lewis, including this one. See his entry for references to critical discussions of Joyce and Lewis by Hugh Kenner and Adaline Glasheen (pp. 265–66).

5. Margot Norris discusses the bric-a-brac of the *Wake* as the material for *bricolage* in *The Decentered Universe of "Finnegans Wake"* (Baltimore: Johns Hopkins University Press, 1976), pp. 130–40.

6. Adaline Glasheen, *Third Census of "Finnegans Wake": An Index of the Characters and Their Roles* (Berkeley and Los Angeles: University of California Press, 1977), p. 145.

7. See the initial section of chapter four, "The Myth of Joyce's Impersonal Narration," for my formulation of the problem the term *teller* names in literary studies. Teller (or narrator) can be no more absolutely distinguished from author than from tale. Joyce capitalizes on the resulting ambiguities in all his fictions. The concept of the narrator has come in for much abuse in Joyce studies. It seems incontrovertible that Joyce's narration forces us to reconsider any unquestioned notions we may have about the narrator as a unified self and about narration as voice. But it is equally true that Joyce, knowing the traditions of narration in English fiction and realizing his readers would come with predictable expectations, decided to play with those traditions by calling them up as well as undercutting them. Consequently, rejecting the term *narrator* absolutely is as reductive for criticism as using it in ways that ignore Joyce's innovations. The best we can do is to use the terms *narrator* and *teller* not loosely but parsimoniously, always remembering that Joyce's narrator and his narration are in flux; they are not stable entities. In the present state of Joyce criticism, the term *narration* is less controversial and less offensive to some critics than the term *narrator*. Actually, the seemingly more objective, safer term is simply a means the critic uses to skirt some of the problems of reading that I try to face in this study. The difficulties will not disappear simply because we change our critical vocabulary (see n.9 below). John T. Irwin has discussed the oscillation between author and teller in *American Hieroglyphics: The Symbol of the Egyptian Hieroglyphics in the American Renaissance* (New Haven: Yale University Press, 1980), especially in "Section 7," "Writing Self/Written Self; The Dark Double; The Overwhelming of the Vessel" (114–29). Irwin focuses on "the constitutive opposition between the writing self and the written self, the problematic doubling of the writer and his book" (120), evoked as a reversal of roles, author and teller speaking for one another. As we shall see, the "Penelope" episode of *Ulysses* provides a vivid example of such a reversal, one in which a character as teller becomes indistinguishable from the author as teller.

8. Various passages in the *Wake* allude to "the hoax that joke bilked" (511.34), including 271.25–29, 274.22, 369.13–15, 375.4, and 580.26–36.

9. In an earlier version of this study (in *James Joyce: An International Perspective*, ed. Bernard Benstock and Suheil Badi Bushrui [Totowa, N. J.: Barnes and Noble, 1982]), at this point I confidently ascribed the narration of I.7 to Shem's brother, Shaun. In doing so, I was working from some unexamined assumptions about narration, especially concerning unified consciousness and teller's voice, that permeate Joyce criticism, as well as most of our criticism of fiction. Not only can I no longer make that ascription, but I would argue that many identifications of Shem and Shaun by critics of the *Wake* need to be reconsidered. Like Ondt and Gracehoper, in Shem and Shaun Joyce creates a double figure, both ambiguous character and ambiguous trope of language, which we understand to be a kind of pun. Like an optical illusion that keeps figure and ground in constant oscillation, the narration ambivalently indicates its origin (in a teller) and its subject matter (as a character) in ways that at once distinguish and identify them. The language will not stay in place, will not stay still. Even so, readers always have to make at least tentative assignments of characters' names (if only to reject them) to the language and actions reported, as I do at the beginning of the section entitled "A Purloined Homeric Correspondence."

10. Leonard Barkan discusses the tradition of such uses of the body in *Nature's Work of Art: The Human Body as Image of the World* (New Haven: Yale University Press, 1975). He does not include Joyce in his study.

11. Brendan O Hehir and John Dillon, *A Classical Lexicon for "Finnegans Wake": A Glossary of the Greek and Latin in the Major Works of Joyce* (Berkeley and Los Angeles: University of California Press, 1977), p. 326. Unless otherwise noted, all glosses involving Joyce's use of Latin and Greek are from this volume.

12. James Joyce, *Scribbledehobble: The Ur-workbook for "Finnegans Wake,"* ed. Thomas E. Connolly (Evanston: Northwestern University Press, 1961).

13. Robert Boyle, S.J., has discussed this passage in his essay "Portrait of the Artist as Balzacian Wilde Ass," in *A Conceptual Guide to "Finnegans Wake,"* ed. Michael H. Begnal and Fritz Senn (University Park: Pennsylvania State University Press, 1974), pp. 71–82.

14. Robert Boyle has suggested a similar interpretation for "chagreenold" as an allusion to Balzac's novel *Peau de chagrin (Conceptual Guide*, p. 76–78).

15. As William York Tindall points out in *A Reader's Guide to "Finnegans Wake"* (New York: Farrar, Straus & Giroux, 1969), "in the Hebrew alphabet aleph is ox, beth is house, gimel is camel" (p. 109).

16. William Savage, *A Dictionary of the Art of Printing* (London, 1841; reprint ed. London: Gregg Press, 1966), p. 248. I draw the information about printing employed in this chapter primarily from Savage and from Philip Gaskell, *A New Introduction to Bibliography* (New York: Oxford University Press, 1972). Gaskell provides a history of book production through the middle of this century. Savage's dictionary includes a great many details concerning the practice and the traditions of letterpress printing.

17. In her *Third Census of "Finnegans Wake,"* Adaline Glasheen suggests that as a verb "pen" means to "shut up" (p. 229).

18. Gaskell, *A New Introduction to Bibliography*, p. 126.

19. In the indispensable first appendix, "An Index of Motifs in *Finnegans Wake*," in *Structure and Motif in "Finnegans Wake"* (Evanston: Northwestern University Press, 1962), Clive Hart lists the "Major Statements" (p. 232) of the letter. He does not mention the elliptical version of I.4.

20. Ibid., p. 200.

21. Clive Hart discusses the longer allusions to Quinet's sentence in chapter seven of *Structure and Motif* (pp. 182–200).

22. In his first appendix to *Structure and Motif*, Hart notes a dozen occurrences of the enjoinder to "stop. Please stop," which he identifies as one of the letter's motifs (p. 233).

23. For this definition of "clayman," see *Webster's Third New International Dictionary*, unabridged.

24. Savage, *A Dictionary of the Art of Printing*, p. 24.

25. Adaline Glasheen links "alcohoran" with Paul Horan (49.15), probably on the basis of orthography (*Third Census*, p. 129).

26. Hugh Kenner, "An Insane Assault on Chaos" (a review of the *James Joyce Archive* and *James Joyce's Manuscripts: An Index), New York Times Book Review*, 22 June 1980, pp. 7, 26–27.

27. Louis O. Mink mentions several interpretations of the diagram while explaining his geographical view in the introduction to *A "Finnegans Wake" Gazetteer* (Bloomington: Indiana University Press, 1978), pp. xxv–xxvi.

28. Cf. "Listen, listen! I am doing it" (571.24). This statement also concludes a paragraph containing references to printing.

29. Gaskell, *A New Introduction to Bibliography*, p. 125.

30. I have more to say about Joycean *Nachträglichkeit* in Appendix 2 and in chapter four near the end of my discussion of the various styles of *Ulysses*.

31. Hart lists "ah ho" and "ah dear oh dear" as the characteristic sighs, respectively, of Mark Lyons and Luke Tarpey, two of the four annalists associated with the four provinces of Ireland. Whatever the specific ascriptions to characters, the proliferating *a*'s and *o*'s often suggest a creating presence of some sort as both end and beginning. For instance, in I.6, the

fourth question (140.8–141.7), whose answer seems to be "Dublin," includes several repetitions of *a*'s and *o*'s. Allusions to the four provinces do suggest the presence of the four annalists, but the *a*'s and *o*'s are linked as well to the *d* and the *n* of Dublin as "origin" and "end" (140.9).

32. As I suggest above (n.9), these identifications are provisional.

33. Jacques Lacan, "Seminar on 'The Purloined Letter,' " *Yale French Studies* 48:59.

34. Besides the essay by Lacan, two other essays related to the controversy are available in English: Jacques Derrida, "The Purveyor of Truth," *Yale French Studies* 52: 31–113; and Barbara Johnson, "The Frame of Reference: Poe, Lacan, Derrida," *Yale French Studies* 55/56: 457–505.

35. Edgar Allan Poe, "The Purloined Letter," in *Selected Writings of Edgar Allan Poe*, ed. Edward H. Davidson (Boston: Houghton Mifflin, 1956), p. 223.

36. Ibid., p. 502.

37. For a succinct discussion of Macpherson, see Brendan O Hehir, *A Gaelic Lexicon for "Finnegans Wake" and Glossary for Joyce's Other Works* (Berkeley and Los Angeles: University of California Press, 1967), pp. 393–97. O Hehir provides a list of discussions dealing with Joyce and Macpherson.

38. Richard Ellmann, *The Consciousness of Joyce* (New York: Oxford University Press, 1977), p. 94.

39. O Hehir and Dillon, *Classical Lexicon*, p. 86.

40. Michael Groden, *"Ulysses" in Progress* (Princeton: Princeton University Press, 1977); Michael Seidel, *Epic Geography: James Joyce's "Ulysses"* (Princeton: Princeton University Press, 1976). Stuart Gilbert was the first critic to point out Joyce's use of Bérard in his *James Joyce's "Ulysses"* (1930; 2nd rev. ed., New York: Vintage Books, 1952).

41. Hayden V. White mentions the meaning of *Punicus* and provides a brief comment on the Punic Wars in *The Greco-Roman Tradition* (New York: Harper & Row, 1973). O Hehir and Dillon's *Classical Lexicon* sometimes glosses "Punic" as "Phoenician" (e.g., for 32.6), but sometimes as an allusion to Bérard (e.g., for 123.25).

42. Ellmann, *JJ* 556, 721.

43. The other references to phoenix are too numerous to mention. The list in Glasheen's *Third Census* is the most complete, though it omits 621.1.

44. In a related vein, David Hayman discusses texts by later authors who follow in the wake of the *Wake* in his introductory essay "Some Writers in the Wake of the *Wake*," in *In the Wake of the "Wake,"* ed. David Hayman and Elliott Anderson (Madison: University of Wisconsin Press, 1978), a reprinting of *TriQuarterly* 38 (Winter 1977). There are examples of this sort of temporal reversal among literary texts within the *Wake* itself. For example, as I point out in the next section of this chapter, the text discussed toward the end of I.5, apparently Shem's rewriting of Homer, is said to have inspired "the tenebrous *Tunc* page of the Book of Kells" (122.22–23). But the inspiring text seems also to be Homer's much earlier rewriting of "a Punic admiralty report" (123.25). As in the relationship of narration to narrative in *A Portrait* as I describe it in chapter two, for Joyce looking forward and looking back are indistinguishable acts.

45. Thomas Goddard Bergin and Max Harold Fisch, trans., *The New Science of Giambatista Vico: Revised Translation of the Third Edition* (1744; Ithaca: Cornell University Press, 1968), especially sections 404–6 and 779. For discussions of the relations between tropes and narrative, see Hayden White, *Metahistory: The Historical Imagination in Nineteenth-Century Europe* (Baltimore: Johns Hopkins University Press, 1973) and *Tropics of Discourse: Essays in Cultural Criticism* (Baltimore: Johns Hopkins University Press, 1978). In his doctoral dissertation, "Bygmythster Finnegan: Etymology as Poetics in the Works of James Joyce" (University of Connecticut, 1976), Seàn Golden provides confirmation for my general sense of Joyce's use of etymology to generate narrative. Golden focuses on etymology as part of a poetics of composition he calls "etymythology." He traces Joyce's

knowledge and use of etymology and examines the influence of Vico, Bérard, and Ernest Fenollosa. Golden also discusses Joyce's knowledge of Celtic onomastic and toponomastic tales. He outlines the ancient art of Irish storytelling as mythologizing through punning. Golden's commentary provides a context for understanding Joyce's use of puns that complements the one I present here. His focus on the connections between actions and names in Irish narratives is especially relevant to my interpretation of the *Wake*'s title. For related treatments of Joyce and etymology, see Hugh Kenner, *The Pound Era* (Berkeley and Los Angeles: University of California Press, 1971), pp. 94–120, and "Joyce and the Nineteenth-Century Linguistics Explosion," in *Atti del Third International James Joyce Symposium* 14–18 June 1971 (Trieste, 1974), pp. 45–52. A. Walton Litz provides a helpful commentary, "Vico and Joyce," in *Giambattista Vico: An International Symposium*, ed. Giorgio Tagliacozzo et al. (Baltimore: Johns Hopkins University Press, 1969), pp. 245–55.

46. This symbol and the others Joyce used in writing the *Wake* are discussed at length in Roland McHugh's *The Sigla of "Finnegans Wake"* (Austin: University of Texas Press, 1976).

47. Glasheen's *Third Census* contains specific references to these figures.

48. See J. G. Keogh, "*Ulysses*' 'Parable of the Plums' as Parable and Periplum," *James Joyce Quarterly* 7 (Summer 1970): 377–78.

49. The notion that a text can take the form of a rosary is not wholly fanciful. Examples of such manuscripts are not unknown in the history of book production. For instance, in India palm-leaf manuscripts were sometimes produced by incising circles of palm leaves with characters. The circles were then combined to form beads and strung as a rosary. As part of the 1982 Festival of India, the British Library exhibited such a manuscript, a nineteenth-century version of the *Gītagovinda*. See Jeremiah P. Losty, *The Art of the Book in India* (London: The British Library, 1982), p. 8.

50. Atherton, *The Books* (1959), p. 101.

51. E. H. Gombrich, *Art and Illusion: A Study in the Psychology of Pictorial Representation* (New York: Pantheon Books, 1960), pp. 4–6. Gombrich is reconsidering Ludwig Wittgenstein's use of the figure in *Philosophical Investigations*, trans. G.E.M. Anscombe, 3rd ed. (New York: Macmillan, 1968), p. 194 (section II.xi). Gombrich discusses optical illusions of various sorts in "Part Three: The Beholder's Share" of *Art and Illusion*, especially in chapter eight, "Ambiguities of the Third Dimension." The standard modern work on optical illusions is S. Tolansky, *Optical Illusions* (Oxford: Pergamon Press, 1964, 1967). See in particular "Chapter X. Illusions Involving Oscillation of Attention." In the conclusion to his study *F. H. Bradley* (Revised Edition) (Hardmondsworth, Middlesex, England: Penguin Books, 1969), Richard Wollheim mentions "reversible 'figure' and 'ground' designs" as evoking a transforming experience that may lead to a vision of the universe as a "seamless whole" (pp. 276–77).

52. Glasheen has a lengthy comment on Joyce's use of "seven" in the *Third Census* (p. 259).

53. Savage, *A Dictionary of the Art of Printing*, p. 93.

54. Ibid., pp. 757–58.

55. In a lengthy parenthesis to *Structure and Motif*, Clive Hart points out some specific parallels between ALP's monologue and another story in *Dubliners*, "Eveline" (pp. 53–55).

56. J. S. Atherton, "The Identity of the Sleeper," *A Wake Newslitter* 4 (October 1967): 83–85.

57. Michael Seidel discusses Vallancey together with Bérard at the beginning of *Epic Geography* (pp. xii, 17).

CHAPTER TWO

1. Geoffrey Hartman, "Milton's Counterplot," in *Milton: A Collection of Critical Essays*,

ed. Louis L. Martz (Englewood Cliffs, N.J.: Prentice-Hall, 1966), pp. 100–108.

2. Laurence Sterne, *The Life and Opinions of Tristram Shandy, Gentleman*, ed. James Aiken Work (New York: Odyssey Press, 1940), p. 477.

3. Sigmund Freud, *The Interpretation of Dreams*, trans. and ed. James Strachey (New York: Avon Books, 1965), p. 143.

4. Take for instance the adult narrator's presentation in Proust's "Combray" of his boyhood description of the twin steeples at Martinville: "I borrowed a pencil and some paper from the Doctor, and composed, in spite of the jolting of the carriage, to appease my conscience and to satisfy my enthusiasm, the following little fragment, which I have since discovered, and now reproduce with only a *slight revision here and there*" (my emphasis; Marcel Proust, *Swann's Way*, trans. C. K. Scott Moncrieff [New York: Modern Library, 1928], p. 233). After this statement the narrator quotes the revised description. As I shall argue, the process of revision also occurs in *A Portrait* when Stephen Dedalus writes his villanelle, which we may think of as a rewriting of the poem mentioned in II.2. In both Proust's narrative and Joyce's, the quoted text is further revised by being taken up into a larger one, the narrative itself. In each case, the surrounding narration presents the genesis of the quoted text.

5. As I pointed out at the beginning of the last chapter, Wyndham Lewis had attacked Joyce in *Time and Western Man*. As many critics have mentioned, Joyce responds to Lewis in the parable of the Ondt and the Gracehoper in *Finnegans Wake* III.1 (414–19) as well as in other passages. Allusions to Eliot and his works occur throughout the *Wake*. For instance, a reference to Eliot's well-known essay "Tradition and the Individual Talent" occurs in one of the marginalia in II.2, the schoolroom chapter (*FW* 268). The final part begins (*FW* 593) with a parody of "Shantih," the final word of "The Waste Land." Although the thunder in the *Wake* is Viconian, the thunderwords are also a version of "What the Thunder Said," the title of the last section of "The Waste Land." By incorporating allusions to these contemporaries in the pattern of the brothers' antagonism in the *Wake*, Joyce turns each into his own double, into his "shemblable" and his "freer" (*FW* 489.28). These words, of course, also allude to "The Waste Land." The appendix to James S. Atherton's *The Books at the Wake: A Study of Literary Allusions in James Joyce's "Finnegans Wake"* (New York: Viking Press, 1959; reprint ed. Carbondale: Southern Illinois University Press, 1974; second, expanded, and corrected edition, Mamaroneck, N.Y.: Paul P. Appel, 1974) lists numerous allusions to Lewis and to Eliot. Stanley Sultan discusses the relationship of Joyce and Eliot at length in *"Ulysses", "The Waste Land," and Modernism* (Port Washington, N.Y.: Kennikat Press, 1977).

6. In his discussion of Joyce in *The Teller in the Tale* (Seattle: University of Washington Press, 1967), Louis D. Rubin, Jr., asserts that Stephen Dedalus narrates *A Portrait*, but he does not explain his assertion with the kind of detailed examination of the text that I undertake here. He also claims, without convincing discussion, that Dedalus narrates *Ulysses*. Although we may think of the literary labyrinth of *A Portrait* as made by a Daedalian teller, as I argue in my discussion of *Ulysses*, the wandering styles of the later work are better approached as creating the image of a Homeric, Odyssean teller. I reject Rubin's attitude toward *Finnegans Wake*, a book that he excoriates.

7. The most recent review of discussions of aesthetic distance in *A Portrait* is James J. Sosnowski's "Reading Acts and Reading Warrants: Some Implications for Readers Responding to Joyce's Portrait of Stephen," *James Joyce Quarterly* 16 (Fall 1978/Winter 1979): 43–63. Thomas F. Staley provides a helpful overview of trends in the criticism of *A Portrait* in "Strings in the Labyrinth: Sixty Years with Joyce's *Portrait*," in *Approaches to Joyce's "Portrait": Ten Essays*, ed. Thomas F. Staley and Bernard Benstock (Pittsburgh: University of Pittsburgh Press, 1976), pp. 3–24. Staley presents a similar overview in a wider context in his "James Joyce," in *Anglo-Irish Literature: A Review of Research*, ed. Richard J. Finneran (New York: Modern Language Association, 1976), pp. 366–435.

8. I would not, however, disallow completely the application of the term *dramatic* to *A Portrait*, because Stephen mentions it in his exposition of an aesthetic theory to Lynch. I shall

interpret Stephen's use of that term as designating both purely mimetic literary representation and the literary text at the conclusion of the process of creation. In these senses, it can describe parts of *A Portrait*, especially the villanelle and the journal, and portions of *Ulysses*. See chapter four, n.29, in which I comment on S. L. Goldberg's influential but reductive use of the term *dramatic* in *The Classical Temper: A Study of James Joyce's "Ulysses"* (New York: Barnes & Noble, 1961) and in *James Joyce* (New York: Grove Press, 1962).

9. William M. Schutte, editor's introduction, in *Twentieth-Century Interpretations of "A Portrait of the Artist as a Young Man"* (Englewood Cliffs, N.J.: Prentice-Hall, 1968), p. 14. In the fourth section of his introduction to this volume of essays (pp. 10–14), Schutte provides what he calls a "summary account" of the styles that is quite helpful, though brief.

10. The result bears comparison to the work in music of Joyce's Hungarian contemporary Bela Bartók. Bartók's *Microkosmos*, for instance, is both five-finger exercises and the work of the master that constitutes an aesthetic world as microcosm. Given the intimate relationship I discern between the styles of narration and the character's sensibility in *A Portrait*, I find it hard to agree with critics who posit some unbridgeable gap between the book's powerful language and its supposedly puerile central figure.

11. All pointed out by Schutte in his introduction to *Twentieth-Century Interpretations of "A Portrait,"* pp. 13–14.

12. I have adopted the terms *psycho-narration, quoted monologue*, and *narrated monologue* from the typology Dorrit Cohn presents in *Transparent Minds: Narrative Modes for Presenting Consciousness in Fiction* (Princeton: Princeton University Press, 1978). She draws extensively on Joyce for examples illustrating her categories. Cohn originally introduced the term narrated monologue in her essay "Narrated Monologue: Definition of a Fictional Style," *Comparative Literature* 18 (Spring 1966): 97–112. That term has begun to gain some currency among critics of fiction written in English. For instance, James P. Pusach uses it to render *erlebte Rede* in his translation of Franz Stanzel's *Die typischen Erzähl-situationen im Roman* (Vienna: W. Braumuller, 1955) (translated as *Narrative Situations in the Novel: "Tom Jones," "Moby-Dick," "The Ambassadors," "Ulysses"* [Bloomington: Indiana University Press, 1971]). But other English terms have been suggested, including Paul Hernadi's *substitutionary narration* and Roy Pascal's *free indirect speech*. In this regard see: Paul Hernadi, "Dual Perspective: Free Indirect Discourse and Related Techniques," *Comparative Literature* 24 (Winter 1972): 32–43, reprinted as the appendix to Hernadi's *Beyond Genre* (Ithaca: Cornell University Press, 1972), pp. 187–205; and Roy Pascal, *The Dual Voice: Free Indirect Speech and Its Functioning in the Nineteenth-Century European Novel* (Totowa, N.J.: Rowman & Littlefield, 1977). In my review of the books by Cohn and Pascal ("Dual Reflections on Transparency: Consciousness in Fiction," *Comparative Literature Studies* 17, no. 2 [June 1980]: pt. 1, pp. 155–67), I discuss the relative merits of some of these terms. I also deal briefly there with Cohn's commentary on "Penelope" as an example of "autonomous monologue." For a less sympathetic treatment of *Transparent Minds*, one that draws on the perspective provided by Edwin R. Steinberg in *The Stream of Consciousness and Beyond in "Ulysses"* (Pittsburgh: University of Pittsburgh Press, 1973), see Shari Benstock's review in the *James Joyce Quarterly* 17 (Fall 1979): 105–9. Paul Hernadi's review is available in *Comparative Literature* 32, no. 2 (Spring 1980): 207–9. Cohn's book is essential reading for anyone interested in the representation of consciousness in fiction. Hugh Kenner's monograph *Joyce's Voices* (Berkeley and Los Angeles: University of California Press, 1978) also deals with Joyce's techniques for presenting mind, though Kenner does not place them within the continental literary and critical tradition that Cohn, Hernadi, and Pascal—all comparatists—provide. Other treatments of the so-called "stream of consciousness" relevant to the present study are: Melvin Friedman, *Stream of Consciousness: A Study in Literary Method* (New Haven: Yale University Press, 1955); Robert Humphrey, *Stream of Consciousness in the Modern Novel* (Berkeley and Los Angeles: University of California Press, 1954); and Steinberg, *Stream of Consciousness and Beyond*. For a discussion of

techniques for reporting speech and thought in French fiction, see Stephen Ullmann, *Style in the French Novel* (New York: Cambridge University Press, 1957), pp. 94–120. I am largely in agreement with Cohn's critique of these earlier discussions, which she expresses mainly in the introduction to *Transparent Minds* (pp. 3–17).

13. Jean Ricardou, "Time of the Narration, Time of the Fiction," trans. Joseph Kestner, *James Joyce Quarterly* 16 (Fall 1978/Winter 1979): 13.

14. Ibid., p. 11.

15. Gérard Genette, "Boundaries of Narrative," *New Literary History* 8 (Autumn 1976): 1–13. Paul Hernadi also discusses diegesis as authorial presentation in his article on free indirect discourse, "Dual Perspective."

16. Wayne C. Booth, *The Rhetoric of Fiction* (Chicago: University of Chicago Press, 1961), p. 164.

17. See in this regard A. Walton Litz's Gombrichean discussion of the act of reading *Ulysses* "through a series of perceptual adjustments" in "The Genre of *Ulysses*," in *Theory of the Novel: New Essays*, ed. John Halperin (New York: Oxford University Press, 1974), pp. 109–20.

18. For a discussion of the dates of composition see Schutte's introduction to *Twentieth-Century Interpretations of "A Portrait,"* pp. 5–7.

19. Stanislaus Joyce, *My Brother's Keeper: James Joyce's Early Years*, ed. Richard Ellmann (New York: Viking Press, 1958), p. 244.

20. Ovid, *Metamorphoses*, trans. Rolfe Humphries (Bloomington: Indiana University Press, 1955), Book VIII, ll. 182–88, p. 187.

21. Flaubert's dictum is found in his letter to Mlle. Leroyer de Chantepie (18 March 1857): "*L'artiste doit être dans son oeuvre comme Dieu dans la Création, invisible et tout-puissant, qu'on le sente partout, mais qu'on ne le voie pas*" (quoted by the editors in *CW* 141 n.1).

22. The complicated relations of telling and listening involving the audience's dual participation as performer and observer resemble those of the "Sirens" and "Penelope" episodes of *Ulysses*, which I discuss in chapter four; see n.65 of that chapter. There is, inevitably, some overlap beween my commentary and that of Barbara Hardy in her more general study, *Tellers and Listeners: The Narrative Imagination* (London: Athlone Press, University of London, 1975). Her discussion of Joyce (pp. 206–76) takes a direction different from the one I provide here; she is more concerned with the conceptual implications of form than with the thematics of telling and listening as presented within the narratives. My interest in the latter is primarily as it may elucidate the former.

23. From a more purely biographical perspective, in "The Growth of Imagination" (*JJ* 302–9) Richard Ellmann has discussed some of the ways in which Joyce can be said "to mother and father himself" (*JJ* 309) in *A Portrait* and *Ulysses*.

24. Joyce seems to have derived "gnarly" from the Indo-European "gnārāre," the etymological ancestor of the English verb "to narrate." A "gnarlybird," then, would be one that tells stories.

25. In what is probably the best-known essay on the villanelle, Robert Scholes interprets some of the language of the section as Joyce's "elaborate explication" of the poem ("Stephen Dedalus, Poet or Esthete?," *PMLA* 89 [1964], 484–89; reprinted in *"A Portrait of the Artist as a Young Man": Text, Criticism, and Notes*, ed. Chester G. Anderson [New York: Viking Press, 1968], 468–80). Dorrit Cohn, however, interprets these passages as "reported by a narrative voice that emulates the imagistic pattern in Stephen's mind" (*Transparent Minds*, p. 32). As she comments in a note, while her view is different from that of Scholes, the two interpretations are "not necessarily contradictory" (*Transparent Minds*, p. 276 n.17). In my view, the ambiguity serves to align the processes of interpretation and creation.

26. In her brief discussion of this section of *A Portrait*, Dorrit Cohn points to some of those "places where psycho-narration verges on the narrated monologue, marking a kind of mid-

point between the two techniques where a reporting syntax is maintained, but where the idiom is strongly affected (or infected) with the mental idiom of the mind it renders" (*Transparent Minds*, p. 33). She notes the inclusion of quoted monologue in the section as well.

27. In "Sirens," the narrator emphasizes the allusion to the beginning of "Calypso" (*U* 55) by using the phrase "As said before" twice (*U* 269, 271). Hugh Kenner has commented on this odd allusion by one part of the narration to an earlier part (*Joyce's Voices*, pp. 112–13).

28. Probably the best known example of chiasmus in Joyce's writing occurs near the beginning of "Aeolus": "Grossbooted draymen rolled barrels dullthudding out of Prince's stores and bumped them up on the brewery float. On the brewery float bumped dullthudding barrels rolled by grossbooted draymen out of Prince's stores" (*U* 116).

29. Chiasmus provides a means for suggesting simultaneously a repetition that is a reversal and a cause that merges with its apparently opposite effect. It embodies the oscillating perspective rhetorically, as the Möbius strip does geometrically and as some optical illusions do perceptually. Cause and effect may even be at some temporal remove from one another. I discuss Karl Marx's use of chiasmus to create both these suggestions at once in my essay "*The Eighteenth Brumaire* of Karl Marx as Symbolic Action" (*History and Theory* 19: 58–72). The figure obviously lends itself to the assertion of symmetry within a sequence. When the reversal between beginning and ending of the chiastic sequence represents a lapse in time as well, the replacement of cause by effect at the end of the sequence can suggest the identity of late occurrence with early. This metaleptic implication is especially appropriate for the temporally preposterous aspects of *A Portrait*. Hans Walter Gabler has discussed the overall arrangement of parts in *A Portrait* as a chiastic structure ("The Seven Lost Years of *A Portrait of the Artist as a Young Man*," in *Approaches to Joyce's "Portrait*," ed. Staley and Benstock, pp. 25–60, especially section 3, pp. 49–51).

30. The oscillating perspective is inherent in Joyce's version of the myth, for the story of wanderings, weavings, and maskings is for him also the narrative of homecoming, unraveling, and unmasking.

CHAPTER THREE

1. See, in this regard, Homer Obed Brown, *James Joyce's Early Fiction: The Biography of a Form* (Cleveland: Press of Case Western Reserve University, 1972). Brown provides a great deal of useful material in small compass, including the chronology of the writing of *Stephen Hero* and *Dubliners* (p. 60). In my discussion I consider questions related to those Brown poses concerning the observer in Joyce's early writing. Some of my conclusions vary from his, primarily because Brown provides no close examination of style, but also because in my readings the observer can be teller, character, reader, or some combination of the three. See also Thomas Staley's "A Beginning: Signification, Story, and Discourse in Joyce's 'The Sisters,' " in *The Genres of the Irish Literary Revival*, ed. Ronald Schleifer (Norman, Okla.: Pilgrim Books, 1980). Staley formulates succintly in general terms the place of *Dubliners* in Joyce's development: "Somewhere between the original conception of the *Dubliners* stories and their completion, Joyce moved along a path similar to the one that was to transform the manuscript *Stephen Hero*, a prose work in the tradition of late nineteenth-century realism and naturalism, into *A Portrait*" (p. 124). I would modify this only slightly by saying that the paths are not similar but identical.

2. Apparently basing his discussion on Ellmann's biography, William M. Schutte, editor of *Twentieth-Century Interpretations of "A Portrait of the Artist as a Young Man"* (Englewood Cliffs, N.J.: Prentice-Hall, 1968), p. 6, claims that Joyce essentially set aside the manuscript of *A Portrait* during the period 1908–14 and that he only completed the final two parts in 1914–15 under the pressure of imminent serial publication in *The Egoist*. On the basis of the admittedly incomplete manuscript evidence, Hans Walter Gabler argues at some length for a different view: that Joyce worked on *A Portrait* throughout this period ("The Seven Lost

Years of *A Portrait of the Artist as a Young Man,"* in *Approaches to Joyce's "Portrait,"* ed. Thomas F. Staley and Bernard Benstock [Pittsburgh: University of Pittsburgh Press, 1976]). Besides presenting the available evidence in detail, Gabler makes several helpful observations about the structural relations of the parts of *A Portrait*, especially concerning Joyce's apparent propensity in revision to shift segments from one portion of the manuscript to another. For instance, Gabler suggests that I.3, the Christmas dinner, may originally have been in II. At the least, his comprehensive essay puts the other theory strongly into question.

3. Paul de Man has discussed the ambiguities of the final stanza of "Among School Children" in *Allegories of Reading: Figural Language in Rousseau, Nietzche, Rilke, and Proust* (New Haven: Yale University Press, 1979), pp. 11–12.

4. The most recent cogent discussion of the composition of *Ulysses* is Michael Groden's *"Ulysses" in Progress* (Princeton: Princeton University Press, 1977).

5. Roland Barthes, *S/Z*, trans. Richard Miller (New York: Hill & Wang, 1974). The translator has chosen *readerly* and *writerly* to render *lisible* (readable) and *scriptible* (writable). In his use of these terms, Barthes makes it clear that the categories are not absolutely distinct from one another.

6. This essay and the circumstances of its rejection are discussed by Scholes and Kellogg (*WD* 56–59) and Richard Ellmann (*JJ* 149–54).

7. Dorrit Cohn employs Spitzer's term in her commentary on psycho-narration (*Transparent Minds: Narrative Modes for Presenting Consciousness in Fiction* [Princeton: Princeton University Press, 1978], p. 33).

8. In their critical edition of *Dubliners*, Scholes and Litz devote a section to "The Composition and Revisions of the Stories" (pp. 236–52). This section includes an early version of "The Sisters." The most thorough account of the story and its earlier versions is Florence L. Walzl's "Joyce's 'The Sisters': A Development," *James Joyce Quarterly* 10 (Summer 1973): 375–421. Fritz Senn has pointed out to me another interpretation of the word "inefficacious" that he and J. Mitchell Morse have discussed. The word may be one that the boy learned from the priest in relation to the efficacy of grace in removing the stains of human sin. While this interpretation may encourage us to modify what I have said about the word, it does not undermine my general point. Even if the boy learned the word from the priest, the teller's use of it differs from the religious meaning to which it probably alludes. We can read it as the older teller's ironic use of the priest's diction that entered his vocabulary during childhood. The play of voices and meanings (the priest's, the boy's, and the narrator's) in this interpretation is closer to the oscillating perspective of Joyce's later fiction than the more straightforward view I present in the body of my discussion.

9. There are complicating factors at work in these stories concerning the relations between teller, character, and reader that my analysis, focusing as it does on grammatical markers and syntactic structures, cannot do complete justice. Because these stories are relentlessly lower middle-class and Irish in their setting and characters, the speech that infects the narration is often that of uneducated Dubliners. For instance, as Michael O'Dea has pointed out to me, when we learn that Eveline's father "was usually fairly bad of a Saturday night" (*D* 38), the idiomatic use of the preposition "of " emphasizes a distance between the character in the story and the teller and readers of the story. Such evocations of a character's idiomatic speech suggest that the alignment between reader and teller can include the character's perspective most fully only when the character's speech regularly follows the teller's norms and our own. The characters whose speech comes closest to those norms are the unnamed boy, James Duffy, and Gabriel Conroy. I do not mean to suggest that their speech adheres absolutely to the teller's style of narration. It certainly does not. But the divergence between speech and narration is sometimes less marked in their stories than in the others. In the case of "Eveline," our perspective and the teller's come closest to the character's in one way when Eveline's interior voice stops at the story's end. Then, the mediation connecting and separating reader and character is more the narrator's than Eveline's. And with the narrator's mediations in

Dubliners we can always align ourselves. The various contrasts of voice in the narration used to create distance all resemble the contrast of adult with child; for instance: educated with uneducated, upper class with lower class, cosmopolitan with provincial. Anthony Burgess provides some helpful comments about Joyce's use of Irish accents and idioms in *Joysprick: An Introduction to the Language of James Joyce* (London: André Deutsch, 1973); see especially "The Dublin Sound" (pp. 27–35) and "Dialect and Idiolect" (pp. 36–47). Part of the triumph of Joyce's narration in "Penelope" is the attenuating of reader and teller's distance from the idiom and rhythm of Molly Bloom's Dublin speech.

10. In this regard see Derek Bickerton's pioneering essay "James Joyce and the Development of Interior Monologue," *Essays in Criticism* 18 (1968): 32–46. Bickerton points out that Joyce first experiments with "indirect interior monologue" (his name for narrated monologue, derived from Robert Humphrey's *Stream of Consciousness in the Modern Novel* [Berkeley and Los Angeles: University of California Press, 1954]) in "Eveline" and "Two Gallants" (pp. 35–36).

11. "He may be getting ready to write *Dubliners*" (Barbara Hardy, *Tellers and Listeners: The Narrative Imagination* [London: Athlone Press, University of London, 1975], p. 247).

12. The extremity of the external view in these three stories has, of course, been noted by other critics, for instance Brown (*James Joyce's Early Fiction*, p. 81).

13. I have adopted these terms, like the others referring to representation of mind in fiction, from Dorrit Cohn's *Transparent Minds*.

14. Among the many critics who do not distinguish the boy from the narrator are Brown (*James Joyce's Early Fiction*, p. 21), John William Corrington ("The Sisters," in *James Joyce's "Dubliners": Critical Essays*, ed. Clive Hart [London: Faber & Faber, 1969], especially p. 23, where he refers to the "boy-narrator"), and Hélène Cixous (*The Exile of James Joyce*, trans. Sally A. J. Purcell [New York: David Lewis, 1972], especially p. 371, where she refers to "the child narrator" ["le narrateur enfant"]).

15. In "A Beginning: Signification, Story, and Discourse," his essay on "The Sisters," Staley discusses the story's first paragraph with respect to a wide range of contemporary theoretical speculations concerning beginnings. Together with some of his comments in the essay proper, his notes provide an overview of the relevant criticism of "The Sisters." As Staley rightly points out, Fritz Senn has already begun making the argument for connecting "The Sisters" with Joyce's later work in his essay " 'He was too Scrupulous Always,' Joyce's 'The Sisters,' " *James Joyce Quarterly* 2 (Winter 1965): 66–71.

16. Dorrit Cohn discusses the self-narrated monologue in *Transparent Minds* (pp. 166–72).

17. Hayden White discusses such sequences of tropes in *Metahistory: The Historical Imagination in Nineteenth-Century Europe* (Baltimore: Johns Hopkins University Press, 1973).

18. Robert Scholes, " 'Counterparts' and the Method of *Dubliners*," in *"Dubliners": Text, Criticism, and Notes*, ed. Robert Scholes and A. Walton Litz (New York: Viking Press, 1967), p. 382; preceding quotations are from p. 387.

19. *The Autobiography of Giambattista Vico*, trans. Max Harold Fisch and Thomas Goddard Bergin (Ithaca: Cornell University Press, 1944). According to A. Walton Litz, "Joyce's first reading of Vico . . . certainly occurred soon after 1905, when he took up residence in Trieste" ("Vico and Joyce," in *Giambattista Vico: An International Symposium*, ed. Giorgio Tagliacozzo et al. [Baltimore: Johns Hopkins University Press, 1969], p. 246). According to Stanislaus Joyce, his brother wrote "A Painful Case" in Trieste (*My Brother's Keeper: James Joyce's Early Years*, ed. Richard Ellmann [New York: Viking Press, 1958], p. 159).

20. In *The Dual Voice: Free Indirect Speech and Its Functioning in the Nineteenth-Century European Novel* ([Totowa, N.J.: Rowman & Littlefield, 1977], p. 65), Roy Pascal

mentions two passages, one from Georg Buchner's *Lenz*, the other from Jean-Paul Sartre's *The Age of Reason*, that conclude with the statement "He was alone." Both these passages are instances of narrated monologue, which Pascal calls "free indirect speech." The contrast with the nearly identical conclusion of "A Painful Case" is striking. In the passages of narrated monologue, the narrator's perspective essentially fuses with that of the character. At the end of Joyce's story, the narrator undercuts the sense of fusion by employing psycho-narration instead. Bickerton discusses the ending of two versions of "A Painful Case" in "James Joyce and the Development of Interior Monologue," pp. 36–38.

21. Brown, *James Joyce's Early Fiction*, pp. 90 and 89. More recently Hugh Kenner has commented briefly on the narration at the beginning of "The Dead" in the first paragraph of "The Uncle Charles Principle" in *Joyce's Voices* (Berkeley and Los Angeles: University of California Press, 1978).

22. Joyce uses the adjective similarly in "Wandering Rocks" when he describes Molly Bloom's plump, "generous arm" flinging a coin to the one-legged sailor (*U* 226).

23. Although dated 1897 in the table of contents of W. B. Yeats's *Mythologies* (London: Macmillan, 1962), the *Stories of Red Hanrahan* reprinted in that volume is the revised version, as the title page indicates. As with Yeats's poetry, because of multiple revisions and reprintings, it is necessary to examine the publication history of his stories to determine which versions Joyce might have known at the time he wrote "The Dead." Because the title page in *Mythologies* indicates revision in 1907 with the help of Lady Gregory, it would seem that Joyce would not have known that version of the stories in time. But the title page is misleading. The major revision actually took place prior to the separate reprinting of the Hanrahan stories in 1905 (Dundrum: Dun Emer Press). The revisions made after that date do not modify the 1905 version significantly. On dates of revision and publication, see Richard J. Finneran, *The Prose Fiction of W. B. Yeats: The Search for 'Those Simple Forms'* (New Yeats Papers IV) (Dublin: The Dolmen Press, 1973), pp. 27–30. There are, then, basically two versions of the Hanrahan stories, one from 1897, the other from 1905, both of which Joyce could have known. Even if he did not know the 1905 volume in time, he could have encountered "Red Hanrahan," the only Hanrahan story not printed in the 1897 volume, through its publication in *The Independent Review* in 1903. The details I have cited using the text of *Mythologies* would have been available to Joyce in the 1897 volume and in the 1903 "Red Hanrahan." Though Hanrahan's dying vision did not originally include the four symbols, they do appear in "Red Hanrahan." Details from other stories in *Dubliners* confirm the connection with Yeats's tales. There is, for instance, the transforming of the "great serpent" and the phrase "cast him out" from the end of "The Twisting of the Rope" (1897) into the wormlike train and "cast out from life's feast" at the end of "A Painful Case." The publication history of Yeats's stories is examined and the versions are reprinted in *The Secret Rose, Stories by W. B. Yeats: A Variorum Edition*, ed. Phillip L. Marcus, Warwick Gould, and Michael J. Sidnell (Ithaca, N.Y.: Cornell University Press, 1981). For another interpretation that stresses Irish mythological elements in "The Dead," see John V. Kelleher's "Irish History and Mythology in James Joyce's 'The Dead,' " *Review of Politics* 27 (1965): 414–33. Kelleher comments on various references to Irish history in "The Dead" and identifies possible allusions in the story to an Old Irish saga. While I am not convinced by Kelleher's list of allusions, I agree with the impetus for his essay: to account for the story's resonance by suggesting the importance of Irish history and mythology even in this relatively early work. For a recent commentary on "The Dead" that takes Kelleher's essay as its starting point, see Donald T. Torchiana, "The Ending of 'The Dead': I Follow Saint Patrick," *James Joyce Quarterly* 18 (Winter 1981): 123–32.

CHAPTER FOUR

1. Wayne C. Booth, *The Rhetoric of Fiction* (Chicago: University of Chicago Press,

1961), p. 220.

2. I quote the passage from Flaubert's letters in chapter two, n.21.

3. Some readers may question my use of the word "metaphor" in this section and elsewhere in this study. I use that word in a Viconian way that I outline briefly in chapter one during my discussion of the title "Finnegans Wake." When I identify metaphors *in* Joyce's writings that can be applied *to* them in describing reader and writer's relationships to the tale, I call both aspects of the trope metaphoric. I do so to capture the alignments in the midst of divergences pertinent to Joyce's figurative language as it functions both in his style and in our experience of his narratives. By shuttling between an internal and an external perspective, one pertaining to language and the other to structure, indicated by a single term, we can trace the transforming of trope into narrative, of language as such into story. The relation we experience between figurative language and structure of narration is one version of the oscillating perspective.

4. For discussions of "polytropos," see Fritz Senn, "Book of Many Turns," *James Joyce Quarterly* 10 (Fall 1972): 29–46, and W. B. Stanford, *The Ulysses Theme: A Study in the Adaptability of a Traditional Hero*, 2nd ed. (1963; Ann Arbor: University of Michigan Press, 1968), especially Stanford's comments on Antisthenes (pp. 98–99).

5. *JJ* 47. Ellmann cites Herbert Gorman's *James Joyce* (New York: Farrar & Rinehart, 1939) to this effect.

6. Hugh Kenner, "Circe," in James Joyce's *"Ulysses": Critical Essays*, ed. Clive Hart and David Hayman (Berkeley and Los Angeles: University of California Press, 1974), pp. 348–49.

7. Ibid., pp. 361–62.

8. Richard Ellmann, *Ulysses on the Liffey* (New York: Oxford University Press, 1972), p. 186ff.

9. Rudolf Arnheim, "Perceptual Analysis of a Symbol of Interaction," in *Toward a Psychology of Art* (Berkeley and Los Angeles: University of California Press, 1966), pp. 222–44.

10. Eco has written widely on Joyce, mostly in Italian; for example, in the first edition of *Opera aperta—Forma e indeterminazione nelle poetiche contemporanee* (Milan: Bompiani, 1962), which became after revision *Le poetiche di Joyce* (Milan: Bompiani, 1966). The latter is reportedly forth-coming in English translation as "The Aesthetics of Chaosmos." More recently, in *The Role of the Reader: Explorations in the Semiotics of Texts* (Bloomington: Indiana University Press, 1979), pp. 67–89, Eco has published an essay in English, "The Semantics of Metaphor," that deals with a passage in *Finnegans Wake* III.3. This is a revised version of an essay originally published in Italian ("Semantica della metafora," in *Le forme del contenuto* [Milan: Bompiani, 1971]). Eco's commentary exhibits the semiotic attitude trapped in its stance toward literary language as limited to the conscious mind only. As Eco develops it, that attitude tries to demystify metaphor by reducing it to metonymy. I refer the reader in particular to "figure 2.1" (p. 75), with Eco's accompanying explanation in the essay and to such categorical, reductive statements as the following: "The imagination is nothing other than a ratiocination that traverses the paths of the semantic labyrinth in a hurry and, in its haste, loses the sense of their rigid structure" (p. 78).

11. For a discussion of mind, including a critique of empiricist views, by a philosopher who is not a Freudian but who argues that we need the notions of the unconscious and of repression to account for memory and imagination, see Stuart Hampshire, "Disposition and Memory," in *Philosophers on Freud: New Evaluations* (originally published as *Freud: A Collection of Critical Essays*, 1974), ed. Richard Wollheim (New York: Aronson, 1977), pp. 113–31.

12. See in this regard Freud's brief essay "Remembering, Repeating, and Working-through (Further Recommendations on the Technique of Psychoanalysis II)," *The Standard Edition of the Complete Psychological Works of Sigmund Freud*, ed. and trans. James Strachey et al. (London: Hogarth Press, 1953–74), vol. 12 (1911–13), *The Case of Schreber, Papers on Technique, and Other Works* (1958), pp. 145–56.

13. "Ibsen's New Drama," *CW* 47–67; originally published in *Fortnightly Review*, n.s., vol. 67 (1 April 1900): 575–90.

14. Kenner, "Circe," p. 356.

15. Joyce refers to his "ports of call" in *Letters* I, 204.

16. Other critics have cited this letter and developed the notion of an initial style in *Ulysses*. The first to do so at length was Marilyn French in *The Book as World* (Cambridge: Harvard University Press, 1976). My stance toward *Ulysses* differs sharply from hers. The divergence concerns her division of the book into two parts, her characterization of the teller as a Dantean guide for the wandering reader, and her notion that the teller is malicious. See n.29 below, in which I suggest that S. L. Goldberg's work on Joyce is the source for this negative attitude toward the narrator.

17. The quotations from Homer's *Odyssey* in this study are from the two-volume *en face* edition of the Loeb Classical Library (Cambridge: Harvard University Press, and London: William Heinemann, 1976, originally published in 1919). The prose translations into English in this edition are by A. T. Murray.

18. In *Transparent Minds*, Dorrit Cohn uses some of James's remarks from this preface in developing her notion of the narrated monologue (pp. 99–140).

19. Booth, *Rhetoric of Fiction*, p. 164.

20. James, *Art of the Novel*, pp. 37–38.

21. See chapter one, n.45, for references to scholarly works dealing with Joyce's interest in etymology. In *Stephen Hero* we are told that Stephen "read Skeat's *Etymological Dictionary* by the hour" (*SH* 26).

22. Bernard Benstock discusses the intrusion of "Chrysostomos" in his essay "Telemachus," in *James Joyce's "Ulysses,"* ed. Hart and Hayman (pp. 1–16). In a commentary whose concerns are close to my own, Fritz Senn uses "Chrysostomos" as an example of disruption in narrative that he calls "*metastasis*." See his "Metastasis," *James Joyce Quarterly* 12 (Summer 1975): 380–85.

23. In the Linati schema Joyce uses the symbol for infinity to indicate the episode's time (Ellmann, *Ulysses on the Liffey*, pp. 186ff).

24. Stuart Gilbert, *James Joyce's "Ulysses"* (1930; 2nd rev. ed., New York: Vintage Books, 1952).

25. The last of these renderings is Robert Fitzgerald's (Garden City, N.Y.: Anchor Books, 1963). Fritz Senn provides a more complete list of variant translations in "Book of Many Turns" (p. 46 n.6).

26. John Henry Raleigh, *The Chronicle of Leopold and Molly Bloom: "Ulysses" as Narrative* (Berkeley and Los Angeles: University of California Press, 1977), pp. 228–44.

27. Leo Tolstoy, *Anna Karenina*, trans. David Magarshack (New York: New American Library, 1961), pp. 591–96.

28. Don Gifford and Robert J. Seidman, *Notes for Joyce: An Annotation of James Joyce's "Ulysses"* (New York: E. P. Dutton, 1974), p. 97.

29. I refer to S. L. Goldberg's immensely influential longer work *The Classical Temper: A Study of James Joyce's "Ulysses"* (New York: Barnes & Noble, 1961) and his shorter *James Joyce* (New York: Grove Press, 1962). Goldberg has been the most eloquent spokesman for the novelistic—that is, realistic—view of *Ulysses*. His work has been the fountainhead for interpreting the narrator as hostile (see, for example, *The Classical Temper*, p. 140). His commentaries are intelligent, well-argued, and clearly expressed. And they have drawn high praise (see, for instance, Thomas F. Staley's comments in *Anglo-Irish Literature: A Review of Research*, ed. Richard J. Finneran [New York: Modern Language Association, 1976]). Even now, twenty years after his books' first appearance, some critics treat them as "definitive" (e.g., James H. Maddox, Jr., *Joyce's "Ulysses" and the Assault upon Character* [New Brunswick, N.J.: Rutgers University Press, 1978], p. ix). Goldberg's positions carry the persuasive force of half-truths, and that is a great force indeed. But he is, quite simply, wrong

about some crucial issues concerning *Ulysses*. It is past time for critics to stop applauding his intelligence and critical tact without examining his positions as carefully and as harshly as he examines the views of others, especially those of Hugh Kenner. His notion that the narrator is hostile arises from nothing more substantial than the New Criticism's penchant for projecting its own interpretative stance of distance and its controlling trope of irony into the works it treats. Goldberg's interpretations are flawed in at least two other ways. The first concerns his assumptions about the "classical," which he aligns with the organic, the natural, and especially the *dramatic*. "Dramatic action" (*James Joyce*, p. 99, and elsewhere in both books) becomes the touchstone in his readings. His correlation of the *dramatic* with the narrowly referential and realistic simply cannot be sustained using Stephen Dedalus's comments about aesthetics. Because Joyce pushes the form of fiction to its boundaries, Goldberg's attempt to call what he considers the valuable parts of Joyce's work *dramatic* amounts to denying Joyce's central achievement. As I have interpreted the terms *lyrical, epical*, and *dramatic* in *A Portrait*, they refer to stages of artistic creation. Consequently, a strongly Romantic attitude toward aesthetic creation informs the typology that Goldberg, taking his cue from T. S. Eliot's polemical anti-Romanticism, wants to use to elevate the classical as *dramatic* to our primary standard of value. The other weakness is his failure to deal with the nature and implications of style in *Ulysses*. His comments reveal little sensitivity to Joyce's use of language. Although he faults the middle episodes severely, Goldberg discusses in detail few episodes after "Scylla and Charybdis." Those he does deal with (e.g., "Penelope"), he deprecates for breaking "away from the dramatic action" (*James Joyce*, p. 99), which he assumes to be normative. In my reading of *Ulysses*, the classical temper defines only one moment in the book's oscillating perspectives.

30. Karen Lawrence, " 'Aeolus': Interruption and Inventory," *James Joyce Quarterly* 17 (Summer 1980): 389. In *The Odyssey of Style in "Ulysses"* (Princeton: Princeton University Press, 1981), Lawrence makes the same claim concerning "stability and continuity" (p. 56).

31. Arnold Goldman, *The Joyce Paradox: Form and Freedom in His Fiction* (Evanston: Northwestern University Press, 1966), p. 82.

32. Ibid.

33. Ibid.

34. In *"Ulysses" in Progress* (Princeton: Princeton University Press, 1977), Michael Groden describes the creation of the chiasmus through changes Joyce made after "Aeolus" was published in *The Little Review* (p. 70).

35. Goldman, *The Joyce Paradox*, p. 82.

36. D. H. Lawrence, "Morality and the Novel," in *Phoenix: The Posthumous Papers of D. H. Lawrence*, ed. Edward D. McDonald (1936; reprint ed., New York: Viking Press, 1968), p. 528.

37. Gilbert, *James Joyce's "Ulysses,"* p. 179.

38. The 1934 Random House edition (*U* 170) includes the "n" in "haunched" omitted in the 1961 edition.

39. Ellmann, *Ulysses on the Liffey*, p. 74.

40. I have taken the spelling and punctuation of this passage from the 1934 Random House edition (*U* 163) rather than the 1961 edition.

41. Ellmann, *Ulysses on the Liffey*, p. 78.

42. Ibid.

43. Ibid., p. 83.

44. Ibid.

45. William M. Schutte, *Joyce and Shakespeare: A Study in the Meaning of "Ulysses"* (New Haven: Yale University Press, 1957), pp. 117–19.

46. Ellmann, *Ulysses on the Liffey*, p. 86.

47. On clowning in *Ulysses*, see David Hayman, "Forms of Folly in Joyce: A Study of Clowning in *Ulysses*," *ELH* 34 (June 1967): 260–83.

48. Gifford and Seidman, *Notes*, p. 195.

49. Goldberg, *The Classical Temper*, p. 314.

50. Some readers may wonder, as did one of the readers of this commentary in typescript, about my relatively compressed treatment of the episodes between "Sirens" and "Circe." The styles of the intervening episodes deserve close scrutiny, closer than the discussion I undertake here. But the interpretations I argue for encourage a swift passage to the "Nostos" in the commentary, though not in our encounter as readers with the stylistic elaborations of *Ulysses* itself. That swift passage reflects a retrospective realization that "Sirens" poses the problem of the later episodes in a crucial form and initiates strongly the movement toward "Penelope" as the book's teleology. As Joyce has Stephen say about Ireland, the home he would leave in order to find, the quickest way to Ireland is by a long detour of wandering, "the shortest way to Tara was via Holyhead" (*P* 250). When we are in the midst of reading the late episodes of part II, the detour seems a long one. But once we have come through, from the perspective of our destination, the gap can seem much smaller. Our situation resembles Odysseus's on Scheria. He is both immensely far from home, having traveled widely and for years, and quite close to home, as the brief voyage to Ithaca on the Phaeacian ship indicates. One of my reasons for dealing with the complications of "Circe" at the chapter's start rather than in its normal place was to quicken the commentary's pace from "Sirens" to "Nostos."

51. The 1961 Random House edition has "on reserve" (263), whereas the 1934 edition, which I quote here, reads "one reserve" (259). Fritz Senn has suggested that the sentence includes as well an example of the episode's tendency to quote earlier parts of the book, for "when I was in Wisdom Hely's" has already occurred in "Hades" (114).

52. "Greyedauburn" is hyphenated in the later of these passages in the 1961 Random House edition but not in the 1934 edition.

53. In his letters, Joyce referred to the denigrating voice simply as "I" (*Letters* I, 131) and to the other as "the epic" (*Letters* I, 126). In *Ulysses on the Liffey*, Ellmann links the "I" with "Thersites, the meanest-spirited man in the Greek host at Troy" (p. 110), as does Frank Budgen in *James Joyce and the Making of "Ulysses"* (Bloomington: Indiana University Press, 1960), p. 154.

54. Ellmann, *Ulysses on the Liffey*, p. 109.

55. Goldman, *The Joyce Paradox*, p. 92.

56. A concise discussion of *Nachträglichkeit*, or *après-coup*, is available in the section "Deferred Action" of J. Laplanche and J.B. Pontalis, *Vocabulaire de la psychanalyse* (Paris: Presses universitaires de France, 1967); trans. Peter Kussell and Jeffrey Mehlman, "French Freud: Structural Studies in Psychoanalysis," *Yale French Studies* 48 (1972): 182–86. The *Vocabulaire* has also been translated into English by Donald Nicholson-Smith as *The Language of Psycho-analysis* (New York: Norton, 1973).

57. Ellmann, *Ulysses on the Liffey*, pp. 186ff. All my references to the schemata are from the versions Ellmann prints.

58. As A. Walton Litz has commented in his essay "Ithaca," in *James Joyce's "Ulysses,"* ed. Hart and Hayman (pp. 385–405), "the form of the episode is as much the substance as the actual interchanges between Bloom and Stephen" (p. 386).

59. In her treatment of "Penelope" as paradigm for the autonomous monologue (*Transparent Minds*, pp. 217–32), Dorrit Cohn discusses the episode as standing "apart from its context, as a self-generated, self-supported, and self-enclosed fictional text" (p. 218). While there is much to encourage us to see "Penelope" as different from the other styles, my argument in this study leads to the opposite perception as well (not instead): that despite its seeming difference, including its apparent independence from the other styles, "Penelope" is not wholly separate and does fulfill the Homeric sequence of styles.

60. In his essay "Eumaeus" in *James Joyce's "Ulysses,"* ed. Hart and Hayman (pp. 363–83), Gerald L. Bruns, drawing on the work of Paul Valéry, deals briefly with the way nineteenth-century realism leads to something else. Bruns emphasizes the constancy of the

narrator's speech (p. 368), as I do, but he treats the relationship of artist to citizen only *within* the narrative, which he discusses as if purely referential. In my reading, the play of the language, including its comedy, takes precedence over the narrative that each reader will generate differently in responding to an episode like this one.

61. I am grateful to Fritz Senn for reminding me of the version Lenehan reports in "Oxen."

62. Donald Barthelme, *City Life* (New York: Farrar, Straus & Giroux, 1970), p. 80.

63. In this regard, see A. Walton Litz's discussion, in his essay "Ithaca," in *James Joyce's "Ulysses,"* ed. Hart and Hayman, of the way Joyce was able "to shatter the form of the well-made novel and expose its multifarious origins" (p. 405). Litz captures convincingly the way the episode and the whole book teeter between apparent extremes. Although I am not wholly persuaded by Litz's emphasis on the symbolic and figurative as dominant at the end of "Ithaca," his impetus is surely correct: to suggest the ways in which *Ulysses* moves beyond realism, the nineteenth-century novel, and even the rational mind. I agree completely with Litz that the extremes are not separate: "Like the Viconian *ricorso*. the final moment of 'Ithaca' is both an end and a beginning" (p. 404).

64. It is also the "we" of one of the titles Joyce proposed for the German translation of *Dubliners: So Sind Wir in Dublin (Letters* III, 164).

65. Roland Barthes discusses the "grain of the voice" and "*writing aloud*" in the concluding section, "Voice," of The *Pleasure of the Text*, trans. Richard Miller (New York: Hill & Wang, 1975), pp. 66–67. See also his essay "The Grain of the Voice," in *Image/Music/Text*, trans. Stephen Heath (New York: Hill & Wang, 1977), pp. 79–124; the subject there is music rather than literature. Mark W. Booth has recently provided a suggestive discussion of the relations between singer and audience in the introduction and conclusion of *The Experience of Songs* (New Haven: Yale University Press, 1981). In the second half of his introduction, in which he considers "The Point of View of Song" and "Song as Transcendence," Booth argues that the experience of song for the members of its audience makes them performers as well as listeners. We sing as we listen, and in doing so we align ourselves with the singer, despite any differences in gender. Booth alludes prominently to Victor Zuckerkandl's interpretation (in volume two of *Sound and Symbol*, Bollingen Series 44, *Man the Musician*, trans. Norbert Guterman [Princeton: Princeton University Press, 1973]) of singing as communal activity in which the boundaries blur between subject and object and between the individual and the group. Booth and Zuckerkandl both attempt to define a special kind of aesthetic experience, one in which self-consciousness disappears. For Joyce, song and its implications for singer and listener provide one element in a different but related aesthetic experience that includes writing and self-consciousness as song's counterparts. The phrases from Barthes that I use in my comments on "Penelope" capture the interaction between voice and writing in Joyce's fiction.

66. I take the idea of self-consumption from Stanley E. Fish's discussion of Plato's *Phaedrus* in "Literature in the Reader: Affective Stylistics," in *Is There a Text in This Class?: The Authority of Interpretive Communities* (Cambridge: Harvard University Press, 1980), pp. 21–67; see especially p. 40. The discussion of the *Phaedrus* has been omitted from some other reprintings of Fish's essay.

67. I derive the notion of an infrastructure in the acts of reading and writing that is not wholly accessible to referential language from the concluding section, "Negativity," of Wolfgang Iser's *The Act of Reading: A Theory of Aesthetic Response* (Baltimore: Johns Hopkins University Press, 1978), pp. 225–31. I discuss negativity near the end of my essay on *The Act of Reading*, "The Ambivalence of Reading," *Diacritics* 10, no. 2 (Summer 1980): 75–86.

68. The quotations from Yeats in this paragraph are from *The Collected Poems of W. B. Yeats: Definitive Edition* (New York: Macmillan, 1956). The first two are from part III of "The Tower" (pp. 196, 197); the final one is from part II of Yeats's last poem, "Under Ben Bulben" (p. 341).

APPENDIX 2

1. Claude Lévi-Strauss, "The Structural Study of Myth," in Richard T. and Fernande M. De George, eds., *The Structuralists: From Marx to Lévi-Strauss* (Garden City, N.Y.: Doubleday, 1972), p. 171.

Index